THE

ZENITH

SECRET

A CIA Insider Exposes the Secret War Against Cuba and the Plots that Killed the Kennedy Brothers

By Bradley E. Ayers

"The credible account of clandestine CIA operations against Castro's Cuba adds to the growing picture of covert government activities and may offer some leads to the JFK assassination."

—*Publisher's Weekly,* on *The War That Never Was* (1976), an earlier, censored version of *The Zenith Secret*

The Zenith Secret:
A CIA Insider Exposes the Secret War Against Cuba
and the Plots that Killed the Kennedy Brothers

©2006 Bradley E. Ayers

Vox Pop #5

First Printing, First Edition
Printed in People's Republic of China

Edited by Rebecca DeRosa and Paul DiRienzo
Copy editing by Louisa McMurray and Charlotte Evans
Index by Kristy Tobin

First published May, 2006
ISBN: 0-9752763-8-7

Front cover photo from Getty Images, used by permission.

Distributed to the trade by SCB Book Distributors
Gardena, CA

Published by Vox Pop/Drench Kiss Media Corporation
1022 Cortelyou Road
Brooklyn, NY 11218

www.voxpopnet.net

Bradley E. Ayers joined the U.S. Army paratroops at 18. During 12 years of active duty he became a Ranger-special operations officer and was promoted to captain. In 1963 he was selected by the Pentagon for a CIA undercover assignment. He was one of the first career officers to oppose the Vietnam War. His other works include The War That Never Was and Myths or Messages.

FOREWORD

By James H. Fetzer

Relative to the death of JFK, Bradley Ayers and I have been working opposite sides of the case. In the wake of the fiasco known as "The Bay of Pigs," two Army officers were assigned to assist the CIA in order to strengthen its capacity to conduct paramilitary operations against Cuba. Bradley Ayers was one of those chosen to fill this extremely sensitive function. During the course of his service in this top-secret capacity and subsequent events, he became convinced that some of those with whom he was working had something to do with the assassinations of John F. Kennedy, the 35th president of the United States, and his brother, Robert, who otherwise very well might have acceded to that high office himself. The importance of what Ayers has to tell us, therefore, crucially depends upon whether JFK was taken out by a conspiracy.

If there was no conspiracy after all, then his reports about possible conspirators and their *modus operandi* has the status of fiction, not fact. In order to take rumor, speculation, and especially politics out of the case, I formed a research group that included the best-qualified individuals to ever study the case. These included David W. Mantik, M.D., who holds a Ph.D. in physics and is also board certified in radiation oncology; Robert B. Livingston, M.D., a world authority on the human brain and an expert on wound ballistics; Charles Crenshaw, M.D, a physician who was present when JFK was brought to Parkland Hospital and, two days later, attended his alleged assassin; Jack W. White, a legendary photo analyst who has played important advisory roles related to understanding and portraying the events of November 22, 1963; and, as a later addition, John P. Costella, another Ph.D. in physics with a specialization in electromagnetism, whose research on the Zapruder film would prove to be definitive.

This research program would lead to the publication of three collections of studies by experts on various aspects of the case — *Assassination Science* (1998), *Murder in Dealey Plaza* (2000), and *The Great Zapruder Film Hoax* (2003) — which have had the function of placing its investigation upon an objective and scientific foundation. The most difficult task, it turned out, was to separate the authentic from the inauthentic evidence. Once that had been accomplished, it became relatively straightforward to figure out what took place in Dealey Plaza on that fateful day. We discovered that official autopsy X-rays had been altered to conceal a massive blow-out to the back of the head, that another had been changed by adding a 6.5mm metallic slice; that the brain recorded in diagrams and photographs at the National Archives cannot possibly be the brain of John Fitzgerald Kennedy; that the home movie of the assassination is a recreation; and that JFK's alleged assailant was framed using manufactured evidence.

Michael Baden, M.D., who chaired the medical panel during the reinvestigation of the case by the House Select Committee on Assassinations, 1976-79, has observed that, if the "magic bullet" hypothesis — that the same bullet that hit the back of JFK's neck, exited his throat, entered Governor John Connally's back, shattered a rib, and impacted with his right wrist and lodged itself in his left thigh — were not true, then there had to have been at least six shots from three directions. We have not only proven the "magic bullet" hypothesis is false,

in fact, it is not even anatomically possible, because cervical vertebrae intervene. We have also determined that there had to have been at least six shots
from three different directions. JFK was hit four times (once in the throat from
in front; once in the back from behind; and twice in the head, once from the back
and once from the front); Connally was hit at least once from the side; and a
bystander was hit by fragments of a shot that had missed. These findings provide powerful premises in analyzing alternative theories of the case. The Mafia,
for example, which undoubtedly put up some of the shooters, could not have
extended its reach into Bethesda Naval Hospital to alter X-rays under the control of medical officers of the United States Navy, the Secret Service, and the
president's personal physician. Neither pro- nor anti-Castro Cubans could possibly have substituted another brain for that of JFK. And even though the KGB
no doubt had the same capability as the CIA and Hollywood to recreate a film,
it would not have been able to secure its possession. Nor could any of these
things been done by Lee Harvey Oswald, who was either incarcerated or already
dead. These discoveries were reinforced by identifying over 15 indications of
Secret Service complicity in setting him up for the hit, which appears to have
been a military-style ambush involving elements of the CIA, the military, and
the Mafia. It's not a pretty picture.

That powerful elements of the government had to have been involved has
been substantiated by independent investigators, such as Noel Twyman, *Bloody
Treason* (1997), whose monumental work implicates Lyndon Johnson and J.
Edgar Hoover in an intricate plot, where Johnson's mistress, Madelene Duncan
Brown, *Texas in the Morning* (1997), and his confederate in crime, Billy Sol
Estes, *A Texas Legend* (2005), confirm it. The execution of JFK by elements of
the military, the CIA, and the Mafia, leads to a tangled web of deceit and deception, which would eventually absorb the attention and energies of Bradley
Ayers. This book presents an autobiographical account of his own observations
and experiences, which dramatically confirms the existence of a domestic conspiracy to take out JFK. The author perfectly captures the atmosphere and atti-
tudes supporting the use of murder and mayhem to advance misguided political
objectives. *The Zenith Secret* is a moving personal narration of one man's devo-
tion to truth and makes important contributions to our history.

BRADLEY E. AYERS

PREFACE

I decided to go public with the account of my experiences with CIA/JM/WAVE, and my impressions and observations of that period, when Robert Kennedy was shot in the Los Angeles Ambassador Hotel in 1968.

The "lone gunman" official explanations for the death of President Kennedy, Martin Luther King, Jr. and Bobby Kennedy did not rest comfortably with me. I had seen, heard, and witnessed too much during my involvement with the CIA to ignore the possibility of a quasi-official conspiracy in the murders of three major figures of the 20th century.

My first effort to expose what I knew about the Kennedy administration-CIA secret war against Cuba was *The War That Never Was* published in 1976. The book was drastically censored by the managing editor, Tom Gervasi, at Bobbs-Merrill. On his deathbed in 1985, Gervasi confided to a family member that he had been on the CIA payroll as a "limited hangout" contract operative with the task of sanitizing books written about the agency. *The Zenith Secret* comes to the reader uncontaminated by such editing and manipulations. (Of even greater relevance to the censorship and eventual distribution interference with *The War That Never Was,* former CIA officer William Harvey, known widely for his involvement in early agency plots to kill Castro as a pistol-toting original Cold War "cowboy," became an editor at Bobbs-Merrill, my original publisher, following his retirement from the CIA. I was not aware of this when the publishers contracted the book.)

This book derives its title from the name of the JM/WAVE cover corporation. Behind the paneled doors of Zenith Technical Enterprises, secret actions of the highest order were concocted. The most diabolical and cynical plots were conceived, and incredibly elaborate cover-ups and deceptions devised—most with the knowledge and approval of the "Special Group" and deliberately without the knowledge of the White House. Brashly holding themselves above the law, audaciously asserting that they, better than anyone else, knew what was in the national interest, the Langley "old boy" clique, i.e. the CIA-JM/WAVE covert ops hierarchy, took matters into their own hands. In so doing, they spawned a mind-set, an attitude of almost omnipotent untouchability, wielding a secret power and influence that profoundly affected the course of American history and the world for over 40 years.

The notorious Phoenix Program of Vietnam, Watergate, narco-terrorism and drug smuggling, alliances with mobsters, thugs, and dictators, the Iran-Contra affair, assassinations of foreign leaders and even domestic leaders can be traced to the secret fraternity and its charter that had its origin under the cover of Zenith Technical Enterprises in the early 1960s.

It was into this cauldron of deception, conspiracy, top-secrecy, and wholesale subterfuge that I was plunged in early 1963 as a 28-year-old senior Ranger-paratrooper captain. I had rated in the top 2 percent of my Regular Army contemporaries. The Special Group, dissatisfied with the failure of many of the CIA's paramilitary missions and the loss or capture of valuable assets by Castro forces, selected me as a covert paramilitary-unconventional warfare specialist, to help the CIA upgrade the training of JM/WAVE's exile volunteers who were being sent into Cuba on high-risk black operations. It was the mission of a lifetime, the culmination of all I had trained and prepared for; one that would challenge the best of my skills as a professional soldier.

I had access at JM/WAVE beyond my rank and staff level, and I discreetly took advantage of it. I was inherently curious and vaguely aware that what was going on behind the Zenith charade was of historic significance. I watched, listened, and carefully gained insight into the politics, bureaucracy and inner workings of the station and the agency staff with whom I associated. This helped me perform my assignment more effectively, but also provided me with previously guarded insider's background on many aspects of the station that were not even apparent to agency employees.

As the head of paramilitary, survival and maritime training at the station, most of my time was spent in the field under conditions of physical hardship and high anxiety over the maintenance of security. But because my role was key to the preparation of the Cuban exile volunteers for their operational missions, I had frequent contact with an unholy rogues gallery of the CIA's black operations, the most notorious among the agency's covert operators hall of fame.

Many of these men continued to play key roles in U.S. paramilitary operations, including "off the shelf" private covert undertakings until well into the 1980s. In the late 1970s, the House Select Committee on Assassinations (HSCA) identified several of these CIA career and contract agents as persons of interest in its investigation of domestic and foreign assassinations.

On the darker side, I met and trained sniper teams for Johnny Rosselli, the Mafia hit man hired by the CIA to orchestrate the assassination attempts on Castro. Not only did I associate with these people professionally, I socialized with them, listened to their complaints, was privy to their confidences, gained insight into their loyalties and prejudices, their morality, thought processes, their favored personal trade methods and techniques. It was truly a highly unique experience for a naïve junior officer and the impressions were indelibly imprinted in my mind.

When John F. Kennedy was killed in Dallas on November 22, 1963, my immediate visceral sensing was that, in some way, the forces that had manifested themselves at JM/WAVE were involved in the death of the president. Later, I would have the same feeling after the death of his brother, Robert Kennedy. Everything I've learned since only reinforces that original intuitive judgment.

Now in my 70s, I have not yet rested in my effort to get the full story before the world and into the historical record of our time. All else has had to become secondary. With the issuance of this book, Vox Pop has provided me the opportunity to fulfill a purpose that has consumed much of my life.

I fully expect this account to generate a good deal of controversy in the intelligence community, the media, and the public, both in the U.S. and abroad, just as was the case with the earlier censored version published as *The War That Never Was* in 1976.

The decision to go forward with the issuance of an unabridged narrative has not been taken lightly. The release of *The War That Never Was* and events directly and indirectly associated with providing an insider's account of the Kennedy administration's covert war against Cuba has had a profound impact on virtually every aspect of my life over the past 30 years. The forces within our government that have tried to discredit and intimidate me have never given up, and long ago I abandoned any hope of leading an ordinary life.

I am not naïve about the consequences of revealing government secrets, especially those concerning illegal and nefarious activities by officialdom. I am prepared for what might come with the release of this book. Were it not for the generally favorable media coverage of my work, lots of prayers, and tons of sheer good luck, I would not be around to write today.

Over the years, many have questioned why I would take such risks, not only castigation, but retribution by those who are threatened by my revelations. As a young, idealistic, Catholic officer, my early exposure to the prevailing CIA philosophy of the period—based on "the ends justify the means"—deeply affected my worldviews and perceptions of government. Officially sanctioned duplicity and deliberate deception were a way of life within the agency among career officers. Manipulation, lies, concealment, bribery—the concepts of non-attribution, plausible denial, unintended consequences, stonewalling, and expediency at the expense of human considerations were accepted, common components of the CIA's covert operations as I observed and experienced them. Perhaps I was too steeped in honor as an officer, too vulnerable psychologically to believe in mission and purpose; too impressionable for the assignment I accepted. Ultimately, the failure of our attempts to overthrow Castro's Communist regime—and the wholesale abandonment of the brave Cuban exile volunteers I helped train, fostered a disillusionment and mistrust I've never overcome. This despite the fact that I later volunteered to serve my country in high risk assignments and still consider myself a patriot.

I anticipate there will be official denials of my account, with no shortage of negative commentary from retired CIA and military types, contemporary critics, detractors, and skeptics among the media and general public.

Ringing in my ears, the words of my part Native American mother: "Perseverance, perseverance, perseverance!" And the words of my first newspaper editor, while I was still in my teens: "Observe, listen, record, report, and be loyal to your conscience." Should anyone have doubts about what appears on these pages, should my credibility or accuracy be impugned, or be it alleged this work is a flight of fancy by a delusional, disgruntled old man, I ask this: Why did my CIA boss, at JM/WAVE, Theodore Shackley, make bibliographical reference to the original publication of my account in his provocative 1981 nonfiction book, *The Third Option,* and why would he continue to communicate favorably with me into the early 1990s on matters concerning my writings?

I believe Mr. Shackley, motivated by a sense of historical responsibility, wanted the story told. He knew I could speak out on the JM/WAVE operation when as a former CIA career officer constrained by oath, contract, and loyalty, he could not.

The fact is that aspects of my history with the CIA and my description of events and contacts with various high profile personalities have been referred to and confirmed by recognized, credible authors in more than a dozen nonfiction books over the past 30 years. I do not offer this in defense of my work but as an aggressive preemption to those who would discount it, and I challenge any and all to disprove my words.

As I have gone forth with this effort, as an investigator and chronicler of history, I've applied fundamental journalistic standards in my work: use first person witnessing of events, and when gathering evidence beyond that, require at least two independent sources to corroborate specific information, and finally, ascertain the willingness of said source to undergo polygraph examination. For anyone asking, I, myself, subscribe to these criteria.

As I've documented my account and recorded my observations and impressions, and while unselfishly cooperating with both official and private researchers and investigators, I diligently avoided becoming part of, or pandering to, the conspiracy subculture in America and elsewhere. While I cooperated unselfishly with researchers I deemed responsible and well grounded in their investigative procedures, I found a great many rush-to-judgement dilettantes ready to jump on any nugget of information without verification, who would run with it to enhance their personal wealth and stature. Solving the mystery of the enormity of the assassinations required coordination, teamwork and sharing of information. Envy, bickering, ego enhancement, rumors, unsubstantiated claims, personal attacks, financial gain, shoddy research, exaggeration, even falsification or misrepresentation of evidence and the exploitation of sources were fairly common motives and traits among many in assassination lore and related areas of inquiry. The legitimacy and credibility of all researchers has been subject to question by the media and the public as a result. I've tried to avoid being identified with those who have brought so much ridicule to the serious, productive efforts of many dedicated Americans.

I pray this work—my descriptions and insights—helps fill the plausibility voids that obscure, warp and distract one's understanding and acceptance of the linkage between some of our nation's most unsettling moments, and the secret power structure forged under the cover of Zenith Technical Enterprises in the early 1960s. The philosophy spawned there has wielded enormous influence upon the course of national events for the past four decades. I hope this book will enlighten, alert, and maybe frighten the average American possessing only casual, traditional media-sourced knowledge of CIA and place into proper context the sinister, secret forces that have dominated the major events of our time, depriving the American people of constitutionally established oversight and control of our national destiny.

AUTHOR'S NOTE

I want to assure all who read this book that I realize the gravity and implications of the revelations contained herein, and the affect they may have on the lives, reputations, and historical images of others. I've delayed going public with this account for many years, struggling with my conscience over the profound ramifications and collective consequences it might have.

I ultimately had to face reality, with my advancing age and very limited resources, time was running out for my voice to be heard and the probability it would not be within my capacity to finish the investigative work and share the experiences that have impacted so dramatically on the course of my life and the world in which we live.

Readers looking for good news in this book will be disappointed, unless they see it as a contribution to finding truth. It's my hope the information contained herein will move others to follow the leads provided.

My conscience is clear and I am at peace in the spirit of these Native American prayers that have been the guideposts for my time on this earth and which I now offer in honor of that extraordinary woman I call Pearl:

Prayer for Living

O Great Spirit, whose voice I hear in the winds,
and whose breath gives life to all the world
Let me walk in Beauty.
May my hands respect the things You have made,
and my ears sharp to hear Your voice.
Make me wise so that I may understand the things
You have taught my people, and the lessons
You have hidden in every leaf and rock.
I seek strength not to be more than others
but to fight my greatest enemy—myself.
Make me always ready,
with clean hands and straight eyes
So that when life fades, may my Spirit come
to You without shame.

Prayer for Dying

When it comes time to die, be not like those
whose hearts are
filled with fear of death,
so when the time comes,
they weep and pray for a little more time
to live their lives over again in a different way.
Sing your death song,
and die like a hero going home.

THE ZENITH SECRET

ACKNOWLEDGMENTS

I am deeply grateful to my now deceased great-aunt and godmother, Mrs. Julie C. Hickey, who encouraged me to complete this project. She alone stood by me through the personal trials of many years. Without her generous support and trust, this story would not have been told.

I express my sincere appreciation to the attorneys Doug Weldon, David Fuller, and Alex Simpson who had the courage to step forward and guide me through the production of this book. I also appreciate the Vox Pop staff's patience in working with me, especially the efforts of Rebecca DeRosa.

I dedicate this book to my family, and especially to my three sons, Daniel, Bradley, and Steven, and my grandchildren, with a prayer that they may someday understand my purpose. All in their own way have sacrificed something for truth, because they have been part of me through it all. I also pay tribute to the brave Cubans, those in exile and those who live on under Castro, in whose hearts still burns the eternal flame of freedom.

Finally, I acknowledge the following individuals who have encouraged and supported my cause over the years, in one way or another. I have not, and will not, forsake their belief in me.

Lee Miller; Cynthia M. Graham; Gay Bostock, my original editor (TWTNW); Anthony Summers; Gaeton Fonzi; Noel Twyman; Michael Andregg; Ron Williams; Jim Fetzer; Ryan Ross; Dale Gustafson; Jim Viken; John McDougal; Gordon Winslow; Brian Quig; Dick Franklin; Kathy Stewart; Ted Higinbotham; Shane O'Sullivan; Anita Buck; the office of Russ Feingold; Wisconsin Department of Veteran Affairs; J.R. Freeman; Abbot Mills; Don and Pat Gay; John Timmerman; John Kelly; David Jones; Jane Johnson; Jim DeEugenio; Lisa Pease; Charlie Wolden; Tom Bremer; Roland Buchman; Walter Forbes; Rick Gates; Arnie Hymanson; Jack Lambert; Kris Luchsinger; Darlene Novinger; Jim Placzek; Dennis and Rosemary Ste. Marie; Marv Winters; Diane Sapp, Esq.; Jeff and Terry Rossow; John Woods II; Judge John Tunheim; Tom Keller III, Esq.; Lt. Col. Koy Bass; Jim Boily; Doug Valentine; Sherry Anderson; Chris Igo; Bill Black; Kevin Bakewell; the Baldricas; Jane Christenson; Lincoln Zonn; Jerry Gumbold; Doug and Rita Jenkins; B. F. Kelly; Mark Sarnoff, Esq; John Dean; Lynn Niles; Denny Chambers; Wyatt Earp; Bob Gallivan; Fred Bihler; Joe Hoffman, Esq.; Tom Mulligan, Esq; Bernie Lumbert; David Johnson; Jack Junker; Gary King; Byron Higgins; Jerry Sondreal; Tom Lund; Bob Mahle; Jim Rothstein; Greg Lynch; Attorney Errol Kantor; and John Kraemer.

And to all of you, for the why and how of it, and to all the beautiful women who have touched my life, for better or worse.

Thank you!

Bradley E. Ayers
2006

BRADLEY E. AYERS

PROLOGUE

December 29, 1962, the Orange Bowl, Stadium, Miami, Florida. The tropical afternoon is warm and bright, the midwinter Florida sky is blue and cloudless. At the open end of the stadium, a large American flag waves lazily in the gentle breeze that blows off the sea. Pastel banners ripple gaily above the stands.

The arena is filled with tanned Latino men in shirtsleeves, and women and children in colorful attire. They sit, quietly waiting and expectant. Despite the festive quality of the scene, there is a subdued, almost somber mood in the air.

Assembled on the grassy infield is a group of men dressed in pressed khaki uniforms. They are gathered before a speaker's platform decorated with red, white, and blue bunting, and a podium flanked by microphones, bearing the familiar seal of the president of the United States.

Some of the men use the support of crutches, while others sit in wheelchairs. The group has an unmistakable military quality, yet the men are almost emaciated, too thin and weak to be soldiers. Their starched khaki uniforms fit loosely; their faces are drawn and hollow-cheeked. It is the look of men who have faced death, but their eyes sparkle and their gaunt faces reflect determination and pride: These are the men of Brigade 2506, the Bay of Pigs survivors.

The arena is quiet. A rush of excitement passes through the crowd, then there is a bustle of activity near the speaker's stand. President Kennedy, accompanied by his wife, strides confidently to the battery of microphones. The stadium erupts in cheers and applause as the crowd of 40,000 Cuban refugees rises to greet him. The air is heavy with emotion.

Suntanned and with the characteristic shock of hair, JFK exudes a youthful, casual quality though the set of his jaw conveys the gravity of the occasion. The president addresses the throng before him. His speech is a moving message of renewed promise of freedom for the thousands of exiles who have fled to the United States. Even before the speech is finished, the crowd is on its feet, shouting: "Guerra! Guerra! War! War!" Pepe San Romano, one of the Brigade leaders, still pale from Castro's prisons, steps forward and presents the president with the Brigade banner that flew on the infamous Cuban beach some 20 months before. Kennedy, his eyes glistening, accepts the tattered flag and turns again to the thousands of cheering Cuban refugees. "I can assure you that this flag will be returned to this brigade in a free Havana."

I watched that scene on television in the officers' lounge at the U.S. Army Ranger Training Camp, at Eglin Air Force Base in northwest Florida. Little did I realize that, within a few months, the event would involve me personally.

The promise made to the Cuban people by the president in Miami on December 29, 1962, was more than an emotional gesture. It was a declaration of national policy, one as purposeful as Kennedy's resolution to place an American flag on the moon by the end of the decade. The president's words in the Orange Bowl were a fervent commitment of American support to the cause of the Cuban exiles. It was a commitment that set in motion a series of events that no one could have foreseen.

In the months following the Orange Bowl address, the Kennedy administration enjoyed an upswing in popular support. By the spring of 1963, it was riding a ground swell of approval. In October 1962, following his success in the Cuban missile crisis, Kennedy embarked on his "Strategy of Peace." Cuba no longer dominated foreign policy, but the administration never took its eyes off Castro. The abortive Bay of Pigs invasion in April 1961 remained an embarrassing blot on the administration's record. Castro's flaunted revolution and belligerent posturing were a continuing threat in the Western Hemisphere and a personal insult to the Kennedys. The compassion the Kennedys felt for the exiled Cuban people was poignantly demonstrated when the administration "ransomed" the Bay of Pigs prisoners with $53 million worth of drugs, food, and medical equipment and supplies, all donated without the use of federal funds. The Orange Bowl commitment in December, 1962 followed this action.

The United States had long been committed to nonintervention in Cuba. Although the Cuban missile crisis nearly made armed intervention necessary, the Soviet withdrawal of missiles and the ensuing Khrushchev-Kennedy "understandings" reinforced the U.S. policy of avoiding direct military involvement.

While President Kennedy assured Nikita Khrushchev there would be no U.S. military invasion, his guarantee did not preclude an attack on Cuba by covert means. The CIA, smarting from the failure at the Bay of Pigs, was given another chance to topple Castro. The president, despite his deep-seated mistrust of the agency, directed the CIA to embark on a no-holds-barred clandestine effort to destabilize Cuba. The objective was to overthrow Castro and establish a democratic form of government on the island. The effort was something of a personal vendetta between the Kennedys and the bearded Communist dictator.

For the first time in its history, the CIA was authorized to establish a field station on U.S. soil. Code named JM/WAVE, by early 1963 the Miami station had become the largest in the world, employing scores of CIA career officers and staffers, hundreds of selectively recruited Cuban exiles; storing masses of stocks of "sanitized" non-attributable military supplies, weapons, ammunition, explosives, sleek power boats, yachts, large mother ships, assorted aircraft. There were also dozens of safehouses and remote training sites in Florida, Louisiana, the Bahamas, and the Florida Keys. Costs were of little concern to the Kennedys or the agency. JM/WAVE was given all the tools required for clandestine paramilitary warfare, intelligence gathering, and espionage.

The CIA's secret war against Castro was not limited to clandestine paramilitary activity. Code named "Operation Mongoose," the CIA focused its efforts on every aspect of Cuban Communist life and included international economic and trade boycotts, penetration and subversion of Latin American political and labor organizations and infiltration and coercion of cultural and academic circles. The objective: eliminate Castro and destroy Russia's hold on the island.

The Miami station was headquartered on the sprawling south campus of the University of Miami, near Perrine. It had been the site of a Navy lighter-than-air landing and hangaring base, known as Richmond Naval Air Station until it was dedicated to the university as an academic research facility after WWII. In 1962, the CIA spent millions of dollars refurbishing the decaying wooden barracks and warehouse buildings, converting the facility to serve its needs as a secure base of operations, communications, and logistical support.

The CIA went to great effort to camouflage the true nature of the JM/WAVE facility. Zenith Technical Enterprises, by all outward appearances, was a benign government electronics research and development contractor, ostensibly doing classified work for the Defense Department and other federal agencies in cooperation with the University of Miami. Logically, the front gate to the facility would have a civilian security guard post and anyone entering the grounds would have to display a photo ID card.

But, behind the elaborate facade of corporate trappings and under the strictest security, an extraordinary agenda of black operations was carried out against Castro's Cuba by the CIA: infiltration of intelligence gathering teams, caching of supplies and equipment to support the Cuban underground, commando and underwater demolition team raids; ambushes, sabotage, crop, food, and water contamination—employing the full range of paramilitary and espionage methodology and technology of the day. Most secret of all were the plots to assassinate Fidel Castro, using Mafia bosses and hit men to organize and carry them out. Everything was done with the "plausible deniability" of U.S. government involvement as a primary consideration.

For the first time in American history, an agency of the government was, in effect, given carte blanche to break this country's laws, as well as international and maritime law.

To assure complete freedom of action, the station was "back stopped" (in the jargon of the trade) at the highest levels of all federal, state, and local law enforcement agencies to avoid any interference from those entities. JM/WAVE operatives in the field who, in the course of performing their tasks, were stopped, questioned, or arrested by unwitting law enforcement officers because of suspicious behavior or violations of the law were quickly released via a prearranged coded communications procedure with the apprehending authority.

Amazing as it may seem, the CIA's secret war was, for the greater part, monitored and sometimes micromanaged by a select group of high level Kennedy administration officials from a war room in the basement of the White House. The president, ever wary of being led down the primrose path by the CIA, designated his brother Robert "Bobby" Kennedy, to scrutinize every anti-Castro operation planned by the agency. Bobby Kennedy, chairing the Special Group, as it was known officially, guided the planning and approved each covert action, including many farfetched undertakings and dirty tricks.

While the CIA Cuban desk relished the unlimited logistical and financial support it got from the administration, resentment ran deep among the covert ops "cowboys," who found themselves constantly bridled and often thwarted by changes in mission details and constraints imposed by operationally untutored administration civilian political appointees in the White House basement.

The president was kept fully informed of the secret war by his brother. He undoubtedly knew of the Castro assassination plots and who was involved in the efforts to carry them out. On the other hand, Congress and virtually all other elements of the federal government, as well as the American people, were kept ignorant of this monumental sinister activity.

The Special Group, on orders of the president, made a critical assessment of the CIA's covert paramilitary actions against Cuba in late 1962. The evaluation was not encouraging.

Historically a "cloak and dagger" foreign intelligence-gathering organization, the CIA had little experience in offensive combat operations, as the Bay of Pigs very clearly showed. The Special Group decided to strengthen the agency's paramilitary capability by providing two "advisers" from the regular U.S. armed forces, on an undercover basis.

I was one of the men selected to perform this top-secret mission. What follows is an account of my experiences with CIA and the aftermath.

Bradley E. Ayers
2006

CHAPTER I

It was mid-December, 1964. I was sitting in the Pentagon office of the United States Army Deputy Chief of Staff for Special Operations. My presence there, that gray, chill winter day, has very special significance. It was my last official act as a commissioned officer in the Regular Army of the United States. I had just presented my letter of resignation.

Across the shiny walnut desk that separated us, I watched the youthful, crew-cut colonel look again at the neatly typed document that lay before him. It was the only paper on his usually cluttered desk. He had been my case officer for the past two years. In that time, we had come to know one another well. He had been at once, my superior, my confidant, my ally, and my advocate; my sole link with reality and the security of my military parentage. He knew more about me than any other person in the world and we shared twenty-four incredibly dramatic months encompassing events that profoundly changed the course of history.

Colonel Bond was a chain smoker, and I watched him reach for another cigarette. Inhaling slowly, deep in thought, his cold, blue eyes were fixed on the letter on his desk. As the smoke trailed up between his thin lips, he picked the document up and slowly read it again.

When he had finished, the colonel laid the letter back in the center of his desk, and sat staring at it for a moment. Then he took a quick puff on his cigarette and stubbed it out in the partially filled ashtray. He turned in his swivel chair to look from his Pentagon office out over the Potomac and the gray Washington skyline.

He hadn't said a word to me. I knew him well enough to know what troubled him. It was almost as if I wasn't there. His eyes swept past the Lincoln Memorial, drab in the late afternoon drizzle. Why was he making me wait? Again I wondered what was going on in his mind. Maybe his thoughts were going back to the beginning. Nearly 24 months. It seemed an eternity. He wondered what had gone wrong. He was the one who had screened hundreds of military records and chosen my name for the top-secret mission. He had made the recommendation.

My mind went back to a hazy, warm spring evening in 1963 to see myself as I was then. The image was hard to focus. It was like looking at a different person, someone I remembered but could only vaguely define. I was naïve and dedicated, gung-ho as the slang term was applied then. The military and service to my country was my life.

It had been that way for a long time. Maybe the seeds were sown, growing up in a small, patriotic Minnesota town, during World War II. As the oldest in a middle-class family of four boys, I watched my father enlist in the Navy, even though he was too old for the draft. It was the first time he had left us, and as the eldest boy, I shared my mother's loneliness. I exalted in the pride I felt for my father's action and the war was the focal point during the most formative and memorable years of my life.

Then there was high school, sports, girls, and a typical Midwestern adolescence in the early 1950s. General Eisenhower was my hero and I shook hands with him once while he was on a whistle-stop tour of Minnesota. I remember our joy the night he won the presidential election. Overshadowing it all was the Korean War. My friends, my high school chums, the sports heroes of the day, all were in the fight. Some never came back, and some that did carried the scars of battle. Our best hockey player came back legless, and a basketball star with professional potential lost his arms. Still there was the sense of pride and dedication, and I begged my father to let me quit school in my junior year to enlist. Thank God and he made me finish school.

I made no plans beyond high school because of the war and because I wanted to serve. Dreams of going to college and one day becoming a writer were put aside, and soon after school was out in 1953, I enlisted in the Army paratroops.

The Korean War ended the same year, and, as acting sergeant, with less than two years service, I applied for Officer's Candidate School. By the time I was 28, I had won a Regular Army Commission and outlined a life's career as a professional officer. I married my high school sweetheart and she joined me to share my military life. No matter I hadn't gone to West Point, no matter I had no college. I was working on that. I had stars in my eyes, and I knew hard work and dedication to the service would bring the fulfillment I sought.

I was an infantry officer, and very proud of it. I volunteered for every school and every specialized training course[1] the Army had available. The pattern of my training gradually qualified me as a specialist in "commando" type operations. As a Ranger-qualified paratroop officer, I went on to receive training in survival, physical conditioning, mountaineering, underwater demolitions, SCUBA, and piloting light observation planes. As the years went by, serving in various assignments around the world, I gained extensive experience as a military instructor and operations staff officer. My military security clearance was upgraded to top secret, and I was exposed to a wide range of command levels, working with classified military plans and programs. My boyhood interest in writing led me into a number of security assignments requiring military writing skill.

My wife, our three sons, and I moved from one place to another as I accepted different assignments, serving diligently and "picking up the tickets," of career development. Our lives revolved around the military. I was a professional officer and that was exactly what I wanted to be. It was not always an easy life, but the satisfaction it brought me far outweighed the hardships and separations. It was a secure and positive existence. It was the only life we knew.

As I sat there in Colonel Bond's office, waiting for him to react to my letter of resignation, I was conscious only of all that was behind me. The colonel was still gazing out over the drab grayness of the Washington skyline.

The chain of events that lead me to Colonel Bond's office for the final time began in the spring of 1963. I had held the rank of captain, and as a senior officer in this grade, nearing promotion to major, I was serving as the executive officer of the Army Ranger Training Camp at Eglin Air Force Base in northwest Florida. My family and I had recently returned from European assignment and after a period of schooling at Fort Benning and a short temporary duty assignment, we had rented a house on a secluded bayou and settled down to a period of stability and peace.

The mission of the Ranger Camp was to train volunteer officers and noncommissioned officers in the techniques of clandestine jungle and swamp operations for small units. Initially, I was excited about the assignment. It seemed to be the ideal place for an officer with my specialties and interests. Vietnam

BRADLEY E. AYERS

was just beginning to receive serious attention from the military establishment and the demand for highly skilled Ranger-trained officers to serve as advisors in Southwest Asia was increasing day by day. This fact eventually had an unfortunate impact on my status at the camp. As the executive officer, I was responsible for the overall administration of the installation. I soon found myself spending more time than I liked supervising mess halls and barracks, making routine inspections, completing reports, directing building programs, and managing paperwork. I found less and less time to participate in the tactical training and, more often than not, was tied to my office and desk back at camp. I would have much rather been in the field.

To complicate matters, Lieutenant Colonel Hakala. who commanded the camp, insisted the executive officer keep his nose out of training and stick almost entirely to managing administration of the installation. I performed my duties faithfully, but yearned to join the men in the field patrolling, parachuting, and engaging in the paramilitary training exercises that were going on. I made numerous requests to the camp commander. After persisting with my demands, he consented to let me go occasionally into the field, but restricted my training participation to off-duty hours and after my regular duties had been accomplished. I resented this restriction, but I was pleased to have the chance to get some exposure to training.

I failed to understand the reasons for the camp commander's attitude, and it continued to be a sore point between us. The lieutenant colonel resented my presence in the field. It was almost as though he was afraid I might have some influence on the men who would supercede his position at the camp. Gradually I began to dislike the man, and, ultimately, a real personality conflict developed. In 10 years of service, it was the first real personality clash I had experienced. It seemed to set the stage for what followed.

As the early months of 1963 passed by, I found myself, for the first time, truly dissatisfied and frustrated in an assignment, and almost at open war with a superior. In retrospect, it seems as if I was provoking destiny. Where had I been that warm April night in 1963 when Colonel Bond was making his recommendations to the Special Group at the White House?

On a sunny April day I made my move and requested a transfer. I had marked a training assignment in Panama as my first choice, justifying the selection by emphasizing my extensive background in the type of training that was being done at the Jungle Warfare School. It was a long shot, but just maybe they'd buy it. At least someone up the chain of command would know that I was unhappy as hell.

THE ZENITH SECRET

CHAPTER 2

"Good morning, sir." I saluted smartly. Colonel Hakala returned the salute and then sat back in his chair eyeing me suspiciously. I waited, but he said nothing, and for what seemed an eternity, I stood stiffly. There was no sound except the whirring of the fan. He finally spoke: "That was Fort Benning on the phone. I don't know what the hell kind of strings you've been pulling, but you're to go to Washington and report to an office in the Pentagon in civilian clothes before twelve hundred hours tomorrow."

I didn't realize it at the time, but those few words began the most fantastic adventure of my life. It wasn't until the next day, as I rested uneasily in the cramped passenger seat of the Washington-bound airliner, that I really began to think about the puzzling turn of events. The hours following the surprise announcement had been hectic, and there'd been little time for contemplation. Overshadowing it all was the aura of mystery that surrounded the call from Washington. I was tense with both curiosity and excitement.

Less than an hour before, I'd said goodbye to my wife and sons. I pictured them standing at the airport: Suzie holding the newborn, Steve, and wearing a brave, defiant look she didn't feel, and young Dan and young Brad clinging to the wire fence as they watched me board the plane. It had been the hardest farewell we had ever gone through, because of the uncertainties ahead. The telegraphed orders had contained only the data for my travel. Before, I had always known at least a little of what to expect, and I could confidently promise my wife and sons that I would return. I made the promise this time, but without the confidence. As I boarded, I thought of them all alone in our small house on the bayou, and I felt a great loneliness.

Now, as the jet began its descent, the knowledge that I would soon understand the mysterious orders quickened my pulse and I sat forward, alert. In a matter of minutes I was in a taxicab; a short time later, I found the Pentagon office I was looking for in a restricted area. Small gold letters proclaimed:

**SPECIAL OPERATION SECTION, SPECIAL WARFARE,
OFFICE OF THE DEPUTY CHIEF OF STAFF ARMY OPERATIONS**

I straightened my tie, brushed my suit, and went inside. I don't know what I expected, but it was quiet inside. I presented my orders to the young receptionist. The minutes ticked by. I lit a cigarette and picked up the *Army Times*, trying to find something to occupy my mind. It seemed ridiculous, after all the rush to get there, that I should have to wait. Nearly an hour had passed when a deceptively youthful looking colonel wearing combat decorations dashed into the outer office. I rose at attention. Instead of saluting, he shook my hand.

"I'm Colonel Bond. Welcome to the Special Warfare Section, Captain. Sorry for the delay, but the matter of your mission has us pretty well going in circles. Come into my office. There's a great deal I must talk to you about, and time is short."

I immediately liked his enthusiastic, informal manner. While he closed the door, I stood respectfully at attention in front of his desk, very conscious of my decidedly nonmilitary appearance.

"For Christ's sake, sit down, Captain. In fact, I don't want to see you standing at attention or saluting or doing anything military from now on. During the next several days, you're going to forget every Army habit you've ever learned, so you'd better start right now."

"Yes, sir," I replied automatically.

"Damn it, I said forget the military...don't you understand? Forget the 'sir.' And that applies to everyone around here. From now on you're a civilian."

I could see that the colonel was serious, but it sounded like some kind of joke.

What had I done? I didn't want to be a civilian!

The colonel continued. "I'm sure you're wondering why you've been ordered to the Pentagon under these rather hurried and mysterious circumstances. I'm sorry that we had to do it this way, especially for your family, but there was no other choice."

I watched intently as the colonel lit a cigarette.

"You've been selected, after careful review, to be given an opportunity to volunteer for a very highly classified and difficult assignment. Now, before I can tell you anything about this mission, you must agree to undergo certain tests, including a polygraph. The tests will take three days. Provided you pass them, which I'm confident you will, you'll be given the details of the mission and an opportunity to volunteer for the job."

Colonel Bond looked at me carefully, his gray eyes unblinking. "It is up to you at this point, Captain. We don't have much time, so I must have your answer now."

I hesitated only for an instant. I knew what I must do. "Of course I'll agree to the tests, Colonel."

I could see that he was pleased. "We'll begin tomorrow morning. There'll be another officer undergoing the tests with you; you will meet him in the morning. Register at one of the nearby motels as a civilian. Incidentally," he added, "I must ask you not to call home or say anything about what I've told you thus far, until a final determination is made on your acceptance for the mission. Do not discuss your reason for being here with anyone except myself—is that clear?"

Later that evening, after I had found a motel near the Pentagon, I took a taxi into Washington. I had tried to stay in my room, but I was too restless; the brief meeting with Colonel Bond had amplified my curiosity. As I wandered from the Lincoln Memorial toward the Washington Monument, my presence seemed strangely unreal. Two nights ago I had been in dirty combat dress, parachuting into the mud of an isolated swamp; now, less than forty-eight hours later, I was dressed in casual civilian attire and was under instruction to shed all vestiges of my military way of life. The change was difficult to comprehend.

So too was the mission, as implied by Colonel Bond, and the demand of the tests I was about to undergo. What could I be asked to do that would require such tight security? The question went round and round in my mind. I knew I had to pass the tests: If the mission was so important to the interests of my country, then I wanted the opportunity to try to qualify for it.

Despite my loneliness as I walked along, I was filled with resolve and renewed dedication. It suddenly dawned on me that perhaps my ten years of training had been for this single mission.

Colonel Bond was waiting impatiently when I walked into the Pentagon the next morning. He led me into his office and introduced me to Major Edward Roderick who was to undergo the tests with me. After shaking hands with the tall, thin, conservatively dressed man who I estimated was in his mid-forties, we sat down, and the colonel began:

BRADLEY E. AYERS

"This morning, you'll begin your examinations. I've set things up so you can more or less keep each other company as you make the rounds, get to know each other. You can expect to be working closely together in the future if everything goes OK during the next few days." He paused, watching our reactions. "These tests may get under your skin a bit, but don't sweat it. Just play things straight and don't worry about the results; it'll be virtually painless. Now, before we go, do either of you have any questions?"

Roderick and I looked at each other, and the major shrugged.

"No, sir."

"Damn it, what did I tell you...forget the 'sir' bit. It's for your own good...you've got to think. OK, let's get started." He led us out to the reception room and told us how to reach our first examination. To our relief, the initial step would be a routine physical. Colonel Bond introduced us to his staff assistant, Lieutenant Colonel Frank Garret who would guide us through our processing.

So it began, first with a thorough medical examination, and then an in-depth psychiatric interview. Roderick and I took turns at each examination, and while we waited we talked, though we were uneasy with each other at first. We both had been impressed with the security measures being taken in connection with our prospective mission, and we joked uncomfortably that either one of us could be a plant to test the other's security consciousness and vulnerability. Once that point was aired, we compared notes about our mysterious calls from Washington. I learned that Major Roderick, engineer officer and demolitions expert, had been ordered from an assignment in Massachusetts. He too had departed on short notice, leaving his wife to care for his home and four sons.

We both breezed through the physical and psychiatric examinations and, after a harried lunch, began a series of written tests that took up the remainder of the afternoon. Finally, we returned to Colonel Bond's office to check out for the day. To me, the day had been disappointing: in spite of all the trumped up security the colonel had passed out, it seemed nothing more than routine Army exams that almost anyone could have passed.

The following day was essentially the same. More forms to complete, more psychological tests, interviews with security agents and a lot of waiting between examinations and interviews. Ed and I soon ran out of things to talk about, and we sat silently and restlessly, eager for the testing to be completed.

I couldn't sleep that night. I was troubled by the waiting, bored with the monotony of the examinations, and anxious about the test results. I thought of my family and wondered how they were getting along. It seemed ridiculous that I couldn't call them, but then it occurred to me that that might be part of the testing. And what about Roderick? Was he legitimate, or was he a plant?

I began to wonder about the whole thing. The mysterious orders, civilian clothes, chain-smoking Colonel Bond with his orders to forget the military, my conversations with Roderick, the doctors, the psychiatrists, the screwy repetitive questions and written exams. Maybe I was beginning to distrust myself, I thought, and maybe that's what they want me to do. They wanted to just see how much I could take.

The next morning, Lt. Colonel Garrett told us that a lie detector test, which would take most of the morning, would be the last phase of our security examination. That afternoon, provided the test results were satisfactory, General Rosson, deputy chief of staff, Special Warfare, would brief us on our mission. A nondescript security agent led me into the testing cubicle and explained the equipment and procedures, while Roderick sat smoking nervously in the waiting room.

The small room was bare of decoration, and the pale green soundproofed walls gave it a cold, impersonal feeling. The expressionless examiner, with his conservative gray suit and practiced friendliness, fit the scene perfectly. I had never undergone a lie detector test before, and when he placed the sensors on my heart, hands, arms, and head, I had the distinct feeling that I was the victim in a horror movie experiment. Slowly and deliberately, reminding me to give only yes or no answers, he began.

"Is your birthday the seventh of March?"

"Yes."

"Were you born in St. Paul, Minnesota?"

"That's in my records in front of you. Yes."

"Just answer yes or no. Do you have three sons?"

C'mon, I thought, you can read all that. "Yes."

"Have you ever had an extramarital affair?"

Tilt. I knew the needle jumped. "Ah....yes?"

"All right, please give me the details."

So that's how it works, I thought, not answering.

The examiner stopped the machine and carefully wrote something on my report. "Are you sure you don't want to tell me more?"

"No, that's it."

As the examiner moved to turn the machine back on, I had second thoughts. Credibility, "No, wait a minute; you might just as well know the details. You'll probably just ask me again."

As the man coldly made notes on his pad, I gave him the details of my extramarital love life: A brief encounter or two, a few one-night flings while overseas or on temporary duty. But, just the same, it was very personal, and I found it difficult to talk about. I'd never discussed this aspect of my personal life with anyone, and I resented being manipulated in this way.

"Have you ever been addicted to drugs?"

"No." The questions carried new meaning now and my attitude changed.

"Have you ever been divorced?"

"No."

"Do you profess to be a Roman Catholic?"

"Yes."

"Is your age twenty-eight?"

"Yes."

"Have you ever been a member of the Communist Party?"

"No."

"Do you hold the rank of captain in the Regular Army?"

"Yes."

"Have you ever had a homosexual relationship?"

"No."

"Have you ever cheated on your income tax?"

"No."

On and on went the monotone voice. Christ, I wasn't a Communist or a queer. My whole life had been wrapped up in serving my country; he had no right to question me like this. I was getting angry.

The calm, even voice came at me again: "Please relax, Captain. There's no good reason to become upset. These are just routine questions. Now, are you in good health?"

"Yes."

"Do you smoke cigarettes?"

"Yes."

"Have you ever stolen anything?"

"No." The needle jumped.

He made a mark on the tape, and I knew I'd get that question again, so I told him about the ammunition and rockets I had helped "borrow" from Charlie Company on the range in Germany.

The questioning resumed. There was no clock in the room. I'd had to remove my watch, but I was sure we'd been there four hours or longer. Finally, when it was over, I was visibly shaken. My face was clammy, my throat was dry and constricted, and I was sweating profusely. No one had ever gotten to me that way, and I wanted to get out of there. I felt ashamed; I didn't even feel qualified to wear my uniform.

The examiner showed me back out of the waiting room. I slumped into a leather chair across from Roderick, but he wasn't looking at me. I followed his gaze to a narrow glass slit in the wall above his head. I hadn't seen it before. It was a one-way mirror. Were we being watched even now? I grabbed my suit coat and left. I was still shaking and was bitterly disappointed with myself. I paused at the men's room to splash cold water on my face, then went to the coffee shop to wait for Roderick. I tried to put my sense of failure out of mind, but by the time Ed appeared three hours later, I was prepared for disappointment. He was even more upset and angry with the polygraph session than I'd been. We both expected unsatisfactory results.

Neither Bond nor Garret were in the Special Warfare Room when we returned. We waited nervously as an hour went by, then another. By the time they arrived, my chest was tight and the cigarette in Roderick's hand was shaking.

"Well, you made it. That's the word we've been waiting for." Bond smiled approvingly. "It was a tight squeeze for a while, but you've been found acceptable by the powers that be."

I turned to grasp Roderick's hand to congratulate him. More than anything else, it had been a matter of personal and professional pride for both of us; now we smiled our satisfaction to each other. No longer was there doubt about where we stood; who could be trusted; who was real. We'd passed the first test together and had formed a friendship.

Colonel Bond said, "We're going upstairs to General Rosson's office, where he'll brief you on your mission. He will ask for your decision, so be prepared to give it to him. We have no substitutes for this job, so if you turn this down, we'll start all over again."

Lieutenant General William B. Rosson's name was already familiar to me. He was a personal friend of the president and a long-time military friend of General Maxwell Taylor, the chairman of the Joint Chiefs of Staff. General Rosson held the sensitive position of supervising the development of Special Forces and other paramilitary activities, principally to support the growing involvement in Vietnam. As we hurried down the long corridors to his office, it seemed more likely than ever that our mission would take us to Southeast Asia.

In spite of Colonel Bond's earlier instructions, we saluted General Rosson as we were ushered into his office. The general was a large, bullish man, and his uniform was bedecked with decorations and campaign ribbons.

"Gentlemen, he began, "you are being asked to volunteer for a very sensitive, highly important assignment. In view of the lengthy preliminary testing you've undergone, I'm sure you realize this mission has more than routine security considerations. I advise you keep that paramount in your minds." He paused to stress the importance of his words. "For some time this country has been carrying on covert paramilitary and espionage activities against the regime of Fidel Castro. Some of this has been done through U.S. sponsorship and supervision of exile forces, while other activities are handled indirectly through various Latin American governments. Under no circumstances can the United States become directly involved—not our people or our armed forces—in military activities against Castro. Since the missile crisis, the U-2 flights have been the covert military activity we've conducted against Cuba. Some of the raids and paramilitary operations are being conducted independently by ill-equipped, poorly organized exile groups, but most of the operations are being planned and conducted under the supervision of the CIA, using carefully selected Cuban exile volunteers, from bases in southern Florida and elsewhere in the Caribbean.

"The CIA has not been achieving the success hoped for. The Army has been ordered to provide the CIA direct support in two critical areas—the training of small commando units for raids and infiltration, and the planning and use of the demolitions and explosives."

The general looked at us, steely-eyed. "Captain, you have been selected because of your background and experience in small-unit, waterborne and parachute operations. Major, you've been selected because of your expertise in demolitions. I will not go into the details of your missions except to say that this matter has top priority and is receiving highest attention at the highest levels of government. The mission will require the utmost discretion and flexibility, as well as the highest possible dedication and professionalism. You will have to sever all ties with the Army, forget that you were ever in the military. Colonel Bond's office will be your only military contact, but you'll be expected to uphold the finest of standards of the Army in whatever you do. The mission will be very demanding on your families, but I believe it will be a challenging and very satisfying assignment. If you accept this mission, you will become undercover agents for the Central Intelligence Agency."

His words hung in the silence of the room. "Gentlemen, I would like your decision now."

CHAPTER 3

We sat stunned in silence. For a few moments I simply could not accept what I'd heard. Neither of us, in our wildest expectations, had anticipated that our mission might involve Cuba.

My immediate reaction was to volunteer for the assignment. I'd made a quick assessment, and it appeared to be the greatest opportunity of my career. I'd be able to use the skills I'd worked ten years to perfect and, more importantly, I'd be making a contribution where it really counted, for I could think of nowhere else in the world where my actions as a professional soldier would be more vital. I'd watched the tactical debacle of the Bay of Pigs, and, with others in the military, shared in the anxiety and frustration of the Cuban missile crisis of October 1962.

It seemed fate was giving me the opportunity to become directly involved in a struggle that I had strong personal feelings about, and as one that offered a unique professional challenge.

I had only one reservation: my family. General Rosson had emphasized the importance of secrecy. What if pro-Castro agents discovered my participation in CIA espionage activities? The possibility of retribution—of harm to my wife and sons—had to be considered.

"I'm prepared to take the assignment, sir, but on the condition that measures be taken to protect my family, to ensure their safety and welfare in my absence."

"I also agree to take the assignment, sir," Roderick added, "but I too want to know that my family will be all right."

Rosson looked at Bond as if he hadn't anticipated this. The colonel shifted uneasily in his chair, searching for the right words. His reply was less than reassuring.

"General, there are a number of details regarding the families that we have yet to work out. The matter will be resolved during the next couple days, when we settle on a cover for these officers. However, the CIA has already assured me they will take the families into full consideration—take care of their finances, brief them as necessary, and provide them the same services the military would."

Nodding, the general turned back to us. "Colonel and his staff will work out the details with the CIA, and you can be assured of our support. The colonel will talk to your wives, and you'll be in constant contact with his office, so any problems can be worked out that way."

Assuming he had placated our reservations, he changed the subject.

"Colonel Garrett will arrange your transfer to the agency and will be your administrative contact here. I want to wish you the best of luck and remind you once again that you're being placed in very sensitive positions. Never forget that you're professional Army officers, even though you'll be working with civilians, who do things differently than we do. You'll be on display. There'll be many high–level people in Washington watching what you do."

It was well past duty hours and the halls were deserted when Colonel Bond ushered us out of the office. Ed and I were both excited about the mission. It promised to be the adventure of our lives. We had dinner together that night. It was the first time that either of us had had an opportunity to relax. No longer preoccupied with doubts and questions, we began to open up to each other. We recognized the importance of establishing mutual trust and understanding. Ed told me he'd preferred to be called Rod, an abbreviation of his last name. He also confided that his last assignment had involved inspecting packages for explosives at the White House.

I was impressed. My first impression of Rod as an introverted, conservative, methodical man seemed confirmed. With subdued enthusiasm he quietly analyzed the events of the past few days, while I had a difficult time containing my exuberance. We seemed to balance each other. He was an "inside man," a planner; I was an "outside man," a doer. I liked Rod but found him a bit stuffy. I hoped that he might change once he was exposed to the swashbuckling adventurers and free-spirited soldiers of fortune I expected to find at the CIA.

We received authorization to call our families but were warned not to discuss any of the details of our assignments. It was nearly midnight when I contacted Suzie, and her voice was full of relief and anxiety. I told her I was all right, and as I asked how she and the kids were, my throat ached with suppressed emotion. She said that all was fine. She was doing her best to be brave, but she wanted to know about my new assignment. I told her I was undergoing some interviews and would be here for another week or so, and that somebody would be in touch soon to brief her. She tried to sound composed, but I knew how worried she was. When we finally said goodbye, the pangs of loneliness returned. The excitement over my assignment had all but overwhelmed that emotion, but now my thoughts were again of my wife and sons. I was glad that I'd raised the consideration of their welfare in the presence of General Rosson.

Roderick and I spent another day at the Pentagon while the details of our transfer to the CIA were worked out. It became obvious that the arrangements had some unsettling overtones. The rumored jealousy between the military and the CIA over roles in certain sensitive areas like Cuba was showing through. Our status had become the topic of closed-door conferences and irritating phone calls up and down the Army and agency chains of command as each attempted to gain greater control. Rod and I believed that someone at a high level, probably in the White House, had directed the Army to help the CIA. The Army had probably been reluctant to have their officers placed solely under CIA control, especially when the Army itself wanted to get into the Cuban struggle. At the same time, the CIA was probably not pleased about being forced to accept help from the Army in an area of operations in which they considered themselves expert.

Rod and I realized we'd become bureaucratic "hot potatoes," and our assignment to the CIA was even more complex than it had first appeared. To further that impression, we began to notice a pronounced concern on the part of Bond and Garrett that we might be corrupted and our loyalty to the service undermined by elements within the CIA. For want of a better term, I called it "bureaucratic alienation of affection." Shortly before our transfer, the Army won the right to maintain a fragile link with Rod and me through bimonthly reports that we would prepare, summarizing our activities with the CIA. Never before had anyone working inside the agency been allowed to make reports to the outside on what they were doing.

It was a sunny Saturday morning when we packed our bags and were driven to CIA headquarters in Langley, Virginia. As the Pentagon disappeared behind us, I was very conscious that I was stepping into something unknown, without the security of uniform and rank, without the sense of being part of an organization and a team, without the tangible goals of recognition and reward, promotion and social standing—all of the things that had always been part of my military career. It was saddening and frightening, but, at the same time, my qualms were overridden by the thrill of new adventure.

We turned off the freeway onto a meandering country road, and after driving through a small wooded area and rounding a short bend in the road, we got our first view of CIA headquarters. At the gate, as we waited for the hard-looking security man to call for our entry authorization, I looked at the super-secret complex I'd heard so much about. The modern gray stone building was somberly impressive. From the flat roof of the building protruded a mass of antennas and microwave receivers. Surrounding the entire complex was a high fence topped with barbed wire; security patrols could be seen around its perimeter. In marked contrast to the ominous quality of the command post were the peaceful landscaped grounds within the fence. People sat reading or talking on stone benches under large shade trees, and groups of young secretaries lazed on the grass. It might have been a typical college campus. The impression struck me as oddly incongruous, because I knew the agency was the source of the most diabolical schemes of assassination, revolution, and political unrest. Spying, espionage, and diplomatic intrigue were its stock in trade. So many cloak and dagger tricks executed by our government had been germinated behind the façade of tranquility that lay before me.

A few minutes later we were standing in the cavern-like, marble-columned, reception lobby of the main building. No one except regular agency employees could proceed beyond this point without an escort. Our guide appeared and gave us security identification badges, then took us to the basement of the building, to a section identified as the Cuban Operations Center. Whatever the CIA's role in national policy toward Cuba, it all began and ended within the confines of those walls. Somehow, I had expected frantic activity, as at a military operations center, but it was very quiet, and most of the desks were deserted, even though the Cuban section was in operation 24 hours a day.

Colonel Bond introduced Rod and me to various people, by first name only. I guess I expected them to fit the classic secret-agent image, but the men and women were mostly middle-aged and exceedingly nondescript. They looked up from their work only long enough to say hello and shake hands, then returned quickly to whatever they were doing. It was less than an enthusiastic welcome.

We were first taken to a plush first floor office and introduced to the head of the Cuban desk, Mr. Des Fitzgerald, who hurriedly but cordially welcomed us. Then we were escorted to an adjacent office and introduced to Mr. William Harvey and Mr. James O'Connell, both of whom exhibited an unmistakable air of authority. After a brief pep talk about our mission, they intimated that we would eventually be going to Miami to work directly with the Cuban exiles, but they gave no details. I couldn't help noticing Mr. Harvey carried a large holstered pistol on his waist, visible under his sports coat. As the meeting was about to conclude, I raised again the question of our families' welfare. Colonel Bond looked at me sharply; apparently it was a touchy matter. More and more, Rod and I had been bothered by the way this had been dismissed. When I made the point again, Colonel Bond and Mr. Harvey agreed that further coordination would be made between the military and the agency to ensure the welfare of our families.

With that, Bond[2] left. We were now officially under the control of the CIA. Mr. Harvey called Guy back into the room and instructed him to be our guide

THE ZENITH SECRET

for the next several days. We were told to come back on Monday. It was deflating under the turmoil we'd gone through. As we were being driven back to Washington, I told Rod that by appearance, none of the CIA figures looked like spies or warriors. They were middle aged, and not in the best physical shape by Army standards. Colonel Bond commented most had OSS, WWII backgrounds.

That weekend, because we had nothing else to do, we asked Guy to show us some of the after-action reports on the CIA's paramilitary operations with the exiles in Miami. Rod and I were eager to get some grasp of the mission we faced. The poorly organized reports proved to be of little value. Almost all the specific data—the identification and size of teams and units, the types of mission, geographical locations, etc.—were given in code. When we asked Guy to interpret the code for us, he professed ignorance of it. Whether he was telling the truth or simply following instructions, we didn't know. We gradually figured out that all Cuban operations agent teams had code names that began with the letters AM. AMTRACK, AMARK, AMTHUMB, and AMCHECK were each separate groups of men working independently, but all reporting to the Miami CIA headquarters which was known as JM/WAVE. Other teams and operational bases had similar code names, and nothing was identified in clear text.

Monday began much as Saturday had ended. Rod and I resumed reading the after-action reports, but this time the information was written in rambling, informal memorandum fashion. No effort was made to number or record copies of the routine documents, nor was any accounting system maintained. When we questioned this, we were told the CIA considered everything classified. Therefore, preparation, filing, and disposal of all material was handled the same as the military's top-secret information. The CIA preferred compartmentalization. No one had access to more information or contacts than was necessary to accomplish his or her specific task.

One's status in the control structure determined the degree of access to information, and only a few people at the highest level knew the full story about any particular activity. This "need to know" was, in fact, the basis of their security system. Even husbands and wives, both employed by the agency, often had no idea of each other's duties. The "need to know" procedure was not new to us. It was practiced in the military to a limited degree, but not at the expense of coordination and teamwork. It was obvious that it was the best possible system of internal security and counterintelligence, but we wondered how rigidly it could be implemented in tactical paramilitary operations when it was essential that each person know what everyone else doing.

Because of compartmentalization, no one could fully describe the Cuban program. We tried to piece together how the exiles were trained and organized, how targets and missions were selected and assigned, and how operations were planned and executed. It was the first real challenge of our mission.

After two days at the agency, we learned to adapt to the seemingly undisciplined civilian way of doing things. I began to form some impressions of the agency employees, at least the ones in the Cuban Operations Center. There were many young typists, clerks, office boys, and junior technical people. Few of them seemed to understand the nature and magnitude of the agency's function.

The others, usually in supervisory positions, were older. With the exception of a few attractive young secretaries, everyone appeared quite taciturn. They spent their days pushing reams of paper from one desk to another. They struck me as typical civil servants, amazingly nonchalant about their highly classified work. The daily decisions of these people caused governments to be overthrown, yet with bureaucratic anonymity; they ate their lunches out of paper bags and promptly at 5 p.m. stopped the war. The incongruity grated on my military sense of immediacy and commitment.

As our second day wound to a close without the mention of Miami, Rod confided that he too sensed an air of uneasiness about our assignment. The agency people treated us with detachment and suspicion, regarding us as intruders in their secret, bureaucratic domain. There seemed to be an atmosphere of forced acceptance, and it reaffirmed our belief that we'd been "jammed down the throat" of the CIA by the Special Group.

The next morning we were given a psychiatry-security interview, which, unlike our experiences at the Pentagon, was relaxed and respectful. With our military dossiers in front of him, the doctor asked us to verify some facts given earlier and gave us another opportunity to withdraw from the assignment.

When we reaffirmed our decision, the interview was concluded. Then we were sent to the agency's cover branch. It became obvious to us that our cover was the subject of considerable confusion. I could understand the problem. Our mission demanded much personal freedom, the fact that we were Regular Army officers on active duty had to be kept secret, and our participation in the CIA's anti-Castro activities violated the agreement made between Kennedy and Khrushchev during the missile crisis. Therefore, our cover stories would have to stand up to scrutiny and must conceal our true status even from certain other CIA personnel while simultaneously allowing the agency to provide for the care of our families as military dependents.

I was totally amazed that the cover branch was able to create new people, to change identities, appearances, credentials, passports, or whatever might be necessary for a specific mission. Some agents had as many as three or four identities, each used for different tasks. Characters and personalities materialized and disappeared as if by magic.[3] I came away from the cover branch with a disconcerting awareness. I had always assumed that people were who and what they said they were. Suddenly it seemed apparent that, at least in the CIA, any person could simply be playing a cover role. I resolved that I'd never again accept anyone at face value. I did not know then that my resolve would return to haunt me.

Our basic cover would provide that we—under our real names—had been honorably discharged from the service some months earlier and had gone to work as civilian technical specialists in Army Research and Development. We were to be attached to an Army support group involved in classified weapons and undersea research with the University of Miami. This group was not real, but anyone looking at the records would see documented proof of it.

Our Regular Army pay would be sent directly to the bank, where it would be available to our families, and Rod and I would receive a monthly cash payment from the CIA. We handed over all our military identification, including our "dog tags." We'd walked in as Army officers and we left as civilians.

In the morning we underwent final processing and were given the name and physical description of an agent who would meet our flight at Miami. Rod and I boarded the midday Eastern Electra flight to Miami, which had become known as the CIA Miami "milkrun." It was said that half the passengers on any given day were agency operatives. As we climbed aboard, it occurred to us that if we'd ever had a wish to simply disappear, this was the opportunity of a lifetime.

CHAPTER 4

The man who met us at the airport must have thought we were headquarters VIPs. He kept saying "sir" and apologized for the heat, the crowds, the long walk to the parking lot, and the quarters which had been found for us. Obviously he had no idea who we really were, and nothing was said about the CIA. His instructions were to deliver us to our temporary quarters, in Key Biscayne, to ensure our comfort, and to leave us there. The house he'd been apologizing for turned out to be an elegant, beautifully furnished home, complete with pool and patio overlooking Biscayne Bay.

For the next two days, Rod and I did little more than eat, sleep, drink, and swim. No one visited us and no one called. By the morning of the third day, we were worried. What were they waiting for after hustling us to Miami so quickly? But finally, that afternoon, the phone rang. We were told to pack our bags and be ready to be picked up the next morning by a man called Bob. A brief description of the car and the man's appearance was given.

When he arrived, he introduced himself as Bob Wall, assistant chief of operations at the station. He looked more like my image of a federal agent; he was neatly dressed in a sport coat and tie with a porkpie hat. He was polite and businesslike, but he seemed irritated about having to escort us to headquarters.

In a few minutes we were on U.S. 1, on our way to south Miami. Bob informed us he would look after us until we were assigned within the "company." He knew who we were and a little about our backgrounds. From his comments, it was obvious he held no great affection for the military. I hoped his attitude was not representative of what we'd find at headquarters.

Bob told us not to use the term CIA. When we had to make reference to the agency, we would use the word "company." He went on to explain that the Miami headquarters was covered under a civilian corporation known as Zenith Technical Enterprises. The station, or "company," was located on the University of Miami's South Campus, adjacent to the abandoned Richmond Naval Air Station, which had been developed by the Navy during World War II as a dirigible base. A hurricane had devastated the immense hangars, and only girders and concrete foundations remained. The airfield was still intact but not open for use, except covertly by the agency. Nestled next to the airfield was a cluster of wood-frame barracks and headquarters buildings. The Navy had turned the area—several hundred acres of woodland—over to the University of Miami for field research and for building expansion. At considerable expense, the CIA had refurbished the old wooden buildings and set up operations as Zenith Technical Enterprises, a firm doing classified government research. Later, after we saw the magnitude of the Zenith complex and became aware of the many rumors about its actual function, it was apparent the university could not have been ignorant of its tenant's true identity.

We pulled up in front of a large double gate. A civilian security guard checked Bob's pass, and we drove along a winding road to a low building identified as the U.S. Army Support Group. This was the official unit to which we'd be attached.

We presented our orders to the noncommissioned officer sitting in the office

*The gatehouse at Zenith Technical Enterprises where visitors were
carefully screened by security guards who provided a front for the CIA complex
beyond the patrolled fences.*

and were given our mailing address and a 24-hour telephone number for the
duty officer. After a visit to the security office, where we were given temporary
passes, Bob told us to find a motel somewhere close to the station and suggested
we contact our families after a security briefing on Monday morning.

Rod and I spent the better part of the day searching, and finally settled on
a quiet place off U.S. 1, three miles from headquarters. The Mariner Hotel was
a far cry from a luxurious Key Biscayne house, but it was convenient and fairly
clean. The proprietor and his wife were not overly concerned about the activities
of the guests.

We spent the following day with Bob and his family. I had wondered how
much agents' spouses were allowed to know about their work, and was relieved
to see that Bob spoke about business matters quite freely in his wife's presence.
I was pleased to see this openness, and I hoped I'd be allowed to be just as honest with Suzie. Bob explained that he was a case officer, which meant that he
managed Cuban exile paramilitary intelligence and commando teams. When we
asked specific questions about training and composition of the units, Bob
seemed suspicious and did not answer.[4]

Monday morning we met the station chief, Ted Shackley. As we sat in his
outer office, waiting a little nervously, I saw that they had missed no detail in
setting up the false front of Zenith Technical Enterprises. There were phony
sales and production charts on the walls and business licenses from the state
and federal governments. A notice to salesmen, pinned near the door, advised
them of the calling hours for various departments. The crowning touch was a
certificate of award from the United Givers' Fund to Zenith for outstanding participation in its annual fund drive.

When we were finally shown into Mr. Shackley's office, I was immediately
impressed by the tall, young executive. His post demanded wisdom and professional skill; Shackley had these in abundance. The station chief had to be close
to the president, a member of the inner circle, and Shackley was the kind of man
Kennedy would have appointed.

He welcomed us with poise, a Harvard air, and a Bostonian accent similar
to John Kennedy's. His polished but informal manner put us at ease while his

cool professionalism instilled confidence and respect. It was the first time that anyone in the CIA had made me feel my services were wanted. I felt a renewed determination. After our encouraging meeting with the chief of the station, we began a series of briefings. The staff was organized much the way the military's was, but with a distinct bureaucratic civil-service aspect. The station had separate, distinct departments: personnel (internal administration and finance); intelligence (various sophisticated procedures, including photo analysis and the use of U-2s); operations (planning and execution of operations, recruiting and supervision of Cuban exile agents); logistics (procurement and distribution of all supplies); cover (responsible for providing suitable cover for all station activities, including those of the exiles); security (internal and operational security, including counterintelligence); maritime (planning and supervision of all seaborne operations); communications (all aspects, including coded transmissions, electronics, etc.); real estate (procurement of houses and property, under cover, for use by all branches). A separate branch had been set up, to develop training programs for all Cuban and foreign volunteers because of the need for competent agents.

There were several other, smaller "offshoot" departments that seemed to function independently and had direct access to the chief of station. I felt that the structure was unnecessarily complex, with authority widely dispersed and confused by overlapping responsibilities. It was unwieldy, with too many separate branch chiefs reporting directly to the chief of station. I had envisioned it as a highly responsive, uncluttered organization, but it now appeared to be a sprawling bureaucratic monster.

At first, Rod and I were treated as VIPs. The branch chiefs each gave us the standard, practiced briefing on their operations, but when we tried to question them in depth about their roles, they were evasive.

We soon discovered that no one knew what to do with us, and finally we were temporarily assigned to the operations branch. Dave Morales, chief of operations, a big Mexican-Native American, was the only branch chief who treated us less than respectfully. He ran all the station's activities with a heavy hand and was famous for his temper. We soon learned that no one, save Ted Shackley himself, argued with Dave. To cross him in any way was to invite trouble.

A few days after our arrival, Rod and I attended a full staff briefing; representatives from all the branches were present—a total of 30 people. The briefing itself was disorganized, but I found it enlightening. The plans for two exile paramilitary actions were discussed. The first was a small commando raid against three Cuban patrol boats they expected to find in the harbor on the southern coast of the island. (Roderick got his first assignment when Ted Shackley asked him to review the demolitions plan for this operation.) The second mission was a relatively simple operation in which another commando team was to bury supplies, ammunition, and weapons in special waterproof containers on the southern coastline. The location of the cache would be radioed to one of the intelligence infiltration teams already inside Cuba, who would, it was hoped, recover the supplies and distribute them to other anti-Castro guerrillas on the island. (In missions like these, the commando teams were transported by ship—usually referred to as the "mother ship"—to a point approximately three miles off the Cuban shore; small boats were then lowered from the mother ship, and the teams would proceed ashore in them, under cover of darkness.)

Bob Wall discussed the control the president's Special Group exercised over all operational activities. The station developed plans for operations and

THE ZENITH SECRET

recruited, trained, and equipped Cuban exiles to accomplish specific missions. Sometimes the station originated the mission, based on its own intelligence, in accordance with the objectives of the Special Group. Occasionally, however, the Cuban office at headquarters or the Special Group itself would order a specific mission, which they would keep under constant review. Wall was the first agent we'd met who had expressed the CIA's frustrations over this. The Special Group had the power to approve or deny missions, modify plans, or dictate details as small as choice of specific weapons. They infringed on decisions of case officers and often insisted on last minute changes after months of preparation and training. This was especially irritating, because the members of Special Group were not specialists in espionage and clandestine paramilitary operations. The changes they ordered caused enormous problems for officers responsible for particular operations and, in Bob's opinion, often guaranteed failure before an operation was launched.

The next step was final processing by both the security and cover departments. After yet another security brief—our 10th by count—we were told the complete story on Zenith Technical Enterprises and our alleged relationship to it as Department of the Army civilians.

This DA cover, which had been established at CIA headquarters in Washington, would allow us to come and go around the station and to live "normal" lives in Miami as innocuous government employees. The security branch hadn't confirmed that someone in Washington had briefed our wives, but we were given authorization to call them and let them know we were in Miami, working on a classified research and development assignment. Security also informed us that our families might be allowed to join us in Miami if the DA cover seemed to be working satisfactorily.

At the branch we were given still another complete identity, for use when dealing with non-regular agency employees and the Cuban exiles or when involved in actual clandestine operations. I was given the fictitious identity of Daniel B. Williams, a former military pilot employed by Paragon Air Service. Rod was provided with a similar cover: Paragon Air Service was a legally chartered Delaware corporation, allegedly engaged in various types of air and sea commerce, research and development. This cover company's activities were international in scope and channeled into south Florida and the Caribbean through a complicated network of other CIA paper corporations and false contractual relationships with actual business firms. The firm had a Miami office, phone number and mailing address, bank accounts, lawyers, accountants, and all the other tangible characteristics of a legitimate business. The Paragon Air Service phone actually rang in the cover branch and was answered by one of the station's staff. I could use my new identity just as I would my true one. I could even open a charge account or buy a house. My alias of Daniel B. Williams included an employment record, social security number, character references, and credit record. I had pretty well overcome my uneasiness about assuming a cover and was beginning to see that one could really lose oneself in a false identity. To remember who I was in any particular situation would take practice.

After a much-needed rest over the weekend, we were taken on a tour of the training bases. The CIA had created a sizeable organization of undercover bases amid Miami's bustling civilian populace. I wanted to see how it was maintained despite the inquisitive public, the probing news media, and the constant operational pressure.

One of Bob's "outside" agents[5] took us to the Homestead Marina where we met Rip Robertson, a former Marine. We'd already heard stories about the tall,

Bradley Earl Ayers (1963/1964)
CIA alias: Daniel B. Williams

rawboned man, his daring escapades at the Bay of Pigs, and, more recently, with his Cuban commando group. Rip, in his mid-forties, was a contract employee of fairly long standing with the CIA. Almost everyone held him in high esteem. Like Dave Morales, nicknamed "the Big Indian" (a.k.a. El Indio), to whom he was directly responsible, Rip was said to be stubborn, independent, and jealously protective of his men. From what we had read and heard, Rip's commandos performed well under his supervision.

Rip had apparently not been told much about Rod and me and certainly was not aware of out military backgrounds. We had been instructed to use our operational (Paragon Air Service) cover, and Rip didn't ask any questions. The tour began with us somewhere in the VIP category again, as Rip filled us in on the details of the V-20 boats used in the commando strikes. Their 20 foot V-shaped hulls had been extensively modified and reinforced, at a cost of more than $30,000 each. They were made of double-thick fiberglass to withstand the beating of high speeds on the open seas and to damage from coral and objects submerged in shallow water. Armor plating was embedded in the fiberglass to protect the fuel tanks and the occupants. Plastic foam and rubber, installed in critical places, added protection against the bullets and afforded the crew some cushioning within the open cockpit. Equipped with twin "souped up" hundred horsepower Greymarine inboard engines with retractable outdrives, the boats could travel 35 miles per hour while using no more than 75 percent of their full power.

We boarded one of the sanitized V-20s; that is, all the suspicious-looking gear, such as machine-gun mounts, towing shackles, and special electronic equipment, had been removed or disguised so that the boat appeared to be a common pleasure craft. Two wiry, young Cuban men climbed aboard dressed as fishermen. Rip ordered the operator to open up the boat full throttle as soon we

THE ZENITH SECRET

reached open water, and with that we were on our way.

I had brought a marine chart of the lower Biscayne Bay and tracked our course from Homestead Marina to the west shore of Elliott Key. The water was very shallow—with jagged coral a few feet down—but we skimmed high over it, and the spray soaked our clothing. Rip told us that on the open sea, even on a calm day, the powerful boat skipped like a flat stone from the top of one swell to another, landing each time with a bone-jarring smack, only to launch itself in the air again. I recalled Bob telling us that the "company" was searching for better, stronger craft, and was trying to improve the performance of the V-20. From the moment I saw the boat and felt it under me, I knew I wanted to handle one myself.

It took us about 40 minutes to reach Elliott Key. We pulled into a small dock, partially concealed in the mangroves, near the center of the tiny island. Two unshaven young Cubans met us there with a rusty old homemade car. One man stayed to guard the boat, and the rest of us piled into the makeshift vehicle. With Rip behind the wheel, we bumped over a narrow coral road through the mangroves and stopped in front of an isolated, ramshackle old house surrounded by palm trees and dense vegetation on the ocean side of the Key. Rip explained that this was the safehouse and base of operations for his commandos. The team lived and trained here and were allowed to go ashore to see their families and friends only once every week or two. The CIA rented or purchased dwellings for agents' use and were considered safe and secure after being checked for outside surveillance.

Rip showed us through the old building, which was set up like a military barracks. In the large kitchen, an elderly Cuban cook was busy over steaming pots that gave off spicy but appetizing odors. We proceeded to the equipment shed, and I saw that the group was well supplied with weapons, outboard motors, rubber boats, packs, green fatigue uniforms, and various military hardware. Rip pointed out that everything on the island could have been purchased in most civilian-military surplus stores; theoretically, therefore, the commandos' equipment could not be attributed to direct U.S. military support.

At noon Rod and I had our first real Cuban meal. It was excellently prepared and more than adequate for the 15 of us sitting at the big table on the porch. I was fascinated by the cheerful exuberance, the flashing dark eyes, and the quick smiles of the young commando volunteers. I regretted not being able to speak Spanish and resolved to learn it as quickly as possible. Rip, who spoke Spanish fluently, seemed to enjoy a somewhat fatherly role, and it was apparent that the exiles regarded him with great esteem.

After lunch Rod and I went for a long walk on the beach. We saw no other dwellings or signs of civilization. Elliott Key was an ideal site for a training camp. Rip had told us that the only intruders were weekend beachcombers and occasionally someone seeking help in a boating emergency. Aside from that, the only security problem lay in the island's logistical support: everything—fuel, bottled gas for cooking, fresh water, food, and other supplies—had to be transported from the mainland, and I could see the difficulties involved in shipping in the supplies without creating suspicion.

Later in the afternoon we asked pointed questions about the organization of the team, training procedures, motivation, and assignment of missions, but Rip, like everyone else we'd met, was reluctant to give specifics. I wanted to avoid any sort of confrontation with him, so when Rod continued to press his questions, I excused myself and walked back down the beach. For the first time, I really appreciated the natural beauty of the place. Only the coral reef and the

BRADLEY E. AYERS

vast expanse of the Atlantic lay in front of me. I wondered what the Cuban exiles thought as they looked across the sea toward their homeland.

It was very peaceful in the old house that night. They had to generate their own electricity, so the light was supplemented with old-fashioned kerosene lanterns. In one corner of the main room the Cubans had created a small shrine in memory of the men who had been killed or lost on earlier missions. It seemed to exemplify the camaraderie within the commando team and their profound dedication to their cause.

In the morning, we all waited in line for the toilet. The bathroom facilities on the island were limited: there was no shower, and fresh water had to be conserved. No one bothered to shave, and bathing was done in the sea. Two weeks of island living presented personal hygiene problems, but most of the Cubans had adapted to the hardships.

Training did not begin until midmorning, after all the housekeeping chores were done. The first session, a review of basic weapons, was conducted in the large central room of the old house. The class was presented quite informally, in Spanish, by Rip's personal assistant, a Cuban named Felix. The commando team had been issued a variety of individual weapons, including Colt .45 pistols, M-3 submachine guns (Greaseguns), Thompson submachine guns, .30-caliber carbines, AR-15 rifles, and standard M-1 rifles. Rip said the weapons had been obtained through Canadian or other foreign sources and could not be traced to the United States government. Most of Rip's team already knew the mechanics of the weapons, but while the class was going on, there was a lot of chattering and fooling around with weapons. The Cubans seemed to enjoy the image of commando freedom fighters and acted out their roles with humorous bravado; some of them even wore their weapons and cartridge belts Mexican bandit style. I wasn't ready to criticize this; I realized that the guerrilla image could be essential to maintaining high morale among the exiles, and to suppress their enthusiasm might destroy their will to fight.

The afternoon training session included instruction in the use of six-man rubber boats, and I had my first look at the Boston Whaler, a rather unique fiberglass boat which was well suited for rugged use. The Whaler was shaped like a small barge, and Rip said it was virtually unsinkable. It had a shallow draft hull with tri-V configuration to give it stability on rough open seas. The commandos used the standard commercial Whaler without modification, either the 13 foot three inch version or the 16 foot seven-inch model. The boating class was presented by another of Rip's assistants and, once again, there was a lot of horseplay. The instruction was disorganized. Finally the team tipped one of the rubber boats, spilling everyone into the water, which provided an excellent excuse to halt the training and go for a swim.

Later on, Rip showed us their newest piece of equipment, an item called a silent outboard motor which was about 50 percent quieter than a standard outboard. The Navy had developed it for underwater demolition missions and other clandestine activities. The motors were not available through civilian channels. They were made by the Johnson Company in several sizes. (Rip's men had a 10 horsepower and a 25 horsepower model.) The motor looked like no other outboard I had seen. It was painted a dull Navy gray and had a regulation military appearance.

The evening's exercise was a rehearsal of a proposed raid to destroy a railroad bridge in Cuba. Although the mission was not yet approved, the team had spent several weeks preparing for it. There was no railroad bridge on Elliott Key, so the commando team had constructed a crude mock-up out of barrels and

THE ZENITH SECRET

driftwood planks back in the mangroves. They had rehearsed the raid several times, so no pre-mission briefing was given. As soon as it was dark, the 12 Cubans donned their equipment and went down to the dock. We watched the men climb into two six-man rubber boats, which were towed from the dock by the Boston Whaler and released several hundred yards offshore. This action simulated the release from the mother craft.

While the commandos were paddling the rubber boats ashore, Rip, Roderick, and I walked through the mangroves to a prearranged landing point about a half-mile from the house. We hid in the dense vegetation and watched the raiding party come ashore and conceal the rubber boats. Although the men paddled the boats quietly, once they were ashore they completely disregarded noise discipline. Talking and clanking the equipment would have given away their position quickly in the real situation.

Keeping ourselves out of sight, we followed the commandos to the mock-up railroad bridge. The team moved quickly, but, again, there was too much noise. They would never have made it if there had been reasonably alert guards on the bridge. The attack itself was disorganized. There was no fire squad, no provision for security, and apparently no basic tactical organization as I had known in the military. The entire raiding party walked straight to the objective and set the simulated charges (small cans of gasoline), and when the charges detonated, everyone scattered. No rallying point had been established, and, as it turned out, two team members failed to show up at the rubber boat site for the return to the mother craft.

Confusion reigned. Finally Rod and I went back to mangroves and found the two frightened, embarrassed Cubans who had become separated from the withdrawing force. Reunited, the team paddled back along the shoreline to the dock in front of the safehouse. Rip said little on the way back, and I was sure he was ready to light into the commandos for bungling the rehearsal, especially in the presence of visitors. From my military viewpoint, the exercise had been almost humorously amateurish. But when we returned to the house, Rip said nothing. There was no critique and no after-action commentary. Instead, the men immediately devoured an enormous stack of sandwiches and black coffee.

They didn't bother to clean their gear, and as soon as they had finished eating they went to bed. I lay awake a long time that night, not able to accept what I'd seen. Rip, as the case officer in charge of the team, was obligated to correct their tactical errors. These men's lives, and the success of their missions, rested on his ability to train them. I felt it was a serious oversight to allow the exercise to become a farce and to ignore the blatant errors which, in the real situation, could kill them.

CHAPTER 5

In a bare rear office next to the training branch, armed with a typewriter and a continuous supply of coffee, I worked on my report for two weeks. Cal, the chief of training, and his assistant Rudy, accepted it with mixed emotions. On one hand, I was proposing a new training empire for them; on the other, if my recommendations were implemented, it would increase their workload 500 percent. By this time I had determined that Cal and Rudy had some reservations about this expansion of their responsibilities, but there was little they could do to stop me. I was functioning directly under the chief of station. They set about revising their manpower charts and equipment lists in anticipation of my recommendations being accepted by the chief.

I had requested an appointment with Ted Shackley for Friday afternoon but when I went to his office, Maggy, his secretary, said he was too busy to see me. If I left my report with her, Ted would read it over the weekend and meet with me Monday morning. I was quite disappointed. Not only was there the question of my going on a mission, but I anticipated questions about and, perhaps, resistance to my recommendations. We could be doing with the Cubans what the Army does with men in basic training, except that in our situation it would have to be done entirely covertly amid a very active and curious civilian community. Obviously, security could pose problems, but I felt I had the answers in the report. Moreover, I knew that Dave Morales would object like hell to the new prominence and control of the training branch in the selection and development of the teams. He would take offense, especially at my recommendations concerning the increased participation of the team case officers. I was concerned about Ted reading my report while I was not present: because of the weight that Dave carried with Ted, my whole report could be thrown out on his recommendation.

When Monday finally came, I was nervous. As I sat across from Ted's desk, he began by telling me that he'd been reading my reports to Colonel Bond and it appeared that Rod and I were adjusting pretty well to the new routine. Then he got right to the point.

He reviewed in detail each of my recommendations, and it turned out that Ted had been thinking of a training reorganization along much of the same lines. He said, however, he'd have to discuss it with the various branch chiefs before making a final decision. In the meantime, I was to make a detailed reconnaissance of the Homestead-Everglades training area for the paramilitary, boat-handling, and survival portions of the new program and let him know what I came up with in the way of suitable training sites.

Now was the time, I knew: "Ted, there's one more step I feel I must take if I'm to make a really sound judgment on the abilities and training needs of the teams."

"I know what you're going to ask. You want to go on a mission, don't you?" I nodded.

"I would expect that from you. What do they call it in the Army—gung-ho, or something like that?" As I expected, he then launched into the usual policy statement about the participation of Americans and the intervention of U.S.

armed forces in Cuba. "And you especially, my Army friend, are prohibited from getting yourself involved. It would create an international incident if you were compromised."

I had heard it before: the answer was no. Before I had time to protest, Ted continued:

"I think we might investigate the possibility of your going on a mother ship with one of the teams to the drop-off point at the Cuban three-mile territorial limit. But until we make a decision, I don't want you to say anything about this to anyone."

Hot damn! I nearly saluted—then remembered my civilian cover—as I thanked him and quickly left his office.

Under temporary cover as a real estate broker and developer, I began my search for a training area, concentrating mainly on the southern tip of the Florida peninsula and the keys. Occasionally Cal, the chief of training, his assistant Rudy, or Larry, one of the training instructors, accompanied me and from them I learned a great deal about the lives of CIA employees. More and more I saw them as typical government civil servants; they could just as well have been working for the IRS or Department of Agriculture. Gone forever were my expectations of dashing, romantic, swashbuckling "soldiers of fortune."

After days of traveling and walking over some of the most desolate, swampy, insect-infested areas in southern Florida, I was able to narrow down the possibilities to three general areas: upper Key Largo, including Linderman Key and the "Pirates' Lair" island safehouse owned by the University of Miami; the Old Card Sound Road area on the west side of upper Key Largo, and the Dynamite Pier area opposite and east of it; the Flamingo-Cape Sable area on the southernmost edge of the Everglades National Park.

My preoccupation with the training program kept me away from most of the day-to-day happenings at the station, but since I was anticipating a possible mission with the commandos I felt it absolutely essential to keep abreast of what was going on in Cuba. During late May and early June 1963, there was a pronounced increase in exile raids and bombings, refugee escapes, and other indications of internal unrest. One of our groups conducted a successful commando raid in Camaguey Province, and someone else blew up a ship in Havana Harbor. The newspapers said secret exile frogmen had done it, and Castro blamed the CIA. Naturally, we all rejoiced when anything like this happened, but at no time did anyone acknowledge, even in private, that our people had been involved. Publicly, the station and its various cover companies were kept out of the spotlight, despite the intense curiosity of the Cuban-exile community and the press.

Customarily, either by prearrangement through exile operatives or because of their own wishes to capitalize on the political impact of such incidents, one of the splinter groups of independent Cuban exiles, such as Alpha 66, would publicly take credit for the raids. Roderick and Bob Wall were able to give me some general information, but I had to closet myself in the super secret intelligence branch "reading room" to get detailed data on the enemy's activity. Usually this was contained in lengthy daily reports, which included the latest U-2 photos of the island (missions were still being flown almost daily), summaries of smuggled letters and reports, and U.S. and foreign press clippings. Oddly, no one questioned my self-authorized access to such highly classified information.

Having been schooled at the Army Chemical Warfare School at Ft. McClellan, Alabama, I was intrigued by reports of herbicides being used to

The V-hulled 20' runabout, with powerful inboard/outboard engines, was reinforced and modified with steel plating and gun mounts, and used as the primary boat for commando raids against Cuban coastal targets.

destroy agricultural crops in Cuba. During this period I also began a detailed study of the Cuban coastline and the general topography of the island. I was determined, if allowed to accompany a team, to be fully prepared for any eventuality.

The staff meetings I attended were long and boring. The little time that was devoted to discussing training matters proved to be of scant value. No one present had been exposed to the hardships and dangers imposed on the Cuban volunteers during the missions, and therefore no one could really understand what was required to prepare them. Most of the staff members admitted their ignorance and, in the end, recognized the merit of an improved program.

The Big Indian, Morales, was the exception to this. As I had anticipated, he raised objections to almost every one of my proposals. Operations seemed interested only in final production, turning out teams and missions in quantity, and depending entirely on the inherent capabilities of team members rather than making the effort to train them properly. An expanded, mandatory training program would encroach upon their dominance at the station and threaten their bureaucratic empire. I had sensed this attitude. In not one of the post-mission briefings did Operations accept any of the blame for losses and failures. It was always because the team was "stupid" or because "those are the breaks." I called it the Bay of Pigs mentality.

Despite Operations' objections, Ted Shackley accepted my recommendations almost to the letter. Ted informed me that I was to be permanently assigned to the training branch to set up and supervise the new program. Two weeks later I was on a V-20, speeding through the darkness, about to intercept a large mother ship lying at anchor some several miles off Islamorada. Our Cuban operator expertly turned the craft and came about on the lee side, then maneuvered it beneath the overhanging hull of the looming vessel. We were surrounded by blackness. Silently, a line was thrown from the deck above us and a cargo net was dropped over the side. We clambered up and over the cold, slippery rail of the Rex, a converted Navy World War II patrol craft.[6]

As the V-20 sped back toward the Florida coast, the full implications struck me. We were on our way to Cuba.

The roar of the departing V-20 was quickly swallowed by the sounds of the sea and the noise of the larger ship's diesels as they throbbed to life. I looked

THE ZENITH SECRET

back for a moment. The lights of Miami glowed to the north. South, toward the Straits of Florida and the Communist island, there was only dark, open sea. To the east I could see Alligator Reef and the slowly moving lights of a large tanker in the shipping lanes of the Gulf Stream, miles from our position. It seemed unreal, as if I were standing on the edge of the world.

Ted Shackley had approved my recommendations only a few days earlier. I never really believed he would let me go. When he gave me his approval, I was a little stunned. My activities during the next two weeks were to be known to only a few. As far as my contacts at the station were concerned, including Rod and the staff of the training branch, I was on an extended reconnaissance trip. That story fit in so well with what I had been doing for the past few weeks, that nobody would question it.

There'd been a week of briefings: meetings with the case officer and his Cuban-American go-between, Marcus; more briefings, and more meetings. We waited. The sea, the weather, and the moon phase all had to be right; and even more important, the Special Group in Washington had to okay the mission. That approval had to come through only this morning. Marcus was along on the mission. Like me, he was allowed to go with the team to the drop-off point. When I learned we would be together throughout this phase of the mission, I was very pleased, for he was an excellent translator and guide. Although Marcus had not been told of my military background, I'm sure it was apparent to him: his awareness became a kind of bond between us. Since he was well educated and had military training, I wondered why he was not permitted to lead the team instead of doing the "leg" work for the case officer. The superficial answer was, of course, that he was a United States citizen and therefore could not actually participate in anti-Castro operations. The truth of the matter, I think, was that his case officer found him so valuable in his role as a go-between that he simply refused to risk losing him on a real mission.

The team was less highly trained than their case officer had led me to believe. They were fairly typical of the other commando teams. Those six members were what was left of one of the very first units the CIA supported after the Bay of Pigs. The group had numbered 20 to 30 men, but some had been killed or captured in earlier operations, had quit in frustration, or were dismissed for security reasons. Rip Robertson had given them their earlier training, and when the larger group disbanded, the six men were passed off to a new case officer.

Marcus was assigned to supervise the six men and care for their immediate needs; he had worked with the group for nearly a year and claimed to have great confidence in it. Two men had been fishermen and had no formal education or training of any kind; they did know boats, however, and had firsthand knowledge of the Cuban coast. Two men had been sugar cane farmers, again with no formal education, but they were well adapted to hard work. One man had been a taxi driver and, another, a cook in a large restaurant. The taxi driver, obviously better educated, more alert, and more worldly than the others, was the team leader. All of the men were in their late 30s or early 40s.

During the week of intense preparation, the team's behavior had been pretty much what I had come to expect. Despite what Marcus had told me about their eagerness to return to Cuba on another mission, the men didn't display much enthusiasm. We went through the briefings, and one hurriedly improvised rehearsal, almost routinely. They said little and asked few questions, except for the team leader, who was very emotional and very confident.

The men had been housed in a comfortable safehouse on the outskirts of Coconut Grove in south Miami. They'd been living there, in almost total inactivity, since their last mission. It bothered me most that they appeared to be out of condition to confront the hardships of another mission. With the exception of the team leader, the men were flabby and soft. Their only exercise was an occasional swim in the small pool beside the house. The CIA case officer had made no provisions for physical conditioning, and the men had become indolent.

My observations were borne out when we went to Flamingo two days before the mission. The rehearsal, in addition to being poorly organized, was conducted in the early evening, in only partial darkness; and although there wasn't nearly so much lifting, paddling, wading, and walking as would be done on the actual mission, the team returned completely exhausted.

I was watching off the port bow, and soon the blink of the signal light from the smaller sister ship—the decoy vessel that would accompany us to Cuba—dotted the blackness. It was her acknowledgment that we'd weighed anchor and were under way. She would follow us at a distance of ten miles, using her small radar receiver. Radios would be used only in the event of an emergency.

This mission was relatively simple and, if discovered, theoretically untraceable. The minesweeper, owned and registered as a Costa Rican commercial salvage vessel, had sailed to the rendezvous point from its home port in Central America. (The crew of the ship was entirely Cuban or Central American.) It was to carry the team to the drop-off point three miles off Cuba, where the commandos would debark and make their way ashore in two rubber rafts with silent outboard engines. The team was to bury four specially designed cache containers at a specific point on the coastline. Later, agents already in Cuba would recover the cache. The exile volunteers would lie in hiding until the following night. At midnight they would return to the mother ship in the same manner.

While the team was ashore, our vessel would put out to sea and conduct a sea bottom survey in international waters. The smaller decoy vessel—a converted oil-rig patrol craft—would remain in close proximity. In the event that the operation was discovered, the faster steel-hulled vessel would attempt to distract the Cuban patrol boats and draw them away from the mother ship long enough for the team to escape.

The decoy vessel, U.S. registered and officially operated by a phony Delaware CIA petroleum corporation, was supposed to be doing offshore oil research and mapping. This allowed it regular and unquestioned access to U.S. ports, which was essential to the second phase of the mission. Also, should the smaller vessel come under attack, its operation as a U.S. craft would permit the use of American air and sea for its protection. (The crew members of this boat also were Latino.)

The role of the second vessel during the later phase of the operation was vital, for it would transport us back to the U.S. After the team made its rendezvous with the mother ship, the decoy vessel and the Rex would sail into international waters and, on the third night, rendezvous off Grand Cayman Island. The commando team, Marcus and I, would then transfer to the patrol craft, while the minesweeper would go back to Costa Rica to await another mission.

After checking on the team members—they were now asleep—Marcus took me down to the galley and introduced me to Captain Luis and his first mate, Enrique. The captain, a stocky, distinguished looking man in his late 40s, wore a gleaming .38-caliber revolver holstered on his belt. Enrique was thin and rangy, with the look of the sea about him; the deep lines etched in his leathery, tanned skin told of a lifetime of sailing.

Captain Luis spoke excellent English, and since he had been on many similar missions, I was most interested to share his firsthand knowledge of Castro's defenses. For the next hour we sipped bitter Cuban coffee as he explained in great detail the modus operandi of the Komar-class coastal patrol boats supplied to the Cubans by the Russians. I was amazed to find that he even knew the names of the Cuban commanders and crew members of some of the fast, heavily armed Soviet crafts. His information on the frequently changing routes and schedules of the coastal patrols was less than 24 hours old. He also knew the exact locations of the powerful coastal searchlight and gun placements in the area the team would be infiltrating.

I had to admire the CIA's ability to secure such complicated intelligence and disseminate it to Captain Luis; there were always two or three operations taking place simultaneously, in one phase or another. Once again, the magnitude and expense of the CIA effort against Castro was obvious. Despite the captain's thorough knowledge of the enemy's defenses at sea, he and Marcus had only sketchy information on Castro's shore surveillance. They knew that the Communists used radar, lookouts, and foot patrols with dogs, and had a network of civilian informers, mainly loyal fishermen and coastal residents. The specifics were supposed to have been part of the intelligence given to Marcus by the CIA case officer who had briefed the team, but the case officer apparently had forgotten to include this information. It would be a touch-and-go situation once the commandos had gotten past the patrol boats.

It was well past midnight when I went below to my small, shared cabin in the forward part of the ship and in minutes I was asleep. Awakened to the same monotonous engine throb that had put me to sleep I realized we were rapidly approaching Cuba, and tonight we would launch the operation.

I joined Captain Luis on the bridge, and for nearly an hour he explained the mechanics of the reclaimed World War II vessel. He showed me the elaborate electronic navigation gear and communications equipment that had been installed by the CIA. I was startled to learn that, despite all the equipment, the captain was navigating by dead reckoning alone, with only an occasional cross-check by LORAN (a worldwide, long-range commercial air-sea navigation system). Except for the usual multilingual banter coming over the standard commercial ship-to-shore radio, no other equipment was on. I asked Captain Luis how the station contacted him to give last minute information or instructions and I learned that the special high-frequency radio was turned on only for limited periods at specific intervals. The captain showed me the 40mm deck cannons mounted fore and aft and two .50-caliber machine guns set amidship. These weapons, and the small arms available to the eight-man crew, were the ship's only defenses. All of the heavy guns and ammunition were encased in innocent looking plywood boxes that had quick release devices to permit easy access. With such limited armaments, I hoped we wouldn't find ourselves in a situation where the boat would have to defend itself: it would be no match for the well-armed, faster Russian boats. The two six-man rubber rafts to be used by the team were covered by a heavy tarpaulin on the lower deck near the stern of the ship.

Below the main deck, the peeling bulkheads were wet with condensation and the pipes were leaking. Captain Luis and I walked through the ship and he introduced me to each of the crewmen. Their eyes flashing, and their skin glistening with sweat, they went about their tasks with pride and enthusiasm. When the captain had finished showing me around, I concluded that the Rex was a noisy, leaking relic, continually in need of repair, but otherwise seaworthy.

BRADLEY E. AYERS

Front view of the Navy Patrol craft, Rex, a CIA raider anchored within sight of former President John F. Kennedy's West Palm Beach retreat.

After the noon meal, the team went back to their cabin to rest; they would remain there until supper, when we would gather for a final briefing. In the midafternoon Captain Luis calculated our position: we were on schedule, somewhere between Cuba and the Dry Tortugas. By dusk we would reach the drop point.

I was alert with excitement as I went below to the galley to join the others for supper and the final briefing. It had been a very warm day and the air below deck was unmoving and rancid. Captain Luis, as was his practice, began the meal with a prayer, then opened a bottle of Portuguese wine and filled each man's small tin cup. I could only pick at my food, but the Cubans attacked the heavily oiled meal with gusto. Afterward, the cook placed blackout covers over the small windows and briefing began. We were now about 12 miles off Bahia Honda, on Cuba's northwest coast, and traveling southwesterly at about five knots.

Instruments and sampling probes had been dropped overboard and were being trailed behind the ship, in accordance with our cover role. The ship would remain on its present course and speed until it reached the drop off point near the village of Dimas, southwest of the Cayou Jutias beacon, at midnight. The vessel would be approximately three miles off the Cuban coast at a time when the two Cuban patrol boats covering the area would be farthest away. As the minesweeper continued to move slowly, the team would launch the rafts, get aboard, start the silent engines, and release their line to the mother ship. All of this had to be done in complete blackout and as quietly as possible.

There would be no turning back, even in the event of discovery, because once the team released the tow line, the mother ship would continue under way to clear the area. Using a compass and visual landmarks on the coast, the team would make its way across the shallow coastal shelf to their landing point.

THE ZENITH SECRET

Hopefully, the silent engines would work, but if they failed, the men would paddle the rubber rafts. Meanwhile, the smaller decoy vessel would move to a point some five miles off Sancho Pardo Bank and, with lights ablaze and engines running loudly, would attract the attention of shore lookouts and the Cuban patrol boats. The decoy vessel would be in international waters, so there was little the Communists could do but keep it under surveillance and, we hoped, be distracted from the team and us.

Tension mounted as the briefing continued. We were all sweating profusely in the small, closed space. The commando team leader, visibly nervous, drew on the back of a nautical chart a rough sketch of the coastline near Dimas. He spoke in Spanish to the team and Marcus translated for me. The launching and the boarding of the rubber rafts were routine; each man knew his assignment. The silent engines would be mounted and started immediately while the boats remained in tow. When the ship reached the drop point, Captain Luis would momentarily rev the engines as a signal to release the line. The two rafts would then proceed shoreward. Once inland, the team would locate a safe hiding place and stay there until dawn.

At first light, the team would bury the cache containers in the mangroves that fringed the shoreline. Then two of the men would move several hundred yards inland to observe the road that ran along the coast from Dimas to the village of Baja. If the team was detected, Castro's men would probably use that route to reach the area; approach from the sea by any sizable boat was impossible because of the shallow water. In addition, the team might be able to pick up some valuable information while watching the road. When it was sufficiently dark, the team would reassemble, uncover their rubber boats, and, this time using only paddles, row back to the rendezvous point. Besides using the compass on the return trip, they would have an RDF receiver to home in on the mother ship.

Captain Luis would have the mother ship in the vicinity of the rendezvous point for one hour, from 0200 to 0300. If for some reason contact was not made, we would return at the same time the following night. After that, the team would be presumed lost. The decoy vessel would play essentially the same role during the recovery phase as it had during the drop, and, of course, would take us back to Florida.

All illumination on board the ship had now been extinguished, and there was only stifling heat and the eerie redness of the blackout lights. In the equipment room, Marcus and I helped the men secure their gear. They wore dark clothes, heavy work shoes, and either dark blue baseball-type caps or wool watch caps. They carried compasses, machetes, entrenching tools, rope, canteens, and ammunition pouches attached to standard Army pistol belts. Two men carried light packs, one containing rations and the other containing a small, specially developed long-range radio transreceiver. With the receiver, they could talk with the mother ship and, under optimum conditions, with CIA reception stations at various locations throughout the Caribbean. The team leader wore a .45-caliber pistol in a shoulder holster, while each of the other men carried a standard M-3 .45-caliber submachine gun and four clips of ammunition. All labels and identifying marks had been removed from the equipment.

When they finished dressing, Marcus checked the men again, and then gave each a small emergency survival kit containing fishing gear, water-desalinization and purification chemicals, secret writing materials, Cuban money, morphine, and a special capsule containing a painless, rapidly acting lethal poison. The contents of the kit would be used at the discretion of the individual, depending on the nature of the emergency. There was no question about the morality of this procedure.

I was troubled by the loose, careless way in which the men wore their equipment. It could easily be lost and was hazardous in other ways as well. I told Marcus to have the men jump up and down in place. He looked at me quizzically but passed my instructions to the team. The clank of metal against metal filled the cramped room. We securely taped the loose straps and buckles; then Marcus handed me a .45-caliber pistol in a shoulder holster and buckled a similar weapon around his waist.

The deck was black. In the distance to the west, lightning flickered and a roll of thunder could be heard over the low growl of the diesel engines. To the south, beacons and scattered lights marked the coast of the Communist island. Off our stern, the bright lights of the decoy vessel were visible. The team moved to the stern and, with the help of the crew, began to uncover the rubber boats. Loud talking, cursing, and the clanking of deck fittings were quite audible over the drone of the ship's slow-turning engines. Marcus tried to quiet the men, but they persisted with their talking. Captain Luis shrugged, as if to say it was impossible to keep them quiet. I believed him. But I was sure the Cuban patrols would have heard us by now.

We all worked to slide the heavy neoprene rafts gently over the rail and lower them to the water so that they'd land right side up. Two of the commandos were lowered to the rafts, followed by the heavy, silent engines. It was still terribly noisy. I looked at my watch; time was slipping by quickly. One outboard engine started immediately, but there was trouble with the other. The team continued talking and cursing as the tools and the outboard fuel tanks clanked against the metal cache containers. We seemed very close to the shore, and I was tense, expecting to hear the first burst of machine gun fire that would signal our discovery.

Finally the cargo net was cast over the side and the remaining team members clambered over the rail and down to the rubber boats. Marcus, the captain, and I watched from the stern as the two small boats became dark blobs trailing a hundred feet behind us in the phosphorescent wake. Both silent engines were running and the rafts were still held by the tow line. Captain Luis went to the bridge, and it seemed an eternity before he revved the diesels. The Cuban coast was very near: the captain had violated the three-mile limit and we were within one mile of the shore. We watched the tow line go slack; then the rafts were lost in the darkness.

As Captain Luis altered the ship's course and headed west, away from the coast, Marcus and I retrieved the line and stood at the stern of the ship, looking shoreward. There was an air of anxiety, and no one spoke very much; our thoughts were with the team. The crew silently resumed its routine, and Captain Luis and Marcus turned in for the night. I couldn't sleep, for my mind kept retuning to the many questions raised about the operation and to my frustration over not being able to go ashore with the commandos. I returned to the bridge, pulled some life vests from a nearby locker, made a crude bed, and lay down. Except for the stars and the heat lightning on the horizon, there was only blackness. I dozed fitfully and got up at first light to see if any word had been received from the team. So far, nothing had been heard.

The sea was flat, the sky heavily overcast. The air was stagnant and very warm. The hours dragged by. We were somewhere off the Dry Tortugas, again trailing the undersea instruments from the jutting long booms. Occasionally a crewman would start the winch motors and reel in the heavy cable to inspect the research devices, for we had to continue to play the role. To pass the time, Captain Luis told stories of his days as a cruise-liner captain sailing out of the pre-Castro Havana. Finally, late in the afternoon, we changed course and headed southeast, back toward Cuba. We continued to move at about eight knots as twilight fell, and as soon as it grew dark, the research instruments were recovered. None of us had slept very much during the long, boring day, but as the time for the rendezvous approached, fatigue gave way to alertness. Moving slowly, under blackout conditions, we edged closer and closer to the shore.

By midnight we could pick up the lights of the coastal villages. The over-cast sky and the blackness of the night made them seem especially bright and close. Again, our maneuver had been timed to slip between the patrol boats and the radar fans. This was the most dangerous phase of the operation. If the team had been captured or followed, Castro's militia would be waiting for us. Captain Luis guided the ship closer and closer to the coast. At 0200 we picked up the lights of Dimas, and Captain Luis cut the diesels to idle speed. We waited in silence as 15 minutes passed, then 20. At 0230, and still no sign of the team. Captain Luis stepped nervously into the wheelhouse to check the RDF transmit-ter.

Suddenly there was a splash near the side of the ship, and an aluminum paddle grated against the thick wooden hull. Marcus and I rushed to the star-board side and peered into the oily blackness. One raft, with three men aboard, was just visible in the water; Marcus half-whispered directions to the comman-dos as they maneuvered the raft alongside the ship. As the men noisily climbed the cargo-net ladder with the help of Marcus and the crew, I continued to search the darkness for the second raft. The lights of the decoy boat flickered in the dis-tance. I could almost feel the presence of a Communist patrol boat in the dark-ness, its crew ready and waiting for the order to open fire on us. Time was running out.

Marcus joined me at the rail, breathless, and informed me that the other raft was far behind. The team leader was in that one, and they had with them a wounded Cuban who had escaped from the militia that afternoon. Dogs were tracking the man when he stumbled upon the team.

I'd just glanced at my watch when the first burst of gunfire spat from the dark shoreline, the slugs raking the water somewhere in front of us. I threw myself on the deck, grabbing Marcus as I dropped. There was more gunfire and the familiar sound of an M3 submachine gun. I peered cautiously over the low gunwale. There were moving lights on the shore, dogs barking, and more machine-gun fire. This time the slugs struck our ship.

Castro's men were firing in the direction of the fleeing raft. Because of the way the rounds were striking, it was quite obvious that Captain Luis had again guided the Rex much closer than authorized—probably no more than about a thousand yards off shore.

"There they are, Marcus! There they are!" I shouted, pointing into the darkness. I could just make out the shape and hear the splashing paddles of the other raft; it was less than one hundred yards from the minesweeper. At that moment Captain Luis revved the engines, and I knew he was going to make a run for it.

"For Christ's sake, tell Captain Luis to hold on for a few more minutes," I ordered.

"They're almost here!"

Marcus got to his feet and raced for the ladder to the bridge. There was another burst of fire, and the lead slammed into our vessel with a dull thud. The powerful lights on shore now silhouetted the commando raft as men paddled frantically towards us. Rifle shots echoed and kicked up small geysers in the water around the fragile rubber boat. The team members aboard our craft made no effort to return the fire, but a crewman uncovered one of the machine guns on the upper deck. He grabbed a belt and the receiver slammed closed. The gun jammed.

The raft was now less than 50 yards away. There was another burst of machine-gun fire from the shore, followed by an agonized cry from the commando boat. It was sinking. It had been hit, probably many times.

At the machine gun above me, the crewmen were working frantically with the stubborn weapon. In an instant they had it cleared and had opened fire in the direction of the shore lights. Two of the commandos from the sinking raft were in the water, struggling to swim toward the ship, but their heavy equipment made it impossible, and they cried out for help. Marcus and Captain Luis opened one of the life rafts lashed behind the bridges and pushed it over the side. It crashed into the water directly below me, scattering paddles and life vests. The steady pow-pow-pow of the heavy machine-gun sounded above me, and some of the lights on shore disappeared.

Marcus raced down the ladder from the bridge and joined me as I climbed down the swaying cargo net. The two swimming commandos reached the life raft and, hanging from the rope ladder, we held them until they had a firm grasp on the netting. There was another burst of machine-gun fire from shore and the glare of the light beam on the scaling hull. The commandos already aboard the ship took positions near the stern and began to open fire with their submachine guns, but it was useless; the range to shore was too great. The two Cubans with us at the net were crying hysterically. Marcus called for the crew to give them a hand up the net, and then he and I jumped into the life raft. With the only paddle I could find, I began rowing toward where I'd seen the rubber boat sinking.

The crack of bullets was sharp overhead. Most of the fire came from our own ship as the heavy machine gun continued to pump away and the commandos fired blindly with their submachine guns. A desperate cry, "Amigo, amigo, here!" led us up to the rapidly submerging raft. Only two chambers remained inflated, and the weight of the silent engine was dragging the raft to the bottom.

The commando team leader was clinging to the rope handholds with one hand. His other arm held the unconscious form of the wounded Cuban they'd helped to escape. We pulled the men into the life raft and I paddled frantically, while Marcus tried to help by scooping water with his hands. The firing from our ship continued.

When we finally reached the side of the Rex, two crewmen met us at the bottom of the net ladder and pulled the commandos aboard. Marcus and I quickly tied off the life raft, and as Captain Luis poured full power to the idling diesel engines, we climbed up into the clutching hands of the crewmen who were hanging over the gunwale. Beams of light and machine-gun fire continued to rake the water as our old vessel shuddered to life and turned her stern to the island,

THE ZENITH SECRET

CHAPTER 6

Captain Luis, Marcus, the commando team leader, and I were standing in one of the small crew cabins on the Rex. The flat seas and still air of the previous night were gone; now, wind and rain tore violently at the superstructure of our ship, making it roll and slam down with a sickening jar as it crested each gigantic swell.

The storm was a blessing. It had engulfed us shortly after we'd begun our run from the Cuban coast. If there had been any patrol boats in pursuit, they were lost behind us somewhere in the storm. Now, running blackout with diesels turning full power, it looked as though we'd made a nearly clean escape.

I looked down again at the young Cuban on the stretcher in front of us. A makeshift medical table had been hastily erected, and Captain Luis and Marcus had been working feverishly over him since he had been pulled abroad with the commandos. Just below his right shoulder blade was a large, jagged hole which could have been made by a bullet or knife. The wound filled with bloody froth with each irregular breath he took, and there was nothing we could do but cover it with an emergency dressing. The rest of his back, shoulders, and head were covered with linear bruises and welts, obviously the result of a severe beating with a heavy instrument. He'd lost a lot of blood and his skin was deathly pale. He hadn't regained consciousness, and unless he received immediate medical help he would die.

For that reason, Captain Luis had decided to disregard the planned rendezvous off Grand Cayman and instead head directly for the nearest medical station, which was on Key West. He'd already radioed headquarters to ask for emergency air evacuation of the wounded man, but the storm was part of a larger weather system, and even the Coast Guard ships and planes would be unable to reach us before morning. At my suggestion, as a precautionary measure, Captain Luis radioed the decoy vessel, advised them of our intentions, and asked that they follow us closely as possible.

There was nothing we could do now for the wounded Cuban, so Captain Luis returned to the bridge and I went to the galley, where I hoped to begin making notes for my after-action report. Marcus stayed behind with the unconscious man in hope that he would regain consciousness long enough to tell us who he was and what had happened.

Marcus had conducted a quick debriefing of the men after we were clear of the coast, but they were too frightened and exhausted to give more than a sketchy, disjointed account of their actions. From what we were able to piece together, everything had gone according to plan until late that afternoon. They'd buried their cache containers and moved to a hiding place in the mangroves several hundred yards down the shore. While four of the men rested, the team leader and one of the men who had grown up in the Dimas area had gone inland to observe the road from the fishing village. They heard and saw nothing unusual. It was dark when they made their way back to the rest of the team. When they arrived, they found the wounded Cuban escapee hiding with the others. In his flight from the pursuing militia, he'd sought refuge in the mangroves and had walked up on the sleeping commandos. In the absence of the team

THE ZENITH SECRET

leader, and despite the man's admission that he was being hunted by the militia, it was agreed that he could stay and try to escape with the team. It was not clear whether he had the wound at the time or it had been sustained in the gunfire during the commandos' escape. Nor was it clear why he'd been taken into custody by the militia or how he'd gotten away. The effort to help the beaten man to the hidden rubber boats had delayed the team's departure. The militia, close behind, apparently found the commandos' hiding place just as they embarked in their boats a short distance down the coast. The militia either saw the rafts departing or heard the paddles or other noises made by the fleeing men.

Questions about the mission pounded away at my tired mind. I put my head down on the stained galley table and tried to sort out the facts, but soon the roll of the ship lulled me and the throb of the diesels filled my head. I lapsed into a deep sleep. I awakened immediately, it seemed, but when I looked up sunlight was streaming through the portholes. The cook had removed the blackout disks and was noisily clanking around the stove. It was morning, and the weather was changing. Something else had changed too, I suddenly realized. I could no longer hear the monotonous tone of the ship's engines. The vessel was still rolling and pitching in the heavy seas, but we were not moving.

I raced to the bridge, looking for Captain Luis. The first mate, standing by the wheel with a concerned look on his face, motioned to the engine room. I found the captain in the bowels of the ship, between two enormous diesel engines, with two sweating, grease-smeared crewmen. They were talking excitedly in Spanish. The captain turned and looked at me. "I'm sorry, my friend, but we have just lost the use of one of our engines. We've tried to fix it, but it is impossible. In these seas, it will take us forever to reach Key West."

"The Coast Guard," I said quickly. "A helicopter or seaplane—we can get the wounded man aboard."

The captain cut me off: "I have already requested their help. But the seas are much too rough to transfer the man to an airplane, and he'd never make it anyway."

We hurried to the small room where Marcus had spent the night with the wounded man, who was still unconscious. Captain Luis spoke to Marcus in Spanish, and then said to me, "We can try to put this man aboard the decoy ship. It is much faster—it would make it to Key West in less than two hours."

It was the obvious answer. The captain radioed headquarters and outlined his proposal. After a delay of several minutes, the answer came back. The wounded man and those who were to return to the United States—the commando team, Marcus, and myself—were to transfer to the decoy vessel and got to Key West. A Coast Guard cutter was already on its way to meet us. Captain Luis was to change course and return to his home port. Act without delay, the message concluded.

Some hours later, the eight of us sat around a wobbly kitchen table in a grimy little stucco house on Stock Island just off Key West. There was very little talk as we awaited the arrival from Miami of the team's case officer. A feeling of emptiness, both emotional and physical, pervaded the atmosphere. What had taken place during the preceding five days now seemed strangely unreal. Fresh clothing, a shower, shave, a good meal, and the better part of a full night's rest had put a lot of distance between us and the danger we had experienced. There was lingering sadness over the death of the young Cuban. The transfer at sea, in a crudely rigged boatswain chair, had been too much for him; he had died a few minutes after we'd gotten him aboard the decoy craft. There was consolation only in that we had tried to bring him out with us. Who he was and what he'd done remained a mystery.

It was midmorning when the case officer burst through the front door of the safehouse. Under his arm was the morning newspaper containing stories of another raid on the Communist island. Castro once again accused the CIA. Fortunately, according to the descriptions and information in the paper, Castro had many of the facts wrong, but there was enough correct data in the story to identify the incident as our recently completed operation. Castro claimed that the one boat had been sunk and all aboard had been captured or killed.

The debriefing continued throughout the day. Except for answering the officer's questions to me, I withheld comments about the mission. The story unfolded as each of us had lived it and, despite the problems we'd encountered, the case officer seemed satisfied with the outcome of the mission. Somehow, I didn't feel that Ted would be quite so pleased. By late afternoon the debriefing had ended. I had spent part of the time drafting my after-action report but, for some reason, I just couldn't keep my mind on it. I needed to get away for a while, and the case officer suggested that I take his car back to Miami. He was going to spend the weekend in Key West with his men, and I was no longer needed.

I drove slowly along the nearly deserted overseas highway. The sun was setting over the mangrove bay heads in the bay to the west. Latin music played softly on the radio. For reasons I couldn't explain, my cheeks were wet with tears for the first time I could remember.

There was important news waiting for me when I got back to the station that night. The CIA and Colonel Bond's office had worked out an arrangement for my wife and three sons to join me in Miami. My first reaction was sheer happiness. But, I wondered how Suzie would take to the cloak-and-dagger business. She already had a bad case of nerves, and not having Army friends around in addition to not knowing where I was or what I was doing, could make it even worse.

On Monday I went to the station early, hoping to get a good start on my after-action report. I was beginning to organize my thoughts about the mission, and I wanted to make sure the report was accurate and fair and, most of all, an adequate justification for my going along. If the report failed to prove the value of my participation, I could not expect to go on another mission.

Using the back office in the training branch (I told Cal I was preparing a reconnaissance report for Ted Shackley, and he didn't question where I'd been for two weeks and left me alone), I worked on the report for the better part of a week. The conclusions I drew were similar to those made in my earlier training report: the exile volunteers needed better physical conditioning, training in the use of seacoast survival techniques and equipment, training in stealth and noise discipline, and training in small-unit tactics, especially patrolling and security. I could justify each of my conclusions now with observations made on an actual mission.

Ted Shackley wanted as few people as possible to know about my trip to Cuba. I asked his secretary, Maggy, who else might see my after-action report. I was mostly concerned about Dave Morales' reaction to my critical observations. Although obligated by professional conscience not to gloss over the failings and inadequacies I had observed, I didn't want to aggravate the Big Indian with my criticisms if it could be avoided. Maggy detected my concern.

"Dave is away for a while in Mexico. Possibly Gordon will see it."

I knew she was referring to Gordon Campbell, the deputy chief of station, who I had not yet met.

Dutifully, I spent the next day talking with the finance, real estate, and security experts at the station to begin making arrangements for my family's move to Miami. I'd spoken with Rod and was surprised to learn that he had no intention of having his family join him. Since he would probably retire within a year or so, he could see no reason to move them down from Massachusetts.

In fact, he confided, he was thinking of requesting relief from the CIA assignment anyway. Nobody in operations, especially Dave, would listen to what he had to say, and he was constantly being sent on "Mickey Mouse" research projects that never materialized. On top of all this, the Special Group in Washington was keeping such a tight control over the choice of targets and the types of weapons that it was nearly impossible to properly plan anything.

I encouraged Rod to reconsider, but he refused and I went ahead with arrangements on my own. It wasn't so simple as a permanent change of station in the military. Everything had to be coordinated between the Army and the CIA, double administrative red tape, and all of it had to be done under my cover as a Department of the Army civilian. What's more, Suzie would have to make the move on her own. With the establishment of the new training program, I couldn't spare a minute to help.

Maggy called the next day to tell me the after-action report was completed and I could look over it. She had thoughtfully made an appointment for me with Mr. Shackley for that afternoon. Minutes later I was sitting in her office looking over my work. I was quite conscious of her as I waited to see Ted. So much so, that I was nervous as a schoolboy, and unable to say anything very meaningful. Just as well, I thought; my wife will be here in a few weeks.

The meeting with Ted went well. He'd already received the case officer's report on the mission and also one prepared by Marcus and Captain Luis. As we talked about my conclusions, I got the impression that he already knew the real shortcomings of the commando team and that my report simply reinforced his evaluation. After all, he'd already approved the new training program, and now he wanted me to go full speed ahead with it. A few days later someone handed me a message about a social gathering scheduled for the following Sunday. I was to call Maggy for details.

When I called her she gave me an address on Key Biscayne. I asked her if I was expected to be there and she said no, only that there was going to be someone there from headquarters that I might like to see. Dress was informal. It sounded interesting, and I decided to go. I'd never been an enthusiastic partygoer, but Suzie enjoyed bridge, the officers wives' club, and the command parties we had to attend. I resisted the idea of attending them, but now I was actually excited about being invited. This would be my first CIA social function, and it would be very interesting to see that side of the agency social life.

With the address Maggy had given me, I turned down a shrub-lined drive and into a small parking place behind an expensive stucco house overlooking Biscayne Bay. The home was near where Rod and I stayed when we first arrived in Miami. I recognized a number of cars as Zenith vehicles sporting unusual radio antennas, but there was nothing exceptional about this kind of gathering on exclusive, ultra-discreet Key Biscayne. I struck the bronze knocker on the carved-wood door, and in a few moments a slide opened and someone asked for my name and security ID card. I passed it through the small opening and a butler let me in.

In the living room the guests were chatting around a table of hors d'oeuvres. It reminded me of a political fund raising party or one of those intolerable military social functions. I felt out of place and went directly to the bar and asked for a Manhattan. I was ordering a second drink when I heard a familiar voice behind me.

"Well, I see you've found the bar, young man."

I turned. It was Colonel Bond. I hadn't expected him to be in Miami. "I hoped to see you," he said. "There's a lot of interest in what you and Major Roderick are doing down here."

After chatting for a few minutes, Colonel Bond said something about having visited my old haunts at Eglin AFB while on a VIP briefing tour. I asked if he, personally, had talked with Suzie while at Eglin. He said Col. Garret and someone from CIA had contacted her. I left it at that. Taking me by the arm, he introduced me to some of the guests. I shook hands with Mr. Harvey and Mr. O'Connell. Both addressed me by my first name. There were several people I recognized from Zenith. Most of the guests were elderly or middle aged. CIA career people, apparently from Washington. Some, by their bearing and manner, were probably former military officers. I met Mr. Hunt, one of the few present there who looked the part of a classic intellectual espionage type. With Hunt was a Cuban introduced as Mr. Artime. I spotted Mr. Fitzgerald and he acknowledged me with a nod of his head. Colonel Bond told me it was Richard Helms, head of CIA covert operations, standing next to him.

Relaxing from the Manhattans, I laughed, realizing that most of the people looked gentle and conservative. Yet when they pulled a string, men lived or died. These men around me were guiding our national policy toward Cuba.

Suddenly there was a stir of activity near the courtyard door. The reception line was breaking up. Apparently the VIPs, whoever they were, were leaving. As they passed through the living room, they talked amiably with some of the guests. One man, his back to me, caught my eye. He was younger than the rest, and his full head of hair was conspicuously longer, reaching his collar. He was slim, with a wiry, catlike stance. He wore a corduroy sport coat and loose, baggy slacks. His hands were thrust into his pockets and his shoulders slumped forward, casual, almost sloppy. There was something about him I remembered from somewhere. He must be an important athlete, I thought, or someone I've seen on television.

I approached and observed the tan, youthful face, the boyish grin, the shock of hair falling over his forehead, the piercing blue eyes, and high pitched voice with an unmistakable Boston accent. It was Robert Kennedy, the president's brother, the attorney general! I wedged my way even closer, and as he began to walk toward the front door, I thrust out my hand. Robert Kennedy shook it, smiling warmly.

"Good to see you."

It wasn't every day that one met the attorney general of the United States. It was rumored that Robert Kennedy had great influence in the administration, and I'd heard he chaired the Special Group. He was appointed by the president to keep an eye on the CIA. His presence tonight reinforced my belief that the Cuban situation and Castro were prime concerns to the White House. I believed that President Kennedy's promise to the Bay of Pigs survivors was more than just an effort to pacify the exiles. There was something special going on. I was thrilled to have some small part in it.

I threw myself into preparing the new training program with gusto after that, and for the next two weeks there wasn't time to think of anything else. Larry would continue to teach basic weapons, use of the compass, land navigation, and other miscellaneous subjects, just as he had in the past. It was decided that his two weeks of instruction would be received first by any newly recruited exile. Walter, a training instructor, and Rudy would continue to teach tradecraft, and their programs would remain pretty much the same. The volunteers would receive this training immediately following or concurrently with their instruction from Larry.

Theoretically, after these two phases of basic paramilitary instruction, the volunteer would have enough fundamental knowledge to go into the field. Those exiles whose primary function involved handling larger boats and engines, such as the V-20, would receive specialized training during this concluding period. Ideally, a team would complete training and shortly thereafter embark on a mission while still somewhere near a peak.

To make the whole program truly effective, we would have to convince the operations people of three necessities. I knew it would not be easy. We'd be bucking the Big Indian all the way.

First, operations would have to make teams available for an adequate period of time. In the past, the case officers put teams in the existing programs and took them out at their own discretion. Often the Cubans got only a small portion of the training necessary for their particular mission. I drafted a minimum and optimum schedule for each program; Cal would have to take a firm stand on enforcing it with the case officers.

Each team or individual was usually assigned a specific task by operations. Some would be commandos, some infiltrators. Some would go in clandestinely and live "black," while others might make a clandestine infiltration but live in the open in their home community, under some sort of cover. So it was essential that the instructor know something about how the men were to be used. This could most easily be accomplished by the case officer's observing the team and working directly with the instructor.

When I'd asked why the case officers seldom observed the training of their men, Dave had become very angry and stated adamantly that the case officers didn't have time to spend in the field. There was no real solution to this problem except to rely on the responsibility and dedication of the individual officers. But, to prod them and the operations branch in general, we had to set up a system of written training evaluations of each team and individual, to be prepared by each instructor as he completed his phase of the program. Since the officers usually became personally involved in the quality of the men recruited and their potential for success, I hoped that each officer would be inclined to look at his team's training performance as a reflection on himself. In a great many cases it was the case officer who provided the real leadership and motivations for the Cubans, and his presence, or lack of it, in training usually had a considerable impact on them. The second necessity was to develop this kind of conscientiousness.

Third was the problem of maintaining proficiency among the exiles. Often a mission would have to be scrubbed just as a team had completed training. This was sometimes due to the events in the target area and sometimes to the policy decision by the Special Group in Washington. Many times a team would sit, closeted in a safehouse somewhere, waiting for a new mission. This was demoralizing for the men and often resulted in loss of the tactical skills and physical fitness they'd achieved during training. We set up a special schedule for condensing training or review periods for agents who were idle. The case officers could put their men into this modified program to keep them on their toes and help overcome the boredom and tension of the periods between missions.

After we hammered out the sequence of programs and the basic concepts surrounding their implementation, I returned to the field to get on with establishing the final phase of training, survival and small-unit operations. I would have to put the program together from scratch and supervise it until it could be turned over to someone else.

Having selected the upper Key Largo area as the best place for survival and small-unit training, I spent the next two weeks ordering equipment, drafting lesson plans and exercises, and searching for a safehouse to use as a base of operations. I rented boats on several occasions to become familiar with the waterways. Besides needing a place to house the teams at the beginning and end of the training periods, I would have instructors to house, equipment and boats to store, and vehicles to park. The 60 mile drive from north Key Largo to Miami was just too much. Valuable training time would be lost, and the exposure on the overseas highway was too great a security risk.

With the help of the real estate man from the cover branch, I finally settled on a complex of three houses on Plantation Key.[7] (The run to the training area could be made by vehicle or boat, and although it was a bit longer than I liked, we could arrange to travel when there would be minimum traffic.) The houses, set on stilts, were well back from the road and protected by a screen of thick tropical shrubbery. There was adequate sleeping space for up to 15 men. One house would be used by the team undergoing training; the second house would be for the two or three Cuban instructors whom I hoped to recruit and train, and it could also double as a mess hall and classroom; the third house would be used for storage of large equipment, and there was a small room that I could set up as an office and communications center.

The property was already under agency control, having previously been rented by one of the cover companies for use by one of the commando groups. I was told the commandos had never used the houses, so the cover was still intact. If we were careful and didn't bother the old widow who lived next door, we would be able to use the property without suspicion or interference from other residents on the Key. By the last week in June, I had the physical organization at both the safehouse complex and the training area pretty well completed. José Clark, one of Larry's Cuban instructors, helped get things set up, and by the time we had finished he decided he wanted to continue working for me.

There were times during this period, especially after enduring a senseless delay at the hands of the agency civil servants or encountering a tangle of seemingly endless bureaucratic red tape, when I would stop and wonder if the situation in Miami was typical of all CIA operations. All the fumbling and internal wrangling—was that the way our country's super secret warriors did business? On one hand, the attorney general showed personal interest in what we were doing, but on the other hand, orders for equipment were often delayed because the clerks in the supply branch took two hour lunch breaks. I could not understand how, if the administration was really serious about getting rid of Castro, such inefficiency could be tolerated.

I tried not to let these feelings affect my personal relationships with the agency employees and I kept my doubts out of the reports to Colonel Bond. But I did talk to Rod about them. He'd made many similar observations while working in an entirely different phase of the JM/WAVE operations. But he was basically a technician and somewhat apart from the human realities of the conflict. He didn't know about my trip to Cuba, and he couldn't fully understand my concern about the exiles and the morality of the whole situation. Nevertheless, we'd discuss our thoughts for hours at a time, usually over a bottle of scotch, in his motel room or mine. Rod described an interesting new guy, a Colonel Rosselli from Washington with whom he was working in operations.

After one of those long sessions on a Friday night, after I had been in the

THE ZENITH SECRET

Keys for a week, I decided to try to forget things for a while. I drove back to the quiet little cocktail lounge in the Caribe Motel in Homestead where I'd stopped several times on my way from the Keys to Miami. As soon as I walked in, I noticed a very attractive woman sitting at the end of the bar. The bartender apparently had just finished telling her a joke, and her laughter was a happy, refreshing sound. I bought her a few drinks, and it didn't take me long to realize how much I wanted her. She went back to my motel room with me.

BRADLEY E. AYERS

CHAPTER 7

The next day I felt terribly guilty. I hadn't been unfaithful to my wife in years. Suzie heard my voice crack over the phone as I told her I loved her, and when the boys talked, tears came to my eyes. I told her that I needed them with me, and she said they could finish packing and be on their way in a couple of weeks. I hadn't found a house yet, but I was looking. We'd figure something out. The important thing was we'd be together.

It was summer now and the heat and mosquitoes were even more intense. José Clark and I had to devise and construct all of our own charts and training aids. I would sketch them out and write the words in English. José would then translate them to Spanish and advise me on nuances of the language. For the infiltration teams, we developed several grueling reconnaissance exercises, using the large, tightly secured Southern Bell Telephone microwave facility as our objective. It was an ideal, real-life target: the trainees could not allow themselves to get caught, for the high chain-link fences were electrified and the watchmen were armed.

I hoped to recruit some additional Cuban instructors during this period and instructed José to be on the lookout for the "right" kind of men in the growing exile community in Miami. Southwest Eighth Street was rapidly becoming known as Little Havana, and the word quickly spread through the close-knit community when "someone" was looking for a person with particular talents.

This grapevine proved to be a real headache in terms of security, but it had advantages when we had an immediate need for a volunteer with specific skills. We hoped the agency's security screening would weed out the undesirables—the double agents and the Castro plants and informers who abounded in the exile community. Frankly, I didn't worry about the Cubans as much as I did some of the heavy drinking, loud-talking American agency employees who frequented bars in south Miami.

We settled on two as potential instructors and one as a combination cook, housekeeper, and equipment maintenance man. I would keep one instructor and the housekeeper and Dewey would train the other man as his assistant.

Dewey, a former Navy warrant officer, was responsible for the small boat training. He had been working with two to five man infiltration teams for nearly a year. Small boat training had been nonexistent until he joined the station and put the program together from scratch.

I'd had no time to search for a house for my family or make any preparations for their arrival, and they suddenly drove up in front of my motel one Sunday afternoon. But an unexpected message was waiting for me at Zenith the next morning. The chief of the intelligence branch would be on vacation for a few weeks and wanted my family and me to live in his home and care for it during his absence.

It was even stranger now, I thought as I drove to Plantation Key, to leave the whole world of Bradley E. Ayers—wife, sons, identity, the whole existence—and step into the identity of Daniel B. Williams for the next two weeks.

Before leaving for the Keys, I stopped by the station to pick up a few supplies. There was a note on my desk. I was to see Gordon Campbell, the deputy chief of station, before leaving. I'd never met him. What the hell? I thought Campbell's office was in the building next to Ted Shackley's. But when I got there, Maggy told me to go to the second floor of the old barracks, a floor above my own office in the training branch. I'd never been in that area of the building.

I walked back to my building and went upstairs. Campbell's office was well-decorated, with all sorts of Zenith Technical Enterprise corporate plaques, alleged product displays, photos, and mementoes. His secretary buzzed him on my arrival and I was escorted into his plush office.

Campbell came around his desk, introduced himself, and shook my hand. I judged his age to be around 40 and he appeared to be in robust physical condition. Dressed as if he had just come off the golf course, tanned, clean shaven, with a trim build, balding blond hair, and penetrating blue eyes, he greeted me cordially. I liked him immediately.

"I've been wanting to meet and welcome you to the station. I'm sorry it's taken me so long. I want to tell you we appreciate what you're working on. I also read your after action report and I think you know what needs to be done."

I told him I'd do my best and we exchanged a few thoughts about the exile training program. As I left his office, he told me to be careful and that he would be seeing me again.

José was already at the safehouse when I arrived shortly after noon. He had brought Miguel and Mario, the two assistants I'd interviewed several weeks earlier. Their clearances had come through only a few days before. I welcomed the two men and briefly told them what we had planned for the next two weeks. They would learn chiefly by watching José and me as we taught classes and by on-the-job exposure. Mike, as Miguel soon became known, would be an assistant instructor, and Mario, the older of the two, would serve as the cook and housekeeper. While José gave them a detailed briefing on the new training program and issued them field equipment, I got ready to receive the first group of exiles.

The team that arrived a short time later proved to be ideal "guinea pigs" for the trial of the survival and small-unit-operations training program. The four men, headed by an intense, alert Cuban school teacher, were accompanied to the safehouse by their CIA case officer, Jerry, who had just arrived at the Miami station. This was his first exile team. I was pleased to see that he was highly motivated, and unlike the older, more experienced case officers at the station, he communicated his enthusiasm to the team.

Jerry briefed me on the team's mission. The group was to make a clandestine infiltration by rubber boat somewhere in Pinar Del Rio Province. They would carry with them a powerful shortwave transmitter. After landing and moving inland, they hoped to join a small anti-Castro guerrilla force that had recently been creating havoc for the Communist militia in the province. It was hoped that the infiltrators would become integrated with the counterrevolutionaries and would be able to establish a clandestine link by radio with the CIA. With the radio and the team leader's influence on the guerrilla leader, it would be possible for the CIA to direct the actions of the small force and coordinate its activities with our own commando and sabotage efforts. If all went well, the team would remain in Cuba indefinitely.

Jerry also gave me a run down on each man's background and function within the team. All of the men were under 30, each had at least the equivalent of a high school education, and each spoke some English. They had already undergone tradecraft, weapons, small-boat, and communications training. To my disappointment, after he finished his briefing, Jerry excused himself, explaining that he was in the process of recruiting another team in Miami. He promised to be back later in the week, and with that, he wished me luck, and left.

Things went much more smoothly that I anticipated. We spent the remainder of the first day teaching the team how to select, wear, and secure their field equipment. We showed them how to take care of their gear and protect and waterproof leather and metal items. Mike adapted quickly to his role as assistant instructor and was soon working alongside Joe and me. Meanwhile, Mario, a former seaman and ship's cook, organized things in the kitchen and familiarized himself with his housekeeping duties.

The rest of the program fell into place just as readily. All the planning, the frustration, and hard work, when my idea seemed an almost insurmountable goal, paid off. The schedule held up well and there were no security problems. No one bothered us at the safehouse, and we saw no one in or about the training areas. The exile team quickly absorbed the survival instruction we gave them. We were impressed with the way they were able to adapt to the physical hardships required of them despite their lack of training.

The leader confided that one thing the team feared most was to land on Cuban soil stranded without food and water. Therefore, the men were intensely interested when we showed them how to spear fish and trap small game with crude devices, how to get water from a cactus, and how to build a high and dry shelter in the mangrove thickets. On the rugged seacoast around Dynamite Pier in north Key Largo, we taught how to identify dangerous or poisonous plants, fish, animals, and reptiles. This sparked rounds of hearty laughter as I had the Cubans handle some nonpoisonous snakes in order to overcome their fear of them. At first, touching the scaly, writhing reptiles produced expressions of revulsion and disgust. But when the team leader, after my demonstration, mustered all his courage and put a big rat snake inside his work shirt, the others, including my instructors, had no choice but to follow suit. Latin masculine pride could clearly be used to our advantage, I learned. There were few, if any, snakes in Cuba, but learning to overcome this kind of fear was another step in gaining confidence.

We supplied the men with raw fish and coconuts, as well as emergency rations from a stock we had laid away at the safehouse, and they did their own cooking when out in the field. In this way we controlled their diet and provided adequate nourishment without losing sight of the course objectives. Long hikes and swimming were included in the team's activities when they were not involved in controlled survival instruction. By the end of the first week the infiltrators began to show the effects of living outside. Tanned, lean, dirty, and tired, but sharp-eyed and a little more confident, we took them back to the Plantation Key safehouse for showers and a weekend of rest.

The second week moved just as well as we introduced the use of boats. First, we taught them how to tie knots and build simple rafts from natural materials, which complemented their earlier survival training. We used areas hidden deep in the swamps of saltwater creeks that ran through north Key Largo. We introduced the men to canoes, kayaks, the military-type raft, and the standard Boston Whaler skiff. Although the team had already undergone small-boat training with Dewey at Flamingo, nearly all their work had been on the open water near Cape Sable. Now they learned to navigate and manipulate their boats through the narrow saltwater canals that were similar to those along the Cuban coast.

We ran a number of exercises of this type, each a little more complex and demanding. As the week came to an end, I felt they were ready for a final test:

THE ZENITH SECRET

We used the well-guarded telephone company microwave transmitting station on Old Card Sound Road, on the edge of the Everglades, as a "live" intelligence target during training.

the telephone company microwave station on Old Card Sound Road.

The only major criticism we had was the age-old problem of noise discipline. Despite this shortcoming, I was satisfied with their performance. Filthy and exhausted, we all rode back to the comforts of Plantation Key safehouse complex that night. We had given our best to the infiltration team, and they had responded favorably. We were on our way.

I saw my family that weekend, very briefly, because on Sunday I had to write the after-training report on the last team. There was also equipment to order, groceries and supplies to buy for the forthcoming weeks, and equipment that had to be cleaned and maintained. I did the report on the patio at home so I could be with Suzie and the boys for a little while. They were getting along fine, but she hadn't found a permanent home for us yet. Then, jamming my briefcase full of reports, orders, and papers, I jumped into my car and took up the life of Daniel B. Williams again.

For the next four weeks it went like that, and at times it seemed as though my real identity had ceased to exist. The second and third teams were not nearly so responsive as the first, and despite my complaints to Cal, neither case officer observed the training. It was midsummer in southern Florida now, and the heat, humidity, and mosquitoes were at their peak; there seemed to be no way to dislodge the officers from their air-conditioned offices.

The intensity of our schedule, the physical discomfort, the confidences we

BRADLEY E. AYERS

shared about the teams, and the long hours of being together in the swamps or at sea fostered a close bond among José, Mike, Mario and me. Although I was in charge, our camaraderie transcended our official relationship. There was no doubt about anyone's dedication to the cause; we never even discussed it. They knew I would not stand with them in the mud and heat, going without sleep and the comforts of my family and a staff job in Miami, unless I believed in them.

We always looked forward to the evening meal, for we would usually snack on survival rations with the trainees during the day and by nightfall were ready for something more nourishing. We would be instructing the course indefinitely, while the trainees were there for only a couple of weeks. Mario, aware of this, would go to great lengths to prepare the most exotic Cuban dishes he could. He would pack the hot food in vacuum containers, and as soon as it was dark, Mike or José would take the jeep back to the safehouse and pick it up for us.

While the exiles were learning survival and tactics, we, the instructors, learned how to cope with the grueling physical demands of the program and gained confidence in our ability to conduct the training without detection from outsiders. The greatest hardships were heat, humidity, insects, and fatigue. At first we all wore khaki or gray work clothes and boots, the dress commonly worn by surveyors and construction workers anywhere, but the clothes were much too heavy. They would quickly become saturated with perspiration and cling to our skin, and heat rash soon followed. Our boots would fill with water as we tramped through the swamps.

It didn't take us long to change our daily uniform. Mine became a tank-type bathing suit or shorts and tennis shoes without laces. José cut the legs off his khaki trousers and got rid of his shirt but kept his boots. He still disliked the idea of walking over hundreds of creeping, crawling small animals in the swamps and on the jungle seacoast. Mike kept his long trousers and a T-shirt, but exchanged his boots for sneakers. We each carried a hunting knife and a compass on a belt, and José, who was a gun fanatic, always had a small-caliber pistol concealed somewhere on his person. At night we reverted to work clothes and boots for protection from the mangrove branches, thorns, and shrubbery.

We slept in jungle hammocks slung near the water's edge to catch any breeze from the sea. Mosquito netting was essential. The insects were so bad that one could not venture forth without saturating his skin and clothing with bug repellent, and, even then, in a matter of minutes the salt-marsh mosquitoes seemed to become immune to it.

I insisted that each team carry a small military radio at all times. We kept another radio with us near our base campsite or hidden in one of the boats. In this way, we were in continuous contact with the groups no matter where they were. The trainees were instructed to remain hidden from any road or waterway, unless they had reason to be moving on it, and from the moment they arrived in the training area, we tried to make them cautious about being seen even by the instructors. We restricted our meetings and formal classes to places where there was a single route of approach, either road or waterway. An observer, either José or Mike, was posted to give us warning of the approach of any interlopers. When someone came, the trainees would scurry to hide themselves and wait until the intruder was gone. In 1963, any Cubans in the Keys were automatically suspected of being engaged in some anti-Cuban activity, so it was safer to keep them completely hidden.

The intruders were fishermen looking for good angling waters. While the trainees were concealed in the brush, my assistants and I would pick up our fishing poles and play out our cover as sportsmen. Much to our frustration and

THE ZENITH SECRET

anxiety, the fishermen would sometimes linger for several hours as they tried their luck, and we would simply have to wait until they were gone to resume training. These delays were costly, but none of the fishermen ever pressed us for information or inquired about our presence.

Occasionally someone with a legitimate inquiry would appear on the scene. The same precautionary measures would be implemented, and if the visitors didn't approach me directly, I would intercept them and ask if I might help. Sometimes, especially around Dynamite Pier, where the agency had worked out cover lease arrangements with the owner, I would demand the reason for the visitors' presence and order them off the land, but I always tried to avoid doing this, because it would immediately foster suspicion. Usually the visitor would turn out to be a real estate agent or some law-enforcement representative, and I would implement our carefully rehearsed cover story: My men and I were mapping crew employed by Paragon Air Service and were doing survey work in connection with an aerial photography contract. Since we were doing some blasting in the area as part of our research work, we would advise the visitor to leave for his own safety.

Luckily, we had few security problems, but one presented a particularly disturbing quandary for me. A uniformed officer from the U.S. Fish and Wildlife Service walked in on one of our training sessions at Dynamite Pier one sweltering day. He politely asked for my ID and began to question me about the apparent environmental damage that had occurred at some of the bay heads and Everglades shoreline on Blackwater Bay and further to the south. I told him I knew nothing about it and the area was somewhat outside my "company's" (Paragon Air Service) zone of interest. (However, I knew Rip Robertson sometimes used that general area for training his commando group.)

I feigned concern for my (cover) company's possible liability and agreed to meet the officer the next day at Jewfish Creek Marina where I would accompany him in his boat to inspect the damaged area. As soon as he left, I called the JM/WAVE security branch from the pay phone at Ocean Reef. I didn't know what I was getting myself into, but explained to security that cooperation with the officer made better sense than aggravating his suspicions, thus jeopardizing the security of my training operations in the area. Security agreed.

The next morning I met the officer and, in his official U.S. Fish and Wildlife outboard, traveled south for nearly 30 minutes. He showed me several acres of mangrove bay heads (small islands) that were virtually devoid of foliage. It was June in the tropics, and they should have been lush with vegetation of all kinds, crowded with birds and other wildlife.

As we approached and observed each of the sites, I detected a strong, unnatural odor like rotten eggs combined with something that smelled of petroleum, like kerosene or diesel fuel. There was no indication of a fire. The mangroves were an ashen color, the remaining leaves wilted and brown. Fallen leaves and dead or wilted foliage covered the mud surface and littered the water under the mangrove roots. The defoliation was virtually complete. There wasn't the slightest indication of any wildlife except for scattered remains of cormorants, gulls, and fish. An ominous, deathlike stillness hung over the devastated islands.

The officer took me to two other locations further to the south, toward Flamingo. We were getting fairly close to Dewey's training area and I became concerned he might become involved in whatever was going on. We looked at two other locations on the coastal Everglades mainland of Flamingo, each of them more than an acre in size, that exhibited the same apparent damage as the bay

Dynamite Pier of Upper Key Largo was selected as a site for the commando survival training program. The isolation of the site also made it an ideal jumping off point for anti-Castro operations.

heads and also had the same pervasive, pungent odor as the islands to the north. It was quite upsetting, given the typically thriving, rich, natural abundance of the coastal area which was protected as a national park.

The wildlife officer suggested the damage resulted from some sort of industrial toxic chemical that had found its way into this remote area. The matter was under investigation and soil and water tests were underway. He told me he had come to Dynamite Pier because it was known my aerial mapping company was in the Keys doing petroleum source research and exploration. I informed him my crew had never been in the damaged area.

As soon as the officer dropped me off at Jewfish Creek, I reported what had transpired and what I had observed to both security and cover at the station. I was advised to go back to my training area and not be concerned about the matter. That was it.[8]

When the trainees were occupied with independent practical exercises in the field, José, Mike, and I would fish together or skin-dive around the old bridge pilings in Steamboat Creek. We caught lobster, snook, and trout that we'd send back to Mario to save for a later meal. In the evenings we would sometimes fish for tarpon with the live shrimp that Mario sent at suppertime. These evenings helped break the boredom and drudgery of the weeks in the field, but we were thankful when we finished our third straight training cycle and learned that we'd get a two-week break. Weeks in the mangroves had taken their toll. I was thoroughly exhausted but pleased as I locked the safehouses and headed for Miami.

It was great getting back to civilization. The sweet smell of oleander drifted through the jalousie bedroom windows and mixed with the mouth-watering smell of steaks grilling on the patio. What a welcome contrast to the heavy, sulfurous stench of the mangroves, rotting vegetation, and dead marine life that pervaded the swamps.

The boys were splashing in the pool, and I could hear the clink of ice on glass as my wife mixed martinis at the bar near the fireplace. I had been back

THE ZENITH SECRET

from the Keys for several days now, and the scene was typical of the pleasant evenings I enjoyed with my family between training cycles. Tonight was special though, because we would be entertaining our first guest in our new quarters. My friend, Ed Roderick, was coming for dinner.

Suzie had found the house while I was away, and it proved to be a pleasant surprise in that it was not what I would have expected her to choose. But of course the agency real estate people had provided some assistance and possibly influenced her selection. She had always leaned toward the conservative, functional simplicity fostered by her middle-class Midwestern background. The new home was a rather esoteric combination of Oriental and Polynesian styling. Done in soft grays with bright red and yellow accents, it seemed slightly garish; yet the Oriental peaked roof, the overhanging beamed eves, and the intricate masonry screens gave it an exotic, mysterious quality.

The house had come completely and beautifully furnished, and we had a six-month lease on the property. The "company" would pick up the tab and we'd pay the utilities. Suzie and the boys seemed very happy, and I was doing exactly the kind of work I enjoyed most. I was looking forward to having dinner with Rod. I'd been out of circulation at the station for several weeks and was eager to bring myself up to date.

Rod had been drinking before he got to the house that night. In fact, he confided, he and the recently arrived Colonel Rosselli were working on plans to ambush Fidel Castro and had been on a weekend binge together. They'd become close friends as they spent time together; their drinking friendship was a natural extension of their on-duty relationship.

While we ate I discussed my training activities and made a point of bringing up the matter of case officers and their lack of attention to training. I hoped that, through Rod, the word would get back to operations. When we finished dinner, I turned up the stereo to cover our conversation as Rod began to tell me about the new things "in the air" at the station. It seemed that the administration was ready to begin making an even more concerted effort to unseat Castro. The election year of 1964 was rapidly approaching, and President Kennedy's Cuban policy critics were putting on the heat. The Special Group had already removed a number of targets from the restricted list, and there were more to go. It was up to the CIA, specifically the Miami station, to plan the new missions, recruit and train exiles, and mount operations to strike the Communist dictator where it really hurt. Other espionage activities were being carried out to coincide with this paramilitary effort, and still more attempts to eliminate Castro were being devised. Then he dropped it. He told me Rosselli had high level Mafia and Havana connections. I was speechless. The American government collaborating with organized crime? I couldn't believe it. I was anxious to meet this guy.

With Russian help—including the delivery of a new, faster, better equipped coastal patrol craft—Cuban defenses had been tightened and sophisticated. The last American attempts to penetrate with larger craft such as the Rex and Leda had ended in near disaster. Though Rod didn't know about my trip to Cuba, I was tempted to vouch for that revelation.

In the future, Rod said, operations hoped to rely on smaller, faster, lightly armed boats that could make it all the way across the Florida Straits and slip quickly through the Communist defenses. Several new V-20s had been developed with a fuel capacity sufficient to assure at least a one-way crossing of the straits. The little boats, with their commando teams aboard, could slip under the radar, through the canals and shallow water, and into the target area. The commandos could make their strike and withdraw quickly the same way. It was

BRADLEY E. AYERS

52

felt that the smaller boats, with a speed of 50 miles per hour, could outrun any of the Communist boats.

When I raised the question about the "one-way" capacity of the small craft, he explained that the new concept would entail pulling one or more of the little boats behind converted commercial fishing trawlers to a point somewhere off the Cuban coast. The boats would then be released for their mission but would return to the United States on their own.

To me, it sounded feasible. Large commercial fishing trawlers often towed boats of the V-20 class. The small boats put the nets out and, when they were full, dragged them back to the larger boat, where they were hauled aboard and emptied. The cover possibilities intrigued me.

The more Rod talked, the more enthusiastic I became. I asked if anyone had thought about training for boat operators. I knew there were few, if any, Cuban operators available to the station who had the skill for this kind of operation. No one had really thought about that yet, Rod answered. Nobody at the station really knew what it was going to entail. Ted Shackley had just returned from Washington and was setting up a series of briefings on the new operations.

Gradually, an idea began to take shape in my mind. I started to say something to Rod, but then Suzie joined us, and the three of us spent the rest of the evening making small talk. It turned out that Roderick was as much of a bridge fan as my wife. With my concurrence, they made plans to get a neighborhood table formed for some of the evenings when I'd be away.

It was well after midnight when our heads began to nod and yawns interrupted the conversation. I insisted Rod sleep on our patio couch. He had had a lot to drink, and he'd already had an accident with his JM/WAVE leased car, an incident that might have gotten us both returned to the Pentagon had I not interceded with Bob Wall and the chief of security at the station.

The next morning, over coffee, I asked Rod how he was getting along with Morales. Sober, his response was guarded. He said he understood what Dave wanted and how he expected things to happen in operations. He volunteered that in his present work with Rosselli, Morales was directly calling the shots and that Rosselli and Morales were obviously very close. Rod was going to go with the flow and not make any waves.

Having finished my training reports for the period and gotten up to date on other paperwork, including a summary of our activities to Colonel Bond, I spent the next few days with my family. We had a good time, but I was preoccupied with the idea that was taking shape in my mind. Although it was my weekend off, I went to the station periodically to check for messages and make calls to keep my Cuban assistants on their toes. I also spent the better part of one day making the required quarterly parachute jump to maintain my hazardous duty pay allowance. Secretly I hoped the long-standing rumor of a commando parachute drop into Cuba might materialize, and I wanted to be ready. The Miami station had made arrangements for me to jump with the Air Force para-rescue team at Homestead Base. No one asked any questions; nevertheless, it felt strange to return to the military environment in civilian clothes.

We jumped over the Everglades from the SB-16 Albatross Seaplanes. I had never jumped from that type of aircraft, but the frop of the chute opening was a familiar and comforting sound and the orange and white canopy blossoming overhead a welcome sight. It was a good jump, and with the end of the week I felt rested and ready to return to work. I would see Cal on Monday morning as a start toward implementing my idea; it was the first step toward a series of events that would ultimately take me to Cuba for the second time.

CHAPTER 8

"Damnit, Cal, the case officers can't find out how their men really work in the field if they don't take the time to observe them. As effective as our training reports might be, I'd be damned if I'd take someone else's word on the evaluation of my men!"

I was upset and Cal knew it. During the six weeks that the new training program had been in effect, not a single station representative had visited the field to see what we were doing, not even Cal, who was chief of the training branch. I could see that he was a little embarrassed. It was the first time I had expressed my aggression with agency employees.

"You know just as well as I do, what we've said about some of the Cubans they've sent us for training," I continued. "They're not capable of anything, much less becoming secret agents. So what happens in operations when we tell them that? Do they just throw our reports away? The logical reaction would be for the case officer to get his tail down to Key Largo and find out what his men really look like and, if necessary, take issue with my evaluation."

Cal turned away from me and looked out the window. "Brad, we all have a great deal of confidence in what you're doing down there, and maybe we feel it's best not to look over your shoulder. You're supposed to be the expert in these matters."

"There's more to it than that, and you know it. I'm fully aware of operations' attitude toward training. They don't believe in it and the Big Indian is not going to push his case officers out of that air-conditioned building to go to swamps and look at Cubans, no matter what."

Cal looked sheepish. He wasn't about to take on the powerful chief of operations; it was part of the politicking that leads to promotions.

"I know we can't get into a battle with operations over this thing," I went on, "but from a purely practical standpoint, I've got to know more about what operations wants and what skills and techniques are being demanded as new missions and priorities are set up. I'm supposed to tailor the training to the needs of the teams, but how in the hell can I do that if we don't coordinate with the case officer? As things stand right now, I see them for about an hour when they bring a team to the safehouse and not again until they pick their men up. It's not enough and it's not fair to the Cubans."

Cal turned to look at me. "Once again, we have to depend on your good judgment. You've got a point, though. How much longer will you be here before going back to Key Largo?"

"I've got a week until we start another cycle."

He thumbed through a stack of papers on his desk. "There are going to be several briefings next week on some new concepts and targets that have recently been authorized by the Special Group. Since these missions will probably use new techniques, you might want to sit in on the briefings. The training branch may be getting into the small boat business deeper than we are now."

Giving no hint of my conversation with Rod several days earlier, I said that it would be a good idea for me to attend the briefings.

"Okay, I'll check it out with Ted. If he has no objection, you can sit in with

THE ZENITH SECRET

me. They were going to restrict the attendance to branch chiefs only, but maybe an exception can be made. Be here at one o'clock on Tuesday and Thursday unless I notify you otherwise."

I attended both briefings. All the branch chiefs were there as well as Mr. Fitzgerald and Mr. Harvey from Washington accompanied by Ted Shackley and Campbell. Dave Morales introduced Mr. David Phillips who was identified as a coordinator for the new initiatives with the exile political organizations.

The briefings were far more interesting and revealing than I had anticipated. There was no mention of the Kennedy administration as being the motivating force behind the new anti-Castro effort, but I'm sure that thought was in everyone's mind. Instead, the intelligence people took great pains to present a detailed estimate of the situation, one that certainly justified any action the United States might choose to take against the Communist regime. I had caught up on the daily intelligence summaries and realized that much of what was said was old hat, but all put together, Castro loomed as an even larger threat to the security of our country and the entire Western Hemisphere.

There now were credible reports of increased Russian assistance in Cuba—the delivery of new, more sophisticated weapons and equipment, and the arrival of more Russian advisers. Reports that some antiballistic missiles had never been removed from the island continued, but the intelligence people claimed that U-2 photographs had not confirmed this. Castro was known to be training agents and commandos to be sent to other Latin-American countries to create political unrest. There was mention of the possible construction of a Russian antiballistic missile submarine base on the southern coast of the island.

More Cubans were being imprisoned, tortured, and killed for political reasons. Many were trying to escape, so Castro had drastically improved his coastal surveillance. Based on what the intelligence experts had learned, we had every reason to be concerned for our safety. The administration was justified in and intent on making a concerted effort, within the limits of the Khrushchev-Kennedy agreement, to protect our national interests.

The CIA, and hence the Miami station, would continue to play a major role in the anti-Castro effort and would take the following steps to upgrade it:

• Increase the effectiveness and frequency of hit-and-run raids by exile commando groups against select targets by intensifying security training and cover precautions and improving infiltration and exfiltration techniques.
• Parachute operations were still ruled out, but certain commando groups would receive parachute training.
• Increase infiltration and intelligence gathering operations.
• Support and assist in every way possible the guerrilla bands and counterrevolutionaries inside Cuba. Foment insurrection by encouraging disaffection toward the Communist regime. Aid and resupply the indigenous anti-Castro forces.
• Broaden the scope of paramilitary commando operations to include underwater demolitions teams.

Various diplomatic steps, including the embargo on goods to Cuba, would continue. The Organization of American States was again being encouraged to take a hard stand against Castro, and individual Central and South American countries were being supported in their efforts to ward off his influence.

Privately I had heard that a new effort to assassinate Castro was being organized, and what Roderick had said about certain major targets being removed from the forbidden list was confirmed. The CIA had long wanted to hit some of these strategically important and highly vulnerable targets—principally oil refineries, petrochemical facilities, and telephone/telegraph installations. These facilities represented major investments of U.S. big business, and even though Castro had taken them over when he kicked out the Americans, the corporate directors had believed that one day he would be gone and the installations would be returned to them. These corporate directors had applied political pressure, and the strategists in the administration had found it "expedient" to avoid destroying these targets, even though it would have hurt the Communists. Now, apparently, the president and his advisers had overcome the objections of big business, or were under such political pressure from Castro-policy critics that something had to be done. A series of operations was being planned for early September, only a few months away.

It was exciting news but from a training standpoint the policy decisions presented some problems. The maritime branch had given a complete explanation of the fishing trawler/V-20 operators, which would probably require a new program, because Dewey simply wasn't equipped to do more than he was doing right now. It was obvious that the V-20 course would have to be more complete than our current small-boat program and would demand instruction in procedures and techniques that were presently untried.

Also, authorization to use underwater demolition teams (UDTs) meant that someone would have to remain to recruit and train volunteers for this very specialized kind of work. There was some mention of the Navy's furnishing instructors for this task, but nothing definite was planned. It was clear that unless one of the other station branches got into the training business, Cal's training branch stood to grow enormously within the coming weeks.

It was during the period of these briefings, when I had reason to frequent the operations-branch offices in the building adjacent to mine, that I finally met Colonel Rosselli. While waiting for the briefings to begin, I would usually visit with Bob Wall or Rod. One day I walked into Wall's corner office to see him talking with a dark-haired, sharply dressed man. As I apologized for my intrusion, Wall introduced him as Colonel Rosselli, ostensibly a former Army field grade officer now in service with the CIA as a paramilitary specialist. Rosselli greeted me warmly while at the same time eyeing me carefully. He had a charming manner, self-confident, polished, soft-spoken. Just for the hell of it, I threw out a hook and asked him if he'd ever served with the 11th Airborne Division. He looked at me quizzically, then at Wall, and somewhat embarrassedly said he had not. Rosselli was a presence in and about the operations building for most of the week of briefings and I saw him frequently coming and going from Morales' office.[9] I also observed him consulting with Rod in the plans room and occasionally walking or driving around the JM/WAVE complex with Gordon Campbell and Mr. Phillips, who obviously held a very important position somewhere in the CIA covert operations hierarchy.

Four days later, as I stood again in the stench and slime of the swamps in Key Largo, my exposure to high-level strategy and my hopes of another mission to Cuba seemed little more than a dream. We had begun another training cycle, and time seemed to drag now. José and Mike responded well to my guidance and had even assumed some of my own teaching techniques. They took more and more pride in the program as they assumed much of the actual instruction. This gave me time to work on those portions of the training that needed improvement or modification. I did more writing, committing to paper many of the lesson

THE ZENITH SECRET

plans and exercises which José would later translate into Spanish.

Despite my efforts to keep occupied, the heat, the mosquitoes, and the long days in the swamps wore heavily on my mind. But, just before my departure from Miami, I had been buoyed up considerably. Cal had called me into his office and told me that he had talked with Ted about the problem of case officers' attendance at training sessions. He hadn't made much headway; it seemed that Dave Morales had Ted Shackley convinced that his people were too busy to be standing around in the swamps.

As I turned to leave, Cal rose from his desk. "Ted did say that he'd like to come down to see what you've got set up in Key Largo. He asked me to recommend a date during this cycle when he and I could see some of the boys in action."

I was very pleased, for I knew that the chief of station never visited training sites. It seemed silly to get so excited about a little training inspection, but Cal and Ted would be my first visitors. One was my boss, and the other had the overall responsibility for all station activities; also, they were civilians and I was a soldier representing my service, and I wanted the Army to show up well as a result of my efforts. I also wanted Cal and Ted to share my pride in the way my Cuban assistants were working. Unfortunately, the team undergoing training seemed particularly uninspired, but I hoped that wouldn't be too obvious. I was eager to go on another mission, and Ted's permission to do so would depend largely on his impressions of survival and small-unit program I'd set up.

The training inspection went off without a hitch. I met Ted and Cal at Jewfish Creek late one afternoon and drove them to the campsite near Dynamite Pier. Both had voiced a wish not to be seen by any Cubans, so I had instructed José and Mike to stay with the team until after dark. Mario sent a specially prepared four-course Cuban meal to the training area, and as the two American agents and I ate, I could see that they enjoyed the diversion of an evening of "roughing it," and of course there was always that bureaucratic satisfaction of having made a "visit to the field."

José and Mike were capable of dropping off the team by boat. They performed the necessary supervisory tasks while I escorted Ted and Cal through the various phases of the exercise. After a detailed briefing on the program, we moved to a concealed location on the seacoast. From there we watched the team paddle ashore in rubber boats and move off through the jungle. Despite their lackadaisical attitude during most of the course, the exile team functioned surprisingly well.

Near midnight, when I took Cal and Ted back to their car at Jewfish Creek, they thanked me for the tour but made no comment about it. Despite the smoothness of the exercise and their lack of criticism, I was disappointed by their visit. There had been no mention of new training or of any of the major policy decisions I felt were under way at headquarters. As I drove back to the campsite alone, I felt more left out than ever. When the cycle ended several days later and I returned to Miami for a week's rest, I was depressed and had just about ruled out any personal involvement beyond what appeared to be an indefinite stay in the Key Largo mangroves.

The big break came unexpectedly one week later. During that week I dutifully prepared reports and ordered supplies for the next group of trainees, and even though it seemed futile, I forced myself to read the daily intelligence summaries.

My wife and sons were happy to have me at home for even a short time, but Suzie noticed that I complained a little too frequently about the heat and the hardships of the swamps. My depression soon caused her to reveal her own growing unhappiness. I was away most of the time, and she'd made no friends; none of the agency wives had bothered to call. In the military, a unit welcome party was the usual practice for a newly assigned officer. Even our neighbors seemed standoffish. It was exactly what I'd anticipated, and now I had to stop it. I suggested that we invite some people over for drinks, and even though it was short notice, most of the training branch showed up—Cal and Larry with their wives, and Rudy, Walter, and Rod. It was a friendly gathering, but it soon became apparent that Suzie and I weren't the only ones feeling tense and edgy with our work; the others were experiencing similar pressures. We made small talk at first and tried to avoid any mention of business, but it was almost impossible. We had all drunk a great deal, and gradually the guests excused themselves. Cal and I were alone on the patio, and his wife and Suzie were in the living room.

Cal, obviously a little drunk, began, "You know, the training branch is going to have to set up three new programs in the next few weeks."

"No, I didn't know that. When I'm in the swamps I'm completely out of circulation."

"What do you know about boats?"

"We have the Whaler and other small boats at the Jewfish Creek Marina in Key Largo, and we do pretty well with them, but what kind of boats do you mean?" Damn it, I was slurring my words. I licked my dry lips.

"V-20s. We've got to set up a complete V-20 course, a UDT course, and a surf-landing course." Cal's head bobbed as he talked, and I could tell he was troubled.

My head was clearing. "What have you got in mind?" I tried to sound casual.

He looked at me, eyelids drooping slightly, then averted his gaze. "The whole thing."

"You've got to be kidding. Who's going to do survival?"

"We'll get a replacement to take over for you. I need someone to set up other programs and get them going. Ted and I think you can do it, if you want the job."

Suddenly I was sober. It was now or never. "Yeah, I want the job, Cal, but if I'm going to do it, I want to make one V-20 trip to Cuba so I can do it right."

He looked at me as if I were crazy, but then the women joined us, ending our conversation.

Back in the swamps a few days later, gloom settled over me again. I'd waited anxiously during the rest of the weekend for some indication from Cal that we would continue our conversation. On Monday morning I thought surely he would call me into his office before I left for the Keys, but he didn't. I knew Cal well enough to realize that it would be almost impossible for him to understand why I wanted to go. To him—a career civil servant with eyes on retirement—the idea of anyone wanting to put himself in a physically dangerous position was foolhardy. Ted might understand, but Cal, never.

Yet there was no other way I could have made my wish known. I couldn't have bypassed Cal and gone directly to the chief of station, for I needed Cal on my side. If they were serious about the new training job, maybe he and Ted would see merit in my request. I'd just have to wait and see what happened.

As it turned out, I didn't have to wait long. When we came in from the field on Friday afternoon, Cal called and asked me to come up to Miami for the weekend; he had something to discuss with me about some of the travel plans. I couldn't believe my ears. He told me to set up things so the "boys" could work on their own for the next week. Hot damn, I thought, I'm on my way. I could barely suppress my exuberance as I made the familiar drive up to Miami. I was ready for good news when I met Cal at the bar in the New England Oyster House in Perrine.

But, to my deep disappointment, the "travel plans" that he wanted to talk about did not involve Cuba at all. In fact, he wanted me to travel in the opposite direction, north to Eglin Air Force Base in northwestern Florida. The agency had gotten wind of a new STOL aircraft, a "twin helio" (twin-engine, short-take-off and -landing aircraft) that was being tested by the Air Force at Eglin. The newly designed plane was highly classified, and the CIA felt it might be of some use to them in landing friendly agents in various target areas, such as Cuba, and "snatching" them out again. The craft was supposed to fly low and fast, yet possess landing characteristics similar to those of a conventional helicopter. The agency wanted someone familiar with airplanes, parachuting, and small-unit operations to take a look at the plane and make a report on it for the Miami station.

"You need a break from the swamps anyway, Brad, and Homestead says they can't jump you out there anymore. You can make a jump for pay at Eglin while you're there. It'll be a good change of scenery for you. And when you get back, we want to talk to you about setting up the new training programs I mentioned the other night. There are still a lot of things, policy-wise, in the air, so we aren't ready to go yet. But you can be thinking about it."

There was no mention of a trip to Cuba. "How long can I expect to be gone, Cal?"

"Figure on up to a week or so and you'll be on TDY [temporary duty] from the station while you're there. You can coordinate with the aviation branch people Monday morning. They've got a C-54 leaving Miami International for the panhandle that afternoon."

I felt quite let down that weekend, for I'd been sure that he was going to tell me I could go on an op. To add to my depression, Suzie was very upset because I'd be gone again, for an extended period. But Monday came quickly, and as I sat in an uncomfortable canvas seat on the Air Force C-54, I wondered how José, Mike, and Mario were getting along in the Keys without me. I dozed briefly, lulled by the drone of the big plane's engines, but soon the copilot came back through the cabin, woke me, and said we'd be landing in Tampa in a few minutes.

As the sleep left my mind, I remembered the large black suitcase next to my small flight bag on the floor near the forward cabin partition. The security branch had given me the battered suitcase, bound with a heavy leather strap and secured with a partially rusted lock, as I was leaving the airport. One of the young agents had run out with it just as I was pulling out of the parking lot.

"Hey, you're going to Tampa aren't you? They say you're going to be on the ground for an hour or two there. Could you run this thing downtown? It belongs to one of our guys stationed up there. It's got his clothes, shaving gear, the works. He forgot it here this past weekend."

"Sure," I said. "It'll give me something to do during the layover."

As he shoved the bag into the trunk of my car, he gave me a slip of paper on which were written a name and address in Tampa. "You'll have no trouble locating the place," he added. "Take a cab and turn the receipt in to me when you get back. And, oh yeah, be sure and have Mr. Martinez open the bag in your presence. He's supposed to have the key. That way you'll be sure it's in the right hands. And use your Paragon cover while making the delivery."

Now, the C-54 taxied to the Transient ramp at McDill, and with my bag and the large black suitcase in hand I was soon standing beside the big plane. I had plenty of time, the pilot said; with a new crew the aircraft wouldn't leave for at least three hours. I called a cab and headed for downtown Tampa.

The address turned out to be a dilapidated wooden building on the waterfront. It was a decidedly rundown area of the city, and, in the late afternoon sun, skid row inhabitants were beginning to make their appearance. As I stepped from the air-conditioned cab and it took off down the littered street, the smells of raw fish, stale beer, urine, and greasy fried foods filled my nostrils. A jukebox was playing loudly in a honky-tonk down the street, and two little black kids narrowly missed running me down with their bikes. The name on the peeling, scarred door before me was that of a fish-packing and shipping company. A tattered green shade was drawn over the window, and a "closed" sign was stuck in the cracked molding.

I knocked several times, and when no one answered I picked up the bags and turned to leave. Suddenly a heavy, black-haired man in shirtsleeves opened the door.

"Yes, may I help you? We're closed for the day." He sounded annoyed.

"Mr. Martinez?"

"That's right. What can I do for you, please?" He had an accent.

"Some friends in Miami asked me to bring your suitcase here. They said you forgot it, and since I was coming through Tampa they asked me to deliver it to you."

"Oh, yes." His face softened. "I've been expecting you. You're Mr. Williams. They called and said you were coming."

I was a little uneasy. It was a tough neighborhood.

"Well, if you'll just open the lock to prove it's your bag, I'll be on my way."

He stared at me. "Surely, but I have the key upstairs in my apartment. If you'd like to come with me, I can only offer you a beer, but you are welcome to it. Upstairs, I'll open the bag."

I followed him through a musty, cluttered office that looked like something dating from the late 1800s, past a stained, smelly restroom, and up a creaky flight of stairs.

Martinez, puffing from the exertion of climbing the stairs with the heavy bag, pushed open a door, and I found myself standing in a homey little apartment overlooking the water. The apartment was not air-conditioned, and the aroma of olive oil and black beans was strong.

He gave me a beer, then left the room for a few minutes; when he returned, he put the suitcase on a table and fiddled with the lock for a few minutes. I watched as he opened it.

Inside the suitcase were brown paper sacks of weighty material, to give the bag heft and bulk and a large manila envelope. There weren't any clothes or personal articles.

"I've been waiting all day for this, Mr. Williams, and I'm thankful you brought it to us safely," Martinez said. "This must be a surprise to you. See, no shirts or socks, only an envelope and bags of money." He emptied a bag of rolled bills onto the table, then tore open the envelope and removed a stack of papers, which he thumbed through quickly. While he read them, I lit a cigarette, sipped my beer, and turned to the window, trying to make myself believe what was going on. The sun was gone, and I looked at the big fishing boats moored at the docks directly behind the old building. There was something vaguely familiar

THE ZENITH SECRET

about the smaller boats in the foreground. Martinez interrupted my thoughts:

"Would you like to stay for a Cuban supper? It says here in these papers that you are authorized to accompany us on a little fishing expedition tomorrow night, if you still want to."

Chills ran through me as he spoke. Then I recognized the smaller boats as the brand new, carefully disguised V-20 strike boats.

We sailed for Cuba under a full moon the following night. I was less tense this time. Ships and sea were becoming familiar, and I was at ease with the Cubans. As the only American present and virtually on my own, I felt less compelled to assume a role of responsibility. I had been committed to the role of supervisor and leader, an American representing the benevolent and all-powerful CIA. But now, it was understood that I was an observer and I felt free to join and assist the Cubans in whatever way I could.

The day had been spent in final quiet preparation for the mission, under Martinez's direction. Under guise of outfitting for an extended commercial fishing expedition, the ships were loaded and the smaller boats fueled and checked. Martinez held briefings in a converted walk-in cooler in the fish-packing plant adjacent to the docks. The heavily insulated cooler, with its thick single door, was the most secure area in the old building, and, with the temperature controlled, it was also the most comfortable.

The first briefing, held at midmorning, was for the captains and first mates of the two fishing trawlers that would make the V-20 delivery. Each trawler would tow two V-20s. Three of the small craft, with a total of 12 men aboard, would be released approximately 12 miles off the coast of Cuba, near the port town of Isabela. One V-20 would remain in case one of the primary craft experienced mechanical failure before the mission was launched. Once the commandos were on their way, they'd make their strike and return to the U.S. mainland in the small boats. The trawlers would remain in the general area for 24 hours fishing, with some success, they hoped before returning to the U.S. Depending on the outcome of the commando raid and the public attention that might result, the trawlers would either return directly to Tampa or be kept, as inconspicuously as possible, in other ports. The commandos, I was told, were an experienced group and had had several weeks' training specifically for this mission. However, this would be the team's first exposure to the new V-20s. Supposedly, the commandos had three good operators to handle the speedy little boats.

The commando force, including six men familiar with the Isabela coastal area, would land west of the town, then penetrate almost a mile and a half inland to the site of a railway bridge. The bridge was the most vulnerable point on the vital Sagua la Grande-Isabela railway. The single-track line carried large amounts of freight and produce between the inland city of Sagua la Grande and the port of Isabela. It was one of the key supply lines in the central part of the island. The commando force was to blow up the bridge and destroy telephone and telegraph lines running adjacent to the tracks.

Mr. Martinez, who obviously had an excellent knowledge of the area, presented a rather formidable picture of the enemy defenses. Puerto Sagua la Grande, as the Isabela port was known, was protected by shore batteries and powerful searchlights. Two of the newest Soviet coastal patrol boats kept continuous watch on the harbor entrance from deeper water between Cayo Megano and Cayo Fragoso. The distinct advantage afforded by the V-20s—besides their speed—was that, once past the patrol boats, they could maneuver in shallow water between the shoals and coastal keys, where the larger boats could not go because of their deeper draft. The success of the mission rested largely on speed and surprise, not on secrecy.

I asked Martinez where I might best observe the actions of the trawlers and the V-20s. After some discussion, and considering the fact that as an American citizen I was barred from entering Cuban waters, it was decided that I would remain with him in the backup V-20. He planned to follow the commandos as far as the shallow water, about three miles offshore. We would lie near one of the outer keys until we heard the bridge blow and would then return to the trawlers, some twelve miles off the coast. That way, the backup V-20 would be readily available to the commandos if they needed it during their run to the target area.

After the morning briefing, the trawler captains returned to their crews. Preparations continued throughout the day. Mr. Martinez was very busy, working back and forth between what apparently was a legitimate fish-packing business and the trawlers that were being readied for the secret raid. I was amazed at his nonchalance as he took orders for fish and conducted other regular business from the cluttered front office of the old building and, the next minute, answered complex questions for one of the trawler captains about the forthcoming raid. He struck me as very practical, shrewd, and profit-oriented. In addition to his fish business, he functioned as a mercenary for the CIA, conducting secret raids against Fidel Castro.

About 30 minutes before we were scheduled to sail, two fish delivery trucks pulled into the warehouse, and, after the overhead doors rolled closed, men began jumping out. It was the commando team, previously hidden somewhere in Tampa. I was surprised to see familiar faces among the team and to be greeted again by my old friend Julio from the Point Mary safehouse.

Martinez and Julio gave the commandos their ship billeting assignments, and while the first mate of each vessel guided the men to the boats, the rest of us went back into the cooler for a final review of the mission. Julio, who had impressed me earlier with his readiness, seemed confident and quite determined about the dangerous raid. We boarded the trawlers, and after rendezvousing with the V-20s and towing them a short distance from the docks, we were on our way. It was almost midnight when we churned past the Mullet Key light at the entrance to Tampa Bay and into the silvery swells of the Gulf of Mexico. Unlike the old WWII Rex, the fishing trawlers were relatively new and quite comfortable. The wide-beamed steel-hulled vessels were more than eighty feet long, and each was powered by two giant Caterpillar diesel engines. Despite their worn appearance and stained hulls and decks, the ships were clean and in good mechanical condition.

They were equipped with heavy nets, fish storage lockers, and many winches and hoists. I had never been on a large commercial fishing vessel before, but I knew that the boats could remain at sea for long periods of time and were uniquely suited to harvesting enormous quantities of seafood. The bridges and wheelhouses were equipped with the latest electronic navigation gear and depth-reading and communications equipment. The vessel we rode on had a special shortwave transceiver installed for communication with a CIA control station somewhere in the Caribbean.

We were to sail south around the Dry Tortugas and the Marquesas to the vicinity of Cay Sal, where we would conduct commercial fishing for about 24 hours, until late Thursday afternoon. This would contribute to our cover and give the commandos a chance to check out the V-20s and other equipment. (The small boats, despite their reinforced hulls and towing modification, took quite a beating as they were pulled behind the trawlers. If we encountered rough seas or foul weather, we would need time to dry out the boats and double-check their engines and controls.)

Thursday evening we would move from the Cay Sal area to the Cuban coast and release the V-20s. We were going to spend some time at sea, and I was much better prepared for it this time. As we left the lights of Tampa behind, I found a comfortable place on top of one of the large fish storage boxes and, with the brilliant stars of the tropic sky overhead, promptly went to sleep.

By midday Wednesday we were turning eastward off the Dry Tortugas and heading toward Cay Sal. Julio, the commando team leader, had lived in the Isabela area and knew the railroad bridge and surrounding terrain. Provided the militia was not waiting in ambush, that part of the mission did not bother him. He was concerned about trying to make it all the way back to the Florida Keys in the V-20s; 90 miles was a great distance to travel in a small, open boat. Everything would have to work perfectly; there was no margin for error. Julio had less than an hour's fuel reserve for the speed and distance they had calculated. He knew that the trawlers would be standing by in the vicinity of Cay Sal for a period after the commandos' taking refuge on Cay Sal, as some of the other raiding parties had done in the past, but Julio knew of the recent cases where Castro's men had come ashore there and taken exiles into custody. No, he said, they would make a run for it, all the way back to the United States.

I could hardly blame Julio for his reluctance to try to hide out on Cay Sal. The small, barren coral shoals and scrub-covered outcroppings were little more than tiny dots on the chart. They were surrounded by sharks and were subject to violent storms. I'd heard that the Cay Sal islands were under control of aviation tycoon Howard Hughes, under a lease agreement with the Bahamian government.[10] Hughes, in turn, reportedly made the islands available to the CIA and other United States government agencies for a variety of uses, and many Cuban refugees and fleeing exile agents tried to find safety there. Some were rescued, but many died of exposure, starvation, or thirst. And, as Julio said, Castro had begun to raid the exposed islands whenever he got word of someone stranded there. The islands were virtually impossible to protect because of their number and their location, but they were patrolled regularly by the U.S. Coast Guard as well as by Castro's raiders. The fate of anyone stranded on Cay Sal Bank lay with whomever got to him or her first. Julio and his men would sooner cast their fate with the sturdy little V-20s, which they hoped would get them back to the United States safely.

The weather remained good during the entire voyage to Cay Sal, and the V-20s didn't seem to take much of a beating in the four-to-six-foot waves. The heavy shackles and nylon and rubber towing bridles absorbed much pounding as the trawlers plowed eastward at a steady 15 knots. Freighters and fishing boats continually moved back and forth across the horizon, but no one bothered us. We passed the time by trolling for sharks, cleaning weapons, reading, and going over details of the mission. We arrived south of Cay Sal Bank sometime before dawn on Thursday.

The crews prepared their nets for fishing and used the V-20s to set them out; as they did so, members of the commando team went over the little boats to check for anything out of order. All four boats checked out perfectly. In keeping with our cover as a commercial fishing operation, the big nets were hauled aboard twice each day by the booms and groaning winches, and hundreds of pounds of fish, including eels, rays, octopi, sharks, and other strange-looking sea creatures were dumped into the storage lockers.

At 4 p.m. the nets were hauled aboard for the last time and we turned south, toward Cuba. The wind had switched to the northeast, and the large storm clouds were building north of our position. For the first time since the mission had begun I felt the familiar rush of adrenaline that made me shiver and caused my heart to pump harder. I went below to the small gallery for what now appeared to be the traditional last meal and final briefing.

Time passed quickly as we went through the solemn supper, wishing each other good luck, making final prayers, and passing of a bottle of rum. I imagined that something quite similar was taking place in the other trawler as it followed us into the gathering darkness. Julio's men were more subdued than the Cubans I had accompanied earlier. They ate in silence and showed little emotion as Martinez toasted them and passed the rum.

The rolling and pitching of the ship gradually increased as we ate, and when we emerged on the darkened deck, the wind was still blowing out of the northeast, but velocity had increased to about 15 knots. Low black clouds, scudding southward across the night sky, blotted out the moon for long periods of time. We had counted on a full moon to aid in navigating the V-20s in the shallow water around the keys and shoals that dotted the Cuban coast in the target area. Martinez and Julio were concerned about the change in the weather.

The lights on all boats had been extinguished earlier, and the commandos were gathered in the shadows at the stern of the trawler. One hundred feet behind us, the V-20s bounced and slapped against the water at the ends of their towlines.

We waited in silence, the tension growing. Sea spray came over the low gunwales of the ship, wetting the weapons and equipment. Far in the distance, there was a flash of light off the bow; it came again, at regular intervals. It was the channel navigation light marking the entrance to Isabela harbor. We had reached the release point; it was time for the commandos to board the small boats.

The captain cut back power and brought the trawler around into the wind. The waves now seemed enormous, and the bow of the vessel would tower over our heads, then slam down with a sickening thud. The crew moved to the stern to bring the two V-20s alongside while the captain held power to keep the bow of the vessel facing into the wind. About 400 yards off our port beam, I could barely make out the other trawler, maneuvering as we were. All of us were soaking wet from the spray that doused the pitching vessel.

With the help of some of the commandos, the trawler crew pulled the violently bobbing V-20s up to the stern quarter on either side of the larger vessel. Despite their heavy rubber bumpers, the small craft pounded against the side of the larger boat, and I could hear the crunch of breaking fiberglass from time to time as it struck the steel hull.

Martinez stood next to me, grasping the handholds, as I was, to keep from being tossed to the deck. I could see the concern on his face. We turned and moved toward the bridge. The captain met us halfway and, hollering over the noise of the diesels and the wind, said that headquarters had just sent final okay for the mission. With Martinez, who may have been thinking of requesting a change of plans, I returned to the stern of the trawler. As the V-20s continued to pound against the side of the larger boat, Martinez inched his way across the slippery deck to Julio and gave him the order to board.

The commando team's effort to get from the stern of the pitching trawler into the bobbing little V-20 was one of the most determined acts I'd ever witnessed. The moon was now completely hidden by the clouds, so we could see nothing of our sister craft. The Cubans boarded one at a time as the rising and falling boats passed reasonably close to each other in vertical movements. Equipment was passed aboard the same way. Finally, a crewmember managed to hand the commandos the .30 caliber light machine gun that would be mounted on the pedestal in the V-20.

It took nearly 40 minutes to load the boat, much longer than we had anticipated. I was greatly relieved when I heard the twin 160-horsepower Mercruisers come to life as the commandos prepared to cast off. With considerable difficulty, Martinez and I boarded the V-20 held off the opposite side of the ship. Despite his size, Martinez showed considerable agility as he bounded aboard the little boat on one of its upward movements. He moved to the controls and turned the key, and one of the engines sprang to life as I jumped aboard.

The lines were cast off and we drifted astern of the trawler to join Julio's boat and pick up the two V-20s from the other trawler. In a few moments we were circling in the heavy seas, with all four boats apparently running perfectly as the trawlers pulled away in the darkness.

The only contact between the V-20s was visual, and with the moon behind a cloud, we were virtually blind. The plan for approaching Isabela harbor called for Julio's and another commando boat to run abreast of each other, using the harbor entrance light as a guide until we were about a mile from the mouth of the channel. The other commando boat and our backup craft would follow about a 100 yards behind the lead boats, close enough to maintain visual contact. About a mile off the light, we would turn slightly to the northwest and head for the Cayo Sotovento light, we would turn sharply to the south, through a narrow channel, and skirt the large mangrove key. We would proceed southeastward, in the deeper water between a series of mangrove bayheads and coral outcroppings, to a little point of land. The V-20s drew nearly 24 inches of water, so after we made the turn at Cayo Sotovento light we'd have to move carefully to keep from running aground. It would be impossible for the Cuban coastal patrol boats to follow us there, but if we ran aground we'd be sitting ducks for the shore batteries as well as the larger enemy boats outside the shallow reef.

With Julio in the lead, we turned toward the flashing light nearly 12 miles away and took up our approach formation. I looked at Martinez standing beside me at the wheel of the V-20 as we were caught in a brief period of moonlight. Earlier in the day he had changed his usual sweat-soaked white shirt and black trousers for a gaudy blue and white Hawaiian sport shirt and tan Bermuda shorts. With wide collar flapping and spindly legs atop tennis shoes, he was a comical sight in our situation; almost ridiculous, I thought. And then I remembered that neither of us had even bothered to carry a gun. We had no weapons, and we were only a few miles off the Cuban coast, under the most dangerous circumstances. I glanced at Martinez again. Hell, he looked like a drunken millionaire on a midnight cruise off Miami Beach. Then another thought struck me: there was no place else in the world I would rather have been. This was it. I belonged with these people.

We had been running toward the light for a long time. Too long, I thought. We were running slower than planned because of the rough seas. I couldn't talk to Martinez over the roar of the engines, but he must have been thinking the same thing. He glanced at his watch repeatedly, wiping the saltwater from his wrist to look at the glowing dial. The light of Isabela harbor was much farther away than it had seemed from the trawler.

The boats were running well and we saw no sign of the coastal patrol boats. As we drew closer to the channel entrance, the lights of the town became visible in the background. Martinez concentrated on following close behind the lead

V20s. As Julio slowed his craft gradually and made the turn to the northwest, parallel to the coast, Martinez did the same, then increased the speed of our boat to keep pace with those ahead.

We were moving along well and were nearly to the Cayo Sotovento marker when suddenly the lights of a large boat appeared directly in front of us. It was a coastal patrol boat, coming in our direction. Almost as soon as we saw the lights of the enemy boat, a searchlight shattered the darkness, and for a moment the four speeding V-20s were caught in its powerful beam. Julio changed course and we followed. He was making the turn to the southeast; we would soon be in shallow water. I glanced around to see other lights flick on as the patrol craft was alerted. Apparently, we'd surprised them as much as they'd surprised us. There was no gunfire, for we had maneuvered away from the beam of the searchlight.

Julio and the commandos gunned their boats to full speed, and Martinez did the same. The boat seemed to leap out of the water as we made the turn into the relative calm of the shallow water. We passed black clumps of mangroves with only inches to spare as we ducked behind the protective bayheads. According to our plan, Martinez and I were supposed to turn around at this point and return to the trawlers, but we both knew that the Cuban patrol boat, even though it had lost us in the mangrove keys, would be blocking our avenue of escape.

We rushed headlong toward the coast, the inboard engines in the four boats screaming in unison as we skimmed across the coral shoals. Suddenly I heard an agonizing engine whine and a loud crackling over the noise of our motors. Martinez and I, looking in the same direction, saw one of the speeding commando boats strike something in the water and hurtle into the air. It hung there for an instant in the spray, silhouetted in the moonlight, then crashed down, spilling its occupants into the water. We'd lost Julio's boat in the darkness, and we and the other V-20 had inadvertently run into the shallow coral flats. Martinez reached for the throttle, but it was too late. We struck the shallows, and the boat rocked crazily as the fiberglass keel ripped against the jagged coral. The momentum carried the boat forward and it landed, as I clung to whatever I could, waiting for the crash I knew would come. Martinez was frozen behind the wheel.

We hit once and bounced back into the air like a skipping stone. I was thrown forward in a half-somersault at the first impact, striking my face and mouth against the top edge of the windshield. I felt my front teeth splinter. Stunned, I turned slightly, and as we hit the second time, my head struck something. Martinez was gone. I felt no pain, only soft, warm blackness as it closed around me.

THE ZENITH SECRET

CHAPTER 9

I was conscious of brilliant orange, yellow, red and blue particles exploding in the blackness of my mind. Then, the staccato crack of machine-gun fire made me realize that I was looking at ricocheting phosphorous tracer rounds arcing across the night sky. The Cuban patrol boat was pouring a steady stream of fire into the small island between our position and the edge of the shoals. The beam of a spotlight swept the tangled vegetation, and the machine gun continued to probe the mangroves. Apparently they'd lost us as we turned shoreward around the keys and into the protective flats. Now we lay disabled, with two boats aground less than half a mile from the alerted defenders. I was sure it would be only minutes before the Communist gunners found us. Somewhere ahead, Julio and the other commandos were continuing toward the landing site on the coast. They must have been oblivious of our plight.

I pulled myself to my feet. My upper lip was torn and bleeding and my front teeth were broken into jagged splinters. My hand, touching the throbbing lump on the back of my head, came away warm and sticky. I could barely move my arms and legs. Martinez was lying in the stern of the boat, moaning and holding his left arm. Across the shallow water, less than one hundred yards from our position, I saw the other V-20. The commandos were in the water around the craft, struggling to free it from where it hung on a coral outcropping. It would be only moments before the patrol boat would hear their frantic splashing and excited conversation. We had to get out of there quickly.

The patrol boat poured another burst of tracers into the mangroves; the rounds pinged crazily into the sky as I moved to the rear of the boat.

"Martinez, we've got to get away from here. Can you get up?"

"My arm...must be broken. We are aground. Where are the other boats?" He groaned.

"Martinez, try to get up. Only one boat is with us. Julio and the other one must have gotten through OK."

I helped the big man to his feet. Blood trickled from an ugly cut on his forehead, and his left arm hung limp and useless at his side. He was biting his lip in pain. He inched forward to the steering wheel in the sharply tilted boat. By this time, the commandos had freed their boat and were pushing it through the shallow water toward us.

Part of the stern of our V-20 was in the water. Martinez turned the ignition switch, and to my surprise the port and then the starboard engine sprang to life. Apparently they had not been damaged, and if the outdrives remained intact, we had a chance. The big Cuban, his gaudy sport shirt now darkened with blood, moved the throttles forward with his right hand. The engines groaned and churned, but we didn't move.

The other boat was now alongside our craft. In a brief period of moonlight, I could see a long, ugly gash on one side above the water line. One of the outdrives had been sheared off. In the darkness I couldn't tell if any of the commandos had been injured, but all four were wading knee-deep in the shallow water, so at least they could still move.

Another burst of machine-gun fire shattered the night, this time farther down the coast. The patrol boat seemed to have passed us by and was probing the small island east of our position.

Martinez, regaining his composure, shouted for the commando operator of the other V-20 to try to start his one remaining engine. His comrades boosted the man into the boat, and to my amazement, it rattled to life. It didn't sound good, but it was running. The other three Cubans tugged on our V-20 to free it from the coral and mangrove roots. Martinez gunned the engines as I jumped overboard to help the Cubans. Rocking and pushing, we backed it into deeper water. The thick, reinforced fiberglass hull proved its worth. Despite the shattering impact, the bottom was still intact.

The three commandos stood in the water, waiting for Martinez's instructions. Should they continue or turn back? We had to decide quickly. Their boat contained one-third of the explosives necessary to destroy the bridge, and their team was vital to the success of Julio's mission. In an instant, Martinez decided.

"Take our boat. It still has two good engines. Get the demolitions into this V-20, quickly!" he shouted. "You must follow Julio. We have no time to spare." He pointed toward what we all hoped was the coastline.

I helped the commandos transfer their equipment and heavy satchel charges into the backup craft. While the commandos clambered into our boat, Martinez and I painfully went over the side of our craft and into the commandos' boat. We would try to make a run for it, back to the trawlers, while the commandos continued their mission.

The commandos disappeared in the blackness behind another low growth of mangrove. Then, with the single engine vibrating loudly, Martinez brought our boat around and headed toward the channel. The sky was overcast again; the blackness ahead was ominous. There was no sign of the Cuban patrol boat as we rode between the dangerous shoals and tangled bay head. I didn't know how Martinez was navigating, but as long as we didn't run aground and the luminous compass needle showed us moving generally to the north, I didn't care.

Looking around our craft, I saw the commandos had left much of their equipment. There were several packs lying on the deck, one Browning automatic rifle, a full belt of magazines, and a .30-caliber light machine gun swung loosely in the pedestal mount. A full box of ammunition was on the mount, and a belt was chambered in the gun. A flashlight and other miscellaneous gear cluttered the deck.

We approached the last small island screening us from the open sea.

Martinez increased power, and the damaged engine chattered agonizingly in its loosened mounts. I strained to see into the blackness in front of us. I knew we'd pick up the Cayo Sotovento light soon. The chop of the shallow water gradually rose to the familiar swells of the open sea. We had only a short distance to go to safety.

As we swung around the last small key, a large boat suddenly loomed dead ahead in the flashes of the Cayo Sotovento light. It looked like a battleship, stretching across the entire channel, blocking our escape. It was the Soviet patrol boat; it hadn't moved down the coast, but lay in wait for us at the mouth of the inlet. Martinez, steering with one arm, reached for the throttle. It was run for it or turn back. A powerful spotlight flicked on and caught us fully in its intense glare.

Martinez hit the throttle, and the damaged engine hurtled the craft into the blackness ahead. Instinctively I moved to the pedestal mount and opened fire in the direction of the moving spotlight that tried to follow us. We were less than 200 yards from the patrol boat, and I could hear the slugs clanking off its armor plating. I kept firing, almost unaware of the stream of tracers directed toward us. I kept firing until the light went out. Then, almost magically, it was quiet, and Martinez and I and the growling little V-20 were alone in the darkness of the open sea.

We continued northward, hoping we'd be able to find the trawlers in the darkness. We reduced power to conserve what life might be left in the damaged engine. Bucking the stiff northeast wind and heavy seas, the disabled V-20 labored up the seemingly endless swells, and then topped the rolling crests and wallowed sickeningly in the valleys. There was no way to trim the boat, and holding the wheel required constant effort and attention. Martinez and I took turns steering and bailing out the water that gushed through the tear in the side of the craft. There were times, out there in the dark, when we seemed to be hanging somewhere between the conscious and the unconscious; Martinez and I said very little, but we both sensed that we were walking the very thin line between life and death. I made him put on a life jacket and put on one myself.

But there was no place for fear—only anger. I cursed my own stupidity for getting caught in this predicament, and I cursed the Army and the CIA and the whole "real" world that, otherwise, seemed so terribly important. What in the hell was I doing here? I asked myself over and over. Then my thoughts turned to the four commandos who had also run aground and who had chosen to continue their mission. Even now, they were probably facing much more than we were. I swore and bit my lip in frustration, my jagged teeth cutting into already swollen flesh.

Martinez lost consciousness sometime during the night while I was at the wheel. The cut on his forehead was no longer bleeding, but I could do nothing about his broken arm. Shock and exhaustion finally overcame him and he collapsed on top of some life jackets on the wet deck. It seemed as though the sea had swallowed us up, and I concentrated only on holding the wavering, luminous compass on a northerly heading.

Eventually I became aware of a pale light in the sky to the east; it slowly became pink and blue, and the shape of gray clouds became visible. Dawn was breaking over the Caribbean. The water around the little boat was an incredibly deep azure blue, and flying fish skipped from swell to swell around us.

Martinez looked peaceful; if he wasn't dead, I concluded, he was certainly sleeping comfortably. The pain at the back of my head and at my mouth had become a dull ache, and then, thankfully, had turned to numbness.

I left the wheel to check the radio direction finder, which we'd turned on to help locate the trawlers. The instrument bore several sharp dents. I knew we couldn't depend on its readings, and there was no indication of a signal from the trawlers. As the golden ball of the sun emerged from the sea, my eye caught a flash from something off our port bow. I scanned the horizon and, after a few minutes, picked up the shape of a distant ship. I went back to the RDF and made another signal scan. Suddenly the beep-beep was loud and clear and pointing directly at the ship on the horizon. It was one of our trawlers, and soon the sister ship was in sight too. I reached down excitedly and pulled Martinez's leg to awaken him. As he stood, we both thanked God.

I vaguely remember bringing the V-20 alongside the nearest trawler and helping the crew pull Martinez aboard. His eyes were glazed; he was in shock from the pain of his shattered arm. I started to protest when he gave instructions to scuttle our battered V-20. Then I realized that, to preserve the innocent appearance of the trawlers, we would have to get rid of the small boat. Besides the damage inflicted when it ran aground, the thick fiberglass hull now bore

THE ZENITH SECRET

several more holes, which had unquestionably been made by bullets. There was no place to conceal the V-20 on the trawler. I watched a crewman lower himself into the craft, pull the drain plugs, and release the lines that held it to the larger boat. In a few minutes only the windshield and bow remained above water, and then, as if to blot out any memory of our harrowing night, it disappeared into the swells.

They took Martinez and me below and splinted his arm. He was nearly delirious from pain, but with the help of a drug he soon fell into a deep sleep. There was nothing to be done about my own injuries. The bump and lacerations on the back of my head would heal themselves, and the swelling of my upper lip would recede. My two broken teeth had been capped as a result of an earlier parachuting injury, and although the caps and a bit more of the teeth were gone, most of the remaining teeth, uppers and lowers were grotesquely loose in their sockets and something had happened to my jaw as I could barely open and close it. There was a large bleeding cut on my tongue. The pain in my back and neck made it almost impossible to move.

I wanted to lie down and rest, but the thought of the commandos somewhere on the Cuban coast remained in my mind. The trawlers had seen no sign of the raiding party, nor had there been the telltale explosion they'd hoped to hear or see when the railway bridge was blown. They could have been out of hearing distance, however, as we were miles away, somewhere south of Cay Sal.

It was as close as we dared get to the island after the events of the previous night. If any of the commandos needed us, they would have to seek us out where we were.

The northeasterly wind had died down and the sun was rising white-hot in the morning sky. I drank rum until I felt an emptiness that sapped all of my remaining strength; then the captain helped me into a bunk, as the world dissolved around me.

When I awakened, it was dark and the trawler was under way. My mouth and head felt better. Martinez, in a bunk across the cabin, was still asleep. One of the crewmen came in with food and coffee, but I couldn't eat. There'd been no word from the raiding party, and we were now proceeding, at reduced speed, back to the United States. There was nothing more we could do. I drank some cold water and went back to sleep. When I awakened again, it was just getting light. I went up on deck to have a cigarette and watch the sun rise. That's when we sighted the refugee boat.

It was an odd-looking craft, lying still on the calm sea, about two miles off our bow. The vessel had the lines of an ancient Phoenician sailing ship, with a large tattered square sail that hung lifelessly in the gray morning light. It had no lights and flew no flag. There was an eerie quality about the boat, and as we neared, we saw no sign of life. The vessel was listing badly and appeared to have been abandoned. As we drew closer though, we saw that the dark lumps on the deck were human forms. They must have been sleeping; as the noise of our diesels grew louder, they began to stir, and a man stood atop the low cabin near the mast of the old boat and waved frantically in our direction.

One of the trawler crewmen had awakened Martinez, who had come up to the deck and now stood beside me. As he spoke to the trawler captain, the other crewmembers joined excitedly in the conversation. Cuban refugees...escaping from the Communist island...adrift and in need of help. I caught the words over the loud throb of the diesels. I knew that thousands of Cubans tried to escape like this—some lashed themselves to rafts and inner tubes or hung on to anything that would float them away from the slavery and horror of Cuba. No one knew how many had been carried out to the open seas only to perish. Now we had to decide whether we should risk our own security to help them.

Martinez barked out instructions to the trawler captain as we came alongside the old boat. There were a few bodies still on the deck, persons too old or sick to stand, but the others were waving excitedly at us. We bumped hard against the wooden side of the old boat as thin arms strained to reach for the lines we tossed down.

There were 15 refugees—an odd mixture of young and old, including a small boy and two infants—and they cried with joy as the trawler crew helped them aboard our boat. They had been at sea for nearly a week, adrift and moving farther and farther from the Florida coast. They'd lost their small engine on the second day, and by the end of the third day all food had disappeared. They'd consumed their last fresh water the night before, and with the onset of the northeasterly wind they had all but given up hope. As it was, an old man and woman were unable to move, very close to death.

All of the refugees were suffering from exposure. They were badly sunburned, and the saltwater had dried their skin so much that it was cracking with open sores and swollen with infection. When they gulped the fresh water we gave them, many immediately became ill and had to vomit over the side of the trawler. Despite their excitement at having been rescued, there was an air of calmness and acceptance about the group. The leathery old fisherman who owned the crudely equipped boat had promised to carry them to safety.

They must have had blind faith in him, because they crowded around and patted him on the back. It was as if they had known all along that they were going to make it.

Martinez and the crewmen circulated among the refugees, exchanging stories about the fate of friends and relatives, gathering information about their homeland and answering questions about America. Martinez ordered the crew to cut the old boat adrift, then went to the radio on the bridge. The trawler was badly crowded now, and some of the refugees needed immediate medical attention.

Martinez contacted a Spanish-speaking station that I assumed to be a CIA relay point somewhere in the Caribbean. Permission was granted to alter our planned course and proceed directly to Key West. The Coast Guard and the immigration authorities would be notified. The other trawler would continue to Tampa. Martinez also asked, in code, about the commandos. There was still no word from them; headquarters had no information.

The captain estimated our position was nearly 50 miles east of the Dry Tortugas, heading due west. We would have to turn north to reach Key West. As the captain brought the trawler around, Martinez radioed instructions to the other fishing boat. We pulled away from the old sailboat that had carried the refugees from Cuba; it lay low in the water, stained and scarred from years of good service under the old fisherman's hand. It seemed appropriate somehow, that the vessel's final voyage had given its master a new life. I looked at the old seaman as his derelict craft disappeared off our stern. He watched in silence until it was gone; his face showed no emotion.

The trip to Key West would take three to four hours, so I went on deck to find a place to wait. The cabins had already been given to the old man and woman and the infants and their mothers. Space was at a premium, but I found a spot on some nets by the stern. The crew had stretched a canvas between the booms to give some protection from the sun, and I lay back to study the refugee passengers. That's when I became aware of the Cuban girl and her family.

THE ZENITH SECRET

I noticed the boy first. He reminded me of my 3-year-old son. There was the same quality of angelic, boyish innocence. He was asleep on the young woman's lap. His strong, tanned face looked peaceful and his small fingers were wrapped tightly about the woman's thumb.

I looked at the young woman holding him. At first glance, she seemed to have typical Cuban peasant features. High cheekbones, full lips and long, flowing, coal-black hair, but, looking more carefully, I discovered something different about her face: it was longer, not the round, open face of a peasant, and it was strong, like her son's. She was dozing against a stack of life jackets. Her hair was pulled back, revealing a high forehead. She was not a large woman, but there was a kind of lithe firmness to her appearance. The full rise of her breasts, her long, graceful hands holding the boy, and her grimy but dainty bare feet attested to the fact she was very much a woman. God, what a place to be thinking about sex!

I wondered how she had found her way aboard the old sailing boat. She must have guts, I thought. I wondered where her husband was…maybe still in Cuba, maybe dead or an exile…hell, maybe one of our commandos. In all this misery and hardship, she remained strong and beautiful.

I suddenly realized that she was awake and aware of my gaze. She looked directly at me, as if she were reading my thoughts. Her large dark eyes burned through me. I averted my attention, cringing in embarrassment. I remembered my appearance—swollen lip, missing teeth, unshaven face. Still feeling her eyes on me, I stumbled to my feet and smiled at her. Almost tripping over the nets, I made my way to the forward part of the ship.

The rest of the voyage was uneventful, and I avoided the stern of the trawler, where the Cuban girl remained with her family. It was stupid, I knew, but she had made me feel oddly self-conscious, and I was very much aware of her presence on the crowded vessel. There was little we could do for the refugees except try to make them comfortable, and the crew was circulating among them to help wherever they could. I stayed on the bridge and made notes for my report

Swaying palm trees, white sand beaches, and crashing surf seemed surreal during the bloody secret war we conducted. Pleasure cruisers like this often returned bullet-riddled and barely afloat with wounded refugees.

BRADLEY E. AYERS

on the mission.

When we sighted the navigation markers off the Marquesas Keys and the trawler turned into the channel that led to port, the refugees, aware that comfort and safety were only a few miles away, clustered excitedly at the rails to get their first glimpse of the United States. As the skyline of Key West gradually became discernible, a Coast Guard patrol boat met us and led us into the commercial fishing docks. I could see a knot of people and various official and emergency vehicles gathered at one of the piers. Some of the refugees began to cry and hug one another or make the sign of the cross. I watched the Cuban girl and her family stand calmly at the rear of the trawler, the young boy wide-eyed and clutching the woman's hand. Word must have spread quickly through Key West that a boatload of refugees was about to arrive: by the time the captain had backed the trawler into the narrow berth pointed out by the Coast Guard, the crowd had grown to several hundred. A cheer went up, and the Cubans on shore began calling to their countrymen on the board.

We could not leave the trawler immediately. First the Coast Guard came aboard and talked to Martinez, the captain, and me. Apparently the CIA had briefed them earlier because they didn't press us for information. A Coast Guard lieutenant took me aside and said there was a car waiting to take me to the Key West Naval Air Station as soon as I was ready to go; a message was waiting for me there.

Immigration and naturalization authorities came aboard, as well as two doctors from the Department of Health. All this time, the crowd on the dock kept growing. A contingent of Navy Shore Patrol showed up to keep the onlookers back and to form a cordon for the refugees. Nearly an hour after docking, the first Cubans were helped off the trawler. It was an emotional moment at first as the two old people were moved by stretcher to the waiting ambulances. The small babies and their mothers were taken to the hospital van, and then the rest were led to a bus. Many people wept openly, and as the Cubans passed their exiled countrymen behind the cordon, they reached out to touch one another between the uniformed shore policemen.

I sat on the bridge of the trawler, alone, and watched the refugees go ashore. Some of them needed help walking, or limped painfully from weakness and exposure. But they all moved with resolution, and their expressions were of gratitude and hope. They believed that fate had delivered them to the land of the free.

The last refugees to file off were the young woman and her son, followed by the older couple they were traveling with. As she reached the pier, she hesitated and turned. For an instant her eyes fixed upon me.

With the refugees on their way to the processing center, our work was done. The doctors examined Martinez and me and ordered us to the hospital.

As the doctors were completing their examinations, a man I recognized as a JM/WAVE security officer arrived. He had a brief, hushed conversation with the doctors and showed them his credentials. Then he came over to Martinez and me and instructed us to go with him. He addressed me by my first name and seemed quite sympathetic about our injuries and ordeal at sea. He said nothing about the mission. Concerning my injuries, I was to tell the medics I'd been in an automobile accident and use my Department of the Army cover.

He drove us to the infirmary at the Boca Chica Naval Air Station. At that point, Martinez and I were separated. It took several hours for the doctor to thoroughly examine me, take X-rays and perform other tests. They stabilized my jaw after packing something around my loose teeth, suturing my tongue and

THE ZENITH SECRET

upper lip cuts, bandaging up various external cuts and taping my back and neck to restrict painful movement. They wheeled me into a private room with a bed where I was given medication and a sedative. Just as I was about to lapse into a drug-induced sleep, the security man came into the room and handed me a typed note. It was from JM/WAVE and advised, if I were physically able, to connect with the daily Air Force Key West-Miami-Eglin daily milkrun flight out of Boca Chica as soon as possible and continue with the helio flight test. The sedatives hit me as I finished reading and I lapsed into dreamless sleep. I never saw Martinez again.

Twenty-four hours later I was on my way to Eglin Air Force Base, in the same lumbering C-54 in which I'd started the journey almost a week earlier. It was past 10 p.m. when we reached Eglin. I checked in with flight operations and was given a room in the Bachelor Officers' Quarters for the night. The twin-helio testing would begin in the morning; they'd waited for "someone" from Miami to take a look at it. I hadn't had supper yet, so I dashed to the officers' mess. Afterward, I persuaded the bartender to let me have a bottle of rum to take to my room. I had intended to call home but decided to wait until I was rested and knew my schedule for the week. I took four good slugs out of the bottle and gratefully pulled the covers around me.

I felt good and well rested when I awakened the next morning. But then I thought of the commandos on the railway-bridge raid. I still had no knowledge of the outcome of the mission, and, of course, no one at Eglin was even aware of it. Before meeting the Air Force crew who would introduce me to the twin helio and conduct the demonstration flights, I called Suzie.

Without my asking, she told me that there had been an article in the paper several days earlier about some commandos who'd made a raid on the northern coast of Cuba. Castro claimed that the attackers had been beaten off and that one boatload of commandos had been captured. He blamed the raid on CIA mercenaries based in the United States. "Just thought you'd be interested," Suzie concluded. I wondered which men had been taken. Castro always exaggerated, but he certainly must have been referring to our raid.

The helio testing turned out to be interesting, but the aircraft didn't seem practical for what the CIA had in mind. It was complicated and required skilled piloting.

On Thursday morning I made a parachute jump from a C-54, and in the afternoon I went to Niceville, where we had lived before my assignment to the CIA. I walked down the narrow dirt road to our old house. All was quiet, except for the sounds of children playing in the Lions Club Park.

We had been immensely happy there, secure in the life we'd chosen for ourselves. But it was all so different now, and no matter how badly part of me wanted to go back, it could never be the same.

I stood for a moment, before walking to the little Catholic Church we had attended each Sunday. For the first time in a long time I prayed.

It was dark when I caught a cab back to Field 3. The next morning we flew to Miami, and when I finally got home, late that afternoon, I found it difficult to talk to my wife. There was just too much under the surface that I felt I couldn't tell her. I knew she wouldn't understand anyway.

I did my best to play down my obvious injuries. The parachute jump I took as part of the twin-helio test at Eglin was a convenient way to explain my broken front teeth and the still-tender bruise on the back of my head. I'd sustained minor injuries like that before while jumping. My sons took delight in kidding me about the missing teeth all weekend, but I was able to get an emergency dental appointment for Monday morning to replace the caps.

I tried to reach Cal and Rod, but both were out of town for the weekend. My anxiety over the outcome of the commando raid kept growing; Suzie showed me the newspaper account she told me about on the phone, and it contained no mention of the other two boats, nor were there any details of the railway bridge destruction.

Much to the annoyance of my wife, I spent most of Sunday completing my report on the twin helio and going over my notes on the V-20 operation. After seeing the small boats in action, I had formed some definite conclusions. The most serious problem with the V-20s was navigation in shallow water, assuming that the operator had the skill to recognize the natural clues to areas of deep water. He would first have to see them. The shallow water operations would have to be run under clear night skies.

After turning in my report at the station on Monday, I met with Cal and Rudy. During my absence they'd begun detailed plans for the new training programs. No longer did there seem to be any question about my role. A replacement had already been requested from CIA headquarters in Washington to take over the survival and small-unit-operations program, and he was expected to arrive at the Miami station within days.

"How long will it take to get a man read into the program down there so he can handle it completely?" Cal asked.

"If José and Mike had no problems without me last week—and you say they had none—then one training cycle will be adequate. I can take the guys through the program, and if he uses the two Cuban instructors properly, there shouldn't be any problems. What specifically do you have in mind for me after that?"

Cal and Rudy looked at each other, as if neither wanted to speak first. Rudy finally started: "Brad, Cal is leaving the station for a new assignment in Washington. It will be some weeks before we get a new training chief, so I'll be in charge. I'm going to have my hands full just taking care of what we've got going now, so we want you to take over a bigger share of the field training."

"Will it include the new programs?" It was better than I'd thought. I had now been on two missions to Cuba and had started the Key Largo program. I was confident and ready, convinced that by playing a larger role in the training I'd be able to make a greater contribution to the cause of Cuban freedom fighters.

"We want you to take charge of all small-boat training," Rudy continued. "This will include the survival program you have in Key Largo and the small boat training at Flamingo. We want you to set up a V-20 program, and also a UDT program, somewhere else in the Keys."

"You won't be doing this all by yourself, of course," Cal said. "Your replacement will take over the survival thing and work for you there. Dewey will continue to run the smaller boats out of Flamingo, under your control. The Navy is going to send us a special UDT instructor detachment to conduct the program, and the maritime branch here will provide some help in getting the V-20 training going."

"We've spent a lot of time discussing this with Ted," Rudy added. "We feel you're the logical person to pull the whole thing together and get it moving. But you belong to the Army and you're only on loan to us, so we don't want you to feel you're being ordered to do this. For all we know, maybe you're ready to go back to the Army now, and this new job would certainly tie you here for a while. We want to consider you and your family as fully as possible."

THE ZENITH SECRET

If there had been any question in my mind before, there was none now. It occurred to me that maybe I should discuss things with Suzie, but this past weekend she had again expressed her growing disenchantment with my CIA assignment, and I knew damned well she'd be happier if I pulled out. But I couldn't; I knew what I wanted, and that was to help the Cubans in whatever way I could. Family would have to come second.

We began that same afternoon, and I was goaded to even greater determination when I learned that only Julio's boat had made it back to the States. They'd limped into Islamorada the previous day after an incredibly harrowing escape from Cuba. The other boat got lost and ended up on Cay Sal. Fortunately, our own Coast Guard picked the exiles up there. Apparently, Castro's claim of capturing one boat was correct. The details weren't clear, but it seemed they'd run aground and been surrounded by militia men somewhere near Isabela. The railway bridge had been partially knocked out, and extensive damage had been done to the telephone lines. The station learned a lot from the mission, but the loss of four exile agents and several boats was a high price to pay.

The weeks that followed my meeting with Cal and Rudy were frantic. The new training programs were top priority as anti-Castro operations increased. I knew my way around now and had begun to adapt to some of the CIA administrative procedures and policies. I had cultivated some casual friendships in the various branches that were important to my training activities, and these paid off handsomely as I set up the new programs. I had especially good luck working with the logistics, security, and real estate people. It was through the latter of these that I was able to establish bases for the two new training courses.

The UDT setup was organized quickly. We needed an isolated house that could accommodate up to 15 men, had access to water, a boat dock, and a swimming pool for the initial UDT instruction. For advanced training we'd use the open sea and the Flamingo area. The Navy was going to send five of their newly organized SEALS force to conduct the instruction, and we planned to train up to ten Cuban agents at a time. With my background in combat swimming, scuba, and demolitions, I was able to outline a training program and order the essential equipment before the Navy instructors arrived.

I wanted to keep all of the training programs within a reasonable distance of one another so that they could be controlled and coordinated. At the same time, we couldn't saturate any area and create a security problem. With the assistance of the real estate representative from the cover branch, we found and rented a suitable piece of property in Key Largo. By the time the Navy men arrived and the operations branch made Cuban UDT candidates available, we had only to move in and begin training.

A site for the V-20 training base was more difficult of a problem until I remembered the safehouse complex at Linderman Key. "Pirates' Lair," as local fishermen nicknamed the site, lay amid the tangle of mangrove islands and canals between Elliott Key and Key Largo. The elaborate complex of houses and docks had been constructed many years earlier by a millionaire as an island hideaway. It was just that. Attempting to reach it by boat even in daylight was challenging.

The complex had four houses which were dispersed about the heavily wooded three-acre island in such a manner that only one could be seen from the single deep-water canal that strung its way through the mangroves. The central house was an ornate two-story gabled mansion of antebellum design.

The front was decorated with stucco pillars that supported a second-floor balcony. The upper rooms opened onto the balcony, and a cupola on top of the house provided an excellent lookout for the entire area. The rooms were richly paneled and thick dark oak and mahogany beams supported the ceilings. A large fireplace took nearly all of one wall in the main living room. The house was the natural choice for a combination barracks, mess hall, and classroom for the Cuban trainees.

Another house was located near the water's edge, adjacent to the docks. It was a less elaborate structure but of more modern design. The single story rambler had a large living room, kitchen, and two small bedrooms. No boat could approach the island without being seen from the house. This was the logical choice for an office and communications center, as well as a home for the instructors.

The other two houses were wood-frame utility quarters. One housed the big Onan diesel generators that provided electricity on the island, with bedroom and lavatory facilities for a caretaker. The other was a dilapidated structure that could be used only for storage. A large wood and concrete dock and an old marine railway fronted the island on the channel side.

The major disadvantage was the problem of logistical support. The only source of fresh water was rain, but the old cistern system for trapping it was inoperable. Our water would have to be brought in by barge every two weeks.

Diesel fuel, as well as bottled gas for cooking, would also have to be transported to the island. Besides the cost involved, this meant that "outsiders" would have to visit the base to deliver these goods, because we didn't have the ability to transport them ourselves. A maintenance and housekeeping crew would have to be kept on the island at all times to keep the generators running and the water system in operation. This continuous manpower could be difficult to supply, and more people would have to know that we were on the island.

The Pirates' Lair complex appeared to be an ideal base for the V-20 training, otherwise. The dock facilities were adequate for berthing several "sterilized" boats, and the modified strike boats could be hidden in the narrow canals that laced through the mangroves on the opposite side of the island. Classes could be conducted indoors and outdoors near the center of the island without observation from passing boats. The island was big enough to do some physical training, and the living facilities were adequate for the twenty or so people who might be assembled there at any one time. The site was already under the control of the CIA, through the University of Miami, which had inherited the island complex through an estate grant. An American husband and wife team, hired by the station, manned the facilities already, so the quarters could be made livable with minimal effort.

The establishment of the new programs demanded every bit of my time and energy. I had virtually no time to spend with my family, and when I did get home I was totally fatigued and very poor company.

My replacement for the survival course soon arrived from Washington. He was a bright, enthusiastic young Army lieutenant in good physical condition. He loved the out-of-doors and learned quickly, and with José and Mike backing him up, he rapidly took charge.

The UDT instructors arrived from the Navy, but because of their security clearances, it was necessary to keep them away from the station. However, I was eventually able to arrange for the young officer in charge to work out of the station. That simplified the logistical and administrative burdens of the UDT program, which otherwise would have been left to me. Dewey's small-boat training at Flamingo carried on without interruption.

As the training activities began to function smoothly, I was able to devote

THE ZENITH SECRET

more time to the V-20 training at Pirates' Lair. The maritime branch provided two Cubans who could be trained as instructors. An American contract agent, a former ship's engineer named Dick, was hired as the permanent maintenance man and caretaker. I hired two more Americans on contract to work with me in conducting the program. Don Cabeza was a former charter fishing boat captain, fresh off the fast, expensive boats on Miami Beach. He was supposed to be a skillful sailor and an adventurer of sorts. Because of his Cuban ancestry and bilingual skill, I planned to rely heavily on him as one of my chief instructors. Arnie, the other American, was a Miami diving bum with a rather shady past. He had considerable experience as a boat operator, so I hired him as an assistant instructor. Each of them was "boxed" and underwent thorough screening by security.

Gradually, my personnel requirements were filled, supplies and equipment were ordered and boats were found. I had to do a lot of scrounging for equipment, especially boats. Eventually word got back to Morales that some equipment was being diverted from Rip and Grayson's commando groups and he went ballistic. Cal and Rudy eventually had to get Shackley to intercede. He issued instructions to the chiefs of maritime and logistics branches to give my new undertaking a high priority. Rip was directed to loan me one of his training V-20s. I was directed to go to Rip's Marathon safehouse on the west shore of Florida Bay and run the V-20 back to the Pirates' Lair safehouse complex, where I'd turn it over to Cabeza. Logistics gave me a car to deliver to Rip in return.

On the way down U.S. 1, I stopped at the Green Turtle Inn in Islamorada for a bowl of soup. It was early afternoon and most of the lunch crowd had left. But near the back of the restaurant, seated at a large circular table, were Dave Morales, Mr. Harvey, Gordon Campbell, Mr. Phillips, and another man, possibly Rosselli, whose back was turned to me. They apparently had stopped for lunch and drinks. I don't know if they recognized me or not. As was the practice in such situations within the agency, there was no acknowledgment either way. Discreetly, I got my soup to go and quickly left. It was the first time I had ever seen the station hierarchy in the Keys and out of their air-conditioned offices. It was encouraging, maybe something big in the offing, I thought.

Rip wasn't at the Marathon safehouse when I arrived. One of his men gave me the keys to the V-20 and I handed him the keys to the car, then I ran the boat back up north to the lair. In the battered V-20 were two unmarked five-gallon cans, partially filled with a liquid that gave off the same odor I had smelled while touring the defoliated areas with the wildlife officer, and they were the same kind of containers we had helped load on CIA mother ships bound for Cuba.

By now the Miami CIA station had set up its own small marine and boat shop in a dilapidated garage-warehouse off Southwest 117th Avenue in south Miami. I worked closely with the logistics people, who were operating the shop on a 24-hour basis to keep pace with the ever-increasing demands of operations and training. In a matter of hours they could convert standard, commercially manufactured boats of various design into rugged fighting or infiltration craft. When the modifications were completed, the boats were painted or rigged to look like common fishing or pleasure craft. We got two modified V-20s and a small Boston Whaler for training at the island, and a creaking old 30-foot Chris-Craft cabin cruiser for transporting personnel and equipment from the mainland.

By August, all the programs for which I had been given responsibility were actively engaged or ready to begin. I'd spent four incredibly busy weeks putting things together, when the threat of a major hurricane finally provided an oppor-

Our operational boats were dispersed throughout the Bahamas under various cover corporations. Some of the boats were converted oil rig patrol craft like the one shown just right of center in this photo.

tunity for a break. As the storm approached, the safehouses in the Keys and on the island were boarded up, and all boats were moved to high ground and filled with water so that they wouldn't blow away. Dick stayed alone at Pirates' Lair to ride out the storm, while everyone else went home to the mainland.

Cal was leaving the station for his new assignment in Washington, and since our social activity had been nonexistent for weeks, Suzie suggested we give him a goodbye party. The usual crowd from the training branch assembled at our house late that afternoon. Everyone had left the office early because of the impending storm, and many had already had a drink or two earlier in the day, for there had been little else to do. Torrents of rain swept from heavy gray clouds, and the winds were steadily increasing to gale force. As the storm raged outside, the liquor and conversation flowed freely inside, and everyone seemed more than ready for a party.

That is, everyone but Suzie.

She was strangely withdrawn, despite her earlier enthusiasm for the gathering. I couldn't help noticing her more-than-frequent trips to the kitchen to mix herself another drink while our glasses were still half full.

We collided by the bar once and I put my arms around her. "Anything wrong, hon? I love you."

Her eyes were glazed and she turned her cheek. Coldly. "No, of course not." I squeezed her. The drinking went on.

Inevitably, as the evening wore on, the discussion turned to the CIA and what each of us was doing in Miami. Suzie, whose unhappiness was even deeper than I'd realized, chose the occasion to level a cutting verbal bombast at me, the CIA, and everything related to either.

"Your work is nothing more than a series of lies," she burst out suddenly, eyeing us all angrily. "Everyone I've met down here is so personally mixed up they can't live a normal life. You're phonies. The company warps and perverts

THE ZENITH SECRET

and changes everybody who comes in contact with it." She turned to me, tears welling in her eyes. "Just look at yourself; you don't even know who you are anymore!"

She began to cry and ran to the bedroom. We all sat in shocked silence. Her words hung in the room while the wind and rain whipped through the blackness outside.

BRADLEY E. AYERS

CHAPTER 10

The hurricane that we prepared for bypassed Miami, but the storm of resulted Suzie's outburst raged on. The guests had the presence of mind to simply say goodnight and leave. There were no words after the party or the following day. Initially I was angry, because I'd warned her of the potential difficulties even before she came to Miami. My earlier misgivings about my family joining me now seemed well-founded. My new responsibilities in the training program were distracting me from my role as husband and father.

Suzie wanted me to request a transfer back to the Army. I tried to explain that I was approaching the most challenging and important part of my work, but our discussion degenerated into an argument. I slammed out of the house and ran along the dark, deserted wet roads that bordered the cane fields near the house. When I could run no more, I returned home to find that Suzie was sleeping in the children's room. I left the house early the next morning, before anyone else got up.

My office at the training branch was a picture of mass confusion when I got there. My chief instructors were trying to arrange for trailers to move boats back into the water and expedite supply equipment deliveries held off because of the impending storm. But I was happy to have something to throw myself into; it took my mind off the problems at home. We finally got things straightened out by noon. The survival course in Key Largo, small boats at Flamingo, and the UDT program began new training phases. Once I had my chief instructors on their respective ways, I turned my attention again to the new V-20 class, which would begin that week. Rudy gave me a "pep talk" before I left the office.

"Brad, we all had a hell of a good time at your party Saturday night, and I know Cal really appreciated the gesture."

"I'm really sorry about Suzie's outburst. As you know, we've been apart a lot, and, with the kids and all, it's been hard on her. Our life here is so different from what we experienced in the military."

"Look, don't make excuses. It isn't the first time agency people have heard that kind of talk, and it won't be the last. You know, my wife and I split up more than ten years ago, and I've been alone ever since. It takes a lot to hold a family together under some of these assignments. The record speaks for itself: the CIA has a higher separation and divorce rate than any other government agency."

I'd heard that before, but it had never meant anything until now.

"Anyway," Rudy said, "Ted and all of us are anxious to get the V-20 program going. Keep the office informed of any problems."

"I think we're pretty well set, but there is the problem of a cook and housekeeper for Pirates' Lair. The couple who've been looking after things are going to leave."

"I'll see if we can get somebody from maritime," Rudy said. "What you really need is a ship's cook, or someone with that kind of background."

"What I'd like is another married couple team. The island is a lonely spot, and there will be times when I'll need to use the cook as a watchman and caretaker. Could you find me a good, elderly Cuban couple to handle the job?"

Rudy promised to see what he could do, and with that I left to meet Don, my chief instructor. He took me to Pirates' Lair in our Chris-Craft, and during the trip I couldn't help worrying about Suzie's outburst. She knew a lot about what the Miami station did, and if she got unhappy enough and I didn't give in, she could very well expose the whole thing. The more I thought about it, the more it bothered me. All she'd have to do was plant a seed of doubt in the mind of someone from the station, and he'd report it to security. I had to convince them that I could keep her under control, or else we'd be on our way back to the Army.

When we reached the island hideaway, everyone was busy preparing for the arrival of the training group that night, and there was a refreshing sense of purpose in the air. Don, Arnie, Dick, and I went over last-minute details—one of them being the problem of hiring a cook—and then Don and I took the Chris-Craft over the training area to review the program we'd set up.

I'd worked closely with Don in setting up the course. I'd incorporated into it all those facets of V-20 operation I'd observed on my recent mission to Cuba, and Don had contributed his own ideas. We'd come up with an intensive three-week program that included basic seamanship and small arms, to be taught principally at the island safehouse complex. Physical conditioning was to be integrated throughout the daily activity. As Don and I toured the area and went over the plans, I was once again impressed with the young seaman's technical knowledge and his understanding of the training objectives. I just hoped I could maintain his enthusiasm and interest over the long, difficult weeks ahead. He was more accustomed to the various pleasures of Miami Beach bars than to the isolation and austerity of island life.

On occasion, Don took me to an area near Alligator Reef light that was teeming with grouper and snapper. The water was crystal clear, the underwater visibility at least 100 feet or more. We decided to do some snorkel spearfishing. I spotted a huge grouper hiding in a coral cave in about thirty feet of water and, with speargun in hand, dove to reach it. The fish was stationary in its shallow cave, but, to my frustration and distress, I kept running out of breath before I could position myself to spear it. Again and again I'd have to surface to get my breath. I decided then and there to quit smoking. I climbed into the whaler and grabbed my Salem cigarettes lying on the seat. I hurled the partially open pack overboard, the loose cigarettes splayed out against the late afternoon sun and clear blue sky. That was the end of my smoking, one of the smartest things I ever did.[11]

Our first group, 15 Cubans, had been selected from the crews of bigger vessels operated by the station. They'd been chosen by their respective case officers, on Ted's direction, and turned over to operations for placement on the V20s. Theoretically, each man had already mastered basic seamanship. All were young, hardy, and intelligent enough to qualify for training in the strike boats.

Many of the maritime case officers complained to me that we were getting their best men, but I had little sympathy. The success of future missions depended heavily on the skill of the V-20 operators.

For the next two weeks I divided my time between my training courses. It was hectic and tiring, and much of my time was spent traveling between training sites. But things went more smoothly than I'd expected. The paramilitary training program was complete, progressive, and balanced; it provided the basic skills necessary to accomplish and survive missions. The size and complexity of the program now exceeded my most ambitious expectations. The amazing thing was that we were doing all of this in virtual secrecy amid a very active civilian

The Pirates' Lair safehouse complex on Linderman Key was a major CIA training site. On this secluded, small island we taught advanced small boat training (V-20s) and Maritime Basic Training. The large house in the foreground served as headquarters.

community.

With a feeling of satisfaction and accomplishment, I drove home after we finished training. In my exhaustion and pride, I'd nearly forgotten about the tension on the home front, so I was totally unprepared for what I found. I found Suzie passed out on the chaise lounge in a dark corner of the patio. Kneeling, I put my arms around her. I carried her to the bedroom, and then, after looking in on the boys, who were sleeping peacefully, I put on my shorts and sneakers and ran through the night until the pain inside was overwhelmed by physical exhaustion.

My work with the CIA and the Cubans and my deep feelings about it were driving us farther and farther apart, and I began to think seriously about requesting a transfer back to the Army. The training programs were all set up and operating well. I'd done my job, and I could go back now with no questions asked. I had almost decided to write to Colonel Bond, but when I got to the station the next day Rudy called me into his office.

"Two things for you, Brad. Number one, I think we've found a Cuban couple to do the cooking and housekeeping at Pirates' Lair. They've already been screened and cleared. Operations says they're good people; they recently escaped, but when they were living in Cuba they helped some of our agents, and, from what I understand, they were damned lucky to make it out alive. You can interview them at the refugee center near Opalaka Airport sometime this week.

He paused for a moment, then continued, "Brad, there's something pretty big going on around here. I think they want us to do some special commando training for them.

He handed me a slip of paper with a name and license plate on it. "You're to meet this fellow—the license number of his car is on the paper—and he'll drive you to the meeting place."

The following day the Cuban couple arrived. I recognized the plump, gentle-looking woman: she was the one who'd been with the beautiful girl on the trawler. Her husband had shaved—that's why I didn't know him immediately.

They didn't remember me, so I gave no indication that I knew them.

I wasn't sure if they were aware that I was connected with the CIA, but the man made a point of saying he was eager to work with other exiles. I told them I'd call the center the following day to arrange for their travel to the island, if they wanted the job after thinking things over. It seemed agreeable to them, but as I rose the woman spoke quickly to the interpreter.

The interpreter said, turning to me, "there is just one more thing they would like to ask you. They have a daughter, 24, and she has a 4-year-old son. The girl has no one else since her husband died, and she and the boy have lived with her parents for some time. Could they go to the island, too? The girl is a very good cook and a good worker."

I was going to say no, but then I hesitated. "Let me think it over and talk with my supervisor. I'll call you later this week and let you know definitely." I thought about the beautiful Cuban woman and our strange silent exchange on the trawler. What an odd turn of fate that our paths should cross again and that I should be confronted with this decision.

Speeding westward along Tamiami Trail I thought about how unusual it was for Rudy to get excited about anything that was really important. As the acting chief of training, he should have gone to this meeting, but he had deferred to me. It seemed odd, as did all the secrecy. When I asked the young driver where we were going, he replied that the trip would take slightly more than an hour; we were going to a meeting place in the Everglades. He didn't elaborate.

We pulled into a truck stop at the junction of Tamiami Trail and Highway 27, and another man—a Cuban whom I'd never seen before—checked the license of the car and climbed in. No one spoke as we drove down the long, slightly traveled highway and eventually turned onto a dirt road bordered by a canal. After about a mile, the driver pulled over. An airboat was waiting in the canal, and in moments we were noisily skimming across the saw grass as dusk settled over the glades. I wasn't surprised since long ago I learned to expect the unexpected from the agency.

After nearly 30 minutes of travel across open swampland and deep canals, we turned under some overhanging trees and pulled up to a small dock behind another airboat. A sign on one of the rotting timbers read "Waloos Glades Hunting Camp—No Trespassing." It was nearly dark, but I could see two small Quonsets with lights burning in the windows. Some men were standing around a campfire in the middle of the clearing, and in its flickering light I could see two helicopters parked in the shadows. One was a military Bell H-13 with the identification numbers taped over, and the other was a civilian chopper with the name of a West Palm Beach air service on the tail rotor boom.

We walked to the fire and a young man handed us cups of coffee. I had never seen any of the men before. Soon the door to one of the Quonsets swung open and four men emerged. As they moved into the circle of firelight I recognized Gordon Campbell. I had seen him only a few times since my brief meeting with him, but had been impressed with his polished, slightly flamboyant executive manner. I caught my breath at the appearance of the second man. It was the attorney general, Robert Kennedy.

The four men talked in low voices for a few minutes, and then the attorney general came over and shook hands with each of us, wishing us good luck and God's speed on our mission.

Hell, I didn't even know what my mission was. His white teeth flashed and sparkled, and I felt a strange sense of strength and resolve when he grasped my hand. Then he and one of the Cubans went to the civilian helicopter, and in minutes it took off. Now I understood the need for extra secrecy. If the president felt strongly enough to send his brother, something very big was being planned.

BRADLEY E. AYERS

When the helicopter was gone, the deputy chief of station came over.

"Williams? Please come with me." As we walked to one of the Quonsets, he said, "The reason we've got you here and the reason for all the secrecy is that we just got the green light from upstairs to go ahead on some missions we've been planning for some time."

We entered the Quonset. It was brightly illuminated by several Coleman lanterns, and there were charts, maps, and other papers on a table in the center of the room. Campbell closed the door behind us and turned to face me.

"We're very pleased with the way you've handled the training setup for the station so far, and we've made that known to your people at the Pentagon. We know it hasn't been easy for you and your family."

A chill ran through me. Did they know Suzie and I were having trouble?

"You'll be happy to know that the Special Group has finally given us permission to use two-man submarines to strike Castro's ships in the harbors. Some of your UDT people will be involved in that. And next week Rip's boys are going to Eglin for parachute training, so an airborne commando raid may not be far off. But right now we've got a go-ahead to hit one of the major oil refineries from on the island. All we've got to do is get a commando force in shape to do the job."

So, the Special Group had finally put the interests of big business second to national interest. The president and his brother were tough, smart politicians: the elections were getting closer.

"We want you to take a commando force of 12 men and give them six weeks of the toughest, most realistic training you can. We want you to teach them survival and get them physically toughened up. Then we want you to run some exercises for them and, finally, set up a rehearsal for the actual raid, and do it over and over until they have it down blindfolded. During this six weeks we want you to eat, sleep, and live this mission with the Cubans, 24 hours a day. We want them ready to go by mid-December."

"Where do you want the training done?" My mind was already racing with ideas.

"We've got a house on the south end of Elliott Key that's never been used. We want you to take a look at it, and if it's all right, you can run the training from there."

He pointed to a spot on the marine chart in front of him: the southern tip of Elliott Key. I had been there a few times, but I'd never seen the house.

"You'll have to keep up with your regular duties in addition to working with this commando group. Again, no one is to know that. Dave is sometimes a little bit difficult, so you'll deal directly with me on anything you need. Use the telephone, and we'll meet away from the station. After you get set, I'll give you a complete scenario for the mission and as much data as we have on the target itself."

He waited for a moment, as if expecting some reaction from me, but then continued before I could say anything.

"If you use the Elliott Key site and work these commandos into the areas you're already using, you should be able to make appearances at your other programs often enough to take care of them. You can also coordinate the use of some of the boats, especially the V-20s, when the people at Pirates' Lair aren't using them."

I was surprised that Campbell knew so much about my training activities. They certainly had done more thinking about this refinery raid than I would have expected, in view of what I'd seen before at the station.

THE ZENITH SECRET

"It sounds as though it will work, but I want to look at the Elliott Key site. I've got so damn much going on in that general area now. Besides all my training, Rip has his commandos just up the Key, and Rosselli has his group at Point Mary some of the time." This operation was to be top secret, and I was concerned that I'd run into my own people some night, chasing down the same canal.

"That's the key to it. With you doing all the training coordination, you can make sure there won't be a slip-up. And let's face it, you know the area and schedule better than anyone else. We want the men moved to the training base this weekend and to start training on Monday. Can you do it?"

"I think so. Who and what can I get for help?"

"The fewer people out there, the better. I think you can get by with a cook and housekeeper. I don't want these commandos to miss any training because of housecleaning chores. We don't have much time."

"My outside man, Karl, will help you with logistics. Take the deliveries and carry the items to the island yourself. Order as little as you have to from logistics, and buy all of your own food."

He took a key, a roll of bills, and a receipt book. "Here's the safehouse key and $1,000 to get things moving. Let me know who you want to take as a cook and housekeeper so I can clear them first. Remember, no one leaves there, once aboard. Call me by Saturday to let me know how you're coming along."

I signed the unmarked, commercial cash-receipt and went back to the fire. Campbell introduced me to Tony Sforza the commando-team contact man, and Karl,[12] then he led me to the H-13 helicopter and instructed the pilot to take me back to Tamiami Airport and then return for the rest of the men.

The next morning Rudy was anxious to know how I made out at the meeting. No problem. I told him; operations just wanted to use some of our training areas and boats for forthcoming mission rehearsals. Our training fleet had grown to nearly 20 boats, I said, and I could coordinate it all directly with the operation people. There was no need for him to get involved. Rudy liked that; at this stage of his career, he avoided involvements whenever possible.

I'd already begun to plan for training. As in some of the other courses, the first step would be to go over the wearing and use of equipment, then go into survival. I could plan the rest of the training as we went along, and I could borrow boats and other heavy equipment from some of the other courses as we progressed.

The only real problem seemed to be finding a cook and housekeeper for the six-week period. I had to find him someone new. I guess it had occurred to me earlier—we could hire the daughter of the couple I'd interviewed for the Lair

The Elliott Key safehouse proved to be an adequate, if somewhat austere, dwelling. The single-story wood-frame house, set well back from the coast in a cluster of majestic Australian pines, was large and weathered.

Apparently built as a vacation retreat or a fishing camp, the building could accommodate a good number of people. The room was bare of furnishings except for a massive wooden table made from a ship's hatch cover and about a dozen roughhewn wooden chairs. A thick layer of dust covered everything.

It would be primitive living. Without electricity and running water, a cook and housekeeper would have plenty to do. It wasn't going to be easy or comfortable for any of us, but the site was suitable. It was concealed from passing boats; there we no roads on the island, so any intruders would have to come by foot; and there were many good training areas around the house.

I then called the interpreter/case worker at the refugee center, who said that the couple, the Avilas, had decided to work for my company. I also told him about an opening for their daughter at another research site. He said he'd talk to the girl, whose name was Eleana, and suggested I call back. The next morning, after learning that Eleana would take the job I called security and ordered the polygraph test.

The call from security came the next morning, just as we were finishing breakfast. I took the call on our bedroom extension, where I could have some privacy.

"The girl looks all right," the security officer said. "She's had a pretty hard life, you know. She lost her husband at the Bay of Pigs and was left with a son. She and her family have really caught hell from Castro because of her old man's involvement with the invasion. That's why they finally made a run for it."

"Does she know what she's getting into now?" I asked.

"She has an idea. She's a pretty dedicated, idealistic woman, with a deep-seated hate of the Communists and Castro. I don't know what you've got in mind for her, but she seems as though she can take good care of herself. I don't think she'll take any crap from anyone."

I thanked the agent and hung up. Now for the confrontation with my own female ball-of-fire. I went back to the kitchen. Suzie was at the stove, her back to me.

"Hon, something has come up," I said quietly. "I'm going to have to go in to work later this afternoon. I've got to take some people on a boat ride tonight; probably won't be home until late. I'm really sorry, but that's what that call was about."

She turned to face me. She was shaking.

"Get out of here! Pack your bags and stay out! You're never around here anyway. Why don't you just go and stay with your greasy Cubans and your queer, phony civilian friends. You're part of them now. You're not an Army officer, or even a part of this family anymore!"

That hurt. I could feel my own anger rising, and I clenched my fists in frustration.

"Go ahead, hit me. You've learned to fight dirty from the CIA. But I'll tell you, lay a hand on me and I'll march right out in the middle of this street and tell the whole world about you and the company. I won't quit until you're finished with this Cuban mess."

It was no contest. I went into the bedroom and threw some clothes into a bag. The boys were huddled around their mother when I came back out.

I detested being alone. The memory of all the Sundays I'd spent by myself in Miami returned to plague me. I went down to the Black Point marina and spent the afternoon fishing, trying to keep my mind off my family. As evening settled over the area, all of the Sunday fishermen left, and it was nearly deserted when Tony pulled up to the dock where I had the Chris-Craft moored.

The men piled out of the car and I motioned for them to put their gear in the boat and go aboard. I was about to ask Tony where the new housekeeper was when I realized I'd mistaken her for one of the men. In the dim cabin light on the boat, I could see her talking quietly. Her long black hair was pulled tightly to the back of her head, and she looked younger than I recalled, her face more innocent and more beautiful.

As I boarded the boat and started the engines, Eleana looked at me. Our eyes met for an instant, and I saw her sharp intake of breath as she recognized me. Then, just as quickly, her face was calm as she regained her composure and continued talking to me. In minutes we were chugging across Biscayne Bay to the Elliott Key safehouse, under a brilliantly starry sky. I led the group ashore and through the pines. Using the powerful flashlight, I showed them around the house and instructed them to make themselves at home. Soon the shutters were opened and the lanterns were lit, giving the old dwelling a warm, pleasant glow. The Cubans chatted excitedly about their temporary new home and seemed enthusiastic about their extended stay on the island.

I spoke to Eleana briefly, apologizing for the lack of privacy she would have to endure. In my haste to set up the commandos, I had forgotten about a separate bedroom for a woman. We decided to convert the back screened porch for her use, and with the help of the commandos a bed was moved and blankets were hung as curtains over the screens. I was delighted to discover that she spoke excellent English—better than any of the men in the group. She would be able to make supply lists and help with translation.

The transfer of the second group of commandos went smoothly. Before I left Black Point I had made arrangements to meet Tony late in the week to get background information on each of the men, which would help me in planning the training. I'd intended to return home that night after delivering the commandos, but something made me hesitate. I left the Chris-Craft moored offshore and took a walk down the beach. Far at sea, the lights of a freighter moved slowly southward. It was very quiet as I began to walk back to my boat. The lights from the island house glowed invitingly through the underbrush, and I could smell the familiar aroma of cooking oil as Eleana prepared a late-night snack.

When I reached the point where the path led back to the house, I stopped and looked at the Chris-Craft. I started toward it, then turned and walked back up to the house. I would remain there with the Cubans rather than face the turmoil at my own home. Thus began the most intense emotional and physical experience of my life.

CHAPTER II

The hot, humid, summer days that followed were incredibly busy. I worked with the refinery raid group from dawn till well after dark each day at the Elliott Key hideaway, seeking to blot out the pain and anxiety over my confrontation with Suzie. But there were times, especially at sunset, when the loneliness cut so deeply that I had to go off by myself so that my feelings wouldn't be apparent to the others.

I remained at the island for the first week to ensure that the daily training schedule was well established. I tried to set up a routine that was not too regimented yet afforded maximum use of the coolest hours of the day for heavy physical work. From the outset, I sensed that they were a unique group. None of the 12 was over 35-years-old, and all but two were married. Most of their families and relatives remained in Cuba, which seemed to be the principal motivating factor. At rest periods and during meals they talked almost constantly about returning to Cuba or getting their families out.

Physically, they were much hardier than the majority of exiles I'd worked with. The men were accustomed to using makeshift equipment and living austerely. For nearly a year they'd worked through one of the splinter exile political groups in Miami, training and running raids on Castro pretty much on their own. Their operations usually were funded by pooled contributions from large groups of exiles or from wealthy Cubans who wished to gain political stature in what they hoped would emerge as a true government in exile.

During the first week there, we began to follow our exercises with a jog. Eleana joined the men for calisthenics, but when she tried to follow us on the first morning run, dressed in boots and fatigues like the commandos, I had to suggest she return to the kitchen. Her duties there were far more important than running with the men, regardless of her personal wish to share their hardship.

After breakfast, the men would assemble in the living room/classroom. Early in the week I discovered that there was no team leader upon whom I could call to pass orders. Tony had assigned the responsibility to an older, articulate commando, but in practice he was nothing more than a go-between for two younger dominant men who each controlled roughly half of the 12-man group. I learned from Eleana that this division of authority was well defined and based on subtle but profound ethnic and political differences. From the very beginning, leadership of the group was a very serious problem, for it was necessary that a single strong leader emerge as the training went on and the mission grew near.

None of the commandos spoke good English, and my Spanish, although improving, was not good enough to present formal instruction. Eleana came to my aid and served as an interpreter in the early morning classes. We went into subjects such as map reading, use of the compass, camouflage and concealment, night and day movement, and hand-to-hand combat. I tried to set things up so I could get away at about midday to visit one or more of my other training programs. Each of them was functioning smoothly, but I had to make these visits anyway, as well as call in to the training branch, to maintain the appearance of my usual routine.

It took me several days to adjust to the demands of my new dual role. At first I was torn between the needs of the commandos on Elliott Key and my own need to keep up with my other responsibilities. When I was away from Elliott Key I worried about what the men were doing. I was fully aware of their inclination to follow the path of the least resistance, and in my absence and without a strong leader it was probable that they would slack off.

I felt an urgency to discuss the leadership aspect of the mission early on with Mr. Campbell. I tried on several occasions, when going ashore for supplies, to contact him by phone at his private number. Each time, his secretary said he was traveling and unavailable. So, I decided to talk to Karl about the problem, for whatever it might be worth. By this time I had the impression that Karl was very much involved in the Elliott Key project and all it entailed. Campbell had placed no restrictions on what I might discuss with his right-hand man.

My trip across the bay was faster than usual, and I arrived at the restaurant near the Coral Castle ahead of our scheduled meeting. I saw Karl, Dave Morales, Rosselli, and Mr. Phillips sitting at a table near the back of the room. When I saw all but Karl leave, three to the same car, I went back to meet him. Over a beer, I told him of my concerns about the leadership of the Elliott Key group and asked him to discuss my observations with Campbell. Karl was pretty savvy and he agreed. On the way back to Black Point I pondered Karl's apparent familiarity with the principal staff at JM/WAVE as I had observed it. I was impressed. Karl was obviously something more than the typical logistics gofer.

After the meeting with Karl, whenever I had serious matters concerning personnel, security or logistics at Elliott Key, I would try to communicate with Campbell by some secure means.

Radio contact from the island was both insecure and quite often subject to interference and signal range limitations, despite the fact we had erected a tall, portable Army surplus antenna. Thus, I would have to steal time from supervision of training and get to the pay phone at Black Point or drive into the station in south Miami. By this time, most of the staff in operations, intelligence and logistics knew me by sight. Despite my unkempt "swamp man" appearance—deeply tanned, with shaggy sun bleached hair, often unshaven and unwashed, dressed in work clothes and boots usually reeking of sweat and unpleasant natural odors—I would make the rounds. Out of curiosity mostly, I would go to intelligence and try to catch up on the daily summaries.[13] Then I'd go to operations, B.S. with Roderick, and check in with Bob Wall. I also developed a friendly dialogue with case officer Tom Clines in the course of training one of his intel teams. He referred to me as the "swamp man" and continues to today.

Of course, on schedule, I'd have to deliver my activity report bound for Colonel Bond at the Pentagon, and that would give me an opportunity to visit briefly with Maggy in Shackley's office. I was always relieved when I was able to avoid Morales because his presence for me was like a threatening dark cloud.[14] When I completed my business at the station and before heading back to the Keys, I'd call Suzie to see how things were going with her and the boys and get an update on any news from our families in Minnesota.

When going ashore, I always tried to be back at the island by late afternoon, in time to conduct a critique and summary of the day's training. We would assemble in the living room and the Cubans would describe what they'd learned that day; then I would offer my observations. The men were usually responsive and enthusiastically interested after a day's work, and often the discussion would branch off into other subjects. Sometimes we had to terminate these sessions to allow Eleana to serve supper.

We ate all meals family-style at the large table in the living room. The Cubans seem to prefer this to the military-style chowline I'd experimented with in some of the other programs. With Eleana's help, I worked out a menu that was relatively simple to prepare yet was low in starches and fats, which was quite a challenge, considering the usual Cuban diet. But Eleana was an excellent cook, and from the very outset the meals were the high point of each day.

I encouraged the men to keep occupied when off duty. Within a week or so, some began to do wood carving, two became household carpenters and handymen—much to Eleana's delight—and two others dug a small plot and planted a garden. I couldn't help thinking, morbidly, that the men would probably never see the results of their plantings.

The men constructed a small shrine in the living room, and the handymen built a rough kneeling bench. This was our church. As we became more relaxed with one another, it was not uncommon to see one or more of the men praying at the shrine during the week at any time.

I devoted most of the early training to seacoast and mangrove survival. In groups of two, I turned the men loose by themselves in the field for the first time. They were to sustain themselves for three days, with only basic equipment. This was the first real test of their endurance.

By early evening the on-shore wind was blowing and the rain was a steady downpour. I moved through the thick underbrush, checking each of the teams in their crudely built shelters. It was well after midnight when I got back to the safehouse, but Eleana was still up. Dripping wet, I headed for my room to change into dry clothing, but almost involuntarily I stopped short as I passed her, sitting at the table. Apparently she had just bathed, for she wore a heavy dark robe and her long black hair hung damp and loose around her shoulders.

Her skin seemed to glow in the soft light from the kerosene lamp, and a clean, woman scent mingled with the fragrance of her perfume. She was busy with the sewing in her lap and didn't look up.

Neither of us had acknowledged our strange encounter on the trawler, and so far our relationship had been polite and businesslike. Now, suddenly, I was very much aware of her womanliness, and that for the first time the two of us were alone in the old island house. The sound of the wind slamming a broken shutter brought me back to reality. I went to my room and took a shot of rum.

At the end of the week I went ashore to see Tony. But the meeting was disappointing. He gave only a brief background sketch on each of the men, but, from spending so much time with them, I already knew most of what he told me.

All of them were from the central part of Cuba, and all but three were tradesmen—carpenters, electricians, plumbers, or mechanics—which made them especially desirable, because a good knowledge of mechanics was vital to the success of the refinery raid. Two of the men were fishermen, and the one they looked up to as a leader had been a small businessman in Havana.

I brought up the odd division of the leadership in the group, but Tony was unwilling to discuss it beyond saying that it had been the only way he could bring 12 men together. I was deeply concerned about it. We'd already used valuable training time without establishing the command relationship that could ultimately mean the success or failure of the mission.

I stole a few hours' extra sleep the next morning, then went out to Coconut Grove, where I was to meet Gordon Campbell. He and his wife lived on a yacht moored at the Dinner Key marina. I walked down a long concrete pier, past sleek, expensive cruisers, and finally found Gordon's boat. Both he and his wife—an attractive bikini-clad silver-haired woman—were well into their

THE ZENITH SECRET

*The Cuban exiles who volunteered their services to the CIA were idealistically moti-
vated but, as a general rule, pitifully unprepared for the dangers and physical
demands of clandestine warfare.*

Sunday afternoon martinis.

As he mixed me a drink, he asked, "What do you think of the men? How do
they look—morale, interest—you know, guts for the job?"

"They look very good so far," I replied, "but there's one big problem, the
commandos have no real leader. The team is split into two distinct, separate
groups of five and six men each...and they seem to want to stay that way. As
long as I give orders, there's no problem, but when they're on their own, the so-
called leader makes suggestions and the other two follow only if they feel like it.
It's too loose to be effective under pressure."

"Goddamnit, if a leader is a problem, then you find one! The case officer for
these boys will be down from Washington in a few weeks. He's been with the
Cuban desk studying the situation and he's well-read. Porter is young but he
knows his stuff. I've assured him you'd have the team ready to go."[15]

Had I heard right? Somebody who worked behind a desk at Langley was
suddenly going to appear on the scene and take over where I left off? Just like
that, I'd train them and someone else would step in and simply "assume" control? I started to say something, but caught myself. This was something totally
beyond my control, and no good would come from an argument with Campbell
at this point. I took a big swallow of my drink. "I'll continue to do my best on the
leadership situation. Gordon, I can assure you that having a leader would make
my own work much easier. More importantly, these are good men, and they
deserve a good leader."

The anger passed from his face and he mixed us both another drink. "All
right, let's go below. I have the charts and photos, and we'll go over the mission
from the beginning to end."

For the better part of the next two hours we pored over refinery blueprints
and incredibly detailed U-2 photos and recently smuggled-out snapshots of the
target. The time schedule was set in the familiar D-day, H-hour military terminology, and Campbell would not tell me when the raid would be conducted. We

BRADLEY E. AYERS

had to be ready to go anytime after the first of December. He wanted at least two rehearsals completed by then, and there was little time left.

Our discussion terminated when Mrs. Campbell came down to the gallery carrying drinks for all of us. She chided us for spending the "glorious Sunday afternoon" talking business, and threw her heavily oiled, deeply tanned body into her husband's lap. Her obvious attention seeking embarrassed me, so I drank quickly, thanked Gordon, and said I'd contact him.

It wasn't until I'd left the yacht that I realized Campbell hadn't given me the exact location of the refinery; he'd said only that it was on the south central coast of Cuba. It probably had been intentional, I concluded, but I had enough data to get well into advanced training and preliminary rehearsals anyway.

The mission was a big one, all right, and tough. In a very complex, pre-cisely timed raid, the commandos would destroy the fuel storage tanks, dock, and ship-to-shore product-transfer pipelines of the refinery. As I drove home, I reviewed the details Gordon had given me. Two fishing trawlers would be used as mother ships for three V-20s. At a shallow water point about a mile from the target, one boat would land and the team would go ashore, under cover of dark-ness. The other two boats would wait offshore, among the mangroves, for com-pletion of the first phase of the mission.

The landed commando team would move down the shore to the pier that supported the pipeline. They would kill the guards on the pier, and then elimi-nate the watchman in the small tin shack at the end of the pier. This accom-plished, they would signal the other two V-20s to come to the end of the pier, where the boats would be tied until the mission was completed.

The commando team would then move down the pier and around the refin-ery yard fence to a position behind a low hill that was about eleven hundred yards from the brightly illuminated cracking towers and processing facilities. Two 81mm mortars would be set up; from an observation position on high ground; their fire would be guided into the refinery proper. White phosphorous ordnance would be used, in the hope that the cracking towers would catch fire immediately and the surrounding fuel storage tanks would explode. Approximately twenty mortar rounds would be fired into the refinery.

Meanwhile, time-activated demolition charges would be fastened to the pipeline pier, and "clams" (round TNT charges with magnetic devices to hold them to metal objects) would be attached to the transfer pipeline. By the time the entire commando force withdrew, the refinery would be engulfed in flames.

As the two V-20s pulled away, the timer would activate, and the pier and pipeline would explode behind them. The commandos would return to the trawlers waiting several miles off shore. Another time-activated explosive would destroy the beached V-20 .

Monday morning began another week of training at Elliott Key, and I gave the commandos their first real information about the mission. Earlier, Tony told them only that they would have an opportunity to strike one of the major strate-gic targets in Cuba. Like myself, they'd been awaiting the details.

My announcement of the refinery target at first brought awed silence, then whistles of astonishment and approval. As the magnitude and significance of the mission struck home, the men shook their fists, cheered, and clapped one another on the back. This would be one of their first real opportunities to hurt Castro. The commandos' mood quickly changed to deadly serious concentration as I outlined the general plan.

Rather than try to break down the already established division of the force, I decided to try to capitalize on it. I designated the smaller, five-man group as the "killer-fire support team." They would go ashore first, I explained, eliminate the guards, and then cover the approach of the other team. The larger group, designated as the "mortar-demolitions team," would land at the end of the pier after it was cleared. Four of them would move, under the protection of the killer-fire supported team, to the low ground, where they would fire their mortars. From the high ground overlooking the refinery, the team leader would direct the fire.

Meanwhile, the two-man demolitions crew would plant the charges on the pier and the pipeline. When the mortar crew concluded the firing, they would withdraw under the protection of the fire support team, which would also be located on the high ground. The fire support would follow and the demolitions team would join them after they activated the charge. Then the entire force would return to the V-20s and make its withdrawal.

Although I had been working with Cuban exiles for many months, I had to keep reminding myself that they were civilians, and what appeared to me as a logical, routine maneuver was to them almost totally foreign. Their questions and apparent inability to grasp quickly the tactics of the raid made it very clear that we still had much work to do. Enthusiasm was not lacking, however, as the men expressed which tasks they wanted and began to assume the roles they wished to play in the actual raid.

I tried to direct the session toward the obvious difficulties of the tactical maneuvers. A high chain-link fence with barbed wire on top ran along the road-way from the refinery to the pier, then into the water well beyond wading depth, adjacent to the pier. The killer team would have to climb over, cut through, or swim around it. The watchman's shack at the end of the pier was quipped with a telephone and a floodlight illuminating the entire dock, so both the phone and electricity lines would have to be cut. There were a number of other problems that I tried to discuss with the men, but they were too excited and couldn't stop chattering about the mission. The team leader, who I'd hoped would begin to play a more dominant role as the mission was laid out, said very little.

That afternoon I visited my other training sites, leaving the men with instructions to work out designations of individual tasks and responsibilities in the mission. That day marked the beginning of a number of subtle changes in our life at the hideaway. The men began to exhibit a new, stronger sense of pride and purpose, and they spoke with confidence and determination. The raid was on their minds constantly and they talked of little else.

We now shared a tangible goal and when we gathered for work, meals, or friendly discussions, there was a feeling of community that I'd never experienced before. We had our differences, of course, but we all put our personal interests second to those of the group.

Eleana played an increasingly important role. Her meals continued to be a key factor in the general morale. Aware that food was our only luxury, she used her resourcefulness and imagination to produce excellent, nourishing meals, and soon gained the commando's respect and consideration. They placed her on a pedestal of sorts and would do almost anything to make her job easier and her stay on the island more comfortable. From the outset she had assisted me with the language translation, but now she also prepared the shopping lists and supply orders, and helped when I began to plan the technical details of the raid. For security reasons, I was not able to bring to the island any of the refinery photographs or other classified data, so all diagrams and layouts had to be fabricated at the safehouse. It quickly became apparent that Eleana was just as intent on making the refinery raid a success as were any of the men. She often would stay up with me late into the night, making charts and diagrams and assisting with Spanish terms and interpretations that made it easier for the men to understand. Aware of the leadership difficulties within the group, she began to serve as a go-between between the commandos and myself. She had a way of smoothing differences and she could put the men's bravado in its place with her quick wit and sharp tongue.

While the men were in the field on the reconnaissance exercises, I turned my attention to setting up a rehearsal raid. I was pleased to find that the Cutler Ridge power plant, on the shore of the bay in south Miami, would make an excellent "live" target. The surrounding terrain was similar to that revealed by the U-2 photos of the target area in Cuba. There was a fence around the power plant; the layout of its towers and tanks resembled that of the refinery facilities; and a long stone jetty that ran out into the bay could be used to simulate the pipeline pier. The water approaches were not nearly so deep as those to the Cuban site, but that would not pose major difficult. The power plant was surrounded by residential homes on large wooded lots, which meant that there would be much community activity around the target area. This was desirable, because the men would have to escape detection, just as in the actual raid.

I drew a series of sketches comparing the power plant to the refinery. From the outset, I wanted to tie the two very closely together so that when the commandos rehearsed at the simulated target, they'd be thinking of the actual one.

Next, I had to find a way to take the men on a daylight walk through the area so that they could familiarize themselves with the terrain. Difficult as this might be in terms of security, it was necessary in order to avoid having one of the commandos stumble into someone's backyard during the actual rehearsals, which of course would be conducted at night.

Eleana suggested, almost jokingly, that we make it look like a Sunday school outing. At first I laughed, but then it occurred to me that we could pose as a nature study group on a Sunday field trip to examine the local flora and fauna. We organized what we were confident was the first Cuban exile nature study club. Eleana was designated as the first and only guide-lecturer, and we even gave the club a prestigious-sounding name: the Pan-American Nature Wildlife Study Group. I would borrow the Chris-Craft from Pirates' Lair, and the following weekend, dressed in our Sunday finery (the only "casual civilian" clothes any of us had at the commando base), we'd cross Biscayne Bay and study tropical plants and animals in their natural habitat—right next to the Cutler Ridge power plant.

When I told the men about our plan, I thought their laughter would cause the old house to collapse around them. We all had been working very hard for more than a month, and the comic novelty of the Sunday excursion was a welcome relief from the serious routine. When I briefed Gordon on our plans for the "nature walk," he too caught the element of humor. It was the first and only time I heard him laugh. On the appointed day, armed with pencils, notebooks, magnifying glasses, sample jars, and sack lunches, we set forth.

There were a few fishermen and a pair of lovers in the area, but they paid no attention to us as we moved around the facility and the adjacent wooded area. Whenever someone passed, Eleana launched into a lecture—in Spanish— on any rock, tree, or bird that happened to be near, and the commandos feigned intense interest. Passersby never stopped to listen or even seemed curious. As soon as they passed, I would resume my narrative of the raid, struggling to conceal my own amusement with the antics of the Cubans. The reconnaissance went off without a hitch.

THE ZENITH SECRET

CHAPTER 12

Communications between Elliott Key and the mainland had been a problem from the very beginning. We tried several different VHF and UHF radios, but our generator set-up was inadequate for the power demands. This combined with atmospheric interference made them almost useless. As our mission preparations advanced, the difficulty in reaching the station became a significant hindrance.

The only way I could maintain the secure contact with Gorden Campbell, Karl, and Tony was to go ashore to the pay phone at Black Point.[16] This was annoying because the trip back and forth by boat across lower Biscayne Bay took nearly two hours, requiring me to be away from the commando training activity underway at a very critical time.

Equally frustrating were instances when, after going ashore, I was unable to speak directly with Gordon, Karl, or Tony and had to leave a callback message. Then, I'd have to stand around, waiting in a location that was always a security concern, for the return call. The problem became more and more aggravating in October and early November as we intensified our training for the refinery raid. Sometimes I'd go for days without contact. On other occasions I'd get word that Campbell and Karl were out of the area and was given no idea when they might return my call. I would angrily return to the island feeling very much on my own.

Tony was somewhat more accessible from his safehouse in Coral Gables, but he did not have access to the station and was not privy to the details of our assignment on the island. I knew he was also busy working with several other exile groups. Despite these problems, I concentrated on teaching men the techniques and skills necessary to their specific tasks in the mission.

I was greatly relieved when I received word to dispense with mortars as the primary weapon for shelling the refinery and to use the 3.5 rocket launchers instead. With their lack of previous exposure to mortars, I had seriously doubted that the commandos would become proficient in time for the raid. The rocket launchers, being direct-fire weapons, were much easier to use. The gunner could direct his own fire simply by watching the strike of the round. We planned to fire the armor-piercing rockets into fuel storage tanks to puncture them. With the flammable contents of the tanks running from the holes, we would fire white phosphorous to ignite them. A major disadvantage of using the rockets instead of the mortars was that the four-man firing team would have to move much closer to the refinery itself, exposing themselves to possible detection by the sentries patrolling the fence. The back-blast from the rocket launchers could be seen at night, revealing the firing position. The teams would have to be covered by the fire support elements at all times, and they'd have to get out very quickly—preferably before they came under return fire from the refinery.

It was decided that a two-man killer team would eliminate the guards. These men would come ashore with the first V-20, as part of the killer-fire support element. They would approach the pier under the protection of the three other men in the group, who would take up firing positions near the fence. The

To rehearse the demolition phase of commando raids, especially the placement of explosive charges called "magnetic clams," used on oil refinery pipelines, we conducted training exercises using the Key West water supply pipeline running from Homestead, FL as a dummy target.

pier, which ran more than 250 yards into the bay, was enclosed by a 10-foot-high fence, so it could not be boarded from the water. We would have to draw the sentry, who was stationed at the shore end of the pier, away from his post long enough for a man to scale the fence.

We planned to do this by creating a disturbance in the water about 50 yards from the shore, next to the pilings. One man would swim out to that point and splash around in a manner which would cause the sentry to leave his post and investigate. Using a rope and grappling hook, the other member of the killer team would scale the fence, sneak up behind the preoccupied guard, and kill him. With the same rope, he would pull his teammate out of the water and over the fence. Both men would sever the power and phone lines and go to the tin shack, where they would kill the watchman and signal the other two V20s waiting about a mile offshore. I spent many hours working with the killer team, teaching them stealth, hand-to-hand combat, and the use of knives and garrotes. Much to my surprise, they learned quickly, often practicing on each other or on one of their fellow commandos with such aggressiveness I worried we might have a real killing, albeit accidental, right there at the training base.

The two Cubans who served as the demolitions team—and who were also the primary V-20 operators—had used various types of TNT charges and plastic explosives on earlier commando raids. I concentrated on showing them how to use the "clams" and the time-delay fuses to ignite the charges. Though, it was impossible to set off live charges at the training site, but we made several night trips to the wood jetty at Dynamite Pier to practice setting pier demolitions, and two other trips to Key Largo where we simulated "clam" charges on the large U.S. Navy pipeline that supplied the Florida Keys with fresh water from the mainland.

The first rehearsal was a colossal failure. I let the Cubans run the operation from beginning to end and tagged along, silently, as an observer. Noise and light discipline were disregarded, and the first V-20 landed in the wrong spot.

BRADLEY E. AYERS

The killer team forgot to cut the simulated electricity and phone lines on the pier. The rocket launcher team made so much noise before they moved close enough to fire their weapons that the real security guards at the power plant directed spotlights toward them. Why we were not discovered and rounded up by the Dade County sheriff that night and put in jail, I will never know.

The men knew they'd made a mess of the rehearsal, and, like athletes after losing a game, they berated themselves and one another. If the rehearsal served any purpose at all, it was to sap a lot of the bravado that had been growing over the preceding weeks. For me, it was a painful revelation of how much work we had to do before the group would be ready for the actual mission. All the doubts and misgivings about the actual raid—some of which I'd suppressed from the day the mission was announced—came back to me.

But we had to go on, which meant more rehearsals. The commandos knew I was dissatisfied with their performance. Instead of tearing into them, I asked each man what his job was supposed to be. As they talked, they realized where they'd failed. As the critique ended, I could feel a renewed sense of determination in the room. I had planned to give them a night off between rehearsals, but when I felt the momentum pick up, I scheduled another rehearsal for the next night.

Eleana was not directly involved in the tactical aspects of the rehearsals, but she sensed that I was still troubled about the men's performance the night before. The next afternoon, as I was making notes on the coming rehearsal, she came into my office. "Dan, you know the men feel very bad about what happened last night." She hesitated, then went on, "But I can see you are blaming yourself too, and this is not a good time to let down."

"I have no intentions of letting down. It's just that we're so pressed for time, and I'm at a loss to know how to improve things. I guess more rehearsals are about all we can do."

She looked at me. It was the same direct, penetrating stare I'd felt on the trawler the first day I saw her. "You can train and rehearse from now until there is no Cuba, but that will not make things any better with these men."

I felt my hackles rise. So now, at this late stage of training, this young Cuban woman was going to tell me how to run the commando force. I started to say something, but she continued: "Blaming yourself, blaming the men, more rehearsals, beating yourselves to exhaustion before you even get a chance to strike Castro—it's not necessary. These men will do just about anything you tell them."

"What the hell is that supposed to mean?" I felt that she was playing games with me.

"Danielito." Her face softened as, for the first time, she used the affectionate Spanish version of my name. "You know what I mean. These men need a leader, that is all. They would do anything for you."

"Well that's just impossible. You've heard about Americans in Cuba. Hell, I'm sure the whole United States Army would be invading the island right alongside your people if the president would let them. What's more, I was sent out here just to train these men, nothing more.

"Look, I can teach them everything I know. I can provide them with all the equipment they need; I can even provide the moral support required. But I can't make soldiers out of them if they don't want to be."

The words had a hollow sound; I was passing the buck, and she'd made me feel it even more strongly. Eleana started to leave, then turned back with the same glance she'd given me when she'd left the trawler. "Danielito mio, they

THE ZENITH SECRET

want to be soldiers; all they need is a leader." The louvered door swung close behind her.

We ran the second rehearsal that night, and, whether because of what Eleana had said or because of my own frustration, I pushed the commandos through the exercise myself. The men were deadly serious and put forth a concerted effort. It was a complete transformation, and as if by magic, things fell into place. The mistakes that were made were minor. The commando force had finally become a working unit. As we roared back across Biscayne Bay, three boats speeding together in close V-formation, I think we finally realized that the job really could be done.

I gave the men that night off. We were all exhausted, though spirits were high. The tension was there, but it was accompanied by a sense of strength. I brought several bottles of rum back from the base to take the edge off things. Eleana, sensing the men's attitude, cooked an especially filling and tasty meal, and after passing the rum around the table, we all turned in.

The next day dawned like all the others at the base. The men, well rested and excited about the rehearsal scheduled for that night, were more talkative than usual. After an early lunch, I called them together to go over the plan for the night's exercise. The living room buzzed with excitement and anticipation as we gathered around the old table.

I was halfway through the briefing when the sound of a light plane flying low over the house interrupted our concentration. Probably just a fish spotter making a turn back out to sea, I thought, and continued talking. In a few minutes the plane was back again, this time lower and louder. It was my policy that if a plane flew low over the house, the men were to remain inside or move into the woods and remain out of sight. The press sometimes used planes to search out exile training bases, and the presence of a large number of men was always a giveaway. I told the men to keep their places and went outside to get the identification number of the intruding aircraft. In a few moments it was back again, skimming over the treetops. I immediately recognized the plane as the single-engine Cessna based at the CIA headquarters in Miami.

As it flew overhead, a white object was released directly over the old house. It was a roll of toilet tissue, streaming out as it fell. It landed only a few feet away as the plane turned to make another pass over the island. The center tube of the tissue roll had been closed with masking tape, and the word "OPEN" had been scrawled on the side with black marking pencil. Hastily, I opened up the tube and pulled out the paper inside. It was Campbell's printing:

NOVEMBER 22, 1963
PRESIDENT KENNEDY HAS BEEN SHOT BY AN ASSASSIN. SUSPEND ALL
ACTIVITY. KEEP MEN ON ISLAND. COME ASHORE WITHOUT DELAY.
GORDON

For a moment I was frozen to the spot. I looked into the cloudless sky, waiting for the messenger plane to drop something else. But it was gone. A picture flashed through my mind in exaggerated slow motion: a peaceful, sunlit morning at Point Mary months earlier. The crack of a rifle fired by an anti-Castro sniper shatters the quiet, and a cormorant, sitting on a mangrove root five hundred yards away, explodes in a burst of crimson and black, leaving only bits of feather to float on the blue water.

CHAPTER 13

We were paralyzed; all of our activities frozen at the moment we received word of the president's shooting. I returned to CIA headquarters in Miami to learn that the president had been assassinated. It was an incomprehensible turn of events, and the station was in a state of total confusion. Rumors of conspiracy and Cuban involvement in the assassination ran rampant among the employees. Certain individuals and pro- and anti-Castro organizations were put under continuous surveillance. The FBI and the Secret Service descended on the Zenith complex to review security dossiers and files on exile organizations. They, and certain agency security employees, seemed to be striking out wildly, searching desperately for any clues that might give reason to the nightmare in Dallas.

People involved in the training programs were only on the fringes. Within a few hours after the president's death, those of us who were not required for immediate duty were told to return home and stay near the telephone. In accordance with orders, I made sure that all my instructors confined their Cuban personnel to the training bases. I directed that radios and television sets be on so men could be kept abreast of developments.

It was late afternoon when I left the Zenith complex. Most of the offices were deserted; desks were left cluttered and scraps of paper littered the floor. Phones rang, but no one was there to answer. Half-empty cups of coffee remained where they'd been set down when the dreadful news spread through the station. A small portable radio, the announcer recounting the horror in Dallas, sat on the security guard's desk at the headquarters building's entrance. The guard's pistol, ready for immediate use, lay beside it. As I walked by and flashed my security pass, I could see tears running down the elderly man's cheeks.

I wondered how the commandos and Eleana were getting along, and for an instant I thought of going back to them. But then, as I climbed into my car, the impact of what had happened began to dawn on me. Suddenly I felt totally exhausted and wanted very badly to go home to my family.

I found Suzie sitting in front of the television set, her eyes red and swollen. She said nothing as I came into the house. Once again, I was propelled from the world of Daniel B. Williams and the CIA to the world of Bradley E. Ayers, career Army officer with wife and family. I sat down next to Suzie and put my arms around her, and she leaned against my chest, sobbing.

"I knew something terrible was going to happen...ever since the missile crisis when we sat on the dock at Niceville that night and almost waited for the Russians to put a bomb on Eglin. And when you had to go to Washington and come down here...it was the end of something for us, Brad. What you've been doing here, it makes me feel dirty and evil. You wait, you'll see this whole Cuban thing and the CIA blow sky high. I just know the president is dead right now because of all of this."

I guess I felt that way, too. A lot of the station people did, right from the moment they heard the president had been shot. There was some connection, and we felt it strongly.

The television droned on, the network cutting back and forth between

Dallas and Washington, giving more details of the assassination. Then the oath-of-office ceremony in the jet, and Lyndon Johnson became the new president. It unfolded like a doomsday soap opera created by a madman. The family, the president's brother—I had seen him only weeks before—the country's leaders frantically trying to bring reason and order to a nation seemingly gone berserk. And the feeling of guilt began to spread as the drama unfolded. I felt angry and frustrated. Life for my generation was tainted. Things would never be the same.

While the nightmare events continued to unfold in Dallas and Washington in the days following the assassination, we tried to continue our work as it had been before the president's death.[17] Two things became obvious almost immediately. One, at our operational level there was a total vacuum of policy. Virtually all paramilitary activity remained frozen, and no one could even guess when or how station operations would be resumed.

Two, an undercurrent of suspicion and paranoia developed at headquarters as a result of the official and semiofficial witch-hunts that were being conducted throughout various government agencies.

As conspiracy rumors swept the nation—many of them connecting the assassination with Fidel Castro and the Cubans—the CIA, especially the Miami station, found itself in a particularly sensitive position. Because of Lee Harvey Oswald's alleged participation in pro-Castro demonstrations, considerable public attention was focused on revolutionary Cuban groups in the United States. Activist paramilitary organizations came under suspicion because of their alleged dissatisfaction with what they believed was Kennedy's "soft line" policy toward Cuba. The CIA was intimately involved, directly and indirectly, with a number of these anti-Castro groups. A rash of sensational news stories, and later a book, *The Invisible Government,* by David B. Wise and T.B. Ross, focused additional public attention on the agency and the activities of the Miami station. Some of the writers accused the CIA of being responsible for a conspiracy leading to the assassination; others merely reflected on the irony of Kennedy's concerted effort to assassinate Castro and his own murder in Dallas at that time.

We attended meeting after meeting—that was really all there was to do. We were instructed to tighten our personal security, review personal contracts in the community, and review our cover stories. We were cautioned to avoid fraternization with the Cubans outside the realm of our duties. We were cautioned about press contacts and alerted to various investigations, both official and private, that were under way. We were told to play down, under all circumstances, our involvement with the Cubans.

While we waited for someone to make a decision, the days became weeks. No one ever made a firm judgment on what would be done with the Cubans. After discussing the matter with Rudy, I ordered the instructors to resume training and complete the courses they had begun prior to the assassination. More than a month after the assassination that I spoke with Mr. Campbell about the Elliott Key commandos. He directed me to hold off any additional rehearsals but to go on training at a reduced pace.

In that way, we were able to maintain, at least temporarily, some of the momentum that had been building prior to the assassination. I thought it would be only a matter of time before President Johnson directed the CIA to resume its effort against Castro. In view of the president's tragic death, which was rapidly beginning to appear as a martyrdom for the cause of freedom everywhere, I was convinced that now, more than ever, we would be allowed to strike the Communists. Certainly the new president would carry out John F. Kennedy's promise to the exiles.

Gordon Campbell and Karl had all but disappeared during this period and the Elliott Key operation, for which I had been responsible, was placed under the control of the training branch. Cal had departed for a new assignment in Washington at the CIA "farm" in Virginia. Rudy temporarily assumed duties as chief of training. I had always gotten along well with him, and he gave me all the freedom I needed to carry out my tasks.

Eventually, an old CIA training officer, Ernie Sparks, arrived and took over as chief of the branch. Cal, his predecessor, had been the consummate professional—low-key, soft-spoken, polite, considerate, calculating, unexcitable, and nearly always dressed in suit and tie.[18] I soon recognized Cal and Ernie were almost opposites in appearance, manner, and personality. Ernie was well known in CIA circles for his gruff, flamboyant character.

Ernie dressed in Western style, with cowboy boots, jeans, and an open collared riding shirt. Often he would have a big revolver holstered at his side. He was about 50, with gray hair, a droopy moustache, ruddy complexion, and piercing blue eyes. His build was portly but muscular. He could have been a Wild West movie character. He had been nicknamed "Sitting Bull" while serving as a training officer in Guatemala, preparing Cuban exile Brigade 2506 for the Bay of Pigs invasion. As the time went by, I learned he had a penchant for booze, women, and sports cars. Ernie and I got along pretty well, but I often had the feeling he had a hard time taking care of business and that compounded my concerns about maintaining the training structure we had worked so hard to create.

The weeks became months. The tense expectancy gradually gave way to boredom as hope for continued paramilitary action against Castro began to wane. The first signs were almost imperceptible, and I simply wrote them off as normal incidents in the day-to-day conduct of training activities.

Dissipating resolve and growing disillusionment were reflected on the attitude and behavior of all the personnel. It was, initially, more noticeable in the Cubans, first in the volunteers and then in the instructors. The planning of new paramilitary operations, except for those of intelligence gathering teams, all but ceased. Although the previously planned operations, including the refinery raid, remained on the books, very few were approved. As a result, the requirement for new agents was greatly reduced, and recruitment of Cubans was cut back severely, while the pool of previously trained men languished in safehouses.

My Cuban instructors, many of whom had worked with me from the very early stages of the program, began to give in to the effects of the interminable wait for a policy decision. They began to complain about equipment and living conditions. I was deeply hurt when I had to fire my old friend José, the survival course instructor, because he severely damaged a boat and motor through sheer carelessness.

Eventually the American instructors also began to reflect the despondency that was spreading through the organization. Discipline at the training bases suffered, and I frequently had to intervene in these problems. Finally I began to feel myself slipping. I became dissatisfied and frustrated. I had hoped to keep spirits alive through my own enthusiasm and determination, to motivate both Cubans and Americans by setting the example.

The one bright spot in my life, besides my sons when I could see them, was the commando base at Elliott Key. More than any of the people I worked with, the Elliott Key group reflected my own mood and my belief about the future course of anti-Castro operations. We had accepted the slowdown, feeling it was only temporary. For that reason, we had to pace ourselves and work diligently to maintain our paramilitary skills. We refused to accept the growing belief that the United States was turning away from Cuba. During this time, the seed planted in my mind earlier, by Eleana became my secret fantasy. I began to visualize myself no longer as an adviser but as the leader. Since we were no longer under pressure, and time was not a factor in our activities, I had no qualms about going to Cuba with the commandos. I spoke of this with no one, because under the circumstances, it seemed a totally preposterous idea and, more than ever, contrary to policy.

As 1964 drew on, the focus of attention was shifting even more to Vietnam. The military, virtually ignored at the Bay of Pigs, and given false starts at the 1962 missile crisis and the French colonial adventure in Algeria, ambitiously sought an outlet for its pent-up frustration. In the evolving age of "limited, nonnuclear war," it sought desperately for a "brush fire" to extinguish. The proponents of paramilitary and counter-guerrilla warfare, represented by the Green Berets who had contrived to impress President Kennedy, carried on a sales campaign for the United States involvement in Vietnam that would have put any public relations firm to shame. The career-officer corps of all the services sought a "gentlemen's" war—one which would guarantee limited combat exposure and unlimited opportunity for promotion and command empire-building. There was something for everyone in Vietnam, and it was far enough away to virtually eliminate the possibility of war reaching U.S. soil. More important, Vietnam was remote enough, culturally and racially, so that war there could be staged and looked upon in a detached fashion by the American public.

I had been away from the military for more than a year, but I felt what was happening. It all pointed toward Vietnam: Green Berets, helicopters, jungle warfare, and the inscrutability of the Oriental, the mystery and tantalizing danger of fighting Communist guerrillas in the Asian rain forests. Even the national press picked up the spirit of the new adventure. For career Army officers, there would be medals, combat infantry badges, command assignments, and spot promotions. All they had to do was jump on the Vietnam bandwagon.

Suzie picked it up quickly. She saw it as a chance to escape her unhappiness in Miami and a proper way for me to return to the regular military. At first her efforts at persuasion were coy and indirect. She read me portions of letters from friends, news reports mentioning fellow officers in Vietnam, and promotion lists from the *Army Times*. Everybody was volunteering, she said. Then she became more direct: that's where the real fighting is. If you're so damn hungry for battle, go where things are really going on. Eighteen months over there will go by like nothing at all, and by the time you come back you'll be a major and will have forgotten about the CIA. Forget about the Cubans,forget about the Cubans,forget about the Cubans. Her voice constantly echoed in my mind.

For months it kept building until Suzie gave up. In spring, 1964, she announced she wanted to take the boys back to Minnesota for a few weeks to visit her parents. The lease was up on our house; we both knew she'd never come back. It was something we couldn't discuss, and in order to conceal our emotions, for the welfare of the children, we carried out the pretense. Quite coincidentally, I received permanent change of station orders (PCS) assigning me to the CIA for an indefinite period. Apparently the agency liked my work.

If there was anything beneficial about the slowdown following Kennedy's death, it was the gradual culling of marginal personnel from the exile force. I dropped two men from the Elliott Key team and several Cuban instructors. What remained was a force of highly motivated, well-trained volunteers who were willing to wait, train, and tolerate the personal hardships inherent in their work. In the summer of 1964 the CIA in Miami probably had a smaller more effective exile paramilitary force than ever before.

There was considerable talk among the exiles—as well as official discussions within the CIA and elsewhere in the government—of shifting the base of operations from the United States to some sympathetic Central American country. A good deal of exploratory planning was done, but the Cubans were unable to find a leader with the ability to command such an undertaking. Exiles were also warned not to attempt raid or other paramilitary actions from U.S. bases, and stiff penalties were imposed on raiding parties that attempted to slip through the official restrictive cordon that was drawn about the southeast coastline of the United States.

As my frustration grew over the interminable wait for renewed anti-Castro action, my Army career, my family, and the life I had once known seemed to have passed me by. I worked hard and tried not to allow my personal unhappiness to show through to the men. But my anguish must have been apparent to Eleana. She began to say things to buck up my spirits and motivate my daily efforts with the commandos. She'd always done this for everyone on the base, but now her effort seemed directed more toward me.

It was inevitable under the circumstances, I suppose, that our hard shell would finally crack. It happened rather innocently. We had run low on kerosene when I hadn't been able to make a supply run to the mainland because of a storm. Eleana told me there would not be enough fuel for the next day's cooking. It was nearly midnight, but the storm had passed and the water was calm. I could make a run down the to Pirates' Lair and pick up enough fuel to last us until I could make it to the mainland the following day.

When I told Eleana my plans, she asked if she could come with me, and maybe stop to see her parents for a little while.

We loaded the boat and soon were skimming along the familiar channels to Pirate's Lair. Eleana went ashore and visited her parents while I filled the kerosene cans and loaded them back onto the boat. When Eleana came back to the dock, she whispered her thanks for the chance to visit her parents and jumped into the boat. We headed back around the island toward Elliott Key. As was our practice, I ran black—no running lights. The moon was full, stars incredibly bright, the sky clear in all quadrants.

Eleana stood close to me as we glided among the narrow canals, and when we swept around the last one and sea opened up magnificently in front of us, her shoulder touched mine.

"Danielito, it is my birthday today. That is why I wanted to see Mama and Papa. They gave me something; would you share it with me?" She held up a small bottle. "It is special Cuban wine, only for birthdays."

I cut the engine and let the boat glide to a stop near the end of the canal. The sea, bathed in the moonlight, lay before us, and we were surrounded by the silence of the night. She pulled the cork and offered the bottle to me. I drank deeply, the wine cold and light and sweet in my mouth. She drank too, as we sat on the wide seat to admire the night.

"Danielito mio, you are so troubled. Sometimes I cry for you because I know you are so badly hurt inside."

I looked in her face and saw tears in her eyes. And then we were in each other's arms, releasing everything that we'd kept back for so many months. We made love there, on the seat of the boat, in the moonlight. There was no guilt, only exaltation. I knew then that I loved Eleana, if I had not fallen in love with her long before.

THE ZENITH SECRET

It was difficult to suppress our newfound joy, but we did not allow it to become obvious to the commandos. My desire for an intimate friendship had been growing for many months, and in Eleana I found the depth of understanding and sexual response for which I had longed. Beneath the fiery, sometimes temperamental exterior, I discovered a mature, intelligent, sensitive woman. She demanded nothing of me except the time we shared, and with the reduced pace of the training activity, it was not difficult for us to be together. I made no effort to limit the intensity of my love, even though I knew there could be no permanence in the relationship.

Eleana loved the sea, and in the evenings we took long boat rides along the winding mangrove canals. At first we found it difficult to talk intimately. She was hesitant about discussing her husband and her earlier life in Cuba because she wanted to put these things out of her mind and begin a new life. Yet, when I encouraged her, she spoke warmly and affectionately about her homeland, and there was no question that she longed to return there.

It was mid-1964 now, and the commandos continued to train and work hard each day, but there was also time for play. Eleana and I spent glorious weekends snorkeling and spearfishing on a great coral reef near the island. We swam nude and lay in the sun and made love unashamedly in the water, on the deck of the open boat, or on the deserted beach. I met her frequently in Miami when we went to the mainland for a weekend. I did this on the sly because I did not want the CIA to know of my involvement with her. As if by magic, we would change from naked, uncivilized castaways to tanned, smartly dressed, urban sophisticates, moving among the swinging cocktail lounges in Coral Gables or Coconut Grove. Inevitably, these evenings would conclude in a small, earthy Cuban hideaway near the international airport, the Mi Rinconcito.

It was on one of these evenings that I had my first experience with marijuana. It was well after midnight and people were everywhere, crowded in booths, jammed on the small dance floor, knotted in corners around the tiny tables. From time to time, acquaintances—many of them Cuban women who had become prostitutes—came up to say hello to Eleana and embarrass me with jokes about her blond, blue-eyed escort. Someone handed her a long silver-colored cigarette, which she lit and then handed to me. "Something special from one of my old friends from the island. Go ahead, it will make you feel very good."

My stomach turned. All those years as an Army officer, countless lectures about the dangers of drugs, shakedown inspections for hypodermics, tiny holes in men's arms; addiction making a person's brain go soft, making a man go soft inside. Evil.

I shook my head and handed it back to her.

"Danielito, this is a gift for your love. You can not refuse it from me." She took a deep drag, then wrapped her arms around my neck and ground her mouth against mine, her tongue searching to pry my lips apart. Her touch made me feel soft and pliable. I opened my lips and she exhaled into my mouth, forcing the heavy smoke into my lungs. I knew that it must have been marijuana, because I could feel my chest expanding and a new and different sense of awareness sweeping over me. Tingling, sharp, feeling high. We shared the cigarette after that. We were stoned, and our lovemaking later that night was easily the most intense sexual experience of my life.

So we existed, Eleana and I together, in this rather strange, temporary world. Monday mornings would find us back in our places at the Elliott Key hideaway, and a new week of training would begin. We talked a lot about the exiles' struggle to liberate their country. No longer was my dream of leading the commando group on the refinery raid sheer fantasy. I had decided that, if and when authorization was granted for the mission, I would go directly to Shackley and Campbell and ask permission to go with the exiles. If official permission was denied, I intended to go anyway. I had not worked out the details—I'd do that after the final mission arrangements were made. But I would go, nevertheless. Eleana knew how I felt, and she shared my intensity and encouraged my militancy. She asked me only that I take her along; if anything happened to me, she said, she'd want to die with me. We believed that the refinery would kindle the fire of internal revolt on the island and provide the symbolic light of hope that would rally Cuban exiles everywhere.

Like a gnawing cancer, the awareness that the CIA would not go on indefinitely maintaining a do-nothing exile force and all their equipment weighed heavily on our minds. The cost would eventually become intolerable. So we knew that, sooner or later, either we would be committed to new action or the forces would be disbanded. We hoped for the former, but as the days wore on, the latter course of action appeared more and more a reality.

The order to disband came first to the commando groups that were hidden around southern Florida. Gordon Campbell asked me to meet him for dinner at Black Caesar's Forge. This would be our first face to face meeting since well before the assassination and I looked forward to it. Campbell was at a table near the rear of the lower level dining room. He greeted me cordially, asked about my family and, for a few minutes, made small talk as we ordered our meal. Something about Campbell had changed. I had never seen this smooth, polished man ill at ease. But this night, he seemed edgy, a worried look on his face, and his hands shook a bit as he lit a cigarette. Despite his troubled appearance, speaking to me, he was his usual matter-of-fact, unemotional self, a man who was never out of control.

Campbell explained major foreign policy changes had been made by President Johnson, and the paramilitary effort developed by the CIA under the previous administration was being phased out. The commando group I was responsible for would be given a security debriefing and be terminated with one month's pay in advance. Administrative help would be terminated in the same fashion and sent home. All equipment would be removed, and the safehouse would be thoroughly "swept" for security items, documents, and so on. I had one week to get the job done. Then I was to return to the training branch to supervise the closedown of my other training bases. Were there any questions?

"What do I tell the Cubans, Gordon?"

"You don't have to tell them a damn thing. Just tell them you're carrying out orders. Your company has lost its government contract. You know, nothing more than that."

He excused himself from dinner early, leaving half of a thick, rare filet mignon. I drank what was left of his double martini while anger boiled inside me. My country couldn't do this. But my country had! I never again saw or communicated with Gordon Campbell.

Telling the commandos we were finished was not so difficult as I feared.

There was muttering, disillusionment, disgust, anger, and even a few "I told you so's." But they went ahead silently to clear the base. Boxes were packed and equipment oiled and stowed in permanent containers, and each man packed his small bag of personal effects. I borrowed the Chris-Craft and made trip upon trip back to Black Point, under the cover of darkness, to where the supply truck was parked for the pick-up. It took us three days to clear the base of major equipment.

THE ZENITH SECRET

I knew that the Cubans did not hold me responsible for what was happening. In their eyes, I had long ago ceased to exist solely as a representative of the United States. I was an American, but I was also one of them, and they knew how difficult the time was for me. And so we gathered for the last time in the old house. I dutifully read the security debriefing instructions, then had each of the men sign on an oath of perpetual secrecy about their activities with the agency. Eleana did the same. I had brought wine for our final meal together, and we sat, as we did so many times before, at the large table in the now-bare living room. There were no words of encouragement and hope this time, no talk of the day's training. Emotion caught in my throat as we stood for a final salute to the exiles' struggle, and then, asking the blessing of the Almighty, I proposed a communal oath:

"In the name of God, although we must now separate, let each of us, in his own way; carry on the honorable struggle that brought us together on this island. And may none of us return to this place until we have earned the privilege of returning by fulfilling, each in his own way, the task we have begun here, so help us God."

Eleana said the words, clearly and slowly in Spanish, and the men repeated them after her.

"Salud!"

BRADLEY E. AYERS

CHAPTER 14

The cancellation of the refinery raid and the closure of my Elliott Key base marked the beginning of the end of CIA anti-Castro operations in Miami. The Elliott Key force was not the only one to be disbanded. Other exile groups were being similarly terminated, their hopes dashed, as were my own.

In the days that followed the termination of commando training, I resumed my earlier routine of supervising other programs. These now were little more than skeletons of the original activity we had conceived and worked so diligently to develop. Retraining of select volunteers remained the primary function of the other programs, and they were stricken by the problems of morale and motivation.

Although I suppressed my emotional reaction and tried to carry on with my duties, I burned inside over what I considered a betrayal of the Cuban exiles. As a professional soldier, I could do nothing more than fulfill the responsibilities of my assignment, which I did. But I found the situation more and more difficult to reconcile morally, and I used every opportunity to make my views known to my associates. It must have sounded almost like blasphemy to them, because gradually I sensed a change toward me in the atmosphere around the station.

At first I tried to write off this uneasy awareness as sheer paranoia caused by my abrupt change in routine and my disappointment. I was back on the mainland, spending a great deal of time around headquarters but with relatively little to do. I looked for my friend and compatriot, Ed Roderick, but he, too, had disappeared into the shadows. Morales was not to be seen. It was unsettling to again confront the bureaucracy, which I had been mostly able to avoid while in the field.

I was conscious of many little things that indicated a cloud had been cast over the acceptance I'd won from my CIA colleagues. The agency people now seemed overly polite and too accommodating and cooperative in small, routine matters. I sensed that they were being sympathetic, sharing and understanding my growing resentment, although they didn't really want to become involved, especially with a non-agency "hot head" who thought too much and sometimes said what he felt. It wasn't considered healthy for one's career, and gradually the impersonality I had confronted when I first came to the station returned. It was as if I had suddenly developed a contagious disease but was allowed to walk around free of quarantine.

The closure of the commando base made it necessary for me to move back to the pink stucco safehouse off Royal Palm Drive near Homestead on the edge of the Everglades. I longed to see Eleana, but to try to call or find her in Miami would be a blatant violation of security. I wrote to my wife and sons, and although I was terribly lonely, the isolation provided me with the first real opportunity to think about myself and begin to place in some perspective all that had happened. I was already licensed as a private pilot and, as a diversion I began working on my commercial, instrument, and FAA flight instructor certification at nearby Tamiami Airport.

Several weeks after disbanding the group at Elliott Key, Ted Shackley instructed me to prepare a detailed after-action report on the entire training operation at the island. This provided me with a unique opportunity to make my views known officially. The report undoubtedly would be read at higher levels of the government. For nearly a week, I labored on the document by myself in the safehouse. I turned the report in to Ted on a Friday, and the following Monday he asked me to meet him for lunch.

Ted avoided talking about the report during the meal, and instead kept the conversation light as we discussed a variety of non-business subjects. I sensed that he was waiting for the right moment to talk about something weightier and finally, as we drank our brandy, he came to the point.

"Brad, that was a very complete report on the Elliott Key project you turned in. It will certainly be of value to anyone else confronted with that kind of crash project."

I thanked him.

"You got carried away with your own political philosophy in the conclusions and recommendations, though, don't you think?"

"There's nothing in that report that's not true. When I talked about morale, motivation, and spirit, and how essential these factors were to getting a mission accomplished Everyone knows these things are true. Can anyone deny that we've pulled the rug out from under the exiles' effort?"

He looked down at the drink in front of him and tapped the glass uneasily. "Look, you've done a good job for us. No one here is going to disagree with what has happened. But there are some things you just can't change. One of them, obviously, is the policy of this administration. Why beat your head against a wall over something you can't even begin to influence?"

I felt the adrenaline surge. "Sir, if more people in the agency would speak up and tell Washington what a tragic waste this is and that this is a rotten betrayal of the Cubans who are willing to die to free their country, then maybe the president wouldn't blunder on with the Vietnam thing."

Ted looked me straight in the eye. "You don't hear very well, do you? I'm going to say it again. You've got a whole career in front of you. You've got a hell of a good foundation, and the efficiency reports that have come from us are damn good. Further, we're recommending you for a Purple Heart and the Combat Infantry Badge. But you're going to louse yourself up so bad, if you continue swimming upstream, that no one will want you anywhere. Damn it, play it smart. It's for your own good."

He paused then added; "There is no way in hell, my friend, that you are going to change the course of things in the Johnson administration. He's going for Vietnam, and, for all practical purposes, Cuba is going to remain as is, barring some unforeseeable provocation. There isn't a damn thing you or I or the agency can do about it, so forget your personal interest."

I started to say something about the Cubans we'd trained and how they believed in us, but he cut me off. "Brad, the company and I both think a lot of you. We'd like to see you come out well in this assignment. You've worked damned hard without a break for nearly two years. I know it's been tough in the field and especially the last few months without your family. Why don't you take a week or two and fly back to Minnesota to see your wife and kids? It would do you a world of good.

"Oh, Brad, you know it's going to be a lot easier to accept this whole thing if you break off your association with the commandos. You know what the rule is about associating with exiles unless they're cleared by the agency. Even a former employee is not considered secure after he's left the payroll. Just a friendly suggestion."

He had said nothing about Eleana, but he must have known. It was a tact-ful suggestion. Not one to be taken lightly, I could tell by the tone of his voice. So that's what was bugging them.

"I haven't seen any of them since we came ashore three weeks ago. I'm not going to violate security regulations, and I don't want to get myself in hot water. But since you brought the matter up, I do want authorization to see the girl who worked at Elliott Key one more time."

Ted Shackley was certainly not a moralist. I felt it was better to have it out in the open, for I had nothing to hide.

"Okay, but wrap it up with her this time. Break it clean, for your own good."

I walked to my car with his warning stinging my ears.

I mulled over what Shackley had said for several days after the meeting. Maybe now was the time to begin patching things up with my family and look-ing toward my own future. With what was happening in Miami, it didn't seem likely that my CIA assignment could last much longer despite the fact I'd been permanently ordered to the agency. At this point I knew I could easily use both my family and my Army career as justifications for turning away from the Cubans. I was a professional officer and could easily take refuge in the excuse that I was simply following the dictates of government policy. But that was the kind of rationale that I found so despicable in others, and I could not make myself buy it.

After several days of wrestling with my conscience, I arrived at a compro-mise: I'd go to Washington for a few days and attempt to get a better picture of my career status and immediate Army future by talking to the career manage-ment department. That would make Suzie happy, of course, and I could write her a nice long letter about eventually getting back to our military way of life.

The other side of the compromise was much more appealing: During my visit I'd have to talk with the people responsible for my present assignment with the CIA, both at Langley and in the Pentagon. These people occupied places of real power and influence. Maybe I'd even see Mr. Fitzgerald who handled Cuban affairs at the agency, and General Rosson, who was in charge of the Army's Special Warfare Operations. When I returned to Miami, I could say goodbye to Eleana and, symbolically, to the other exiles, knowing that I had pleaded their cause at the highest levels of power accessible to me.

Three days later I checked into a motel near the Pentagon. From the moment I stepped into the cab at National Airport, I was aware that the mood of the city had changed. The assassination still clouded the seat of government, and a cold, somber atmosphere that was deeper than bereavement over a phys-ical death had replaced the warmth of the Kennedy administration. The smiles and color were gone.

My trip to Washington was a dismal failure. I'd had to wait three hours one day to spend just five minutes with Colonel Bond, and that five minutes was interrupted by no fewer than four telephone calls, all apparently dealing with special forces' commitments in Vietnam. The colonel, who looked older and more harassed than I remembered, thanked me for my regular bimonthly summaries and complimented me on the excellent reports he'd received from the CIA. He could tell me little about my next assignment, but advised me that undoubtedly, after Miami I might continue with the agency in Vietnam. My position, the whole issue of Cuba versus Southeast Asia, was symbolized by the new maps of Vietnam hurriedly tacked over the maps of Cuba on the walls of his office.

The Cuban section of the CIA was even more discouraging. I learned only that the CIA's role in anti-Castro operations was shifting from paramilitary action to passive intelligence gathering. They did say they'd like to have me stay on and continue with my work if I wanted to, but this would be with infiltration teams. Commando operations were being phased out.

Three days later, back in Miami, I desperately wanted to see Eleana. She had moved in with another Cuban woman when the base closed and had told me of their intention to live there until we could meet again. There had been no promises; I'd told her only that I'd received other orders and would see her as soon as it could be arranged.

I found Eleana at the Mi Rinconcito with her girlfriends. It was early when I entered the softly lit Cuban bar and it instantly brought back memories of the pleasant evening we'd spent there. Eleana was radiant, more beautiful than I had ever seen her. Her eyes flashed when she saw me walk in, and she threw herself into my arms.

For a while, it was like old times. We danced and held each other close. There were no thoughts of tomorrow; both of us were clinging to the moment, for different reasons. The knowledge that I would have to say goodbye to her was like a cold, dead, weight inside me. Later, we drifted from the Mi Rinconcito to a motel near the airport.

Eleana was more a woman now; the commandos and the exile struggle were secondary to her own needs. As morning came, she talked about getting an apartment so we could live together. She had found a job, and we could continue to work together with the Cuban freedom fighters if that was what I wanted. She begged me to stay with her.

I was torn inside as never before. I could not say goodbye to her this way, and in the end I compromised myself again. I told her I would have to go away from Miami for a while, a flying job in Central America. But one day I would come back to resume my work with the exiles and, I hoped, I would find her. We would make no promises, because both our lives were changing. She was beginning a new life with her son in the United States, and she should do it freely. My work was unpredictable; I traveled frequently, and our life together would be anything but stable. In the end, we resigned ourselves to parting.

We made love a final time, in a rumpled bed bathed in sunshine. Afterward, I took her back to Mi Rinconcito. She kissed me goodbye quickly, and when she jumped from the car she didn't look back.

I could not deny that all logical indicators pointed toward a return to the Regular Army and Vietnam. As I had volunteered for the CIA assignment, I was free to request a release at any time. But my emotional involvement was so great by now that I couldn't do it. I still clung to the hope that a change of national policy might be forthcoming or that Castro might provoke the United States into renewing paramilitary activities.

During one of these times, when my hope was renewed, I developed a one-man sales campaign for a new approach to covert paramilitary operations in Cuba. During my early research I had made a detailed study of the topography of the island. The Zapata Peninsula was an extensive swampy area of several hundred square miles located on the south-central coast. It's a virtually uninhabitable mangrove and freshwater marshland, laced with streams and canals and subject to frequent flooding. Only alligator hunters, a few fishermen, fugitives and desperados frequented the area.

Castro had used the Sierra Maestra Mountains to hide his anti-Batista guerrilla forces. The rugged, wooded terrain served as his base of operations and made it difficult for the Batista militia to seek out and destroy his revolutionary bands. Castro knew the mountains, and most of the people who lived there still remained loyal to him. But could we not use the swamps of the Zapata Peninsula for the same purpose for which Castro used the mountains?

I called my plan the "Pantano Concept," using the Spanish word for swamp. The CIA could plant a guerrilla force in the swamps and use the marshland as a base of operations. Its central location, isolation, proximity to Havana, and line of communication made it geographically ideal.

My plan included infiltration of the commandos, extended re-supply of guerrillas, proposed demolition targets, and ambush operations and raids of various types. Finally, I worked out a plan for evading counter-measures that Castro could be expected to take, and a last-ditch plan of emergency withdrawal of the forces should that become necessary. When I had finished the lengthy, minutely detailed, fully supported proposal, I gave it what I felt was my ultimate personal endorsement: I included a personal letter to the CIA chief of station, volunteering to train and lead the commandos myself.

To make the whole matter quite proper, and ensure that none of my CIA superiors would be offended, I submitted the paper through official channels, beginning with my boss, Ernie Sparks. But Ernie exhibited little interest and only wanted to know if I really thought it was wise to add my personal letter of commitment to the study? I told him that I felt morally compelled to endorse the plan with my own offer of participation. I didn't see the comments he added to the paper, but after a few days it was sent on to the front office. Days passed and Ted finally called me. It was a good study, a fine idea, and represented a lot of thought and research, he said. Unfortunately, the proposal was not in consonance with current policy. My plan died, just like that.

My embers of hope were fanned again, in a different way, a few weeks later when Ernie instructed me to report to the chief of station's office for a special meeting. I was not disappointed with what the meeting turned up. Ted informed us that Manuel Artime, the young, politically ambitious Cuban who had figured prominently in the Bay of Pigs operation and who had emerged as one of the more important exile leaders, was being given the endorsement of the Johnson administration for the purpose of forming a new government in exile. Artime's all-Cuban political and military organization would be based, clandestinely, in Nicaragua and would train a new exile military force to conduct both covert and overt tactical operations against Castro. The operations would exclude the use of any American personnel. CIA assistance would be limited to placing advisers with Artime's staff in Nicaragua. It was hoped that the popular, youthful militant would be able to unify the politically fractious exile community and ultimately seize power from Fidel Castro.

Artime was in Miami, ready to begin the formation of his organization. I heard rumors to the effect that the United States had given him more than a million dollars to establish his base. Certain agency staff members had been designated to present a series of briefings for Artime on particular intelligence or tactical specialties. I had been selected to tell him how to establish and conduct a simple paramilitary training program. In essence, over a period of several days I was to show Artime how I'd set up my program for the CIA and how it operated, and give instruction in the basic techniques of survival and covert small-unit operations.

I assembled the necessary materials, charts, tables or organization, equipment samples, and other paraphernalia. Three days later, I met Artime at a plush Tudor mansion adjacent to a Coral Gables golf course. The house—one of the Miami safesites reserved for VIPs and special operations—had been carefully checked by security, and I was warned to exercise extreme caution during my travel to and from the house to ensure that I was not followed. Artime was staying there for the duration of the briefings.

The quick-witted, young Cuban leader immediately impressed me. I had only to look at his face and into his clear, sharp eyes to recognize the zeal and intense ambition that burned inside him. I felt an instant kinship with him, and as the briefings progressed I began to see in him the personification of the exiles' cause. He responded warmly and attentively to everything I said, and the sessions would always last much longer than planned.

Among the numerous phone calls and frequent visits by political aides that interrupted my briefings with Artime, there was one rather strange incident that was, later, to have considerable impact on my life. Two men came to see him one rainy afternoon, and, as had been the procedure, Artime excused himself and went into the study to speak with them privately. I busied myself making notes and reviewing the remainder of my program for the day. The phone rang, and Artime left the two men in the study to take the call. He remained on the phone for some time, and while he was gone, the two Cubans began to argue so loudly that it was impossible for me not to hear them. They were arguing about money, something to do with a large cache that some agents had hidden in the Florida Keys. The argument was primarily over the loyalty of the men who had hidden the money and whether they would join Artime. But one of the men also mentioned, in Spanish, an island with two houses by Angelfish Creek, a metal cache container hidden in concrete under water on the island, a "Castro assassination payment," and the delivery of a half-million U.S. dollars. The men quieted when Artime returned, and I went on with my work, paying little mind to what I'd heard.

For weeks following my sessions with Artime, I hung on to my dream of going to Nicaragua. But nothing ever happened. I never saw Artime again, and rumor had it that his attempt had fizzled. It was said that he'd been unable to pull together the numerous political segments represented in the exile population, and when he failed to demonstrate the political strength necessary to unify his people, the United States government withdrew its support. Artime's scheme died before it ever had a chance. One more spark of hope was extinguished.

It was September and I had been flying a lot. I had passed my commercial pilot written exam, and was working on the flight time requirement. One day, as I completed a cross-country flight, and was fueling the airplane at Kendall Flying School, a man approached and asked to talk with me when I was finished. He was waiting for me in the pilot lounge after I tied the airplane down and made my logbook entries.

The man was dressed in a tan suit and tie, wore dark glasses, was clean-shaven, had a trim physique, and a very smooth manner. I'd never seen him before, but he had CIA written all over him. He introduced himself as Greg Crossman and handed me a business card showing he was an employee of Paragon Air Service, my operational cover corporation. He suggested we take a walk, that he had some information for me.

As we walked in the grass between the parked aircraft, Crossman explained that I had been recommended as someone who might be interested in an "off the record" job. He explained that one of Paragon's subcontractors had some people stranded on the coast of Cuba and wondered if I'd be interested in organizing an operation to return them to the States.

My thoughts immediately went back to my meeting with Colonel Bond and the session I had with Mr. Shackley several days earlier. Rumors had been going

This palatial Coral Gables home was used as a "high level" CIA safehouse and reserved for special VIP activities. I spent a week here with Manuel Artime teaching him the fundamentals for organizing a new Cuban commando training program for Central America. Artime's anti-Castro effort, to be based in Nicaragua, never got off the ground.

around the station that, with the draw-down of operations personnel, maritime assets, support, and technical/signal resources JM/WAVE, a few exile intelligence gathering infiltration teams calling for exfiltration were, in effect, stranded on the island. I had also heard it from some of my remaining instructor cadre with whom I was in contact, as the rumor was already afloat in Little Havana. When I'd asked Ted about it and expressed my concern, he had quickly moved on to other things with the comment that no further operations had been authorized. Apparently this meant even rescue missions.

I told Crossman I'd think about it and get back to him at the number on his card. When Crossman left, I took a jog around the airport perimeter, thinking over his proposal. There was little to ponder. I had opened my mouth to Ted and now I had to put up or shut up. I called Crossman the next day and told him I'd meet him to discuss the task at hand. An Army Ranger never leaves his people behind.

The plan was relatively simple. A Cuban group covertly supported by CIA and headed by Cuban freedom fighter/activist doctor Orlando Bosch would provide the manpower and resources. The concept was to establish a rendezvous point near the western coastal tip of the island. It would be up to the team requesting exfiltration to reach the rendezvous point. Concurrently two V-20s each carrying deflated rubber rafts would leave the lower Keys and make the run across the Florida Straits/Southeastern Gulf of Mexico to a point on the Cuban coast as close to the rendezvous area as possible. This would be done under the cover of darkness, and, weather permitting, on a weekend when watchfulness on both the U.S. and Cuban coasts was relatively lax.

THE ZENITH SECRET

One V-20 with its operator would remain offshore as a back-up while the rescue craft would get as close to shore in the tricky waters as possible. The boat would carry five men, including the operator, with four of the group, one a team leader, to go ashore and move to the rendezvous point to link up with the team to be exfiltrated. The rubber rafts would be inflated only if it was necessary to use them to get to shore in waters too shallow for the V-20.

The team to be exfiltrated was composed of three men, and it was hoped and planned that all would make it to the rendezvous point. The penetration team of four men, on linkup, would provide security at the rendezvous sight and, as rapidly as possible, assist the men to be exfiltrated to the shoreline and the boat, either V-20 or rubber raft. Once at sea, the boats would speed outside Cuban coastal waters, redistribute personnel as equally as possible between the two V-20s and return directly to Key West. Several contingency plans were discussed, including the type weapons to be carried, emergency medical care including rescue at sea if either one or both V-20s should be disabled. Speed was essential to the success of the operation.

Two days later, I met Crossman again at the airport at nightfall and he drove me to a deteriorating old wood frame house just off S.W. 8th Avenue in the heart of Little Havana. He dropped me off and said he'd be back to pick me up in an hour.

I was met at the door by a huge, tough-looking black Cuban. He took me into a room lit by candles. There, I was introduced to Dr. Bosch. He already knew my name and referred to me as Mr. Williams. Bosch, who I had heard about as a militant anti-Castro proponent had a gentle, distinguished quality about him. Casually dressed, bespectacled, with thinning hair, and a slight build, he was not an imposing figure. He spoke very good English, articulating his words and using frequent hand gestures to make a point or describe something. I looked around as we talked. In the shadows I could make out forms. The house was full of Cubans. Whatever Bosch and I discussed was certainly not private.

Bosch needed someone to quickly organize the rescue team and dispatch it. The word coming out of Cuba was that the men to be exfiltrated were on the run from Castro's forces, virtually without food and living from moment to moment in imminent danger of capture and execution. They were still in communication with the agency via radio, continuously expressing the desperation of their circumstances.

Bosch, with non-attributable CIA support, had a base of operations and a safehouse just north of Key West, near Oceanside Marina. He kept his boats there. I agreed to meet him and his men the forthcoming weekend. The rescue mission was set for Saturday night, weather and all other considerations permitting.

Early Saturday, I rented an Aeronca Champ from Kendall Flying School and filed a flight plan to Key West. I told them I'd spend the night in Key West and return the plane on Sunday evening, probably late. Two hours later, I was in Key West en route in a taxi to the address given me by Bosch.

Bosch's safehouse was a big, old decaying two-story stucco mansion a short distance north of the marina. Years earlier, a channel had been cut into the corral next to the building. The V-20s were docked at the marina and could be brought around to the canal for loading. On arrival, I was delighted to find my old friend Julio Fernandez the man in charge. I was also pleased to find the exile volunteers he had brought down for the rescue mission were all men that had been through my training programs, two from the Elliott Key project. It took us only a few hours to work out our plan for the rendezvous with the stranded team. Time would not permit a rehearsal, but the new moon and predicted weather were just what we needed.

Julio brought the V-20s around a little after dusk. I recognized them immediately as CIA/JM/WAVE boats that had been stripped down and handed off to Bosch and his group. Earlier, we had enjoyed a huge Cuban supper and passed around a bottle of rum. We were in very high spirits as we loaded the boats, not without a good deal of loud frivolity, at the narrow passageway cut into the coral channel wall. Shortly thereafter, with well wishes from Julio and the cook, we were on our way southbound, speeding wide open, across nearly flat seas.

I carried a .45 cal. pistol in a shoulder holster; the rest of the men carried M-3 submachine guns. The sea was unusually calm as we sped across the open, often turbulent Gulf Stream. We arrived off the southwestern coast of Cuba in less than three hours and began to execute the established plan. All went very smoothly and, with a little exploring, we were able to get my V-20 with the penetration team less than a hundred feet offshore. We could easily wade through the mangroves to dry land.

I had gotten fairly familiar with the lay of the land in this area of Cuba while studying the maps in preparation for the refinery raid. Better yet, one of my team members had lived nearby the rendezvous point and had good knowledge of the terrain. I let him lead us through the near total darkness with our hearts beating. Ambush was a constant concern.

Just before leaving Key West, Julio had gotten a message from the stranded team advising they were at the rendezvous point, an old barn/cattle shelter about a mile inland. When we arrived, all was silent. We set up security about fifty yards from the structure, only a vague shape looming in the darkness. I made our presence known by tapping two rocks together, and I had one of my men whisper loudly in Spanish. We waited, signaling again and again. An hour went by. There was no response.

Dawn was rapidly approaching and I decided to go in. I took one of the men with me and approached the barn. There was only the sound of our movement through the vegetation. The heavy scent of oleander pervaded the humid night air. But, I could smell death before we even reached the barn.

We entered the old building through a cattle opening. I had my pistol at the ready and a flashlight in my left hand. As we came around a hay bin it was immediately apparent our rescue mission was futile.

Displayed on the manure-covered floor were the bodies of the intelligence gathering team that had been calling for exfiltration. The three men had been killed in a most gruesome fashion. We examined the bodies. Two had been shot through the back of the head, execution style. I recognized the team leader, a man who had been through several of my training programs in 1963. He had obviously been beaten. His trousers were around his knees and his groin was a bloody mass. His genitals had been crudely cut off and jammed into his mouth.

His throat had been slit. I fought to control my horror. The Cuban I brought with me burst into tears and vomited on the spot.

We looked around for the team's radio, a highly sophisticated "burst" receiver-transmitter specifically manufactured for CIA clandestine communications. It was nowhere to be seen. Leaving the barn, we went to a ramshackle building that I assumed housed the farmer who owned the barn. What we discovered was as great as the horror in the barn. The front door was open, and inside the building we found an elderly man, a woman and a small child on the floor of the kitchen area. All had been killed with a knife or hacked to death with a machete. Their faces had been mutilated during the killing.

We could do nothing but report what we had found. Sickened and distraught, we withdrew to the rest of the team and made our way back to the V-20. Well after dawn on Sunday morning, we pulled into the canal next to the old mansion, pretending we were fishermen returning from an early morning outing. I got on the phone immediately and reported what we'd found to Bosch and Crossman. Bosch was livid; Crossman's reaction seemed, on the phone, to be emotionless. I couldn't eat and didn't want to sleep, even exhausted as I was. It was not too late to make noon Mass, so I had Julio drop me off at a church in Key West. After Mass, I walked the rest of the way to the airport, untied the Aeronca and flew back to Miami. What I saw that night would be with me for the rest of my days.

CHAPTER 15

Profoundly disturbed by what I had experienced on the rescue-extraction mission, I called in sick and holed up for several days at the Homestead safehouse. Alone there with my thoughts and vivid replays of the horrific discovery in the Campasinos' barn and home, eating and sleeping were of no consideration. I knew that somehow I had to block out what I'd witnessed and go on. I took to running long distances at dusk, pushing myself to near exhaustion.

The runs, followed by a couple of stiff shots of rum, would knock me out for a few hours, but I'd awaken in the predawn hours only to lie there, staring at the ceiling, the gruesome scene at the farm playing over and over again before me, the images as on a movie screen from which I could not turn away. When I did begin to feel some escape from the mental and emotional torture, the lingering scent of oleander would bring it all back.

Overlaying this torment was an increasing sense of helplessness, frustration, danger, and confusion about my role. No matter how deeply I was repelled by what I'd experienced on the recent mission to Cuba, now, more than ever, I felt I had to do something to get the attention of those responsible for what I clearly saw as the abandonment of the exiles and their cause. While running, and in the solitary quiet of the safehouse, I did a lot of soul-searching, agonizing over my next move.

The Army was my last hope. I had come to respect Colonel Bond as a principled, dedicated professional soldier. If anyone could, he'd understand the tragic mistake that was being made, and he had access to the top people in Washington.

I searched my mind for some act that would give my plea the greatest possible impact. Short of a blatant violation of CIA and Army regulations that might focus attention on the administration's Cuban policy, I had little with which to underscore my arguments. In the final analysis, the only point of real value was my career as a Regular Army officer. Eleven years of service was a lot to risk on any issue, but someone might take notice if that were placed on the line. A resignation in protest. Did I have the guts?

Following my last disappointing trip to Washington, I had written Colonel Bond a letter expressing all that I'd been unable to say when we met. Now, with some desperation in my voice, I called from the safehouse and told him I had to see him as soon as possible. Bond, somewhat reluctantly, agreed to see me, but warned that I should advise the station of my intention to travel to the Pentagon.

I immediately called Rudy. Sitting Bull was away, and I told him I wanted a week's leave to go to infantry officer career management at the Pentagon to look at my file. It was almost a lie, but I did intend to visit personnel if I had time. I made arrangements for a drive-away car (my trips to Washington were made at my own expense, and this was the cheapest way to travel) and departed the next day. Driving straight through, I was in D.C. 24 hours later.

My expectations on this trip were more realistic than on my earlier visit, for I no longer believed that I could have any effect on the course of events that moved national attention farther and farther away from Cuba. Nor did I even believe, as I had so naïvely before, that I might find sympathy for my views. The best I hoped to accomplish was to make a personal statement for the record that I, as an American citizen, believed that the United States was betraying the cause of freedom in our own hemisphere by turning its back on the Cuban exiles; and that I, as a professional soldier, could not compromise my own moral judgement to be part of such a betrayal or to participate in another war contrived and propagated by the military establishment, industrialists, and ambitious politicians for the sake of selfish gain.

Anti-Vietnam views were decidedly unpopular in late 1964, and it was virtually unheard of for a junior officer to take such a position. Quite obviously, the act would place my career in jeopardy. Was I really prepared to back up my statement with resignation? There was little else I could do once I'd made my position known. Nearly 12 years—the most significant years of my life in terms of career and future—gone up in smoke. What then? What about my wife and sons, our financial security and way of life? I had no skills that would be easily applicable to civilian life, with the possible exception of my pilot ratings.

And did I really want to become a civilian? Military life was the only thing I knew. Would my resignation aid the Cuban exiles in any way? That was the real question.

With the demise of Artime's effort, I had begun to seriously consider freeing myself of all government ties and returning to work with the Cubans as an ordinary American citizen. Maybe that would be the best way to aid the exiles and fulfill my personal moral commitment. The idea was exciting on one hand and frightening on the other, for it would necessitate major changes in almost every aspect of my life.

I arrived in Washington to find the same grayness in the air and the same frantic Vietnam-oriented activity at the Pentagon. The 1964 political campaign was in full swing, and one could feel almost feel the morbid, warmongering atmosphere as the president and his opponent, Barry Goldwater, debated only the method and pace by which death and destruction would be wrought in Vietnam.

Colonel Bond listened to me thoughtfully and attentively. A less understanding and patient superior officer could easily have court-martialed me for what I said. I told him about the failed rescue-exfiltration mission. When I had finished, he told me that what I said would be kept off the record. He dismissed me with the simple advice that I follow my own conscience. When I left his office, I felt in some ways like a spoiled child who, unable to get his way, had thrown a tantrum.

To make matters worse, before leaving the Pentagon I learned from Army career management that I was definitely slated for Vietnam when I left my present assignment. Bitterly, I faced the reality of having to knuckle under policy or tender my resignation. From Washington, I flew to my family in Minnesota.

Since the day I'd enlisted in the Army, going home to Minnesota had always been a special, cherished experience like coming into a warm, friendly room from a driving blizzard, a refuge from the cold and hostility outside. This time it was different.

I told Suzie of my wish to leave the service and find a new life. At that moment I did not want to be anywhere without her and the boys, not Florida, not the CIA, and certainly not Vietnam. Suzie pleaded with me to reconsider. More than anything else, she voiced concern about our financial security. And she didn't feel I was psychologically prepared to move away from the idealism, discipline, and regimentation inherent in a professional officer's life.

The alternative was Vietnam. Suzie knew it, and this was the course she pressed for. It was nothing new. Get released from the CIA and request Vietnam, she begged me. It would only be for 18 months or so, and she and the boys would wait in Minnesota. It was at this point our communications failed. Suzie simply could not comprehend the moral compromise I would be required to make in order to comply with her wishes. When we could talk no longer, I told her that I'd already planned to hold off my decision until after the national election.[19]

During this time, an increasing number of career agents were being transferred to Southeast Asia. Some had been with the Miami station for several years and were virtually irreplaceable because of the knowledge they possessed. Yet, to further their own careers or at the request of the agency, they were reassigned and the resulting vacancies were not filled. Depending on the importance of the position held by the staff member, it was customary for the individual branch, or occasionally, the front office, to hold a farewell cocktail party on the eve of the employee's departure. These gatherings occurred more and more frequently as the administration rushed pell-mell into the Vietnam conflict.

The parties were a rare display of social intimacy for the Miami CIA staff, and it struck me as rather odd that this kind of camaraderie should manifest itself at a time when the fire of the station's mission was being extinguished. Some of the warmth and unity would have been very welcome during the peak periods of tension, work, and struggle.

At these gatherings, I often found myself involved in rather deep philosophical discussions with Maggy, Shackley's girl Friday. Over the period of my assignment at the Miami station we had developed a kind of secret understanding that led to a comfortable, platonic friendship.

Whether it was because I'd been deprived of female companionship since I said goodbye to my wife and then Eleana, or for other reasons, more and more I enjoyed my informal encounters with Maggy. It seemed quite natural, since both of us were unencumbered by mates or escorts, that one night after a farewell party we decided to continue our discussions at a cocktail lounge. Several drinks later, we discovered that we had more in common than an interest in national policy and espionage. I was very relaxed with Maggy. She knew of my undercover role as Daniel B. Williams as well as my military status, so there was nothing I had to hide from her. She was also aware of my personal problems, both with my family and with the station, and, I figured, probably about my involvement with the commandos, Eleana, and Elliott Key, although she never mentioned it.

Dawn was just beginning to break when we left the small cocktail lounge. We got the sleepy bartender to sell us a bottle of wine, and Maggy insisted we leave my car and drive her shiny black MG. We put the convertible top down and soon were speeding through the winding lanes of Coconut Grove. Maggy kept urging me to go faster and faster, for the small car was a sheer pleasure to drive, and she knew I enjoyed it as much as she did. The freedom of wind and speed added to our intoxication, and the sensation became a very physical thing. All thoughts about her position in the front office and her possibly being Ted's mistress, became secondary.

I pulled the car off the road and down a narrow trail, leading to a deserted jetty next to the Deering estate on Biscayne Bay. There were no words. When I stopped the car she came into my arms. Because the little foreign car was uncomfortably cramped, we sat on the seawall and drank the wine as we watched the sun rise over the bay. I undressed her, and there, on the flat seawall, we made love, oblivious of the sharp coral that cut our skin.

I found in Maggy the physical and intellectual outlet I needed to better

THE ZENITH SECRET

understand myself, and I was able to look a little more objectively at the moral and professional quandary I faced.

The events of the preceding months—the Artime briefings, the preparation of the Pantano Concept, even the futile rescue mission—had helped release the frustration I felt. But when hope faded for both Artime's effort and the possibility that my Zapata Peninsula idea might be approved, I became more and more conscious of the meaninglessness of my efforts. The training programs were in virtual stand down. Each day's schedule was nothing more than a "make work" routine for the remaining agents. We reached the point where no one seriously believed that President Johnson would change his policy toward Castro. The administration, pushed by the pro-Vietnam military industrial machine, was plunging deeper and deeper into the war, and Cuba was becoming a thing of the past, forgotten.

To complicate the questions I faced, I received a letter from Colonel Bond informing me that I could remain at the agency for another year if I wished. The CIA had asked that both Ed Roderick and I remain in our assignments, and the Army was willing to leave the decision to us. The agency had already offered Rod a civil service position, beginning as a GS-12 or 13, which would be compatible with his military rank. It would be a fine opportunity, he thought, since he had no firm post-retirement plans.

The brief glimmers of encouragement came and went, and with each of them, my disillusionment and bitterness grew. The fact that the administration was turning its back on the Cuban question and breaking the American commitment to the exiles was intolerable to me, and the way in which it was being done was even more disgusting. By maintaining the CIA structure in skeleton form in Miami and showing tacit but unproductive support for Artime, the administration could claim that it had helped the exiles. In this peculiar exercise of political morality and logic, Johnson could claim no compromise on the Castro issue. As men and machines were poured into Southeast Asia, the CIA in Miami maintained a structure for little purpose other than to provide the administration with an answer for the critics and a positive image for historians. I saw it as the ultimate form of political expediency.

Others, especially in the agency, saw it too. But, no one said anything and no one seemed willing to endanger career or image by exposing the fraud and publicly arguing against the administration's policy. I saw that if I stayed with the CIA, I'd be part of the destruction of what I'd helped to build. Could I stand idly by and see my country's investment disappear and, with it, the faith and hope of the Cuban freedom fighters? Could I now contribute to the betrayal of the exiles? Would I not find my hands soiled as I stood by executioners—my peers and supervisors—who did not possess the courage to object? Could I live with my conscience if I did? I wrestled with these questions simply as a man, confronting them with no other standard than my own morality, and my conscience answered no.

The affair with Maggy had gotten out of hand. I felt great sympathy for her. Abstractly, I saw us as two lonely, desperate souls, each with self-made problems, struggling to retain some sense of honor or dignity while confronted by almost overwhelming decisions. In view of this, I was not surprised when she hinted about working out some kind of "arrangement" and, together, remaining with the CIA after my resignation.

One night, as we talked, I experienced an almost overwhelming sense of entrapment. I had placed unquestioning trust in Maggy. Now it occurred to me that there could be another motive behind her efforts to persuade me to stay with the CIA. Maybe it wasn't love. Maybe it was just a clumsy CIA recruitment plot. Perhaps Maggy, in her dedication to the agency, was using my deep feelings for her and my sense of commitment to ensnare me for the agency. Maybe that's what our friendship had been about from the beginning, I thought. Nausea washed over me. Why would any other CIA venture be any different than this: the bodies in the barn, abandoned and expendable.

That was the end of our affair. The next morning I moved out of her apartment and went back to the emptiness of the Homestead safehouse. I never confronted her with my suspicions, but she must have known why I left. She telephoned a few times and told me how lonely she was and how she missed me. But the seeds of doubt about her true intentions had been planted, and I gave her no encouragement.

My experience with Maggy intensified my paranoia. Assuming that my suspicions about the underhanded recruitment effort were correct, and considering the doubts I had always harbored about the agency's sincerity in handling the Cuban freedom fighters, I began to wonder about the ends to which they might go to maintain control over a disenchanted employee. Assuming I rejected them after having the door opened so widely, would they take reprisals? What if they wouldn't let me resign? They had no rules except expediency. Suddenly, the idea of being framed for some criminal act or publicly dishonored and confined became a real fear. My suspicions eroded whatever loyalty I felt toward the agency.

I needed to stay busy doing something productive, and, with time on my hands, I got back to flight training at Tamiami Airport. More and more I realized I had to develop a marketable civilian skill if I were to seriously consider resigning my commission and employment with the CIA. Extended cross-country trips became a wonderful escape from the life I was leading on the ground.

But I was never very far from the reality of my involvement with the agency and JM/WAVE. One day, upon returning from a flight, I was met again by Greg Crossman. He got directly to the point and asked me to help Bosch put together another off-the-record rescue operation. I was very angry. I told him I wasn't about to get more people killed trying to go after agents that were already dead or being set up as decoys. Did he not understand that Castro's militia now probably had one of our radios, and all the codes and frequencies to monitor any operation we might undertake?

Finally, I told him to go back to headquarters and tell whomever was controlling things they should never have left exile teams in Cuba without support in the first place. I told him to get some other fool, as I had no death wish. Crossman took a deep breath and walked away. It was the last time I saw him.

I had recently been treated for malaria-like symptoms. Suddenly, the exertion of physical exercise, the intensity of concentration and planning until late in the night, the worry and loneliness, all combined to take their toll physically. I was struck by fever and nausea that made me so weak I couldn't leave the safehouse. I'd never been so sick before. I was barely able to move from my bed to the bathroom. For hours at a time, I hovered in a state of half-delirium, and at night I was plagued by incredible nightmares. Images of my wife and sons, the missions to Cuba, Eleana and the island hideaway moved together in my mind in a kaleidoscope of painful, bitter memories. I dreamed of returning to Cuba alone to destroy the refinery. I was in the grip of a mass of confused, black thoughts, and overwhelmed by fantasies of death.

I don't know how many hours I lay like that, only that when I awakened the illness had passed and it was daylight. The sun was shining. More than anything else, I felt as though my mind had been washed clean by some invisible force. I was left with one overriding compulsion. I picked up the phone and called Suzie. At that moment, I wanted nothing more than to go home.

If I truly were a professional soldier, I would have to stand and fight where I was needed and where my efforts would be truly meaningful. As long as I was alive, I could stand as a persistent reminder to my country, the military, and the CIA of the betrayal of the exile cause.

CHAPTER 16

Sitting at my desk in the training branch, I was well into composing my letter of resignation when Ernie wanted to see me. Fully realizing my behavior had been pretty erratic over the last couple of months, I'd anticipated an ass chewing or worse. When I entered his office, Ernie stood up, came around his desk and closed the door behind me.

OK, here it comes, I thought, heart pounding, preparing for Sitting Bull's moody unpredictability. As he sat down, he was smiling, almost slyly.

"Brad, I've finally got some good news for you. We've been instructed to set up a small boat surf-landing program for the intelligence infil teams. Seems though there've been some losses when we've tried to put people ashore on the more exposed areas of Cuban beaches. Ted wants us to find some places on the Florida coast where we can train the exiles in techniques that will get them safely landed through breaking waves."

I was dismayed that everything else was being shut down and now this, out of nowhere. Was Ernie telling me this just to prop up my spirits? What he said seemed to contradict everything else that I'd observed going on at the station. Encouraged, I asked him what he wanted me to do.

"Ted is of the opinion that security would be a major headache if we tried to set up something on the Florida Atlantic coast. There are really no safe areas between here and Daytona Beach where we might find desirable surf conditions. We do have some secure arrangements up in northwest Florida around Panama City and Fort Walton Beach, mainly near Eglin. We've got somebody up there to manage things. I think you may have met Karl, who's primarily a weapons man. We'd like to have you look over the area with him and come back with a feasibility estimate. The idea, if there's enough good, breaking surf often enough, is to fly teams up there for a week or so of training. We can securely base them at Eglin."

My thoughts were racing as he spoke. Was this some indication that the secret war would regain momentum? Something about it didn't sit well with me, but I couldn't get a fix on it. There was something about Ernie's manner that made me uneasy. Very fresh in my mind were the extraordinary experiences of recent weeks and my own confused personal situation. Opting for the positive, I agreed to do the reconnaissance and turn in the report on my return.

Two days later, early in the morning, I boarded a C-54 parked well off the flight line at Homestead Air Force Base. I'd done this many times before as we flew to Eglin for my regular quarterly parachute jumps. This time, we'd land at Tyndall Air Force Base to meet Karl and take a chopper to reconnoiter possible surf training sites on the Gulf Coast between Panama City and Pensacola. I knew the pilots, both of whom seemed to be nursing severe hangovers, and they even let me sit in the right-hand seat once we got to altitude.

The flight was uneventful. The Florida autumn weather was perfect—a few high, wispy clouds against the blue above, visibility unlimited except for the usual whitish haze that hung over the beaches and the Gulf horizon. The ocean was a rich azure, the winds almost calm—in all respects, a gorgeous semi-tropical fall day.

Karl was waiting for me in flight operations when we landed at Tyndall. It had been more than a year since I'd seen him. He had changed little, he seemed older, but still wiry, soft-spoken with his distinctive European accent and piercing eyes. He shook my hand. Since I was wearing work clothes, I was surprised to find him in a dark suit, white shirt, and tie. I chided him about his dress; he replied with something about having to meet someone later.

Karl seemed to know exactly what we were about to do as we briefly talked and looked at the map before boarding a black, unmarked H-34 helicopter. Once aboard, we put on flight helmets with earphones so we could converse during the flight and talk with the pilots. The pilots had already been briefed on our interests and after take-off we flew to a point just west of Panama City Beach and then along the white sand beaches of northwest Florida at about 300 feet toward Fort Walton Beach. As we flew, Karl and I spoke and circled possible training sites on the maps I had brought along. The large cargo/passenger compartment door of the chopper remained open. Although we were not wearing parachutes, the crew chief had buckled us into leashed safety harnesses when we boarded so we could access the door and scan the coastline below.

Everything went smoothly until we got to a point off Santa Rosa Island just west of Fort Walton Beach and Eglin Field 9. Suddenly, with no direction from me, the chopper made an abrupt turn to the north and began climbing steeply. I looked at Karl and he seemed impassive. The crew chief, who had never removed his helmet and tinted face shield, remained in his seat opposite the door. I was startled by the unscheduled maneuver, anticipating some sort of emergency had occurred requiring a deviation from our flight plan.

We flew north for possibly five minutes, continuing to climb over the uninhabited wilderness expanse of the Eglin reservation. When I tried to activate my headset mouthpiece, I found it dead. Instead, over my earphones I heard the Beatles song, "Yesterday." What the hell was going on? Our plan for the day had not called for anything like this.

We were pulling a few Gs as the aircraft continued to climb. I gestured to the crew chief and Karl. They ignored me as they motioned to one another over the din of the slapping rotors. Suddenly, the chopper began hovering. I estimated the altitude at about 2,000 feet based on my experience as a parachutist—a typical jump altitude being 1,500 feet. I recognized the terrain below as a bombing range close to Field 11, not far from my old headquarters at the Ranger Camp.

I was frozen in fear and bewilderment as the crew chief unzipped the upper part of his flight suit and began to withdraw a pistol. With that, Karl unbuckled his safety harness and partially stood upright. He took off his suit coat and threw it on the web seat. Then he laid down on the floor of the aircraft in a fetal position, next to the open door. I watched in abject horror as Karl rolled himself out of the hovering chopper. He never looked at me, nor were there any words.

I watched him fall. As he exited the aircraft, he assumed freefall, as in skydiving, a stable body position, spread-eagled, facing the earth below. The helicopter immediately cut power as Karl fell, and in autorotation, began a rapid vertical descent, following the plunging figure. I watched him all the way to the impact with the earth below, face down, holding the spread eagle posture, the white shirt, fluttering neck tie, the gray trousers and expensive penny loafers—the image of the falling body branded in my mind forever.

The descending helicopter stabilized at about 300 feet directly over Karl's inert body. Suddenly, the music stopped. My headset crackled to life. The pilot dryly announced something to the effect we've just lost a crewmember and would be returning to base immediately. Karl's body lay in a small clearing surrounded by slash pine, scrub oak, and palmetto. As we pulled away from the scene and began to climb, I saw three people emerge from the woods and move toward Karl's body.

I began reciting the Act of Contrition, resigned to being the next one to go. I also resolved that the crew chief would have a fight on his hands when it came my turn. For whatever reason, it was not to be my day. I cannot describe my emotional state as the aircraft flew to Field 9 at Eglin instead of returning to Tyndall. I kept a keen eye on the crew chief until we landed. As I left the chopper on the tarmac near flight operations, I saw the Air Force C-54 I'd flown in that morning parked a short distance away. The crew chief of my chopper had remained in his seat, impassive and silent during the brief flight to Field 9, and he disappeared into flight operations very quickly after we were on the ground.

From the time we boarded the H-34 that morning until I walked away from the aircraft that afternoon, I never laid eyes on the pilots' faces. They remained in the chopper after we landed.

I went to look for the pilots of the C-54 that I expected to take me back to Miami. A man in civilian clothes met me at the chain link gate in front of the operations building. I had never seen him before and he introduced himself and flashed his badge identifying himself as an Air Force accident investigator. He wanted to talk to me about what I had witnessed that day. We went into a small room near the pilot's lounge and I told him exactly what I'd observed.

When I was finished, he went to his briefcase and presented me with a prepared statement, essentially confirming that I had seen Karl, identified only as a contract employee of some petroleum research firm in Texas I had never heard of before. The statement simply said I had observed Karl fall from the helicopter in the course of a classified training reconnaissance mission.

Thoroughly overwhelmed and intimidated by what I'd witnessed, I signed the statement because, as worded, it was true. However, it completely ignored any suggestion of the circumstances by which the "fall" had taken place. I was warned not to discuss the incident with anyone, as it was a matter of formal investigation by the Air Force.

I was shaken to the core by the events of the day—terrorized. Karl's plunge to death was no accident. The entire event was orchestrated by whomever controlled Karl in the agency. He must have known his fate, and facing the threat of being shot, he accepted it. Why? Who was Karl, really? What had he done to invoke a death sentence? In all of my relatively brief experience with him I had observed him to be an extraordinarily effective covert operative.

These were my many thoughts as we flew back to south Florida. What in the good Lord's name was I involved in? Why was I made a party to Karl's death? It didn't take major mental exercise to understand the message. It came through loud and clear, and I would never again be the same.

The revulsion I began to feel for the CIA and all it represented was visceral. I sat alone in the Homestead safehouse for a couple of days when I got back to Miami, calling in as an excuse the need to write the report of my reconnaissance for surf training areas. There was no objection or question. How deep were Ernie Sparks and the training branch in all this? I dreaded having to go into the station another time.

In my heart of hearts, I simply wanted to go home to my wife and sons, for better or worse. I was a mess, totally bottomed out. The evening run didn't work. The glass was full.

I sat for hours staring at the typewriter in the silence of the safehouse. At

Karl was a weapons expert and logistics planner. Soon after witnessing his mysterious death, I resigned from the CIA and Army.

times, I was overwhelmed by paranoia, expecting a car with a CIA hit man to pull into the driveway at any moment. Sleep was fitful; I kept all the lights in the house on and slept with my pistol on the nightstand beside my bed.

Who could I trust? Obviously there was a purpose in sending me on the reconnaissance trip, and it wasn't to find surf-training sites. Ernie must have known what it was all about, but how high did it go at the station? Karl had been involved with the upper echelon at JM/WAVE, so logically Ted Shackley and Gordon Campbell as well as Morales had to know what would take place.

And why allow me to witness it—I kept coming back to that question—it could only be to intimidate me, to show me what could happen if I persisted in voicing my discontent and objection to the agency's stance on Cuba and the abandonment of the exiles in the effort to overthrow Castro.

Then these chilling thoughts struck me and produced immediate nausea as I pondered Karl's bizarre death. The alleged Air Force investigator at Field 9 said an official investigation would take place. The only other witness to the events in the helicopter was the crew chief and he disappeared immediately after we landed. I had never really even seen his face—he had never removed his flight helmet and tinted face protector. The pilots, if they were identified, could testify they only became aware of Karl's "fall" after he had left the aircraft, and then they had followed standard emergency procedures by reporting it and flying to the closest airfield. During the entire flight, I never got a good look at them, only glimpses of their helmeted heads throughout the small deck windows.

These realities hit me with sledgehammer impact. What if an investigation pointed to me as causing Karl's plunge from the chopper and his death? It would only take the testimony of someone claiming to have been the crew chief to point the finger at me; the pilots could report all they observed and heard was some commotion in the passenger/cargo compartment in the moments before Karl left the aircraft. My God, it was the perfect setup, and the threat of prosecution could be held over my head by the CIA for as long as I had any connection with

BRADLEY E. AYERS

it. Furthermore, as an active duty Army officer I could be prosecuted under the Uniform Code of Military Justice no matter if I resigned or remained on active duty. There were no statute of limitations for murder or wrongful death under military law. Conceivably, the agency had me exactly where they wanted me, the ultimate means of control.

This was sheer insanity. I looked and felt like hell. I knew I had to get a grip on myself. I hadn't slept, eaten, shaved, or showered since returning from Eglin. An empty bottle of rum on the kitchen counter pretty well accounted for any nourishment I had taken over the past few days. Do something, I told myself over and over again, but what? I took a long run on one of the Everglades back roads, puked my guts out halfway through, went back to the house and got myself cleaned up.

Then I called Maggy at the station. I told her I needed to see Ted as soon as possible. She began asking me questions, both personal and about my situation in general. Had I made a decision about the future, she wanted to know. I deflected her inquiries as politely as I could. "That's what I want to see Ted about." She called back as I was packing my personal belongings and told me I could see Ted in the morning. I was jumping the chain of command, but I didn't trust Ernie.

I made a pot of strong, black coffee, poured a cup and went to the typewriter. I spent the evening preparing a report detailing exactly what had transpired on the trip to northwest Florida and on the Eglin reservation. I tried to document every detail, overcoming the panic I still felt inside, wording the document in the most formal, objective style I could produce. As a further demonstration of what I hoped would reflect a certain professional detachment, I included written descriptions of the surf-training areas we'd viewed to supplement the maps that would go with my report. I wanted to walk into Ted's office and present myself in a way that would not betray my true feelings. I wasn't about to let him, or for that matter anyone at the station or anywhere else, see me sweat.

Ted Shackley saw me almost immediately after I arrived at his office the next morning. He seemed harried and impatient, but he punched his intercom button and told Maggy to hold his calls. I handed him the report and he quickly glanced over it.

"Yes, I heard about Karl. Hell of a situation. He was a good man. Too bad; it's under investigation, of course."

He made no mention of my description of events or the actions of the crew chief in my report. Instead, he asked how I was doing. I was honest and direct with him. I told him I felt I was swimming upstream, fighting the current policy at the station and maybe had burnt myself out. Maybe it was time to leave. I missed my family and I missed the Army. I explained I was considering my options.

"Let me know what you decide. As you know, there are some career opportunities with the company, and you've established a pretty good foundation with us."

I started talking about the futile rescue mission, but he cut me off after a few words. "Yes, we know, we're looking into it."

I then went back to Karl's death, hoping to smoke out something about the circumstances, but then Ted left me hanging with the reply. "These things take time and the Air Force is involved; right now it looks like a terrible accident. If there's a finding, I'll let you know. By the way, thanks for your surf training report."

THE ZENITH SECRET

With that, Ted got up and showed me to the door. I left totally frustrated and more confused than ever. I was getting mixed messages—or I was reading it all wrong. Stay with the agency knowing what might hang over my head, or return to the Army and a career that could blow up in my face with charges at any moment. What kind of future would this be?

It was now, more than ever, apparent to me the only way I might regain some control over my destiny would be to leave it all behind and make a fresh start as a civilian, for better or worse.

CHAPTER 17

The Homestead safehouse with its scent of blooming oleander had, in many ways, become an emotional torture chamber for me. After I met with Ted and firmly decided on a course of action, I went down the hall to the real estate branch and told them I was moving out. Cover was relieved because my living there was not an economical use of the property—it was a big house, the rent, utilities, and maintenance were high, and JM/WAVE funding was being cut.

I met with Ernie and told him I intended to resign and try to make it as a civilian. I didn't mention Karl's death to him and he didn't bring it up. It was as if the incident never happened. I had grown to mistrust Ernie and tried to avoid him as I concluded my duties at the station. Don Cabeza, my principal instructor at Pirates' Lair, took over as chief of maritime training, not a surprising move as he and Ernie had become very buddy-buddy on and off duty.

When I had things pretty well wrapped up, I researched the regulations for the forms and procedures for resignation from the Regular Army. It turned out to be quite simple. Again, sitting at my desk in the familiar surroundings in the training branch, I resumed work on my letter of resignation. In main, it read:

NOVEMBER 20, 1964
MEMORANDUM FOR: WHOM IT MAY CONCERN
SUBJECT: RESIGNATION OF REGULAR ARMY COMMISSION

It is difficult for me to give up a career to which I have devoted a critical decade of my life. My principles as an officer in the United States Army were founded on high ideals of patriotism, public service, and dedication to the defense of our way of life. This makes my decision to leave an emotional as well as an intellectual one.

When I enlisted as a private, I placed complete trust in my country and was convinced of its fundamental infallibility. Now, 11 years later, I find myself totally disillusioned. My goal was not only the defense of our way of life, but to fight for the freedom of those enslaved people whom my country could assist and free. As time progressed and I received broader exposure to the military establishment, I saw, again and again, personal ambition and selfish considerations take precedence over attainment of what I thought was a mutual goal.

Concurrently, because of certain actions taken by my country, I began to question the nature of its goals. I saw my country ignore enslaved peoples in our own hemisphere and pay political and diplomatic lip service, for political advantage. In other areas of the world, this situation was resulting in the loss of American lives.

The country that epitomizes freedom and democracy, and is looked upon as the leader of the free world has turned its back on enslaved peoples less than 90 miles from its shores, as well as other places around the world.

With this reality in my mind and heart, I am submitting my resignation as a Regular Army officer. I remain prepared to serve my country and, if necessary, make the ultimate sacrifice as a soldier, if I am convinced of the sincerity of the task.

THE ZENITH SECRET

Respectfully,
Bradley E. Ayers

BRADLEY E. AYERS
CAPTAIN INFANTRY
UNITED STATES ARMY

The letter was completed and the necessary forms prepared and forwarded to headquarters. What I thought I could never do, I had done. As the fall days dragged by I waited for my orders, fully expecting some hitch would arise because of Karl's death.

Ernie talked to me once more about working for the CIA. Ted Shackley gave me a security debriefing, a profound thank you for my work, and a wish for good luck.

Maggy was out of the office when I went to see Ted. I was relieved I'd not have to say goodbye to her. I was so conflicted. Maggy somehow represented the emotions I was struggling with, and would continue struggling with for years to come: guilt in abandoning what I once so deeply believed in and unselfishly embraced. She was with the CIA, had trusted me as a kindred spirit and allowed me to enter the idealistic inner sanctum of their philosophy and purpose. I had to face the fact I was rejecting their confidence and would leave a significant part of myself questioning my decision and privately regretting I was no longer one of them.

As I was leaving Shackley's office, he said something I've never been able to reconcile. "By the way, just to put your mind at ease; they concluded Karl's death was suicide and the investigation is finished."

The rest of the processing at the station was brief and routine. I was unable to find Rod to say goodbye to him. No one else said much to me as I prepared to leave, and there was no farewell party. But I believed, deep in my heart, that none of them would ever forget me, because they knew why I was leaving.

My orders finally came and overnight, I was back in Washington for the final time as a commissioned officer. I was debriefed by the CIA and said goodbye to the few agency people I knew who worked in headquarters. I surrendered my cover documentation and, in theory, wiped from my mind all that had happened in the preceding two years with the agency. The persona of Daniel B. Williams was placed in a file cabinet somewhere in a basement vault in Langley, Virginia.

Finally, I found myself in Colonel Bond's office for the last time. That's where it had all begun. I came in as I had the first time, in civilian clothes, and saluted him smartly even though I had no obligation to do so any longer. My letter of resignation rested on the walnut desk that separated us.

Bond took my letter and excused himself for a few minutes. When he returned, he was curt and direct. "Captain Ayers, you've made your point and it seems your mind is quite made up. You've been a good officer and we hate to lose people like you. On the other hand, you've got a lot of life ahead and a wonderful family to look after. General Rosson and I thank you for your service and wish you all the best."

As I stood to leave, he came around the desk and took my hand. "Captain, if you change your mind, call me at this number." He handed me a scrap of paper with a number scrawled on it.

BRADLEY E. AYERS

It was dark as I left the Pentagon and a soft, light snow was falling. It was over for me. I sat on a curb in the wet snow and cried like a baby. God help me; God help my country!

I returned to my wife and sons in Minnesota, hoping that a new life was beginning for us. But I was haunted by memories.

The Minnesota winter seemed to have no end. I found warmth nowhere, and the memories returned ever more frequently and with greater intensity. Also, my resignation had made me an outcast within my own family and in the town of my youth. Each day the flames of war in Vietnam grew brighter, and I was painfully conscious of the whispers of small town gossips. The question was why I, a career Army officer, sat on the sidelines while the war raged on in Southeast Asia. It was impossible for me to explain. No one would have understood even if I tried.

For nearly a year following my resignation, I struggled desperately to hold my marriage together and begin a new life as a civilian. I began writing again and sold a few articles to magazines, but it did not bring enough money. Then, using the remainder of our savings and a loan from a close relative, I bought a five-passenger airplane with plans to set up a small charter business. Flying was the only useful civilian skill I possessed, and I had great hopes for one day operating a fleet of small planes and owning my own commuter airline. But my wife refused to participate in the business. She considered it a foolhardy and financially unstable venture.

Eventually, the economic and family pressures following my resignation overburdened a marriage already strained by the events of the preceding three years. I didn't contest the divorce. I gave Suzie custody of our sons and willingly conveyed to her all material possessions except for a few personal belongings, with a profound sense of failure in having shattered the last and most important cornerstone of my life.

Empty and dishonored in the eyes of those closest to me, I could find no reason to remain in Minnesota. By getting way, I hoped to regain my moral and emotional strength. I steeled myself as best I could against the loneliness for my sons and, with a few personal belongings and my dog, flew off in my airplane.

It was inevitable, I guess, that less than 18 months after leaving I landed again in Miami. During the intervening time, my life had become so unhappy, my self-image so distasteful, that unconsciously I was searching for my other identity again. I wanted to return to Daniel B. Williams and finish the task I'd set out to accomplish.

Unfettered by military or government ties, I developed a simple plan of action within a few days after my arrival. I based my plane at the old Tamiami Airport, at Tanner Aviation, and rented a battered, old trailer that doubled as an office and living quarters. I took any flying job I could get, hiring out as a pilot or flight instructor. I let my hair and mustache grow to alter my appearance. I began efforts to reestablish contact with anti-Castro exile organizations to offer them whatever help I could.

Using my old alias, I returned to the familiar haunts in the Cuban settlement in Miami. I let it be known in Little Havana that I wanted to help. I discovered that in the time I'd been away from Miami, the exile movement had drifted into even greater disarray. As far as I could determine, the CIA had withdrawn virtually all support of exile paramilitary efforts, leaving behind deep resentment and distrust of all Americans. Most of the exile community had given up all hope of ever returning to Cuba and, with the aid and encouragement of the United States government and community welfare programs, had

Bradley E. Ayers (1965)
I returned to Florida to work with the Cuban exiles after my resignation from the CIA and the Army.

settled back to enjoy the amenities of life in America. There was no cohesive exile political organization, no positive effort to establish a government in exile, and no single exile leader capable of unifying the Cubans. Despite all indications that my efforts would prove futile, I decided to make whatever effort I could to fulfill the commitment I felt for the dying cause.

The United States government had further tightened its security ring around the militant exile groups operating in the United States. The FBI and the CIA had effectively penetrated all exile organizations to the extent that every plan and the identity of every person involved were communicated to the authorities. The policy of U.S. neutrality toward Cuba was further enforced by the continuous surveillance of the Gulf Coast and south Florida coastline by the Coast Guard and U.S. Customs and Immigration.

I knew the government would show no mercy for me if they caught me actively supporting and abetting the exiles. They could even charge me with using privileged security information to promote illegal action. In 1966, to be an American working with exiles in Miami after the CIA had pulled out was a very dicey business.[20]

Operating undercover (as Daniel B. Williams) and fearing I might be compromised and arrested, I could do little more than advise and encourage the exiles and continue to give them training in various paramilitary skills. Many could not understand why I volunteered my services. Many were suspicious, and for that reason my effectiveness as an instructor and adviser was severely limited. On the other hand, I was suspicious of many of the exiles and, more than ever, learned to look out for myself and keep my ears and eyes open.

The ultimate humiliation came when I was persuaded to meet again with Orlando Bosch's band of supposedly militant anti-Castro exiles. (Bosch was later jailed in Venezuela, charged with involvement in the 1976 bombing of a Cuban airliner that killed 73 people. He was released and came to the United States where President George H. W. Bush pardoned him in 1990.) I was blindfolded

BRADLEY E. AYERS

and driven to the rendezvous point, a dilapidated house somewhere in Miami. There, they offered me $10,000 to use my plane to drop a 500-pound bomb in the middle of Havana. Bosch, who had great political ambition but was given to extremism, would claim responsibility for the brave act against Castro. Their idea was crazy and symbolic of all that was wrong with the exile movement. I was sickened by it.

There was one person, I felt, who would be able to give me guidance before I found it necessary to abandon the cause completely. Breaking every commitment I had made to myself, I located Eleana and telephoned her. A man answered, and in a few moments I heard her familiar voice. I will never forget the conversation.

"Eleana, this is Dan...you remember...in 1963 on the island with the exiles...we worked together."

A pause, then an intake of breath. An instant racing back in time, then disbelief. "Is this some kind of joke?"

"What do you mean? It's me, Dan. I'm working in Miami now."

"Who is this?" she asked, her voice tense.

"My God, Eleana, this is Dan! Don't you know my voice? I have to talk with you."

"I don't know who you are," she said angrily, "but it is not funny. You have no right to call me like this. I am going to tell my husband. You are not Daniel Williams; he died in a plane crash two years ago. It was in the paper, the whole story. Danielito is dead. He is gone forever." She hung up.

I was dumfounded. Crushed.

Had the CIA gone to that extent to ensure my elimination? The agency, godlike, had created an identity, allowed an existence, manipulated, and exploited, and then, when no longer useful, terminated it. Expediency—I should have expected it. I was filling a dead man's shoes! It was a morbidly fascinating comparison to the corruption and death of the exile movement, and now I was living out the unfinished destiny of a dead man.

For days, I pored over old newspapers, seeking an account of a plane crash mentioning my name. I found nothing. Eleana must have been mistaken, or maybe the story had been published only in the Cuban papers, fed to them to solve the sudden disappearance of one Daniel B. Williams. Had he really existed and done all those things with the Cubans? I began to question my own sanity; I had to go back and prove it to myself. Almost frantically, I returned to the Keys. I found the training sites deserted. I walked once again through the mangroves and jungle, but there was no trace of our survival training shelters or the traps and snares we had built. A hurricane had swept the area since I'd been there. I went to the safehouses. Two had burned to the ground and now only the blackened foundations remained. There was no trace of our presence there.

Finally, I drove to Plantation Key to visit the three houses on stilts, the last safehouse complex where I might be able to confirm the reality of Daniel B. Williams. If any of our old sites could have withstood the ravages of the hurricane, it would have been this one. The grounds were deserted, and except for the windows being boarded over, the place looked the same. I tried the doors to each house, but they were locked. I walked down to the water's edge where we had kept the V-20 strike boats protected in a small basin dug into the coral. The pilings and the low dock gave no clue as to what we'd once used the basin for.

Pirates' Lair could only be reached by boat. I drove back to the Ocean Reef Resort on the northern tip of Key Largo, rented a boat and rowed to the Lair. The island seemed deserted. The stucco rambler fronting the docks on Angelfish

THE ZENITH SECRET

Creek was boarded up. I tied off my boat and walked up the path toward the large, turn-of-the-century mansion. Only the foundation remained. There were signs of a fire and other indications from the debris littering the area that a hurricane may have contributed to the destruction of the house.

Then I walked to the east, making my way along an overgrown pathway that led to the above ground concrete cisterns that once held fresh water for the island's residents. I remembered the conversation I had overheard while briefing Artime in Coral Gables a year earlier. I had deduced from what was said that a large sum of money, rumored to be $250,000, supposedly 50 percent of the reward money for the assassination of Fidel Castro, might have been cached either at Pirates' Lair or beneath Rosselli's safehouses at Point Mary. My rather superficial search of the ruins at Point Mary had been fruitless. But I knew we once used the empty bunker-like cisterns on the island for concealing weapons and explosives.

I had no real expectation of finding the money after all the time that had passed, but I was curious to see if there was any sign that something had been hidden there or in the immediate vicinity of the cisterns. I found them heavily overgrown with vines and other tangled vegetation. The very heavy cement lids were in place, and I knew I couldn't move them. The inability to inspect the cisterns made the "legend" of the money even more tantalizing. [21]

Discouraged, I sat down on a coral outcropping to look across the gray, glassy sea before me, pondering what forces had brought me back to Pirates' Lair. It was surreal.

I don't know how long I sat there, but I was startled by the sound of a door slamming. I turned and caught my breath as I saw a man followed by a large German shepherd coming down the path from the stucco house. They walked toward me. It was as if they had emerged from nowhere.

As they drew closer I recognized the man. It was Dick, the old seaman-engineer who had been the caretaker at Pirates' Lair. My pulse quickened. Though I hadn't seen him in more than two years, he'd surely remember me. He had worked for me as a contract agent. I had done favors for him, arranged for his pay, made out his efficiency reports, listened to his complaints, and even covered for his monthly three-day binges when he couldn't make it to work. He and the dog were approaching but hadn't noticed me yet. I stood up, not wanting to surprise them. Smiling, I extended my hand.

"Dick, for Christ's sake, what are you doing here? It's just great to see you again."

He didn't answer. There was no expression; his face was set. He kept walking, the dog at his heels. My throat felt dry. He stopped a few feet from me, staring blankly.

"Dick, it's me, Dan Williams...you remember..."

His face was expressionless, and he seemed to look through me as if I were transparent.

"I've never seen you before in my life."

At that moment, I understood that Daniel Williams and the world in which he had existed had vanished forever. I turned and walked slowly to my boat. Dick, the dog by his side, stood with his back to me, facing the sea and Cuba. As if, in Dick's mind, the slate had been rubbed clean.

At that moment I accepted the fact that Daniel B. Williams was no more.

CHAPTER 18

The encounter with Dick at Pirates' Lair was a soul-wrenching reality check. I resolved not to discuss my JM/WAVE experience with anyone. My immediate family already knew more than they needed to know. I learned early on in life that I coped best with adversity and downturns by staying very busy. So, with this as my philosophy, I threw myself into developing my air charter business. Although I didn't recognize it at the time, full time concentration on business was excellent self-therapy.[22]

I was only casually aware of the Warren Commission's investigation of the president's murder and suggestions of conspiracy raised by independent sources. I knew, of course, the official line: Oswald, acted alone. But I couldn't completely discount what had been the prevailing unofficial word, at JM/WAVE, that Castro was responsible for the death of the president. And, there were lingering thoughts about the rumors I'd heard in Miami, in the Cuban community. Some rumors asserted that U.S. political right-wingers in collaboration with militant exiles had conspired to publicly execute Kennedy.

But I had little time to ponder the principal questions of the crime; who had the motive, method, and opportunity? If there was a conspiracy, who had the power and far-reaching influence to control and manipulate all the different agencies of our government to effect a cover up? What I did know as fact, from my own experience, was the secret war against Cuba effectively ended with the death of the president and America plunged into the war in Vietnam.

Having put my involvement with the exile freedom fighters aside for good, and after hiring out as a pilot on other flying jobs, I established a business plan that involved moving my aircraft seasonally between bases in Minnesota and Florida, this to capitalize on the upscale tourist-sportsman clientele who regularly chartered general aviation aircraft to fly to and from out-of-the-way locations not served by the airlines. A revenue back-up was the air cargo trade.[23]

When winter came, I moved the aircraft to Florida, with a base at Tamiami Airport south of Miami. I was one of the few Florida air taxi operators that flew a single engine over water for extended distances, and that gave me a real price advantage over those who only flew multi-engine planes to the islands.

I always felt a mix of emotions and a certain uneasiness on flights that took me near Cuba. Ever reluctant to file a flight plan to overfly the island (I had no doubt Castro would have loved to get his hands on me), I typically skirted Cuba at or above 12,000 feet, remaining over international waters, even if it took me well out of the way to reach my destination. At altitude, I'd look down on the island, appearing so benign, and ponder the turmoil and how its people and politics had influenced the course of recent history and my life, personally. All the while, of course, I kept my eyes peeled, watching for any of Castro's jets scrambling to intercept me.

Never, during this time, in spite of all the fascinating and unusual people I encountered, the places and unique situations I found myself in, did I breathe a word of my secret war background. Whenever Cuba or the CIA came up, I'd remain silent, deflect, or try to change the subject. I was determined not to resurrect Daniel B. Williams.

I decided to look for a permanent base of operations in Florida where the weather was suitable for year-round flying, even though I knew it would mean more separation from my sons.

Occasionally, charter flights out of south Florida took me to the northwest panhandle of the state, an area I was quite familiar with because of my military and CIA activities at Eglin Air Force Base. The area was growing rapidly, and a new airport had been constructed near Destin, a once quiet but now popular fishing village adjacent to the pristine white sand beaches of the Gulf Coast that stretched from Panama City west to Pensacola. Sport fishing and a thriving seafood industry provided an economic base for the community, and a recent booming vacation and retirement development promised all sorts of business opportunities, including an air taxi service at the new airport.

I was a certified flight and ground instructor, and there seemed to be a great interest in general aviation and learning to fly, especially among the military personnel stationed at Eglin. The potential for a flight school at Destin seemed obvious to me.

On my next flight from Miami to Pensacola, I dropped in at Destin to talk with the fixed base operator, the man who had the Okaloosa County franchise to control activities at the airport. Glois Brand was an older, southern Alabama gentleman, rural in manner and well known in the Southeast as an experienced Gulf Coast, backwoods pilot. He was fully rated for almost anything that flew and was reputed to be a savvy businessman.

Brand was slow and deliberate, and my rather aggressive, youthful enthusiasm for the flying business probably appeared to be that of an upstart.

After several meetings, Brand and I agreed on a joint venture that would allow me to base my charter operation at Destin and start a ground school. I'd be required to share a percentage of my revenue with Brand, and he'd pay me for any flight instruction I'd give when not flying charters. It seemed like a workable deal, and within weeks, I established my base of operations at Destin. I rented an off-airport building for the ground school with an adjoining small office and apartment where I could live.

The sleepy little fishing village, with its vista of the Gulf and fleet of sport fishing vessels, shrimp boats, oyster and lobster skiffs—all of which could be taken in from my apartment—was a welcome contrast to the frantic urbanity of Miami, and I quickly settled into a relatively peaceful routine. The town had several quaint, but excellent seafood restaurants, with simple, nautical motifs that were an unpretentious reflection of the culture of the area. I felt I might have finally found my niche. I wrote to my sons, telling them all about my new home.

When not flying or instructing, I pretty much kept to myself, and I scrupulously avoided sharing anything more than superficialities with anyone. I tried to project the image of a confident, enthusiastic entrepreneur, an asset to the growing community. Watching the sun set over the Gulf was a moving experience, and whenever I could, I'd do calisthenics and run on the beach.

As the sun began to slip below the seascape horizon, with dusk quieting the breaking waves, I would think of my sons, the past, that I was alone, and ask the Almighty and myself, why in the hell was I there?

I was about to find out.

CHAPTER 19

Late one afternoon, while running on the Destin beach, I neared a circle of figures sitting around a small fire. As I ran past, a woman jumped up and came towards me. She and her children had come to the beach to swim and picnic. She had attached the car keys to her swim suit and lost them somewhere in the surf. The family had no way home. They were overjoyed when, after 20 minutes of searching, I found the keys. Lee introduced herself and each of her children. Her husband was an Air Force C-123 pilot serving in Vietnam.

That's how I met Lee, a woman who would share with me a series of choices and developments that profoundly affected the course of our lives.

In the days that followed, I encountered Lee, sometimes with her kids, in and about town. There was a smiling greeting, but no conversation.

When I had no charters scheduled for, a weekend, I'd put up a sign on the main road running past the airport, advertising air rides over Destin and the scenic Gulf coast. One bright Sunday, Lee and her children drove up for an air tour. Lee said she always wanted to learn to fly, and I gave her my practiced pitch about my ground school and flight instruction. Lee was intelligent and classy, yet down to earth, easy to talk with, and still very much the lady in the southern tradition. Her kids were sweet, and in many ways Lee and the children reminded me, painfully, of the family I once had.

While I was very conscious and deferential to her marital status, Lee rather suddenly became an exceptional presence in my otherwise solitary existence.

Some days later, I was running my usual late afternoon route on the beach when I saw Lee on a blanket, sunning and reading. I waved to her as I went by and she waved in return. After thinking it over, I slowed on my way back, and approached her to say hi. She put down the paperback she was reading and we made small talk for a few minutes.

"Have you read this?" she asked, handing me the recently published *Warren Commission Report.* "This is not worth the paper it's written on, and I don't think the American people are going to swallow it. There's more to the murder of the president than Oswald. You ought to read it."

I was a bit taken off guard as Lee continued.

"You've been in government, in the military; you've been around. I'm an Air Force wife, and I've been close to it, too. I'm reading the report for the second time, and when I'm finished, I'll give it to you. Read it and tell me what you think." She seemed quite serious.

Several days later, I found the book waiting for me at the airport office I shared with Brand. Lee had placed it in an envelope and asked him to give it to me. With the time I had to read, it took the better part of a week to plow through the convoluted, confusing document with all its appendices and exhibits.

I discovered the *Warren Report* raised more questions about the president's death than it sought to answer. There was no reference to the CIA's secret war against Cuba, the Castro assassination efforts, and the alliance the agency apparently had with the Mafia (e.g. Rosselli). How could this blue ribbon panel, investigating what might be the crime of the century, have missed, or ignored this extraordinary activity and its political and criminal implications? Of equal import was why? Was the ignorance deliberate?

I was hypersensitive about my CIA connection. Karl's strange death, his resemblance to Oswald, the rumors of CIA involvement in the president's murder, and the virulent anti-Kennedy talk around JM/WAVE all lurked in the back of my mind. Did Lee know something I didn't? Was she who she said she was? Or was she on a fishing expedition with me?

Lee described growing up in southern Louisiana, in the bayou country. She still had family there and had done some TV work in New Orleans. She said, in relation to Oswald's alleged involvement with exile groups in "the Big Easy," that it was common knowledge the CIA had Cuban exile training bases around Lake Pontchartrain ever since the Bay of Pigs. I just listened. She observed the investigation by New Orleans DA Jim Garrison was just getting underway and that politics in Louisiana were totally corrupted by mob influences and the big petroleum interests.[24] She asserted her belief that Oswald, alone, was not responsible for the murder of the president.

Up to this point I had never discussed the JFK assassination with anyone other than my immediate family. I was uneasy. I told Lee I was trying to keep an open mind on the subject, hoping Bobby Kennedy, as the attorney general, would eventually pursue the truth about his brother's death. I avoided any hint of having met RFK in Miami while with JM/WAVE.

Lee told me she and the children were leaving for her parents' home in Louisiana in the next few days to meet her husband who was returning from Vietnam unexpectedly. He had been promoted to major and would be taking a new assignment. My encounters with Lee and her children had been refreshing and stimulating. She and I had become friends, and I hated to see her leave Destin.

She stopped by my office to say goodbye as she and the children left town. I felt a deep sadness as I watched them drive away.

My conversations with Lee about the assassination moved me to take greater interest in the matter. I began watching TV and reading the news regularly as the Garrison Investigation and other inquiries developed. There seemed to be an undercurrent of public skepticism about the Warren Commission's conclusions and other aspects of the report. Several private researchers with excellent credentials were writing books challenging the official position on the president's death and the efficacy of the Warren Report. The possibility of a conspiracy was put forth, and reports by many foreign news sources fueled the theory. I took it all in, keeping an open mind and trying to correlate what I knew about the Kennedy administration's secret war against Cuba, the Castro assassination effort, and the presence of the Mafia's Rosselli at the Miami station.

I had no time, or inclination, to do any research beyond what came my way via the media. I was content with the fervent belief that Bobby Kennedy would bring to bear all the resources of the Justice Department to resolve any controversy surrounding his brother's murder.

Furthermore, I had more immediate concerns. My arrangement with Brand at the Destin Airport had been slowly deteriorating. When he saw me making money, he demanded a larger cut. He stopped selling me fuel for my charters at a discount and began assigning students to a new flight instructor. My ground school enrollments were down, and suddenly Brand announced he was starting his own ground school program at the airport.

At first, I responded in stunned disbelief. The old buzzard had snookered, me. I was sickened by the reality that I'd either have to acquiesce to Brand's greedy exploitation or pull out. I was already stretched to the breaking point and the prospect of another move was quite troubling.

As she was leaving for Louisiana, Lee had asked me to keep watch on her beach house and her personal property stored nearby until plans for the family's next move were confirmed. She gave me the address at her parents' home so I could contact her in the event of some emergency. I wrote several times assuring all was well in Destin, and briefly updated her on the rather mundane developments in my situation without mention of the conflicts I was having with Glois Brand at the airport.

Lee responded with nice little flowery notes, and finally a lengthy letter explaining her husband had been reassigned to an Air Force squadron in Germany and that she and the children would be accompanying him. It was all part of the accepted military lifestyle. Lee said she'd be returning to Destin to pack and supervise the moving of the family's personal property for shipment to Wiesbaden. She was gone for nearly a month.

I was pleasantly surprised when, one day, she came to my ground school office on Destin's main thoroughfare. She appeared somewhat distressed and explained she was on her way to the beach house to begin packing for the move to Germany. Her children had remained with their father to avoid complicating the packing and moving. Lee suggested we meet for dinner that night at one of the local restaurants. I could tell something was wrong.

That evening, she seemed more composed and looked quite lovely. We talked about generalities initially, and I felt comfortable enough to tell her of my festering problems with Brand at the flight school, and that I might be leaving Destin, probably to return to Miami where I still had some viable business contacts. It was the dead of winter in Minnesota, so there was no good business reason to return there.

Wishing to put our conversation on a more positive subject, I began to enthusiastically describe all the benefits of an extended assignment in Europe. That's when she dropped a bomb on me. Lee explained that she and her husband had not been getting along before he went to Vietnam, and she had begged him not to volunteer for a second tour. Now, his second tour had suddenly been cut short, for reasons she didn't understand—possibly because of combat stress. Despite the fact that they'd been married for nearly 10 years and had beautiful children, they were now like strangers to one another.

Lee said her husband had returned from Vietnam profoundly changed. He was drinking heavily and had physically abused her several times. She was frightened of him and didn't want to accompany him to Germany. But, putting her own feelings aside, she was going because of the children and her desire to keep the family together. As she began to cry, I struggled for words, but there was nothing I could say though I had great sympathy for her. All the pain associated with my own marital difficulties came rushing back. My head was filled with colliding, conflicting thoughts.

We sat in flickering candlelight in a shadowed corner of the old nautically decorated supper club. I reached across the table and took Lee's hands. "I feel terrible for you. I know the hurt involved in trying to keep a marriage together. The welfare of the kids has to come first. I had to face that reality when my marriage came apart. There isn't a day that goes by that I don't anguish over being separated from my sons. So I know what you're struggling with, although if something happened, you're the mother and undoubtedly the kids would remain with you. But the whole thing is just hell. Is there any way you can patch it up, go to counseling?"

THE ZENITH SECRET

She leaned across the table and kissed me. "I'll be alright. Let's take a walk on the beach."

There was no moon, only starlight and the gentle sounds of waves as they washed the shore. We walked barefoot in the still-warm sand at water's edge, arm in arm, carrying our shoes and a half-empty bottle of wine I'd taken from the restaurant.

"How long are you going to be in Destin?" Lee was the first person I really felt close to since leaving the CIA and active duty. I didn't want her to leave, but it would be wrong for me to try to influence her decision. Her marriage and motherhood were far more important than my feelings.

"My husband has the kids with him at his parents' home in Illinois. They're visiting there until we fly overseas out of Chicago. I've got about ten days to get things done here and meet them at O'Hare."

My mind was racing. There was something very special about the rapport we shared. I had so much bottled up inside, it was choking me. My conversations with her had stirred so many thoughts. I was attracted to her, and wanted to confide in her, to bare my soul. I wanted her to know me fully before we parted.

"I don't know what the future holds for either of us, but for some reason, I feel a need to talk to you about my past. In some ways it concerns what we've discussed about the president's assassination. My life is kind of a mess, pretty precarious in many ways, and there are some things that are bothering me deeply and may be important. We think alike, and no matter what happens between us, you're the one person I know and trust who could understand and maybe communicate what I have to the right people."

She pulled closer. "Brad, you're frightening me."

We walked in silence for a few minutes and decided to sit for a while in the dunes and sea grass facing the sea and drink what was left of our wine.

After passing the bottle, I spoke. "As you know, my situation here is pretty unstable. I'd love to see my boys, but it's winter in Minnesota and little or no flying. I need to fly back to Miami to see if I can reestablish myself at Tamiami at least until spring. Why don't you fly down with me for a couple of days, get away from all the turmoil for a bit before you leave; and I'll show you around south Florida. The break will do you good. If I help you with the packing it can be done in a couple of days and you'll have some time to yourself to think things over.

And, the trip will give us a chance to talk."

"I'll think about it. Right now, I've got to get our things moved. I'm so mixed up about the future."

With that she began to sob and I put my arms around her. I hadn't been with a woman in more than a year, and the intimacy of the moment was overwhelming. I kissed her. This time it was not a kiss of friendship but one of intense passion. Lee responded.

Her beach house was not far away, and holding each other, we stumbled our way in the darkness across the dunes, the surf crashing behind us a fitting accompaniment for our raging emotions. The electric power had been cut off in the vacated house. Lee lit candles. She led me into the bedroom. There were no words as we undressed and made love.

Sleep was fitful. Lee got up and brewed some coffee over a Sterno can. She brought me a cup and sat on the edge of the bed.

"I'll go with you to Miami and fly to Chicago from there."

I had no flights scheduled. The charter business had dropped off and Brand, the airport operator, may have been stealing my trips. We got Lee's packing done in two days, and the van came on the third to pick up the load.

Everything went quite smoothly, unusual for the typical military move, but then, this was the Air Force with its rule of "zero defects." Lee and I remained together, trying to keep the mood light with music and wine, as we went about the tedium of packing and cleaning the beach house. We were together at night, in my cramped apartment, wordless in love.

Folks in Miami were more discreet and less inquisitive than those in rural areas, and there were no probing questions when I fueled and parked the airplane. I'd wait until later to talk with Tanner Aviation about moving my operation from Destin to Tamiami Airport and basing my business there. I had based my operation there a year earlier and had a good relationship with the management. Lee and the few days we had left to be together were the focus of my attention. We got a cab to a motel on Bird Road, not far from the airport. Bustling, ethnically diverse Miami was quite a contrast from the social atmosphere and pace of life in Destin.

I had promised Lee I'd get her mind off her trip to Germany. So after dinner, we went to the Mi Rinconcito to enjoy some authentic Cuban music. The little club was just as I remembered it. We danced and drank our rum and tonics. The past came down hard on me. I was falling in love with Lee, and I wanted her to know me for everything I was and everything I was not.

"Lee, tomorrow I want to show you around south Florida and the Keys. I want to take you to some places and talk about experiences I had there when I was on active duty. What went down drastically affected many lives and I can't shake it. And I think it may be important to what's happened in our country, the assassination and all. I can tell you there are very few Americans who are aware of what you'll see and hear. You're the only person with whom I've shared this. Things happened here that I think need to be revealed. If something should happen to me, maybe you can pass it on to the right people."

She reached across the table and took my hands, pressing them to her lips. "Are you sure you want to do this?"

"Lee, I need to trust someone. I think I know where you stand on certain things, the assassination questions mainly. God only knows what the future holds for each of us. But, you are my dear friend and you've got a good mind. You'll understand, and I'm confident you can handle it and do what's necessary if something should happen to me. Now, let's dance, beautiful lady!"

We went back to the motel and made love. The next day, we rented a car at the airport and I gave Lee the grand tour. We first went by the home where Suzie, my sons, and I lived in 1963 and 1964 while I was serving with the Miami Station. Then we drove to the former JM/WAVE complex, the buildings boarded up and deteriorating, giving no hint as to what had gone on there. The University of Miami was converting some of the structures to house a primate research program. On the way, I pointed out the old agency marine repair shop. I couldn't believe it, but there were two battered V-20 hulls half covered with vegetation, alongside the padlocked building.

As we drove, I gave Lee a running account of what had gone on at various locations and where they fit into my experience with JM/WAVE. I took her to the mansion in Coral Gables where I had met and briefed Artime, then to Coconut Grove where Gordon Campbell's yacht had been docked. We went south on Old Cutler Road, past several former safehouses, ending up at Black Point where we had a beer at the little dilapidated bar and café shack that doubled as the dockmaster's office. We drove back north and I took her by the Cutler Ridge power plant and told her about the refinery raid rehearsal and what preceded it.

That evening, we ended up at Black Caesar's Forge, and over drinks and

THE ZENITH SECRET

dinner I elaborated on the key personalities I'd encountered while at JM/WAVE, including Rosselli and Karl, and some of the operations I'd been part of. I spared her the gruesome details of the failed exfiltration mission and Karl's strange death. I'd leave that to a more suitable moment. Lee seemed, as I hoped would be the case, absolutely intrigued, and asked many sober, provocative, intelligent questions.

The next day, we took my plane and flew to the grass airstrip at Ocean Reef Resort on the north tip of Key Largo. I let Lee take the controls on the way down, to her delight. Before landing, I circled low over Elliott Key and pointed out what remained of the refinery raid mission safehouse and told her how I had learned of the Kennedy assassination there. We circled Linderman Key and flew just above the water along Angelfish Creek, past Pirates' Lair, and I pointed out the old cisterns, barely visible under the palm trees and Australian pines. I described the turn-of-the-century mansion that had once stood on the island, and how we had used the site as a base for maritime and V-20 training.

Heading south just above the trees, we maneuvered along Steamboat Creek and other areas on the coast we had used for survival and small unit tactics exercises: the microwave tower and the pipeline, our simulated training objectives.

After tying down at Ocean Reef, we rented a car and drove to the Jewfish Creek Marina where I used to dock my boats, then south to Plantation Key where I took Lee to the former safehouse complex where I had based my major training operations. We stopped for a drink and a bowl of turtle soup, the house specialty, at the Green Turtle Inn in Islamorada. This had been the favorite stopping place for the JM/WAVE upper management when they traveled to and from the lower Keys. On the way back north, we visited Point Mary and what was left of the two safehouses that once stood there. I told Lee a little of the "legend" of the alleged money cache, supposedly the down payment for the elimination of Castro, while we relaxed over a glass of wine at the infamous Caribbean Club in Key Largo.

We finished our tour late in the afternoon with a visit to Dynamite Pier and Old Card Sound Road. I described to Lee how Pete, an aging Cuban fisherman and cook, used to bring us delicious Cuban meals twice daily, piping hot, just off the stove, all the way from Plantation Key. It had been the high point of the day for the instructors and me living in the mangroves. The return to these sites evoked all kinds of memories for me, and, on several occasions, brought tears. Lee understood.

It was late when we got back to Ocean Reef, and we decided to spend the night there. Again, Lee seemed totally fascinated by everything I'd shown and described to her. That night, after supper, she sat for a long time alone, looking out to the sea. I was exhausted, mentally and physically, having once again opened more old wounds.

Lee and I had, by being together these days, dug an emotional pit for ourselves. Despite our intimacy, Lee never removed her wedding rings. They were always a reminder to me that her true loyalties remained with her husband and children. It hurt, but I told myself it was right and I had to accept the consequences. Tomorrow, she'd only be a memory.

Early the next morning, we flew back to Miami in time for Lee to catch her flight to Chicago. We didn't say much en route, both, I think, anticipating with dread the inevitable goodbye. I landed at Miami International, parking near the Northwest Airlines gates, and I walked with Lee, carrying her bags, to the terminal.

Everything inside me was begging her to change her mind about leaving, but I knew she had to go. I was in awe of her courage and determination. Her husband was a very fortunate man. I choked on my words as I told her I'd probably be at Tanner Aviation until spring if she needed to contact me, and then I'd fly back to Minnesota and my sons. I asked her to write from Germany and let me know how things were going.

We stood at her gate as boarding for the flight began. We kissed, and she told me she loved me. It was the first time she had said it. We were both crying like children. She squeezed my hand, "Be safe, Brad." Then she disappeared through the door to the ramp leading to the aircraft. I stood there for a while, hoping she might turn around and come back to me. The door to the ramp was closed, and when I saw her plane push back I knew she was gone.

THE ZENITH SECRET

CHAPTER 20

A "graveyard spiral," in aviation jargon, defines a flight condition in which the control of the aircraft has deteriorated beyond the pilot's ability to recover. The plane descends, nose earthward, in ever tightening 360 degree rotations, accelerating beyond its design limits, usually disintegrating in air and impacting with free fall velocity. No pilot ever wants to get into this configuration. Emotionally and psychologically, I felt myself slipping into that hopeless predicament after Lee left Miami. I knew I needed to regain stability.

A year earlier, I had developed a pretty good rapport with a fixed base operator on Grand Bahama Island in the course of flying charters to and from Freeport, the major town and airport on the island. I'd even been invited for dinner and stayed overnight as a guest of the Canadian couple that ran the Freeport Flight Service. Maybe getting out of the U.S. for awhile might improve my attitude about a lot of things, including perceptions of my country and where it seemed to be headed.

Freeport Flight Service had a 1950's vintage Piper Apache, a no-frills, twin-engine old bird with many years of island hopping as their primary charter aircraft. Many customers refused to fly in a single engine plane over water, so I was hired to fly the Apache on call. As most experienced pilots know, the Apache's flight characteristics, should one of its engines fail, are like a rock's. We didn't tell the passengers that, of course, and the price for a flight in the Apache was double that of a single engine charter. We always gave the customers whatever they wanted.

The flying business was good. Development in the Bahamas in the late 1960s was flourishing. The outer islands, Eleuthera and Great Abaco, had been discovered. Closer in, there were new vacation and retirement developments on Andros, and the Cat Islands had become popular retreats for the British upper crust. The centerpiece for this extraordinary influx of getaway investment, some of it legitimate, but mostly offshore hidden illegal wealth (political, gambling, and organized crime interests), was on Paradise Island, and on Grand Bahama at Freeport and West End. The construction industry was booming, and the nearest place to go for goods and services was the southeast coast of Florida.

Historically corrupt, always ready to make accommodation for the right amount of U.S. or British currency, Nassau did what was expedient to further the economic razzle-dazzle. Poverty-ridden islanders suddenly found employment opportunities. They rushed to take advantage of the demand for all varieties of unskilled labor.

Families separated, children were left with the elderly, local businesses and essential trades abandoned, and traditional lifestyles and values cast aside in the quest the islanders naïvely believed would bring them a better life. It was a sad thing to watch.

But I was busy and making a little bit of money for both the Freeport Flight Services and myself. On any given day I might find myself flying people, some breathing and some not,[25] expensive furniture from an upscale shop in the States to the wife of an English Lord in her new mansion on a remote private island, plumbing fixtures and building supplies for the new developments in

THE ZENITH SECRET

time for contractors to meet construction deadlines, live animals ranging from monkeys to lions,[26] or medical evacuations from the islands to Miami. There seemed to be no end to what someone needed to be moved "right now," and I was usually ready to go, barring the threat of a hurricane.

Between trips, most often when a weather system made flying impossible, I had time to myself. My tropical-styled little hotel room might have been great for someone on a brief Caribbean vacation, but the ambience soon wore thin.

I caught the news from the States and read the newspapers. The conversations I'd had with Lee about the Warren Commission findings, my own reading of the reports and the questions it raised, my personal knowledge and observations while with JM/WAVE, the developing Garrison inquiry and its bizarre twists; these things could not be ignored. Where in the hell was Bobby Kennedy? From the little Freeport library, I got the early writings of Mark Lane, Josiah Thompson, Thomas Buchanan, Sylvan Fox, and the works of a few other writers who seemed credible. The fundamental theme, now being vehemently discounted by the establishment media in the States, was the proposition of a conspiracy in the death of the president. What to seemed to be missing in all of this was any direct reference to the Kennedy administration's secret war or the implications against Cuba, the Castro assassination effort and other things that went on in the CIA and JM/WAVE preceding the death of the president. Did all of that occur in a vacuum? Didn't Oswald's apparent connections to both pro- and anti-Castro entities raise some questions?

There was one glaring absence in all that was written alleging some kind of conspiracy in the assassination: a specific definition of a sinister force that had motive, method, opportunity, and the capacity to orchestrate and carry out the cover-up. These questions, more than any others, continued to provoke my interest. Nevertheless, the assassination controversy by no means dominated my life.

I spent many hours alone flying over the vast expanse of the Florida Straits and the Atlantic Ocean. Lots of think time. Ninety percent of my trips were within the legendary Bermuda Triangle, and while I was not superstitious, I knew there were mysterious navigational anomalies in the area, and weather conditions could change very quickly. I carried flotation and survival kits in both my aircraft and the Apache, but some flights carried me over questionably charted islands and waters, with no navigational aids or communications. Rescue in an emergency would be unlikely.

I was busy. Days, weeks, months, literally flew by. Suddenly, everything changed. In mid-summer, 1966, I walked in to the Freeport Flight Service office to pick up my schedule for the day. There was an urgent message: Lee and her children would be arriving on a flight from Germany at Miami International within 24 hours. An airline flight number followed.

The next day, I flew to Miami and went to the rented trailer I had been living in near the airport. I drove the '61 Ford Falcon I'd obtained in trade for flight instruction to Miami International just in time to meet her flight. My head was spinning. As from another dimension of reality, Lee appeared, followed by her three kids, but no husband. She saw me immediately and rushed into my arms, sobbing. She looked as though she'd aged 10 years, still beautiful, but her face was bruised and swollen. I went across to the airport hotel and rented a large room for them.

Her husband accused her of "whoring around" with some of the bachelor officers and beat her in the presence of the kids. This apparently happened several times. The Air Force authorities sent Lee and the children back to the

States. She said her marriage was over, and a divorce was in the works, and that she and the kids were going to make a new life for themselves. We spent the night in each other's arms on a cramped day bed in the sitting room, too emptied of spirit for any passion.

We stayed together, talking like mature adults as best we could under the circumstances, while the children played in the pool and amused themselves for the day. That night, we made love on the day bed as we had in Destin. I noted earlier she was no longer wearing wedding rings.

Her oldest child was capable of looking after the two younger kids for a day, so the next morning, Lee and I took off for Grand Bahama and what might be our future, for better or worse. No question, we were now going to face it together. Lee seemed charmed and a bit overwhelmed with the airport welcome we received upon taxiing up to the terminal. I had told the tower I was bringing in a VIP passenger and the greeters and the steel drum Calypso band went all out for us. I took Lee over to the Freeport Flight Service office to introduce her to the manager and his wife.

The moment I walked in, I knew something was wrong. After briefly introducing Lee, the glum looking manager presented a tan envelope. It was addressed to Freeport Flight Services and myself, and it bore a Nassau civil aviation directorate return address. The envelope had been opened.

"You're not going to like this," he said, as he thrust the envelope at me. No one living or doing business in the Bahamas during that period would be unaware of the political turmoil in Nassau. While the British continued to exercise some sort of symbolic protectorate of the islands, the mechanics of governance were really in the hands of the favored Bahamian good old boys, the old clans and their progeny, controlling affairs on the scattered islands. Lynden Pindling, the prime minister of the Bahamas, had been exercising a faux nationalist, protectionist mantra, demanding that foreigners who wished to live and do business in the Bahamas to pay the piper, a.k.a. Mr. Pindling. Because I was not a resident of the Bahamas, under the new policy, my Bahamian Air Taxi Certification was being suspended, and I was no longer permitted to do business originating on the islands. I had the option of establishing residency and applying for new certification at the outrageous fee of $5,000, plus administrative costs. I saw this as blatant extortion.

There was also the possibility of a darker motivation for the suspension of my flying rights in the islands. Lynden Pindling had been on the CIA payroll during the secret war against Cuba in the mid-1960s for the use of certain islands for covert operations. I learned this from JM/WAVE intelligence reports. For all I knew, he still might be on the take. Had the agency influenced Pindling's action, keeping me from doing business in the islands? I could only speculate.

No matter how attractive the island lifestyle and the idea of escaping from the U.S. and all that it had come to represent for both of us—a growing mistrust of our own government rising out of the murder of the president followed by the insanity of Vietnam—Lee and I agreed the welfare of her children had to come first. She was at loose ends, with a divorce to deal with, and very little money, and no place to live unless she returned with the kids to her parents' home in Louisiana. For a variety of reasons, she was not enthusiastic about doing that.

There was no question about our deep affection for one another, our common interests, and view of the world. We were already bonded in many ways. Wouldn't we be better off together rather than trying to establish a decent life separately? We both had to stabilize our situations as soon as possible.

THE ZENITH SECRET

We kissed and held each other, struggling with so many questions. The immediate concern was getting Lee back to Miami and her children.

On the flight back to Tamiami, embroiled in our thoughts about the future, we said little. A plan was beginning to formulate itself in my mind, a course of action that would give us time to consider where we'd go from here. I kept the idea to myself for the moment.

Lee needed a couple of days to rest and get her thoughts in order, so I flew back to Freeport by myself, gathered my belongings, checked out of my room, collected what was owed me by Freeport Flight Service, paid some bills, and said the necessary goodbyes. Everyone around the airport now knew about the suspension of my flying privileges and seemed to understand what I had to do, including the old B-26 mechanic who was still working on that troublesome starboard engine. With that, I flew back to Miami.

As I flew into the setting sun, the hazy south Florida coastline with the lights of the cities just becoming visible, I kept telling myself the entirely unexpected events of the past week had to have some grand purpose beyond my immediate comprehension.

CHAPTER 21

It was near midnight in late summer 1966 when Lee, her children, and I landed at a small airport about 40 miles from St. Paul-Minneapolis, Minnesota. My primary charter aircraft, a Cessna 206, had again delivered. I had given a kindly, pipe-smoking older gentleman, Jim Miller of St. Croix Falls, Wisconsin, advanced flight instruction and flown to Mexico with him several times years before. Jim had expressed his appreciation for my effort and, when I was about to embark for Florida with my business, he told me to call if I ever needed anything. Jim owned the popular Dalles House bar, restaurant, and motel complex nearby. I knew I could count on him to put us up for a while. Our arrival back in my home area was unannounced.

I walked to the pay phone on the flight shack wall and called Jim. Lee and the children were dozing in the airplane when Jim drove up. Despite the hour, he helped load our baggage and took us to his motel. No questions asked, Jim talked with the desk clerk and drove off. In minutes, we were in a large comfortable room, and sound asleep.

Lee and I had talked at length, after my return from Freeport, about what we should do next, individually or collectively, to stabilize our situations. I hadn't seen my sons in more than a year, and I also needed to face my investors and try to explain the recent developments in the Bahamas. I suggested to Lee that she and the children fly up with me, get away from the oppressive heat and humidity of south Florida for a few weeks, and spend some time in a different environment. School would start soon, decisions would have to be made, and it would be a great northern vacation for the kids before the school year began, wherever that might be.

The next morning, using Jim Miller's car, I set out to deal with the multitude of challenges and responsibilities I now felt were mine. I left Lee and her kids to rest, enjoy the pool, sauna, play area and other amenities at the Dalles House.

I first spent several days with my sons, canoeing on the St. Croix River as I had done as a boy. Then I went to St. Paul, Minnesota and met with my flying business investors, brought them up to date on recent developments, and asked them to allow me time for another try to make good. They mandated that it would have to be made close to home, no more extended ventures into "foreign territory."

The leaves had begun to change and a northern winter would soon be upon us. Lee and I decided to remain together and make the best of things as her divorce proceeded. Her children had to start school, and I had to get my flying business up and running or find a job. I rented a small apartment on the west side of St. Paul, raided my parents' attic for furniture, and got Lee and her kids settled in time for school registration. Then I rented hangar and office space at the St. Paul Downtown Airport, reestablishing my air charter and flight training operation there. To avoid complicating Lee's divorce situation, I fixed up a little cabin on a nearby lake to call home. Lee and I spent as much time as we could together, and shared meals, went flying, or on outings with her kids and mine on weekends. Despite the relocation turmoil, financial stress, ongoing legal concerns, and my business demands, we were surprisingly happy. Lee joined me in the business, looking after the phone, scheduling, bookkeeping, and other office matters when the kids were in school. Early on, I flew back to Miami, cleared my trailer and drove the old '61 Falcon back to Minnesota.

Lee and I[27] remained very much aware of the assassination investigation, the Garrison probe, and the worsening situation in Vietnam, and became increasingly cynical. The long Minnesota winter nights gave us ample opportunity to talk about these matters and our growing disillusionment with our government and its leadership.

However, we had too many personal concerns and demands to cope with to become active in the growing war protest movement in America.

For some time I had, with my limited journalistic background, considered the idea of writing publicly about my CIA experience and what had gone on in Miami with the Cubans. However, by Army regulation as a commissioned officer, I had been prohibited from maintaining a journal or diary.

Even though I had not signed a perpetual secrecy agreement concerning my service with the CIA, I was well aware of the potential legal risks in divulging classified information, especially about anything as sensitive as CIA operations. I was not aware, nor did research reveal, that anyone on the side with the agency had gone public with a first person account in any form. Who would publish it? I also, in good conscience, had to consider my motives for writing. What could be accomplished by going public? Who might be endangered? What were the risks and possible consequences?

April 4, 1968, well after midnight, Lee and I were flying somewhere over northern Minnesota, struggling to stay awake on our way back from a cargo delivery to Winnipeg. Lee had the controls and I was messing around with ADF to pick up a local radio station with music to break the isolating tedium of the flight. There were thunderstorms in the area and a lot of electronic interference. Suddenly the static cleared and I got a clear signal out of Minneapolis. No music, but breaking news, the announcer with a special report: Martin Luther King, Jr. had been killed, apparently by an assassin, in Memphis. More details followed. A sniper with a high-powered rifle was likely the assailant.

Lee and I looked at one another in the reddish dimness of the cockpit, speechless, unbelieving. She began to sob. She had grown up in Cajun-French southern Louisiana, where the black population exceeded the white. Segregation was unknown in Sunset. She had many black and biracial friends; the black community was as much hers as was the white. I had served with blacks, on an equal basis, during my active duty military career and while I was with the CIA. Many of the Cuban freedom fighters were black.

Lee and I had observed the ongoing civil rights movement led by Dr. King to be long overdue in America, and the courageous effort had our full philosophical and spiritual support. The news of Dr. King's murder struck us both with hammer-like force. How could this be happening in America? Another assassination on the heels of the president's death—and apparently under fairly similar circumstances. One could not ignore the possibility of some organized extermination campaign. But who and why?

Even though we had our hands full trying to survive and make a new life for ourselves in Minnesota, we could not ignore the growing social unrest in America. The King assassination aggravated our increasing mistrust of the government. The war in Vietnam had, after the Tet Offensive earlier in the year, intensified dramatically. I found myself flying coffins and body bags, draped with the flag and covered with flowers, at least once a week to the small communities throughout the Midwest. I had to steel myself to maintain the professionalism expected as the remains were moved to and from the hearse. At every destination, grief-stricken family members gathered around my aircraft. On two occasions I transported the bodies of officers I had served with.

Robert F. Kennedy became far more vocal and aggressive following the King assassination in his condemnation of the war in Vietnam and criticism of the Johnson administration. He did not express his opinions about the *Warren Commission Report* and the faltering Garrison investigation. Nonetheless, I remained hopeful that if he were elected, a new official inquiry would be ordered,now, not only into the JFK murder but also that of Martin Luther King, Jr.

Garrison's work in New Orleans had produced a number of interesting leads pointing to CIA involvement in JFK's death: the possible role of the Mafia, and alleged connection between David Ferrie and Oswald, the mysterious and conflicting activities of an individual identifying himself as Oswald in the period immediately preceding November 22, and the indications that the federal government conspired to sabotage Garrison's inquiry. An investigation of JM/WAVE, the Castro assassination effort, and the presence of Rosselli and others with ties to the CIA at the Miami station was absent. I could certainly provide information that might help investigators flesh out Garrison's leads.

Late at night on June 4, 1968, I returned from another mortuary flight and parked my plane near my office at Wings, Inc. at the St. Paul Downtown Airport. From my second story office I called Lee and learned that Bobby Kennedy was in critical condition from a bullet wound to the head.

In tears, I drove the dark streets to Lee's apartment. She was silent as she hugged me. We sat for most of the night watching the TV reports. To me, the pattern in the murders of those who might guide America out of the darkness of the Cold War, racial inequality, social injustice, and the ongoing insanity of the war in Vietnam, was becoming apparent. With Bobby's life slipping after the shooting in the Ambassador Hotel, I vividly recalled the fire in his eyes, his magnetic intensity, the inspiring grip of his hand when I'd last met him at the JM/WAVE paramilitary base that night deep in the Everglades. I felt his vitality, his presence confirming the honor of our purpose. My God, what was happening to my country?

CHAPTER 22

Deeply affected by Robert Kennedy's death, Lee and I talked at length about the Garrison investigation and its bizarre twists.

In the emerging JFK assassination books, researchers often made reference to the Kennedy administration's secret war against Cuba, but many got their facts mixed up with the Bay of Pigs fiasco and the Cuban missile crisis of 1962. There was even some vague reference to Castro assassination plots and possible involvement of organized crime figures who maintained gambling interests in Havana until Castro took over. But the specifics—what had actually been going on at Zenith Technical Enterprises in Miami in the early '60s—remained hidden from all but a few and were really never considered in the scenario of events preceding the president's death.

Because it had not been disclosed, I felt it at least of marginal importance to the public's gaining a more comprehensive understanding of the dynamics which may have had something to do with an assassination conspiracy. Now that Bobby was gone, there might never be a reopening of the official investigation, and in the absence of anyone else with intimate, first-person knowledge stepping forward, it might be my patriotic duty to come forth with all I knew and had observed for the historical record.

The single major thing that struck me was Garrison's published identification of David Ferrie. The David Ferrie pictured in the newspapers closely resembled one of the pilots with whom I had flown from the New Richmond Naval Air Station JM/WAVE headquarters in the spring and summer of 1963. The pilot's appearance was quite distinctive and sitting right next to him in the seat of a small aircraft made it virtually impossible to ignore his facial features. It was not unusual for CIA operatives to disguise themselves, usually with hair pieces, facial hair, glasses, hats, and clothing for a particular assignment. Usually this was done in privacy, away from the station, before embarking on some operation that required the deception. One would not violate tradecraft doctrine by going into the station wearing a disguise or engage in an activity where one's true identity was known, thus making the disguise unnecessary and even ludicrous. Some agents and operatives were really good at the use of physical disguise, but the pilot I flew with was not, assuming he was in fact attempting to alter his appearance. Thus, he became memorable to me. Furthermore, he seemed to look just a little bit different each time I saw him, thus jeopardizing the efficacy of the disguise and creating suspicion. On the first flight, the man introduced himself as Dave, and I never learned his last name (which was not at all unusual in interacting with operatives). Discreetly, I did not ask him if he were disguising himself—I had no need to know.

A second area of significance was Karl's identity and death. I could not put out of mind his extraordinary resemblance to Lee Harvey Oswald. The more I learned about Oswald, the more he and Karl seemed alike—not only in physical appearance, but also in speech and, from the little I saw of Oswald on TV before Ruby killed him, his mannerisms. With all that was becoming known about Oswald's alleged activities in the period leading up to the assassination of the president, the possibility of someone posing as Lee Harvey Oswald had to be considered. And why was Karl eliminated? Could it be that he knew too much?

There were other more abstract questions that remained prominent in my thoughts. What about the anti-Kennedy atmosphere that prevailed, essentially in the Operations Branch under Dave Morales at JM/WAVE, and among some of the contract agents and Cuban exiles in Miami? What about Rosselli and his organized crime connections? I knew that the Kennedy Justice Department had declared war on the Mafia and that Bobby Kennedy was personally orchestrating the battle against mob kingpins. It seemed so odd to me this was going on at the same time that Rosselli had carte blanche access to JM/WAVE and enjoyed a close relationship with Morales and the station hierarchy.

What about the frustration with the Special Group and its micromanagement of paramilitary operations at JM/WAVE? Would Ted Shackley or Gordon Campbell, or even David Morales, devise and conduct covert actions that were not approved in Washington? I wondered if the Special Group authorized the aborted refinery raid that we'd trained for on Elliott Key. Gordon Campbell had restricted knowledge of that activity to a select few at the station, from what I knew and observed.

These thoughts tumbled around in my mind as I considered the wisdom of speaking out about what I knew and might contribute to a broader public understanding of circumstances and activities, as well as the identification of persons that might have some connection with the assassinations of the president and his brother. I was very much aware of being influenced by all the publications that, in 1968, were offering various opinions, theories, and evidentiary constructs defying the Warren Commission's conclusions. I knew that one could be influenced by these writings. If I had something to add to the issue, I wanted my account to be based purely on what I had experienced and observed, coupled with my impressions, and not "polluted" by what others were presenting. Realistically, it was impossible to make a sound judgment about so much of what was being argued in support of assorted assassination conspiracy theories.

The old admonishment, "to thine own self be true," ruled my thinking and my decision process. I talked with Lee about what I was considering, even though I had not arrived at a course of actions. I explained why I felt I had to come forward; she agreed and promised to stay with me. Because I had nothing to work from to reconstruct my account, it had to come from memory correlated with my accumulation of routine records, receipts, flight logs, letters and other personal documents that would help pin down times, places, people and events.

It would not be an easy process. I initially was not even sure of a format for what I had to offer, much less an idea of how to get it into the appropriate public forum. Go to the media, write for publication, a magazine article, a book? I had never written a book before; how might I find a publisher who would believe and work with me?

What about my life with Lee? What would be the ramifications for her children, my sons, my aging parents, my brothers, my flying business investors, and others so vital to whatever stability I had? I struggled with these considerations. And, as a former professional soldier entrusted with highly classified information, did I have the right to arbitrarily divulge what I knew? How would the agency react? For a time I was terribly conflicted. I concluded that my actions were fully justified if the CIA had been involved in the deaths of the president and his brother.

As my growing suspicions suggested, a coup d'etat was at hand. If our Constitutional process and the American people had been betrayed, and I had a patriotic duty to come forth with any information I had that might be relative to

BRADLEY E. AYERS

the treason, any and all secrecy obligations be damned!

I was not yet 35-years-old, but I'd already witnessed a lot, faced unusual challenges, and made difficult decisions. My outlook was one of cynical optimism: anticipate the worse, but expect the best. Seldom in life does a man know exactly what he must do. For me, this was one of those rare moments.

As the controversy surrounding the assassinations became a major issue in America and elsewhere in the world, I spent whatever time I could spare during the last months of 1968 and much of 1969, reconstructing the details of my CIA experience. I created timelines, and organized the people, places and events I felt were relevant. The monetary aspects of the undertaking were never a consideration or motivation. I would accept the consequences of my actions, whatever they happened to be.

About the time I began construction of the hangar complex at Lake Elmo, a quaint, but well-maintained farmhouse on 10 acres of land across the road from the airport was put on the market. Lee and I bought it and worked for more than a year to remodel and paint the farmhouse and the outbuildings, moving in by stages as the work was done. By the end of 1969, we were finally reasonably well settled and had begun to realize some of the stability that had evaded us both for so long.

All of this domesticity was set against the backdrop of the social and cultural turmoil in the late 1960s. Already cynical about the actions of our government, we came to see the war as another major deception. We were drawn to several anti-war rallies and began attending political meetings with a group of patriotic intellectuals who shared our outlook on national policies and related matters.

Despite our many late night discussions and weekend motorcycle jaunts with our friends, Lee and I did not discuss my CIA background or divulge any interest in the assassination beyond voicing generic skepticism of the official investigative findings. We'd agreed to keep that area of our shared interests to ourselves until it was decided how to make it public. Some of our friends were very vocal in their anti-establishment rhetoric, and we'd become aware of the government's apparent intention to crack down on anyone who would dissent in a significant way with official word of policy.

By 1970, I had reconstructed the essentials of my secret war experience and felt fairly well prepared to present what I had to a professional entity that might be able to place it in context and advise me where to go with the information. I talked with Lee about going to the FBI or Secret Service as local and state authorities would have no background or jurisdiction at the level of government that had to be addressed. We both rejected that course of action as almost laughable, because, if there was a cover-up in the assassinations, both the FBI and Secret Service were probably complicit.

I wanted to start with a relatively obscure media entity in the immediate area. I needed to test the waters. I knew nothing at this time of literary agents or publicists; and I was not comfortable going to the popular print or broadcast media for fear of having my story revealed in such a way that would embarrass or endanger my loved ones or discredit my account. After all, it was not a run-of-the-mill confession.

Sometime during our anti-establishment conversations with our academic friends, University of Minnesota professor Dick Franklin and his lovely partner, Kathy Stewart, we had gotten into a discussion about Minneapolis-St. Paul avant garde filmmakers and emerging, super gutsy, free-spirited movie producers. I think we had all recently seen "Easy Rider" and "Deep Throat," both of which were provocative in one way or another. Someone mentioned a company called Somerset, Limited. The word was that one of their producers was working on a project involving the assassination of the president.

I did some further checking on Somerset and learned of its two principals, multi-millionaire entrepreneur Henry (Hank) Flesh and an experienced movie script writer, Ted Higginbotham. I had numerous meetings at Somerset in the weeks and months that followed as Ted, with Hank looking over his shoulder, began to develop a treatment. They would call me in frequently to answer questions and fill in details to "flesh out" the story line as the treatment was being written. They began to express concern the account might be too revealing of possibly actual CIA operations to survive government scrutiny and possible litigation if produced for public consumption. Their reservations and fears reflected their ages, background and the atmosphere in America at the time. Lee and I hated to see the screenplay project languish, but it was apparent that Ted and Hank had way too much at risk, to put money and effort into a project that might only bring them grief, litigation and financial loss. Lee and I went to a posh holiday party at Hank's in late December 1970, and then went home to decide what to do next.

I was now more determined than ever to get the story out, but at what expense, and how? Outside the old farmhouse, a blizzard raged. Lee and I were practicing Catholics, more spiritual than churchgoing on a regular basis. That night we knelt beside one another and prayed for divine guidance. Then, in the spirit of the season, with the Christmas tree lights glowing softly and hope in our hearts, we opened a bottle of wine, jumped into our warm waterbed, and made love.

CHAPTER 23

Lee's landing on the 2,000 foot grass airstrip at the Ocean Reef Resort on the north tip of Key Largo was a flight instructor's dream come true. It was late January 1971. Determined to get her private pilot's license, she was well on her way to soloing. I'd allowed her to take the Cessna 206's controls for much of the flight from Minnesota to Florida, and she'd performed admirably.

The decision to return to Florida had not been an easy one. The Christmas season at the farm had been strained. I stewed over the holidays, a creeping repugnance of my own cowardice seeping into my psyche. Why didn't I have the courage to go forth with my story and let the chips fall where they may? After all, that had been my idealistic motive. With the movie idea, I was backing away from my original purpose and intent. No, if I were going to be true to myself I would have to reveal what I knew in the most unvarnished, straightforward manner.

I shared my thoughts with Lee. Eventually, we agreed the best way to make my account public would be to present it to the world as a non-fiction book. Lee encouraged me to convert my fictionalized screen treatment to book form.

"Lee, do you realize the amount of time it'll take to do a book? Given the precarious state of our finances, with business in the doldrums, I don't feel I can just drop out and spend my days writing. That wouldn't be fair to you or my investors. We're probably looking at four to six months to rewrite the treatment. Secondly, I don't know if I could really deliver a full, accurate account all from memory, here in Minnesota. And, I don't even have a publisher."

She responded, "Well, if you're truly determined to do this, maybe you should head back to the Everglades and Keys for a while. Go back to the scene of the action."

It was that exchange that precipitated events that would ultimately become life changing for Lee and me, and those closest to us.

Once committed to a task or mission, my headstrong nature kicked in. Likewise, Lee tended to be independent and single-minded. When we were on the same track, our teamwork was laudable. It was the dead of winter. There was virtually no flying, teaching, or real estate work to be had. Why not fly to the Keys for a few months and do as much as possible on the book? Refresh area knowledge, visit old sites, recreate maps, take photos, do whatever research necessary.

With a little effort, the logistics were manageable. Lee's children would stay with friends and remain in school.

The married couple renting the apartment I had created adjacent to our old farm home would look after the property and the dogs while we were away in return for a rent discount. The airplane hangar and offices would remain locked up until spring. The plan came together, and on a bitterly cold January morning, Lee and I took off southbound. Saddened to leave her children, Lee shed a few tears as the 206 groaned to altitude. I never ceased being impressed by her courage and unswerving willingness to stand by me.

With Lee by my side, and having resolved to get the book done as quickly as possible, I was a man on a mission. We had told few people about our intentions of temporarily moving to Florida to finish my book. My great aunt, one of my loyal sponsors over time, was the only family member aware of the book undertaking. She understood what I had to do as she slipped me $1000 when I went to say goodbye.

Lee and I wasted no time after landing at Ocean Reef. On our approach to the island airstrip we circled low over Elliott Key, Pirates' Lair, and the Point Mary area in north Key Largo. I was surprised how little the area had changed in the four years since I'd last been there. I recalled from my days with the agency in the Keys a small housing development almost adjacent to the Point Mary safehouse complex. It was quite isolated, there had been homes for rent there, and if we could find something available, the location would put us in close proximity to my old northern Keys operational area

Luck was with us. We found a house to rent by the month near Point Mary the same day. Without unloading our baggage, we drove to Miami. While we had the car, I wanted to revisit and photograph the old JM/WAVE complex and as many other operational sites as possible. Again, we were surprisingly fortunate in this effort, and I found myself surreally transported back in time, as if the buildings, some eerily vacant and dilapidated, were haunted by their extraordinary history. The next day, we drove the Cross Key Highway to Plantation Key, photographed the safehouses and other former operational sites there, had a drink at the Caribbean Club in Key Largo.

The days went by with steady production. No one bothered us; the isolation was soothing and allowed for complete focus on the task at hand. Then, my parents called. They were flying down to visit for a few weeks, so we rented a car and drove to Ft. Lauderdale. We decided to go to the waterfront to admire the many yachts and fishing boats docked at the marinas there. We came across an older yacht, an early 1960s vintage mahogany wood-hulled thirty-four foot Trojan, with a FOR SALE sign displayed on the cabin door.

One afternoon, having completed my day at the typewriter, I called the owner of the boat. He said he would lease it with an option to purchase. We decided to meet in the weeks ahead so I could inspect the boat and take it on a test cruise. Lee was amused by all of this, knowing full well our financial constraints, but she loved boating and the sea, and agreed to look at the Trojan, for whatever the experience might be worth.

A day or so later the quiet of our solitary tropical evening was interrupted by a phone call from Hank Flesh in St. Paul. He asked if I'd been reading the papers. Big-time Washington exposé columnist Jack Anderson, the protégé of famed muckraker, Drew Pearson, was publishing a series of articles naming mobster Johnny Rosselli as one of the key participants in the Kennedy administration and CIA plots to assassinate Fidel Castro. The Anderson stories were confirming everything about my own account of the CIA's secret war against Cuba in the period preceding the murder of the president. He even speculated about Bobby Kennedy's knowledge of the covert war and his remorse about the possible connection to his brother's death.

I got Anderson's phone number and called his office, leaving a message with his secretary about my interest in his recent columns about Rosselli, the CIA and the plot to kill Castro. Anderson called back the next day and asked me to send him a synopsis of my information. I put my summary in the mail immediately. I fully realized that I had my fanny hung out a country mile.

Until this point, there had been no real reason for the CIA, FBI, or any federal agency to become aware or take note of what I was up to. All contacts concerning my CIA story had been discreetly low key and couched in the context of a work of fiction. Almost overnight, following my phone conversation with Anderson, things changed. The first was a sudden, subtle volume decrease on our phone, especially with long distance calls. Then, within days of my communications with Anderson, we were surprised by the visit of a middle age, scholarly looking man. He came to our door explaining he was an archeological researcher from the University of Miami doing a field study of Florida Keys Indians who inhabited the area around the time of Columbus. He asked to walk across our property to a nearby mound believed to be a long hidden camp and burial site. We made no objection to his presence and he returned to our home several more times over the following weeks. Naïvely, we let him come into our home several times. He seemed legitimate. We called the phone company about telephone problems and they checked out the line. The repairman confirmed there was an unexplained power drain affecting our connection.

Nothing could or would be done about it.

Meanwhile, I was taking a break from the typewriter. Kicking around the charred ruins of the old Point Mary safehouses, I came across badly damaged U.S. currency in $20 bills dated between 1966 and 1968. I found the money in and about the partially collapsed coral foundations where the wood houses had rested, and in the surrounding area. A weathered, scorched, but empty suitcase was nearby. Could this have been the money cache I first heard about when I was briefing Artime in the fall of 1964—the down payment on the assassination of Fidel Castro? At first, the dates on the bills seemed odd. They apparently were printed after 1963. But, what a great cover move for the CIA to get Treasury to print post-dated bills, thus establishing plausible deniability in connecting the agency with any earlier covert undertaking. I took the bills, altogether more than $200, to a local bank for verification of their authenticity. The twenties were the genuine item, but where was the rest of the money if in fact the bills were part of the original $250,000 cache? I shared the discovery of the tattered twenty dollar bills only with Lee.

The dialogue with Jack Anderson increased with frequent communications by phone and mail. Anderson thought I would want money for providing him information, but I made it very clear that I wouldn't accept payment except for expenses and only asked that he help me find a publisher for my book in progress. Anderson began talking about bringing us to Washington, D.C. to be interviewed.

While we were trying to work through this, I received a letter from Hank Flesh confirming what he'd told me on the phone about becoming a source for Anderson. He spoke in unmistakable terms: "Frankly, I think you're asking for nothing but disaster if you get mixed up with Jack Anderson and an expose column..." What did Hank mean? Jack Anderson was the one person who seemed to have some grasp of the story I was trying to get out and who understood the importance of it.

As far as I was concerned, Rosselli's improprieties at the Friar's Club in Los Angeles were a sideshow. My confirmation of the mobster's presence at JM/WAVE, the CIA's apparent coalition with the Mafia to kill Castro, and the possible implications of the secret war against Cuba with the murders of the president and his brother were really the essential issues. If collaborating with Jack Anderson would help me get my account substantiated and published, that had to be our first consideration. Lee agreed, and I wrote Hank a short letter thanking him for his advice and told him we were going to proceed with what we felt we had to do.

We tried to stay on schedule with writing while wrestling with how we

THE ZENITH SECRET

might go about cooperating with Anderson. I put in long hours typing at the bench near the basin, and Lee often worked into the night retyping my drafts. So when the owner of the Trojan yacht in Ft. Lauderdale called and invited us to join him and his girlfriend for a three day sailing cruise to Bimini, we were ready for a break. I called Les Whitten, Jack Anderson's assistant, and told him we'd decide about how to proceed while sailing with some friends over the weekend.

That Friday, we secured the rental house as best we could. I padlocked a small closet off the kitchen, placing there our items of most value—camera, typewriter, tape recorder, all my book-related notes and photos, personal correspondence, and other items I needed for the ongoing project. As an afterthought, and I've never been able to fully reconcile all the reasons, I took my partially completed book manuscript, wrapped it in heavy plastic, and hid it beneath a coral outcropping in the mangroves behind the house.

With a rental car, we drove to Miami and met our friends at a posh marina hotel where we boarded their sailboat. After martinis and canapés at sunset, we set out for Bimini. There were strong easterly winds, and as the lights of Miami disappeared behind us, we were bucking eight to ten foot waves. By midnight, the four of us were fully occupied with crewing the boat and keeping it on course. Having spent a good deal of time navigating in the air and on the water in the infamous Bermuda Triangle area, I gradually sensed we were drifting well to the north of our destination.

As tactfully as possible, I explained to the skipper we had drifted north most of the night and probably now were about to sail right through the Northwest Passage and right out into the stormy Atlantic Ocean. I advised him to fire up the small engine and make an abrupt course change, cross wind, almost directly south. Within two hours we had Great Caesar's light in sight and by late afternoon, made our way through the tricky rocks of Bimini Harbor.

I had a hunch my friend invited us on the cruise because he wanted to talk about our interest in the Trojan yacht. Again, I put him off, telling him I'd get back by the end of the month. Later that morning, we cast off for Florida under clearing skies. What a weekend it had been. It had surely served to divert our attention from the book and the Jack Anderson quandary. But not for a moment longer.

I sensed something was amiss as I pulled into the yard at our rental house in Key Largo. I could see the side door that opened onto a screened breezeway was standing open. The breezeway door was ajar. Both had been secured when we left on Friday. All the lights in the house were on. Someone was or had been in the house. Lee and I looked at each other in shock and jumped from the car. It was obvious from the moment we entered the house that it had been thoroughly searched. Every cabinet, drawer, cubbyhole, suitcase, anywhere anything might have been stored had been opened and the contents pretty much dumped on the floor. The padlocked closet had been broken into and most of everything I'd placed into it had been removed and was nowhere to be seen.

Burglars? We quickly surveyed the scene, each going to the areas of our greatest concern. When we met again in the kitchen, there was little need for words.

Other than the contents of the closet and a few of Lee's personal items, nothing of substantial value was missing. Someone had been searching for something.

Lee went to the refrigerator for a cold drink and gasped when she opened it. The Cornish game hens left over from a meal days before were gone, as were some cans of beer, salad and a variety of other foods. She went to the sink. She had washed and put everything away on Friday before we left, but, there in the sink, were the bony remnants of the game hens, and neatly stacked on the sideboard were the dirty dishes and silverware apparently used as someone enjoyed a meal. There was no sign of the six-pack of beer or empty cans.

Someone had been in our home and they had no qualms about letting us know they'd been there.

The missing book-related materials and equipment concerned me most. I picked up the phone to call the sheriff only to find it dead. Outside, I found the line had been cut. What the hell was going on? I told Lee to begin to inventory our possessions, but not disturb anything until we could get the police on the scene. Then I ran behind the house, through the brush and mangroves, to the place where I'd hidden the manuscript. I was relieved to find it undisturbed.

Concerned that whoever had searched our home might return, I left the plastic wrapped box where it was. I went to the home of a couple that lived almost directly across the road from our rental home. They'd seen a car drive up on the Saturday night after our departure and park in the drive next to the house. It was still light, and they watched the men, two, three or more, get out of the car and enter the house. They said the men looked like hippies. The lights went on and there was a lot of banging and crashing, loud talk and laughter. It went on for an hour or more. At first, the neighbors thought they were our friends who had been given access to the house in our absence. But, when the "partying" persisted, they became concerned there was something wrong.

The Point Mary subdivision was quite isolated, with few full time residents. There had been some break-ins in the area before. Finally, after watching what was going on at our home, Mr. Warner called in a report to the Monroe County Sheriff, describing the situation. The response, according to Warner: "We're too busy to respond." With that, the Warners remained awake until the intruders left later in the night. Mrs. Warner confided that they'd been quite frightened by the incident. I used their phone to call the sheriff and report a burglary under very suspicious circumstances, asking for an officer to come out to view the scene and take a formal report.

The following day, a deputy sheriff came to the house to take a report and examine the scene. I had begun to believe we'd been the victims of a highly specific search operation, probably orchestrated by CIA and FBI in coordination with local law enforcement. I explained that to the officer who stared at me blankly as he made notes for his report. He told us that there was little the police could do about the matter and filed the report as Monroe County Sheriff case number 7103305.

Now, it was beginning to come together; the archaeologist's repeated visits, the phone problem, and now the house search. Taken together, one could not ignore that we'd been, and now would continue to be under surveillance by someone who might want to keep me from going public with the CIA story, and was monitoring our every action. Apparently someplace, with someone, we'd struck a very sensitive nerve.

If the break in had been carried out by a federal agency it may have been sparked by a call by Jack Anderson to CIA headquarters in Langley verifying my authenticity. Maybe the CIA needed to know what I had and could deliver to Anderson to corroborate his recent articles on the secret war against Cuba. Agency operatives not only had motive, but method and opportunity during our weekend absence.

If the break-in was any indication of what might come to prevent me from going public, there might be a defense that, to this point, hadn't occurred to me. The agency abhorred publicity of any kind unless it was of its own manufacture or manipulation. Any obvious persecution of a whistle-blower that might attract media attention, possible public sympathy and outrage, would be avoided if at all possible. The CIA did not want to create martyrs. Therefore, if I were in for trouble trying to get my story out, the media might be my best line of defense. Cooperation with Jack Anderson made even more sense than it had previously.

As days passed with not so much as a word from the Monroe County sheriff or any indication of a break-in follow-up investigation by the authorities, Lee and I concluded we'd been the victims of a black bag job.[28]

I informed Jack Anderson of the break-in and things moved quickly after that. It was agreed we'd fly to D.C. and meet with him and Les Whitten on the first of April. In return for sharing what I knew about the post-missile crisis secret war and Rosselli, Jack promised to put me in touch with a major publisher. While these arrangements were in process, we barricaded ourselves in the Point Mary rental home. We prepared to leave at the first sign of danger— overt surveillance or another intrusion. To that end, I contacted our friends in Ft. Lauderdale, and suggested he move the Trojan yacht from the marina where it was docked to his home on a canal in Hollywood. I used a pay phone in Key Largo to make these arrangements, as I was confident any conversation from the house would be monitored.

We landed at Ft. Lauderdale International where we were met by our friends. They drove us to a luxurious home in Hollywood where the aging yacht was now tied up. We promptly renamed it the Abraxas, a Greek term for a talisman or good omen.[29] On the second of April, we flew commercially to Washington, D.C. where Les Whitten met us at National Airport.

We had only carry-on luggage, and were soon driving the dark Washington streets to Jack Anderson's home. On a coffee table, Anderson displayed a series of look-alike mug shots and he asked me to identify Rosselli. Within seconds I pointed out Rosselli's personal characteristics, behavior, dress, even his preferred alcoholic drink. Lee remained silent, transfixed by what was taking place.

This was the litmus test, and I passed with flying colors. Jack asked me if I'd be willing to testify on Rosselli's behalf in connection with the Friar's Club criminal charges he was facing in LA and I told him I'd consider it. He then picked up the phone and called Rosselli's attorney, Adrian Marshal, in California and had a brief conversation with him. My identification of Rosselli, confirming his presence at JM/WAVE, and my willingness to possibly testify to that fact apparently was Anderson's main objective of the evening.

Satisfied, he sat back on a large couch and we discussed my CIA experience. I began to feel at ease with Jack. He said he'd do a column on my story. We then talked about the break in at Point Mary and other ominous happenings of the past two months. He did not look surprised as I told him of my suspicions. I felt he was in sympathy with my purpose in going public as I explained it to him. Finally, believing it best to be completely forthright, I told him of the recent discovery of the tattered $20 bills. I thought he and Whitten were going to leap off the couch.

Telling Anderson about the money find was a mistake because it became a fixation with them. Late in the morning the following day, Les Whitten picked us up at the hotel and took us to Jack's downtown offices. We met Anderson's new assistant reporter, Brit Hume, who tried to help us pass the time while Anderson and Whitten were doing their column for the day. Late in the afternoon, Whitten broke free and sat with us.

"Brad, I'd like to have you make a call. I've got Bill Harvey's number in Indianapolis. You know he's retired now. Why don't you give him a call and reminisce a bit. I'll stay on another line."

"Les, I don't think this is a good idea. What the hell am I going to say to him?"

"Just make like you want to talk about old times."

"Okay, if that's what you want."

After several interrupted connections, I heard Harvey's gruff voice on the end of the line. It was apparent the call was an intrusion as I introduced myself and the reason for my call. I talked about meeting him at Langley in 1963. He seemed all right with that, but when I brought up JM/WAVE, he terminated the conversation. I was not surprised. Covert operators just didn't ring up one another like that. Harvey was too savvy to believe I was calling for old times' sake.

Lee and I were supposed to fly back to Ft. Lauderdale that night, but with the disconcerting developments of the past 24 hours in Washington, and the events in Key Largo, we asked Whitten to change our flight plans to fly directly back to Minnesota. Things in Florida would have to remain as they were for the time being. We arrived back at Minneapolis International around midnight and took a taxi to the Lake Elmo farm. Neither of us had a dime in our pockets after we paid the cab fare.

We'd no more than begun to breathe a bit easier when the first of a series of Jack Anderson exposes of my story began to appear in his syndicated columns. About the time of the second article, I got a call from Les Whitten.

"Jack wants us to fly back to Florida; and he wants you to show me the area where you found the money. We can talk on the way and when we get there. We'd like to leave as soon as possible."

At this point, Anderson had not put me in touch with a publisher or agent. Must I prove myself yet again? I tried to get Whitten to understand the whole money cache thing was totally speculative; the dates on the bills were out of sync with the Castro assassination plot time period. Secondly, we may well have alerted any and all federal agencies with any interest in my going public, to our intentions. Point Mary and Pirates' Lair would be hot spots. At this point, we began to receive threatening phone messages.

I called Whitten back, followed with a letter, expressing my concerns, but agreed to flying with him to Florida in pursuit of the secret money cache story. One part of me hoped it would be a bust, because the hidden funds issue had come to dominate my dialogue with Whitten and Anderson at the expense of many more significant, tangible aspects of what I hoped to deliver publicly.

We flew back to Florida together after meeting in Washington, D.C. and I showed Les around our old training areas and safesites. Les was anxious to get on with the money search, even though in my running dialogue I repeatedly tried to temper his expectations. The money search had become a distraction, as far as I was concerned. Les wanted to spend time looking around the ruins of the safehouses at Point Mary. I thought I had pretty well searched the area weeks earlier for more tattered bills or any indication of a money cache. Surprisingly while kicking around in the leaves and soil, Les found several more bills. He was ecstatic. Now, it was apparent the money issue would dominate his interest in the information I had and might provide. He took the old suitcase to show to Jack.

I had to drag Les away from the treasure hunt so we could visit Pirates' Lair. It could only be reached by boat, so we returned to Ocean Reef and rented a skiff. Lee joined us, and I maneuvered the small craft through the maze of saltwater, mangrove-fringed canals to Anglefish Creek. Les was excited and somewhat fearful as we passed a couple of big alligators, disturbing their afternoon slumber in the mud, provoking them to splash into the water only a few yards from the boat. It was all very familiar to Lee and me, but to the urbane, bookish Whitten, the trip to Pirates' Lair was a wild adventure.

The last time I'd visited the Lair was about four years earlier, when I had the strange encounter with Dick by the cisterns, and the island had been essentially deserted. The only intact dwelling had been boarded up and, to all appearances, abandoned. As we motored around the last bend that brought us in view of the house and dock, it was immediately apparent the island was occupied by someone. Standing near the house and on the dock were at least a half-dozen swarthy men dressed in mixed military-style clothing, some in camouflage fatigues and some carrying weapons. What had we gotten ourselves into this time? I had told Whitten and Anderson the island was uninhabited at my last visit and I truly expected to find it that way on this trip. As we neared the dock area, other men emerged from the house, apparently alerted by the noise of our motor. They more or less assembled on the dock and glared at us. From their posture and manner, it was clear we would not be welcome if we tried to go ashore.

I shook my head indicating no to Whitten and we continued along Anglefish Creek toward the sea. The commando types, from the dock, watched us as I steered the boat down a side canal and out of the sight of the island. As we turned, I spotted two additional military-appearing men near the old cistern at the eastern tip of the key. When we were out of earshot of the island, I cut the motor and discussed the situation.

"Les, I don't think it's a good idea to attempt to go ashore, much less search the island. Those guys look like they mean business, and I got the distinct impression we were intruding on something. Who knows who they are and what they're up to. If you get into a scrape or confrontation out here, you can't just call for the cops. We're 50 miles or so from any law enforcement. If we got into it with those guys, they'd feed us to the gators and no one would know the difference. Best we go back to the Reef now and try later, maybe that gang will leave by nightfall."

It was late afternoon when we got back to Ocean Reef. We were scheduled to return to D.C. the following day. We had to move quickly if we were going to search Pirates' Lair. Later that day, I donned black clothing and charcoaled my face. It was fairly late; lights were ablaze in the house and around the island. Whoever was there did not appear to be making any preparations to leave. Whitten was crestfallen, but not prepared to return to the Lair on his own. He was silent for much of the return trip to D.C.; and I felt he blamed me. I had done my best under the circumstances, and I wasn't about to jeopardize anyone's welfare or aggravate a situation that might interfere with the book I had yet to finish.

After a night's rest and an opportunity to clean up after our strange trip, Whitten introduced us to the D.C. representative of a major New York publishing house. We met with her for nearly an hour, discussing my book project. She had read the Anderson columns with interest. I gave her a copy of the synopsis—I had given the book a working title, *The Captain*—and a sample chapter. Before leaving D.C., I gave Anderson all the tattered bills I'd found at Point Mary so it could be traced by his contact at the U.S. Treasury.

BRADLEY E. AYERS

CHAPTER 24

Jack Anderson published yet another column dealing with our trip to Florida and the search for the money cache, near the end of April of 1971. Lee and I were surprised as we didn't feel newsworthy conclusions could be drawn from our trip to Florida with Les Whitten. Anderson and Whitten milked the escapade for everything it was worth, and, at least, the column didn't condemn me for the situation we found at Pirates' Lair.

Lee and I hoped for a respite from the surprising attention given to my story. It was unfortunate the emphasis seemed to be on the money cache. There was nothing we could do about it, of course, as I'd agreed to cooperate with Anderson and he could exploit the information I'd provided in most any way he chose. I was getting a hard lesson in dealing with the media.

We began to get curious and blatantly threatening messages from a Mr. Blasco making reference to the money cache and its disposition. I relayed these messages, as accurately as possible from my notes, to Anderson and Whitten. My primary interest at this point was a response from the publisher we'd been in contact with in D.C.; the whole money cache matter was quite tangential and had become a distraction.

The D.C. rep for the New York publisher we'd met with finally got in touch, and the word was not what we'd hoped. New York wanted the complete manuscript before making a decision on a contract for the rights to my story.

I didn't have a finished manuscript. Further, I sensed from the editor's remarks the publisher was somewhat less than enthusiastic about going forth with a book that revealed CIA's inside workings, especially one that presented so many sensitive and potentially embarrassing facts. I thought I'd given them all that was needed to make a judgment about publishing my book. This was a new game for me. We reached the conclusion that in all probability no publisher would seriously consider my work until I delivered a finished product.

Accepting that, I felt the best place to get the job done was back in Florida, again at the scene of the action. What's more, we had the boat and airplane there giving us a good deal of logistical flexibility should we be seriously harassed. Finishing the book was now to be my primary goal.

So, I was totally caught off guard when Jack Anderson called and asked that I return with him and Whitten to upper Key Largo to continue the search for the money cache. There had been so many messages from Blasco and others since the last Anderson column, we had to change our phone number.

I strongly urged Jack to postpone an immediate trip to Florida and advised him it was not in my or anyone else's interest to go back down and "stink up the area." We were already high profile enough, and I didn't want anything else to jeopardize the completion of my book.

Despite my words of caution, Anderson and Whitten flew to Florida and hired a local guide to take them to Pirates' Lair. Their search, which proved unfruitful, apparently was a crushing embarrassment because, they'd announced to virtually everyone inside the Beltway they were going to the Keys to bring out a secret CIA money cache. From all indications, they didn't even bother to search further at Point Mary where my and Whitten's discoveries were made. They described their unproductive search in another of their columns on the first of June 1971. My name and the information I'd provided them was used to justify the treasure hunt, but the tone of the column was a somewhat muted endorsement. Jack and Les knew they'd screwed up big time.

Shortly after the column appeared all across the country and God only knows where else, Whitten called to inform me all the tattered bills found at Point Mary had been authenticated by the Treasury Department and they were being replaced and returned to Anderson in the form of new currency of the same value. That was pretty good news. But Whitten told me Anderson felt it only fair that we split the proceeds, some $300 in total, to offset some of the expenses he'd incurred.

From my point of view, the value of the discovery was that it was made near what had been a CIA safehouse complex, where mobster Johnny Rosselli's Castro hit snipers were training. I had personal knowledge of that because I'd been there in the summer of 1963 and witnessed the JM/WAVE-directed activities. I could not explain the out-of-sync dating on the tattered bills, but postdating would certainly have been within the capability of the agency in an effort to obscure any connection to a Castro assassination payoff.

There were other developments, not necessarily directly affecting my project, but disconcerting in many ways. While I had no personal knowledge of the other players identified by Garrison, I felt strongly that David Ferrie had been an operative/pilot at JM/WAVE. Garrison had reinforced the idea that there had been more than one Oswald. I could not put from my mind the clone-like resemblance between Karl and the Oswald I'd seen post-JFK assassination. When it became apparent agencies and prominent individuals were involved in sabotaging Garrison's work, I had to consider there would be threats to my small effort to tell what I knew.

I had a plan to try to make us as inconspicuous as possible while going forward with the book. We drove Lee's '69 Olds to Fort Lauderdale and immediately moved the Abraxas to an off-the-major-waterway marina near the International Airport. And, for the next two and a half months we went back to documenting my CIA experience. We melded into the backwater, live-aboard underclass that hung onto some minimal survival lifestyle on aging boats on the polluted waterways that then laced the outskirts of urban Fort Lauderdale.

Much to our relief, we found matters at relative peace when we arrived back at the farm in Minnesota after the sweltering summer. We were still living with the fallout of the Jack Anderson column series, not quite sure of what might happen at any given moment. Constantly anxious about any word from a publisher or any other entity that might have an interest in the book project, I drove into the city every morning to pick up the mail, and then stopped for coffee at a nearby restaurant.

In retrospect, it was naïve of me to believe I was not being watched. I was about to experience one of the most frightening and life-changing periods to arise from my effort to make my account of the CIA's secret war against Cuba public.

One Friday evening in September, I decided to make the trip to my family's hunting property on Squaw Lake the following day, stay over, and come back on Sunday. Although I no longer hunted, it was my responsibility to go each fall, make sure the property was posted and make a general inspection.

That Saturday morning, I rose early and drove my 1968 Ford Bronco to town as usual. I had been receiving mail at the post office in St. Paul to reduce tampering with our mail. I was back home by 9 a.m. I had already packed my gear for the trip and decided to take my 1969 BMW motorcycle. An hour later, I was heading north for Squaw Lake some 250 miles away.

The trip was uneventful. I stopped for coffee and gas, putting the receipt in my pocket. When I arrived at Squaw Lake, I was chilled to the bone. The little community had a single café and gas station, a general store, a couple of bars, and Leno's Resort. I had been there many times before, and after getting supper at the café, I headed for Leno's for a sauna. The decision to hang on to my gas receipt and my visit to Leno's that night became hugely important.

A guest had to sign in at Leno's, get a towel, and pay the sauna fee before accessing the old rustic wooden facility. I greeted Mrs. Leno and chatted with her briefly. She knew of my family's land nearby and was aware of our annual visits.

The sauna was a great cure for the road chill, and I languished in the heat for nearly an hour. I awakened at dawn with renewed strength and confidence. I made my walking inspection of the land, had breakfast at the café, and headed back south. I arrived at the Lake Elmo farm at nightfall. My homecoming was unremarkable. Lee and the children seemed well. Little did I know that my rather spontaneous trip that weekend would be crucial in the horrific events that followed.

The next morning I rose as usual, helped Lee get the children off to school, and then drove into St. Paul for the mail. I stopped for coffee as usual and scanned through the *St. Paul Dispatch* newspaper. There on an inside page, something caught my eye. It was my image, done in the form of a typical police sketch. The sketch was an artist's rendering of my image from a photograph that Lee had taken of me in the Florida Keys the winter before and which was one of a number of personal photographs that had been taken from the house in north Key Largo (without the palm tree in the background!). Beneath the sketch was a news story reporting the assault and rape of a 9-year-old girl in Mounds Park on the east side of St. Paul over the preceding weekend. The unnamed man in the sketch was the primary suspect based on descriptions provided by children who had been near the scene of the crime. Police were looking for the suspect and asked for the help of the public.

I got to a pay phone to talk to Lee, not sure what I was going to say. Before I even got a word out, she told me that a Sergeant Zacharias from the Ramsey County Sheriff's Office had called a few minutes earlier and wanted to talk with me.

When I arrived at the Sheriff's Office, Zacharias told me I was a suspect in the rape/assault as described in the morning paper, based on information that his department and the St. Paul Police had received from various sources. They not only had my physical description, but my Bronco vehicle identification, color, license plate number, etc. They even had a description of the clothing I was wearing on Saturday morning. Zacharias then read me my rights and asked me if I cared to make a recorded statement.

I told him about my background, the CIA, my book project, the north Key Largo break in, the contact with Jack Anderson and the articles, the harassment, my lifestyle, my relationship with Lee; everything that might be relevant to the matter at hand. He kept trying to hurry me along, and I sensed he already knew much of what I was telling him. He then began to tell me some of the details of the crime. How brutal it was, that the little girl might die or, at the very least, be scarred for life; the trauma to the other children who were alleged to be at the scene. While not being specific, he said the assault had taken place on Saturday morning around 9 a.m. He asked me to give a full and complete account of my whereabouts over the weekend.

Unblinking and hoping not to come across as too anxious, I recited in detail my weekend trip to Squaw Lake. I included verifiable elements, the stops for gas and coffee all for which I had the receipts, the visit to a local resort for a sauna. Everything I could recall, minute by minute from Saturday morning through my return on Sunday night. In conclusion, I told Zacharias that I would be willing to take a polygraph examination, and, because I was not even in the area, had no intention of hiring an attorney. I asked him to clear me as a suspect. After about an hour and a half, Zacharias told me I could leave, but that he might want to talk to me again.

Curiously, when I began to check around the area for the distribution of the *St. Paul Dispatch* containing the police department sketch, I found that it had appeared only in limited editions in the immediate metropolitan area. When I got home, for the first time in our marriage, I lied to Lee, telling her that Sgt. Zacharias wanted information on an incident at the airport. She did not press me.

Several days passed without further incident. Then I received a call from a detective with the sex/homicide division of the St. Paul Police Department. I responded by going immediately to his office in downtown St. Paul to meet with him. He was tougher than Zacharias, much tougher and threatening. I decided I needed legal advice, quickly. I wasn't going to play into the hands of whoever was behind the effort to set me up. This was more than a case of mistaken identity.

With the second police interview I concluded the matter was not just going to go away and that I was, potentially, in huge trouble. I knew no criminal attorneys, having never needed one, so I went to the Yellow Pages. I called Attorney Errol Kantor who calmed me down and I went through the whole thing again, all the background information, the trip to Squaw Lake, the newspaper sketch, the story, and getting questioned by the police.

Kantor believed my extraordinary account. I gave the attorney all the money I had—$50—and he said he'd make a few calls and get back to me. He advised me to say no more to the police and definitely not to agree to stand in a line-up. With that, I went home to Lee and told her the whole story. We both cried uncontrollably.

Kantor called me back to his office the next day. He said he had made a few inquiries and that the assault/rape of the little girl was a crime getting top priority attention by the law enforcement, and they were under a lot of pressure to find the perpetrator. And, in a remark that caused me to freeze in my chair, he said, "The pressure to finger you is a political situation coming from very high up." He would not elaborate, he'd confirmed it—I was being framed!

He warned me against talking to the police anymore. As far as the line-up was concerned, Kantor said he had talked with the Ramsey County Attorney and told him, if they had enough evidence, arrest me; if not, stop bothering me.

The attorney then brought up the invitation I had received to a writer's conference in Rye, New York, taking place the following week. It was an expense-paid, weeklong event. "My advice to you is to go now. Make whatever arrangements you must, but get out of town. Don't make it easy for 'them'—if they want you bad enough they'll come and get you and I'll have to take it from there." I asked Kantor how much I owed him in legal fees and he replied, "Let's see how this works out." To this day, I owe him a profound debt of gratitude for believing in me and for the advice he provided. The important thing was to get out of Minnesota and make myself less available. The next day, I loaded the

BMW motorcycle, and after a tearful goodbye to Lee, left for New York. I felt like a fugitive on the run.

Besides the visits from Zacharias and in light of my absence, someone started a rumor campaign in our home community in Minnesota. It spread quickly that Brad Ayers was wanted on a criminal charge in connection with the assault and rape of a little girl in September. It was a crushing, dastardly act. When I learned of it I swore I would one day even the score with those who were responsible and the way to do that would be to make my CIA book a reality.

Lee flew to New York to be with me several weeks after the writer's conference. We needed to talk and plan our next move. With the pressure still on from law enforcement, I didn't dare return to Minnesota, but I missed Lee and my family terribly. We decided it would be best if I stayed on the move. Lee and I rode the motorcycle to Florida and we had a few precious days to ourselves. She flew back to Minnesota to face the music again while I moved in with an old friend in Coconut Grove. I returned to my writing and was resolute in my determination to finish the book.

Finally, distressed by my separation from Lee and our home, I decided to act. In December, I flew back to Minnesota to reclaim my identity, regardless of the risks. Lee had been contending with the uncertainty and pressures for months. I proposed we temporarily relocate to Florida. She cheerfully accepted the plan, and, over a period of two days, we packed up the Bronco, found a caretaker for the house, and loaded our outdoor gear in a Boston Whaler boat. With our dog and the kids, we set off for Florida and the boat we had lived in the previous summer.

By the end of May, the original manuscript of nearly 400 double-spaced pages was essentially finished. Knowing I could not count on any help from Jack Anderson, I began reaching out to literary agents in New York. Perry Knowlton expressed interest. The school year was ending and the heat, rain, and humidity of the Florida summer was about to descend. With our work done, we longed to return to the farm in Minnesota. The only thing keeping us from going back was the fear of what might be waiting for us.

Then, in June 1972, the Watergate break-in and ensuing investigation changed everything. From the outset of our difficulties which had begun with the publication of the Jack Anderson articles in the spring of 1971, I was convinced that the CIA, FBI, or possibly some ad hoc federal damage control/counter intelligence entity was behind the harassment and efforts to discredit us. It appeared that this effort might have been orchestrated directly out of the Nixon White House, possibly by the same people that broke into the Watergate. The ensuing revelations seemed to reinforce that perception. Some of the Cubans working under E. Howard Hunt and G. Gordon Liddy had worked for the CIA's Miami Station at the same time I was there. The more I learned, the more it became apparent that their pattern of dirty tricks bore close resemblance to those that had plagued Lee and me.

With my mission basically accomplished and with a possibility of a publisher on the horizon, emboldened and sensing that we might now be free to go home, we returned to the farm and tried to pick up the pieces of our life.

Thank God for Watergate![30]

THE ZENITH SECRET

CHAPTER 25

Even though we'd delivered the completed manuscript to Knowlton in New York, Lee and I returned to Minnesota with considerable trepidation. What made the situation worse was our financial predicament. The preoccupation with completing the book, the flights to Florida, the boat, and the inattention to the flying business left us virtually destitute.

Attempting to resurrect the flying business was out of the question. Operating costs for general aviation were escalating out of sight. I met with my investors and honored their wishes to sell the hangar and airplane. I took a job giving flight instruction and teaching ground school and started writing again for magazines and hiring out as a remodeler to help make ends meet.

Meanwhile, Perry Knowlton had talked with several major publishers, but only the Bobbs-Merrill Company of New York and Indianapolis was interested. In 1973, the manuscript was under review by the managing editor, Tom Gervasi.

Unbeknownst to me was that upon retirement from the CIA, Bill Harvey went to work for Bobbs-Merrill. Apparently, my manuscript was intercepted and the book's contents carefully reviewed by the agency and some of its entities. For the next two and a half years, I made revisions and rewrites of the manuscript at the suggestion of Gervasi. The pattern was one of whittling away at those parts that were the most sensitive or potentially embarrassing to the agency. Gervasi explained that Bobbs-Merrill could not accept the libel risks that portions of the book presented.[31] One of the requirements set by Gervasi was that I change all the names of major figures. Also excised was text on David Morales, Rosselli, the use of toxic chemical agents against Cuba, Karl's death, and Ferrie's presence at JM/WAVE. By 1974, I was beaten down trying to make a living and hold my life together. With my marriage to Lee falling apart, I agreed to what Gervasi asked. After all that it had cost, just getting the book into print was better than no book at all.

After rewriting the book for the third time, I sought outside advice from Gay Bostock, a Minnneapolis writer and editor. She read the manuscript and was enthusiastic with what I had. She helped to piece together the elements of the story that were left after the edits at Bobbs-Merrill.

The ordeal of the book (1968-1974) placed too great a strain on our marriage, and Lee and I divorced. She returned to Florida with her children and the Lake Elmo farm was sold, the proceeds divided between us.

In 1975 I applied for a private detective license and wrote to Zacharias asking if my application might be contaminated by having been a subject in the rape/assault incident of 1971.

Zacharias got right back to me by phone and almost apologetically stated it would not in any way impact upon my application process and if I needed his endorsement to please ask for it. I was dumbfounded because only a few years earlier, he had been out to crucify me. He asked me to stop by his office when my book was published, as he'd like to have a copy of it. I was still very wary of him and his intentions. Nevertheless, I brought him a signed copy in June of 1976, shortly after the book was released.

Zacharias took me into his office and shut the door. He told me some odd, extraordinary, and puzzling things. He said the file on the rape/assault incident had been destroyed. This was less than five years after the case was presented to me and my attorney as one of unusual interest by the government and law enforcement. He added that the crime was never solved, but that they thought a man already in prison had done it.

He then told me he had made two trips to Squaw Lake to check my alibi and had also verified my gas and coffee stops. Despite that, he said that he and the St. Paul Police continued to get very precise anonymous tips that reflected an intimate knowledge of me, my pattern of behavior, dress, appearance, etc.— and he became suspicious. He never identified the informant who always used the telephone. He even called the CIA to request the agency's cooperation but they refused. At that point, the county attorney relinquished the pressure to arrest me. I asked him if he knew the damage that been inflicted upon me and my family, the undermining of my marriage, the whole bitter pill. His reply was that he was only doing what instructed to do by "higher ups" and that it was through his insistence that I was cleared as a suspect.

And today, in view of my pragmatic mistrust of government and the law enforcement establishment, I question whether there was, in fact, the rape and brutal assault of a little girl on that September morning in Mounds Park. I am inclined to believe the entire affair was concocted to discredit me, destroy my reputation, ruin my family life, and, if it really worked, to provoke me to self-destruct.

By the fall of 1976, after running a few ads for the book in Washington and New York papers, Bobbs-Merrill's interest in promoting *The War That Never Was* diminished, and it was left to me to arrange publicity for the book on my own. The story never grabbed the attention of the major national media, despite the exposure of the CIA's secret war against Cuba and the agency's association with organized crime. Despite all the promises by the marketing and publicity departments at Bobbs-Merrill, they sponsored only one limited promotional tour in the summer of 1976. The high point was a TV interview I did with high-profile former Johnson-era White House correspondent Nancy Dickinson.

John Rosselli gave limited testimony to the Church Committee in the summer of 1975 connecting Mafia bosses Santos Trafficante and Sam Giancana with CIA plots to kill Fidel Castro. Apparently, Rosselli wasn't questioned about his activities at JM/WAVE. However, because of his testimony and published dialogue with Jack Anderson, the Senate Intelligence Committee Sub-Committee looking into the JFK assassination, became interested in Rosselli and in questioning him. Word was that Rosselli would be called to testify before the full Subcommittee.

In 1976, as my book was being released, I had no knowledge of Rosselli's connections with mob kingpins Giancana and Trafficante. About a year earlier, Giancana had been murdered, gangland style, a few days before he was to appear before the Church Committee. Now, as I was doing my best to promote *The War That Never Was*, in an effort to bring the JM/WAVE perspective to public attention, Rosselli disappeared.

I immediately suspected foul play. Rosselli was too old and ill to run on his own. He really had no place to hide. He would not have had many friends or allies willing to shelter him. Given his close associations with the CIA, I believed the agency probably was involved in his disappearance. The savvy old mobster would only have gone off with someone he absolutely trusted. In August, his body was found in a steel drum, floating in a Florida canal. What immediately occurred to me when I learned of Rosselli's death was that the one person he would have trusted implicitly and might have gone anywhere with was David Sanchez Morales.

Meanwhile, my old nemesis, Orlando Bosch, was in the headlines with his militant Cuban exile group, CORU, and their various bombings and violent anti-Castro activities. Chilean diplomat, Orlando Letelier and his secretary were killed in a car bombing in Washington, and it was rumored that anti-Castro Cubans were somehow involved.

After months of being passed off to Gervasi's publicity and marketing assistants, underlings and junior staff people at Bobbs-Merrill, I finally had a phone conversation with him in early 1977. Gervasi was distancing himself from me and I could no longer count on Bobbs-Merrill for anything.

"Tom," I asked, *"The War That Never Was"* is turning up DOA. I don't get it. There's tons of stuff coming out of Washington that tie into what I know and can elaborate upon; create some stir about my account. I've done everything you've asked and a whole lot more on my own. Bobbs-Merrill can sell more books; I'm willing to do my part. My information is being ignored!"

Gervasi signed off wishing me good luck.

Baffled by Bobbs-Merrill's handling of my book, and now reconsidering what I'd agreed to in the "editing" process, I pondered why the publisher went ahead with the contract and book in the first place. My contemplation led me in a rather sinister direction. While the agency seemed to have escaped relatively undamaged from the Watergate scandal it was suffering from an acute image problem. The hearings of recent years had revealed an operation clearly beyond any oversight and in violation of its charter to engage only in foreign intelligence collection.

The picture being painted was that the CIA was an out-of-control, highly secretive, autonomous, maverick organization, operating without constraint or Constitutional oversight. My eyewitness account of the Kennedy White House Special Group having authorized and micromanaged JM/WAVE covert paramilitary operations put the CIA in a different light. Attorney General Robert Kennedy's presence at JM/WAVE on the two occasions that I observed in 1963 flew in the face of the notion the CIA was engaged in unauthorized activities. Kennedy's presence showed that the agencies activities were fully sanctioned by the White House.

In the fall of 1976, the House of Representatives, finally provoked by the flood of information bringing certain aspects of the *Warren Commission Report* and the circumstances surrounding the death of Martin Luther King into question, had established the Select Committee on Assassinations (HSCA).

Supposedly, this would be a no-holds-barred inquiry. I looked forward to being called to testify about what I knew of JM/WAVE activities and my perceptions and observations while serving with the agency.

Right through 1978, I held out hope the HSCA would seek me out and allow me to put on the record what I might contribute. Years later, when I finally spoke with Gaeton Fonzi, one of the Committee's principal investigators working specifically on CIA, Cuban exile, and Mafia leads, he said they "couldn't find me."

A bright spot in this rather dismal situation was the burgeoning interest of highly credible, respected writers and researchers. Most had publishing contracts with major houses and were accumulating all they could beyond what had been revealed in the media, the course of the various official investigation, and under the Freedom on Information Act, or their private sources.

One winter evening, while chatting at the bar at the Decathlon club in

Minneapolis, I got into a rare, stimulating conversation with a gentleman about my experience with the Cubans and JM/WAVE. He had read my book, so he knew where I was coming from. I estimated the man was about 10 years older than I, and was trim, intelligent, a bit intense. We had to break off our conversation because of a raging blizzard and return to our homes before the roads were closed.

The next time I met him there, he told me that he was a lieutenant colonel, serving as an intelligence officer with the Army Reserve Command. He told me the Reserve was anticipating some sort of role in connection with the "Cuban problem," and I might have something to contribute.

He apparently had access to my official records and suggested I seriously consider reactivating my commission for an assignment with the 13th Psychological Operations Battalion at Ft. Snelling. He implied, given my rank as a senior captain when I resigned, I could be promoted to major within a year. I could not believe my ears. After all that had transpired, the Army might welcome me back?

I agreed and served initially with the psychological warfare unit during the Cuban Marielito boatlift event, then, at my request, with the Federal Emergency Management Administration doing evacuation planning in the early 1980s.[32] But after I found out my promotion to major had not come through, I resigned. My military 201 file, the records of my active duty service, and CIA service, my medical history, and efficiency reports—all had been stripped from the file without explanation or apparent recoverability. I sensed the all-powerful, insidious reach of Langley once again. To this day, despite repeated Freedom of Information Act requests, the records have never been produced. As a result, I've been denied promised awards and decorations for combat service and have been refused Veterans Administration GI Bill disability benefits for various injury claims.

By 1981, all three of my sons were in college, and I seldom saw them. I'd completed work on my postgraduate degree, a Masters in Education, and now at midlife was restless and open to new challenges. I found it impossible to settle into what might have been an idyllic existence. I was working on another book on unexplained phenomena, but remained haunted by the intrigue, excitement, and adventures of the past.

A plan had been jelling in the back of my mind and I decided to implement it. I sold the rustic house I had built overlooking the St. Croix River, temporarily moved into an apartment with my new girlfriend, and bought a 34' Taiwanese trawler in Sarasota, Florida. There, I intended to open a new chapter of my life, a "Travis McGee" existence, moving the boat about Florida, the Gulf and the islands at will, writing, doing some investigating, looking after my retired parents near Venice, and cruising the Caribbean with my dog and lovely new companion.

In the early 1980s, the illegal drug trade was fueling the Florida economy. For many of the same reasons we used Florida as a base against Cuba 20 years before the drug smugglers were using the state and its wild, forsaken wetlands as a base of operations. I decided to offer my skills in the Reagan administration's war on drugs.

The Drug Enforcement Agency (DEA) had just issued a call for recruits in connection with Reagan's drug war. Except for the age factor, I seemed to meet all the requirements. Age appeared to be the only obstacle to hiring, if I passed the background investigation. I was excited. The starting salary was good and I relished the idea of getting back into real action.

What I didn't know at the time was that I'd unwittingly and rather naïvely gotten myself tangled up in congressional and other official investigations of the period. The entire sordid affair is historically known as the Iran Contra scandal that nearly brought down the Reagan presidency. The public revelation of my involvement, a first person account of my experience where I was once again to cross paths with some of my old CIA compatriots and agency proprietary companies from the JM/WAVE era, will be left for another day.[33]

In 1989 during a respite in Minnesota, I received a phone call from a fellow identifying himself as Bob Dorff, a well-connected businessman and screenwriter in Beverly Hills. Dorff explained that he had read *The War That Never Was* and, as a private JFK assassination researcher, was intrigued by my account. Specifically, he wanted to know if the CIA employee I referred to, as "the Big Indian" was David Morales. By this time, I'd been so beaten and bruised intellectually and emotionally by the handling of my book, I'd abandoned concerns about perpetrating Bobbs-Merrill's censorship of my account. I confirmed for Dorff that the Big Indian, El Indio, and David Sanchez Morales were one and the same.

Dorff sounded excited by my disclosure, and he was anxious to meet with me to discuss other aspects of my book. He volunteered *The War That Never Was* might be the basis for a screenplay. Would I be willing to fly to the West Coast to meet with him?

In Minneapolis I had met a wealthy gentleman from Phoenix who had extensive business dealings in the Twin Cities. We shared an interest in boats and he eventually hired me as an investigative consultant. The assignments I was performing for him entailed that I base myself on his sailboat at the Kona Kai Yacht Club on Point Loma in San Diego. This was one of the elite, luxury, live aboard marinas on the southern Californian coast. A huge luxury ship belonging to the Krocs' (the founders of McDonald's) was tied up there among the magnificent yachts of movie stars and other celebrities. One of the amenities of my assignment was carte blanche access to all the club facilities, including the excellent restaurant and lounge.

Bob Dorff kept in contact with me, encouraging a meeting at the earliest opportunity, but it was some weeks later before I could get time away from my assignment in San Diego and drive to Los Angeles to meet him. I drove to his address in Beverly Hills; a cluttered second story office in the heart of the commercial district. Dorff was an affable, heavy-set, middle-aged man, short in stature, a smooth, somewhat affected social manner with a mincing stride and effeminate gestures that I'd come to associate with Hollywood types. He greeted me warmly, and we spent several days discussing my CIA experience, *The War That Never Was,* and the personalities involved. We talked in great detail about Morales and he put me up in his condominium where we conveniently continued our discussions until late in the evening.

At one point, he engaged me in a phone conversation with Gaeton Fonzi, a former HSCA investigator, who had first made a possible connection between Morales and domestic assassinations. Fonzi had written an article about his work for the Select Committee and I urged him to continue his research, particularly relating to Morales. Knowing what I did about the Big Indian, he could well have been involved. I made it clear I had no specific information of Morales' culpability, though. Dorff's principle interest in me was as a source of information on Morales. In exchange for my cooperation, Dorff offered to present my book to an executive at HBO for possible consideration as a made-for-TV-movie.

After returning to San Diego I was having breakfast at the Kona Kai one morning. It was in March 1989. I heard a voice from the distant past. At a large, round table to my rear were a group of men in business suits. The voice came from that table and when I turned to look there was Bob Wall, my initial JM/WAVE case officer, who I hadn't seen or communicated with in 26 years. The men were talking rather loudly and apparently had little concern for my presence near their table. A chill ran down my spine as I heard Wall describe to the group details of the CIA's secret war against Cuba during the period I served with the agency in 1963 and 1964. I kept my back to them and listened. I was astounded, nearly overwhelmed, by the odd coincidence of the situation. The call from Dorff, his expressed interest in Morales, now the appearance of Wall, Morales' assistant, stepping out from the crypt.

I kept my composure, listening to the men's conversation and Wall's continuing comments. This was going to be good! Maybe Wall and his group knew I was there all the time? Was I being baited? Did Wall know of the new interest in Morales via some phone tap or compromise on Dorff's part? I had to try to find out, overcome with curiosity and my need to somehow reconnect with a man that played such an important role in my life. As the men rose from their table to leave, I turned at looked at Bob Wall. He looked almost exactly as I remembered him.

I was about to say something, but it wasn't necessary. Wall recognized me immediately. As we shook hands it was almost as it had been so many years earlier when I first walked into his office. Wall explained he's retired from the agency and was now a consultant with a hemispheric financial group based in Bethesda, Maryland. He claimed he'd been attending a conference of global financial experts at the Kona Kai and had some free time before their next scheduled meeting. We spent the next four hours together talking over the "old days" at JM/WAVE, how our lives had gone since, our families, and all kinds of tangential matters, including CIA-supported paramilitary actions in Central America.

I was astounded and intrigued by Wall's openness and candor. Never once did he bring up *The War That Never Was,* nor did I, letting him guide the conversation. I took him into San Diego to shop for gifts for his family in an old car my wealthy client kept at the marina. We had a drink together. Finally, I queried him about some of the people we'd worked with at JM/WAVE—Shackley, Clines, Sforza, Roderick, and certain case officers I remembered. He told me what he knew about them, rather guardedly I sensed, and respectfully told me Morales and Rip Robertson had both passed away. Wall recalled some of his moments with Morales that coincided with my memories of the Big Indian and we shared some laughs.

I was careful not to press the Morales questions beyond the superficial. After all the years, I could still detect Bob Wall's professional and possibly personal discomfort with the former chief of operations at JM/WAVE. I made no mention of Bob Dorff's recently expressed interest in Morales. Wall gave me his business card when I dropped him off back at the Kona Kai conference hall entrance. I went back to the boat to sit on the deck as the evening fog rolled off the Pacific, shrouding everything in a mysterious grayness. It was not unlike what was going on in my mind as I struggled to fathom the events of the day.

I continued my work for the wealthy Southwest businessman into the summer of 1989, and when it was possible to travel to Los Angeles, I'd visit briefly with Dorff and we'd continue what had become somewhat a brainstorming of JM/WAVE related knowns and unknowns, hoping to piece together bits and pieces of evidence that might point directly to CIA involvement in the JFK assassination. Dorff picked my mind. He continued to focus on Morales. During this time, we were in contact with Fonzi and authors Tony Summers and David Lifton exchanging information and speculating on leads. Dorff, with resources unavailable to most other private researchers, had amassed a significant library of books and official documents, some from the HSCA and other confidential sources.

Dorff and I had quite a lengthy discussion about who actually served as the deputy chief of station at JM/WAVE. Tom Clines was prominent in the operational front offices adjacent to Shackley's private suite in the operations building. But, so was Gordon Campbell. I tried to explain to Dorff there was another very visible executive suite, with all the Zenith corporate trappings, in the building next door to operations. This was the cover office, staffed with full-time secretaries and decorated to appear as a typical business headquarters. Shackley would never be there, but either Clines or Campbell would when it was useful to present Zenith Technical Enterprise's face to world. The Maritime Branch was located in the same building, and for that reason, it was most convenient for Campbell, who was running that branch, to man the cover office. I'd described the physical appearance of both Clines and Campbell to Dorff, and I found it interesting in Fonzi's book there was no mention of Campbell. Campbell was identified in *Deadly Secrets,* however, . This would become a matter of significance in my future work.

Dorff told me that he had a working association with an organization in Dallas known as the JFK Assassination Information Center, directed by attorney Bernard Fensterwald; early JFK researcher and author, Gary Shaw and his assistant, Larry Hancock. He was on the phone with them regularly during my visits to Beverly Hills.

Dorff encouraged my continuing cooperation by facilitating efforts to peddle the movie rights to *The War That Never Was* and the publication of the new book I'd begun on my experience with the DEA and the Reagan/Bush war on drugs.[34] Dorff also covered my expenses when I was in Beverly Hills, allowing me to sleep in his condo. I hoped that by allying myself with Dorff, I might finally realize my literary aspirations while also contributing to what I had trusted to be serious, honorable assassination research.

By the fall of 1989, Dorff, his associates and I had just about explored all the research avenues that might implicate Morales and his connections to the domestic assassinations. My interaction with Dorff had reawakened my long held suspicions that somewhere there was a link between CIA, JM/WAVE, and the assassination of the president, and possibly others, including RFK and maybe even MLK in 1968. It became quite apparent that to carry the research forward a field investigation would have to be mounted to reconstruct the life and activities of the American CIA officer known as El Indio.

At Dorff's request, I completed a detailed affidavit attesting to my knowledge of and relationship with David Morales. What followed was a series of telephone communications between myself, Dorff, Gary Shaw, Attorney Fensterwald, a well-resourced businessman, and Joe West, a JFK Assassination Center benefactor from Houston. It was agreed, that I should open an investigation on Morales. I explained to Dorff and his associates that, as a licensed private detective, I could not undertake an investigation unless I had a contract to do so with a client requesting the inquiry be performed and, at least a minimal retainer paid in confirmation of the agreement.

I required a contract agreement in hand in order to proceed with a field background investigation of El Indio. It was agreed I'd drive to Dallas and meet with Shaw to obtain the agreement and then go to Houston where I would receive a $1,000 retainer from Joe West. It was acknowledged that the retainer would only satisfy the need to perfect the contract. Additional fees and expenses would undoubtedly accumulate and have to be covered. Attorney Fensterwald said he understood this very clearly. This seemed to be a very sincere, genuine commitment on the part of Dorff and the others, especially because Dorff kept advising me to be sure to keep all my receipts and maintain accurate records of my time and other expenses.

I packed the car for extended travel, closed up the townhouse, and on November 27, 1989, departed for Dallas to meet Gary Shaw. I had no idea what may lie ahead. It was another cast your fate into the winds venture. So began the search for El Indio.

BRADLEY E. AYERS

CHAPTER 26

I knew in my guts this one was not going to be a cakewalk. If, in fact, Morales was some part of CIA or related assassination plots—foreign or domestic—the secrets would not be given up easily. I explained this to Dorff and all concerned before deciding to embark on the pursuit of El Indio. The agency would be well prepared to bank the fire, and would, if monitoring the phone and mail exchanges of the preceding six months, know what we were up to.

The JFK Assassination Information Center in Dallas had become a high-profile conspiracy theory proponent in the continuing controversy surrounding the death of the president. The center was a focal point for all sorts of so-called researchers and independent investigators—mostly dilettantes of questionable motive—who had no scruples or sense for critical thinking. Except for establishing legitimacy for my inquiry, I was reluctant to report directly to the center as the field investigation progressed. It was agreed that Bob Dorff, who maintained a modicum of personal security and awareness, would act as a cut-out, an intermediary who would receive my communications as the investigation went forward and send it along to Fensterwald and Shaw.

I had just finished Don DeLillo's novel *Libra*, a sympathetic portrait of Lee Harvey Oswald, and as I made the long drive to Dallas, my mind was occupied with thoughts of the man who allegedly killed the president. Had DeLillo, with his imaginative work, accurately portrayed Oswald, and did it support or contradict the "patsy" theory? The book, albeit fiction, was (from what I knew about Oswald) a well-researched and intriguing piece of work. When I arrived in Dallas on November 29, my thoughts were acutely focused on the events in Dealey Plaza that month, 26 years earlier. I met Shaw at the center and he took me on a quick tour of the exhibit, an impressive assemblage of JFK assassination memorabilia, collectibles, books, and related publications. Gary and I talked over coffee about the Morales investigation and reviewed the arrangements for reporting via Dorff. I'd never walked the ground in Dealey Plaza, so after the meeting with Shaw I toured the area. As a former special operations paramilitary officer, I was interested in viewing for myself what could have been a standard paramilitary style ambush—triangular fire from an overlooking perch (School Book Depository or nearby tall buildings), the overpass, and the grassy knoll. Dealey Plaza was a classic textbook killing zone. I struggled to keep an open mind, but the scene sent chills down my spine. I choked as I imagined the horror of that moment when the fusillade rang out. The execution was exquisitely simple and perfect if, in fact, that's what occurred.

I checked back in with Shaw before leaving for Houston to meet with West. Sure as hell, as I left the center I picked up a tail—two suited FBI types about a half block behind. I ducked into a bar, went out the rear door; then went into a crowded sports bar in an old restored warehouse. I went into the restroom, reversed my jacket and put on the baseball cap I always carried with me when I might be followed. It was late afternoon before I was able to slip out a basement door and get back to my car. I took a circuitous route out of town, thought several times I hadn't ditched my pursuers, but finally got on my way to Houston.

Once clear of Dallas, I called both Dorff and Shaw on their home lines and left word I wouldn't be returning to Dallas soon, at least not until the Morales investigation had been completed. My suspicions about the JFK Center being a possible focal point of interest by those monitoring private assassination research had been confirmed.

I met with Joe West that evening and again the following morning. He quizzed me in detail on what I had on Morales and related CIA-JM/WAVE matters. He didn't seem to quite make the connection to a possible assassination conspiracy and he begrudgingly handed me the $1000 retainer. I drove back north to meet with Shaw to go over the investigative agenda and procedures, and get his signature on the retainer agreement. I met him in Corsicana, Texas, well away from Dallas and the center, and left for New Mexico.

I began a two-month exercise in "wheel spinning." I searched all over New Mexico for any trace of Morales, going on the information I'd gotten from Wall that the Big Indian had originated and died in the state. Old phone books, birth and death records, tax rolls, marriage and divorce records, voter registrations, newspapers, library files, routine public records such as vehicle licensing, obscure and incomplete Native American tribal-reservation records. Nearly all of this had to be done in person where the records were kept, and the quality and availability of the data was often poorly maintained. Compounding the problem was the fact the surname, Morales, was about as common as Carlson, Johnson, and Olson in the northern Midwest. It was tedious, time-consuming, expensive, fatiguing work.

I eventually threw caution to the wind and wrote to Bob Wall, advising him deceptively (the guilt is still with me because it's not my way) that I was doing research for a book on minorities who had prominent careers in our nation's intelligence services. Could he give me more specifics on where I might develop background on Morales or possibly, pass my request on to Ted Shackley? He gave me Shackley's address and I wrote immediately giving him the same contrived explanation to explain my need for information on Morales. I received a cordial response from Ted. Although he criticized me for going public with my views on America's war on drugs,[35] he gave me what I needed for the Morales inquiry. Ted and Bob, my former CIA superiors, wittingly or unwittingly, opened the door to the life of the Big Indian.

With leads provided by Shackley, I was able to do a lot of preliminary investigative work by phone and lay out a precise agenda for continuing in the field. Arriving in Phoenix on February 28, I set about reconstructing what could be discovered there. Through mind-numbing public records searches, scanning old newspapers and phone books, recovering school and church records, I was able to identify persons who likely had some knowledge of Morales' personal and professional life. The next task was to track them down and solicit their cooperation with my inquiry, which I continued to press under the guise of book research. Things fell surprisingly in place, and as March began, I'd assembled a substantial file.

I was able to reconstruct in considerable detail, with supporting evidence, Morales' early life in Phoenix up through the period when he briefly attended the University of Arizona in Tempe in 1944. Utilizing school records, academic yearbooks, church files and other documents, I reconstructed Morales' childhood and adolescence, his educational history, personality, social interaction, and friendships.

He was nicknamed "Didi" by his closest friends and they would continue to call him that throughout his life. David Morales later became known by his "war names" Pancho, or the Big Indian, a.k.a. El Indio (for his massive build and distinct Mexican-Native American features). Morales had a lengthy list of assumed operational aliases outside the CIA and other official agencies. He was remembered as a dark, handsome Latino kid, tough early-on from the barrio streets, yet outgoing, engaging, and, on occasion, aggressive to the point of bullying. He was a good athlete, very physical, with a quick temper. In a fight, he could be quite vicious.

This information led me to several people who had fairly regular contact with Morales throughout his life and proved to be exceedingly valuable sources. The essential substance of my preliminary report was based on interviews with Morales' lifelong friend, Ruben Carbajal; his attorney, Robert Walton; high school classmate (and now TV executive) Delbert Lewis; younger brother Robert Morales. All lived in the Phoenix-Scottsdale area and were reasonably accessible and cooperative.

To some degree, I'd been awed, intimidated, and offended by Morales during my contact with him at JM/WAVE. I even saw Ted Shackley defer to his overbearing manner and imposing presence. Morales seemed, in some ways, larger than life, unreal, callous, insensitive, rude, single-minded, a giant machine in the shape of a man bulldozing its way as it wished. His documented history in Phoenix as a youth, and the interviews with his most intimate associates brought a human perspective to what I was seeking to document, to some degree contrasting with the sinister nature of Morales' work with the CIA.

While my interviews with Robert Morales were not as productive as I'd hoped, the discussions with Carbajal and Walton proved quite fruitful, and provided extremely important and provocative information about Morales' life and activities with the agency. I spent hours talking with them, having ascertained to my satisfaction their reliability as sources.

The summarized statements of each of these individuals were confirming and revealing. Based on their knowledge and association with Morales over the years, they had come to believe that David was a hit man for the CIA. Carbajal and Walton were able to offer astoundingly specific information relative to Morales' high-level agency associates (with whom I'd also served in the 1960s), conversations during which the Big Indian told of his exploits, his various government operational covers and travels, as well as his alleged retirement from the CIA in 1976.

I deliberately kept the interviews freewheeling, unstructured and open-ended. At the end of the day, I documented what I'd heard and cross-referenced it, if applicable, with information from other credible sources available to me. The reports sent on to Dorff were well supported with testimony and corroboration relevant to the interests of my client, the JFK Assassination Information Center.

Implicit in their comments was the apparent rationale that murder in the name of the United States was morally acceptable, particularly if Didi and his associates felt it necessary to protect America. By whose judgment, and where does the killing end?

All sources expressed their suspicions as to the true cause of Morales' death in 1978, which came at a time the HSCA was looking into the JFK assassination. They uniformly viewed Morales as a dedicated patriot, attesting that by their intimate knowledge of the man, David Morales could be counted upon to do the dirty work if he believed it was his duty.

Carbajal reminisced at length about his lifelong friendship with David Morales, sometimes near the point of tears and other times with fits of laughter.

THE ZENITH SECRET

Although I was reluctant to emphasize it in my report because of my inability to explore and verify at the time, I found Ruben's accounts of Morales' frequent trips and alleged business interests in Mexico in the 1960s to be of interest. Morales would always stop by El Molino, the popular Mexican restaurant in Phoenix that had been operated by the Carbajal family for years, to visit with Ruben and have several drinks as he passed through town on his way to Mexico City or Guadalajara. This confirmed what I'd learned of his activities many years earlier while at JM/WAVE.

The restaurant the Carbajal's owned was a fixture in the community. Ruben intimated all sorts of Arizona politicians frequented the eating spot, and that the Carbajal family was quite friendly with the Goldwater clan, including Senator Barry, and his family.

Ruben confirmed that David had left Arizona to attend college in California after being turned down for military service for physical reasons. He left Phoenix for California shortly thereafter, where he attended USC and UCLA. Robert corroborated Ruben's story and added that David had been supported by and lived with a wealthy benefactor in Los Angeles until graduation from UCLA in 1947, when he enlisted in the U.S. Army paratroops. Both Ruben and Robert suggest David was recruited almost immediately into intelligence work and served in Germany.

I had a little information on Morales' activity in California, but as with other aspects of my inquiry, that period of his life would become of particular interest to me only years later. Morales apparently remained on duty in Germany, in some intelligence capacity, until 1953. There, he met his spouse, Joan, who was said to be the daughter of a prominent Boston family. She contrasted greatly with his Cesar Romero appearance and his teaching at a military-dependent school. If this information were correct, Morales could have been involved in the CIA's Berlin tunnel operation[36] (the Berlin tunnel operation was a successful but controversial plan to use tunnels to get intelligence about Soviet troops in East Germany), his involvement with that covert escapade, touted as a brilliant Cold War success for the U.S., would have placed him in early career contact with the likes of William Harvey, Ted Shackley, Henry Hecksher and other key agency paramilitary specialists who later became infamous as the CIA's covert operations masterminds. Carbajal said that at a Washington party for Morales in the 1970s, David's CIA compatriots told him that Didi had been selected by the agency's newly formed covert operations branch in 1948 as one of the first six paramilitary operatives. If this were true, it meant that Morales was recruited by the agency right after his graduation from UCLA.

My lengthy interviews with Carbajal and Morales provided an informal overview of El Indio's exploits with the agency in the years following 1953, as both men recalled it from Morales' visits to Phoenix and their contact with him. Supposedly, Morales was back in Washington attending the University of Maryland in 1953. Shortly thereafter, he was in Venezuela and then Havana, as a U.S. Foreign Service officer. Each of my sources suggested the diplomatic assignments were cover for David's intelligence work, although they had no intimate knowledge of what that might have been at the time. All had heard of Morales' visit to the Eisenhower White House to receive a decoration following the successful overthrow of the government in Guatemala.[37] Of course, they assumed he was wrapped up in the Castro-Cuban controversy well into the 1960s, but only knew he'd returned from Havana after Castro came to power and was working out of Washington and Miami.

I determined from my discussions with various sources that David Morales never attained the rank of sergeant first class in the Army. Corporal was his highest rank. He never served in World War II, nor did he serve in Korea. The tombstone inscription in Wilcox was false. There was no autopsy following his death; none was requested or ordered. The alleged ambulance breakdown in Benson was thought to be a critical factor in his emergency evacuation to the hospital in Tucson. His wife and children supposedly moved to Newton, New Hampshire refusing to comment about David's life and death. I was unable to convince David's brother Robert to obtain a copy of the Tucson medical records and death certificate for me, and efforts to put my hands on them were totally frustrated by the Arizona authorities. During follow-up interviews with Carbajal, Walton, and Robert Morales, after my visit to the Wilcox cemetery, I brought up the apparent recent disturbance of the soil over the area where the casket should have been buried. I asked if anyone had requested an exhumation or movement of the remains to another site. Despite the general opinion that Morales had been murdered—he had once expressed to Carbajal that the agency would take him out at some point—there seemed to be no interest that the grave might have been tampered with as a result of our ongoing investigation.

I gathered from comments by each of my sources that Morales maintained contacts with various political and financial interests in Arizona and Las Vegas, as well as in Washington and cities in Mexico, Central America. and South America. The purpose of his frequent visits to these locations was not known, but David apparently had access to the higher levels of power in government and private enterprise. During the later period of his government service, he was engaged with Ruben, and Bob Walton in Latin American commodities trading and import-export dealings involving Mexican businessmen and government officials. I discreetly avoided raising the question of Morales' possible ties with the Mafia or organized crime anywhere, leaving that for another time. I hoped the information might pop up as some other revelations had.

Morales apparently never made his work with the agency a secret from his family and closest friends. He was particularly vocal about his involvement in the CIA's various undertakings to unseat Castro. He shared his anger and frustration over the failed Bay of Pigs invasions and openly blamed President Kennedy for the slaughter of the exile freedom fighters on the beach.[38] Carbajal and Walton knew David was involved in the secret war that followed in the early 1960s and that Morales was at the center of CIA covert paramilitary operations. They knew he was probably involved in the attempts to assassinate Fidel Castro.

Morales continually expressed a profound dislike for the president, referring to him as a coward and a traitor. Morales' deep hatred for the president surfaced dramatically one evening in the spring of 1973 after a quasi-official CIA social event in Washington, to which Carbajal and Walton had been invited. Everyone had been drinking heavily, but had returned to a hotel room for a nightcap. The conversation turned to President Kennedy. Bob Walton had worked in the early political campaigns of JFK in Massachusetts and had a favorable opinion of the deceased president.

Suddenly, Morales went ballistic and began to rant and curse the Kennedys. He brought up the Bay of Pigs and what he'd experienced on the invasion beaches—his exiles were exterminated by Castro's militia because of no air support—at the decision of president . Morales raved for several minutes, stunning the sensibilities of Ruben, Walton, and Walton's wife.

None of my sources that had been close to Morales ever admitted meeting John Rosselli, but Carbajal was a bit vague in his answer. I suspected he may

THE ZENITH SECRET

have been introduced to Rosselli and I expressed this in my report to Dorff as an area of further inquiry.

To his intimates, El Indio had boasted about his involvement in secret operations in Laos and Vietnam as part of what later was revealed as the CIA's Phoenix Program. When lubricated by a few drinks and with friends, including Ruben at El Molino in Phoenix, he'd talk about torture and assassination techniques he'd used to intimidate and kill Viet Cong loyalists and sympathizers. Carbajal even knew Morales' cover during this period. Because they had business dealings together, Carbajal had to communicate with Morales via AID (the Agency for International Development) with whom David was serving as a public safety and community development officer.

I asked each of my subjects if Morales had visited them during the three years or so he was supposedly assigned in Southeast Asia. Apparently, he stopped over in Phoenix several times on his way from the West Coast to Washington, or on his return to his overseas assignments. I was particularly interested in the spring of 1968 when Martin Luther King, Jr. and Bobby Kennedy were assassinated. None of the sources could pinpoint the dates and times Morales (always unannounced) showed up. During these visits, he sometimes slept over at the Carbajals'. It was during one of these visits, Morales and Carbajal were drinking, as usual that Morales expressed his fear that the CIA would end his life when ready to do so.

Walton, as David's attorney, and Carbajal, as Morales' business partner, had to stay in contact during the early 1970s because of their joint interests in private commercial ventures. They confirmed that Morales, following his work in Vietnam, was assigned to the Pentagon office of the Joint Chiefs of Staff as an advisor on Latin American counterinsurgency matters. He traveled all over South America between 1971-1973 and was believed to be in Chile during the overthrow of the Allende government in 1973. This was of considerable interest to me because I knew that Ted Shackley, in his post as head of the CIA's Western Hemisphere covert operations had orchestrated the coup and that a corporation known as ITT was believed to have provided cover for agency operations in the country.

It was during this early to mid-1970's period that Morales apparently sought to expand his private business interests involving his friends, Carbajal and Walton. He invited them to Washington several times for social and business events at which they were introduced to Morales' agency associates, Ted Shackley, Tom Clines, Tony Sforza, Edwin Wilson, Felix Rodriguez, and others. Carbajal claimed he was introduced to Manuel Artime by Morales on a trip to Miami. A variety of business ventures were discussed on these junkets, including international arms trading and other profitable but high-risk ventures. There also seems to have been a good deal of partying and high living associated with the trips made at the behest of Morales. Carbajal and Walton said Didi was always the center of attention at these get-togethers and his CIA colleagues never ceased with their tales of Morales' covert exploits, including assassinations. Morales could be counted on to "do it" when nobody else would or could. He was described as a back-alley expert.

During the concluding portions of my interviews, I tried to discreetly broach the issue of the Letelier car bombing of September 1976. That was the year Morales announced to his family and friends that he'd retired from the agency.

He and his family had earlier purchased the property near Wilcox, and they returned there to establish a vineyard. I felt a direct "car bombing assassination" question might be a bit over the top in that I'd tried to keep my domestic assassination interest low key.

So far, what I'd gotten was far beyond my expectations. The interviews did confirm that Morales was in Washington and Phoenix in 1976. Carbajal had some business dealings with Sforza who had established himself in Miami and may have traveled to Phoenix with Morales to talk about some import-export venture. I left it at that, not yet connecting dots that would later become important to me.[39] The reader may recall that it was the Letelier car bombing that initially prompted the interest in Morales and Sforza by HSCA investigators.

As I went about my work, I was constantly vigilant for anyone following me or monitoring my activities. I stopped for supper at a little Mexican restaurant I'd frequented a year earlier while on assignment. I left the restaurant at about 9 p.m., and was walking toward my car in the semi-dark parking lot. As I approached the vehicle I could see the passenger side door was open and the shape of someone slightly bent over reaching into the car. I yelled something to the effect, "What the hell are you doing?" as I walked up behind the figure that I now saw as a man. He was clearly rummaging behind the seat where I kept my briefcase. With that, the man withdrew from the car with my briefcase in his left hand and a slim-jim. I was only a foot or so away from him and preparing to wrestle him to the ground when he raised the slim-jim and struck me in the forehead. I was stunned momentarily. The man then turned and ran down a darkened side street with my briefcase.

By appearance, he did not look like the typical street bum car burglar—he was rather stylishly dressed in dark slacks and shirt, had gloves on his hands, was well groomed with a mustache, about 35-years-old, six feet tall or thereabouts, well-built, and around 180 lbs. I ran after the man and saw him jump into a waiting car about a half block away. In the briefcase were my accumulated files on Morales, $300 in cash, my camera and tape recorder. The burglary had all the earmarks of a professional black bag job. They got everything I had on Morales up to that point.

I was deeply cut by the slim-jim and went back to my motel to clean up and treat the wound, which was very close to my left eye. I called Dorff and Shaw and told them what had happened. Then, I contacted the Phoenix Police Department and made a complete report of the incident.

My instincts suggested the car burglary was only the beginning of official efforts to monitor and possibly interfere with my investigation of Morales. I felt I had to wrap up my work in Phoenix as quickly as possible and then lay low for a while. I also had to assume my communications with Dorff were being compromised by phone taps. I finished as much of my work in Phoenix as quickly as I could and set out to confirm El Indio's alleged burial site and develop anything I could in the area where he supposedly retired in 1976.

I arrived in Wilcox, a small, nondescript, high-prairie-desert town in Southeastern Arizona, a few miles north of the Mexican border, on March 3rd. According to Shackley's letter there lay the remains of David Sanchez Morales. It was near dusk as I pulled off Interstate 10, a cold rain was falling from the heavily overcast sky, dark clouds and fog partially obscuring the surrounding mountains. The streets of the aging, Old West community were deserted and dark.

I was anxious to verify Morales' resting place. Given my injury, I knew I needed to take a break, so if I could find the grave I planned to stay at the motel in Wilcox for a day or two. There was only one cemetery in the community, and I thought Morales' grave would be easy to find given his stature. The weather was still damp, cold, and gloomy as I drove to the graveyard. My sleep had been fitful and I was nearly out of money. What I'd learned of Morales in the preceding weeks transcended whatever professional detachment I'd hung onto as I went about probing the past of my former CIA superior.

The burial ground was spread over some ten acres of barren prairie land, mountains in the background, a chill wind blowing across the plain under a leaden sky. I walked the grave markers, row on row, some of the older late nineteenth century interments covered with stones as was the practice then to keep scavengers and coyotes from digging up the remains. There was no sign of a Morales headstone. I drove back into town and found the local undertaker, Dale Carlstead. He gave me a plot map of the cemetery, marked the gravesite for one David Sanchez Morales. What he told me, without undue solicitation on my part, was quite extraordinary in that he knew nothing of Morales' true history.

Wilcox was a small town; the mortician also handled emergency services. He remembered the day in 1978 the emergency call had come in and the ambulance ride to the Morales residence near the ghost town of Dos Cabezas. The interrupted race to Tucson with the stricken man and the unforgettable funeral that followed days later. While I said nothing about my true interests in Morales, other than the fact I was anxious to visit the grave of a man I knew while in government service, I was astounded by the undertaker's detailed recall and impressions of the death and interment of El Indio. His account, sitting in his austere office—appointments right out of a 1940's Western movie set—almost unbelievably coalesced with all I knew and had learned about Morales.

I'm not easily given to superstition, but as I returned to the cemetery with the gravesite plot layout in hand, I could feel the disapproving presence of the Big Indian shadowing me. I went to the plot identified as the Morales grave and found no marker but I did see possible evidence of tampering. I took photographs and was prepared to return to the mortician's to raise the issue. He'd said he hadn't been to the area of the plot for some time.

I found a broken fence post at the edge of the graveyard, returned to the site marked on the plot layout, and began digging where a marker for Morales would be aligned with other headstones. Despite the rain, the earth was hard and the prairie sod tough and thickly rooted. Like a man beset, I tore at the earth with my crude tool, determined to find what I'd come there for. As I hacked away at the ground, I felt the insanity of the whole quest—all that it meant—creeping up on me. There I was, scraping away at the earth, trying to find some remaining evidence of a man who epitomized a mindset that nearly destroyed me and all I believed in.

I looked skyward, then at the earth again, and it was there: the small exposure of granite under about four inches of dirt. It was as if it had been deliberately covered and ignored for years—in spite of the fact the rest of the grave indicated recent upturning. The simple headstone read:

DAVID S. MORALES
SFC US ARMY
WORLD WAR II KOREA
1925-1978

Except for the name and dates of birth and death (if true) on the stone, I already knew on the basis of witness testimony and other evidence the inscription was bogus. It was a CIA-contrived, transparent, cynical effort to obfuscate

Morales's grave; Wilcox, AZ
The stone itself was covered over with 3-4 inches of dirt and sod before I uncovered
it. However, the grave itself appeared recently disturbed.

and conceal the truth about the man I was told rested there. Now, I was beginning to have doubts about whether there were any remains below.

A stiff wind came up, sand, dust, and tumbleweeds blew across the barren graveyard. The headstone could easily be covered over. I had to mark it. I walked a nearby fence line and found an American flag that had apparently blown off another grave. I took it back to the exposed Morales headstone and stuck it into the ground in front of the gravesite. What blasphemy, I thought.

Standing by the grave in the gathering darkness, I visualized Morales' death and burial:

They fly into Tucson, Arizona over a period of 24 hours, traveling singly or in pairs—never more—on different airlines, different flight schedules. Some take circuitous routes, changing planes at cities far distant from their points of departures. It's always done this way when necessary to gather at one location. No easily definable travel pattern, staggered arrivals, no apparent connection between members of this group that would gather, no trail that would lead back to the entity they represented. If they spot one another in the terminal or in public there is not so much as a hint of acknowledgement, even though most had known each other for 30 years or more. Maximum security; it's their way of life.

Undistinguished, businesslike, reserved, inconspicuous, some grandfatherly or professorial in appearance; rumpled dark suits, subdued ties, carrying thin briefcases, they blend with the crowd and move smoothly. In taxis or rented cars they scatter to the finer hotels and resort villas that had been reserved for them under various corporate covers.

THE ZENITH SECRET

The clear, dry desert air, rich with the scent of blooming cactus and sage-brush is refreshing for those who had flown in from Washington, D.C., already hot and humid in late May, or from other crowded, noisy, foul-smelling American or foreign cities. Tucson's informal Spanish/Western ambiance, pastel buildings, cool bubbling fountains, shaded green mountains in the distance, the quaint cow town atmosphere, all reflect a simplicity of life far removed from the purpose of these men who gather from the far corners of the world, like shadows, in the spring of 1978.

Their arrival goes virtually unnoticed, so adroitly do they infiltrate the town. When they have all arrived, there are more than 20. Tucson doesn't know the true identities of its distinguished guests or the institution they represent. Had it become known, it would have made extraordinary news, for these plain, faceless, innocuous men were at the top of hierarchy of America's Central Intelligence Agency. Unbeknownst to the tranquil Arizona community, it hosts the crème de la crème of American Cold War intelligence operatives; world-class experts in international espionage, clandestine plots, sabotage, torture, and assassination.

The men gathering in Tucson live their lives in calculated obscurity. Anonymity is the name of the game; the key to their continued viability as spies. Their deeds of the preceding 30 years, rationalized and performed in the name of freedom, would remain unheralded by the government they served. There would be no public accolades.

Only within this small, unique, select brotherhood would any of them receive recognition for their work. It was one of the conditions they accepted when they volunteered to serve with the agency. It was all part of the concept of plausible denial and it created a very close bond between them. That was why they had gathered in Arizona.

Their presence in Tucson would be brief, not more than 24 hours. They came to perform an almost sacred ritual. One that was becoming more familiar in recent years. They came to say good-bye; to pay their final respects to one of their own.

David Sanchez Morales, the big Mexican-Navajo Indian—the legendary El Indio, the fabled Pancho, the man of 100 faces, the veteran of more than 30 years of CIA clandestine service is gone.

The word went out by encoded cable or scrambled phone message from Langley three days earlier. Morales, officially retired from the agency, was living under State Department cover on a backcountry ranch and vineyard near Wilcox, Arizona about 100 miles east of Tucson. He had returned from a hurried business trip to Miami and Washington complaining of chest pains. A seizure followed. For a while, the Big Indian tried to make light of it—emergency treatment at the small Wilcox hospital and a decision to transfer him to the Tucson Medical Center. The ambulance trip was long and hectic, with a breakdown near Benson, halfway to the hospital. By the time he arrived, he had lapsed into a coma.

Placed in intensive care, with his room secured by sheriff's deputies, he failed to respond. Only his family and closest friends were permitted to see him. Seventy-two hours later, they pronounced him dead. There were no last words, no final confession. He remained unconscious as the Catholic priest administered the Last Sacrament. He was only 53.

So they came together to pay their respects to the Big Indian and his family—his wife Joan, also a former agency employee, and his six children. The agency would assure their future welfare; that was guaranteed, provided that

BRADLEY E. AYERS

there was no autopsy. The telephone call from headquarters, moments after David had been pronounced dead, had been sympathetic and gentle but steady, with measured authority. Everyone agreed, it would be best for all concerned.

With that, only the interment remained—the ritual final tribute by the unique brotherhood, words of support and condolence for the family—a brief ceremony at the small graveyard on the barren plateau overlooking Wilcox. With that, David S. Morales would face eternal obscurity, remembered only by his tightly knit family and the handful of aging spooks that had come to pay their final respects. That's the way Langley wished it, for a lot of reasons.

The men in Tucson rise early that morning. By prearrangement they rendezvous and, in a convoy, begin the drive to the austere little Spanish-style Catholic Church in Wilcox. The 100 mile journey in the secure privacy of the rental cars—all of them swept for listening devices by the agency security team that had been in place in Tucson since Morales' arrival at the medical center five days earlier—provides an opportunity to share their thoughts about the Big Indian: to recall the man, his life and work with the agency. This constitutes a secret eulogy for Morales, a catharsis for the brethren, a last chance to remember a brave comrade in arms. Equally important, it is an opportunity for the counterintelligence specialist accompanying the group to explore options for damage control if the story of Morales' work with the agency ever began to surface.

I thought about what Fonzi might have been doing right then. Fifteen hundred miles away, in Miami, the principal HSCA staff investigator awakens with a slight headache and irritation that make his eyes water. His wife is in the shower. The bedroom in their modest rambler in the Miami suburbs is a mess: stacks of library books, papers strewn here and there; it was chaotic. He had read until 2 a.m., his wife long since in deep slumber by his side. She had become used to the nocturnal reading binges that began when he returned from Washington.

The investigator had taken a few days off from his assignment, ostensibly to relax, spent time with his family, and work on his boat. He tried, but it wasn't working very well. Except for a few urgent phone calls, the days were OK, but cases of documents he'd had time to review in D.C., had become a magnet at the end of the day. Typically, it was futile. He didn't even know what he was looking for anymore—he was on a fishing expedition. He felt frustrated and discouraged, especially with the pressure the Committee was under to get on with its work and come up with something substantial or lose its funding. That, on top of the leadership shakeup and dissension within the group wore heavily on his mind.

But last night? There it was, the last document he had picked up just before dozing off. A typed rough draft item, unsigned, no official heading, informally structured, appearing to be a memorandum for file or record, probably written by one of the earlier Committee staffers maybe a year earlier. He drew deeply on his cigarette, coughed, and read it again. The memo had to do with the 1976 Letelier car bomb murder on embassy row in Washington, D.C. One paragraph in particular catches his attention:

DAVID MORALES aka "Pancho." During the 1950s and 1960s MORALES was Chief of Station for various South American countries, including Nicaragua. He runs with Wilson and Sforza. He is now "retired" and living in New Mexico. He is an alcoholic and possible "weak link".

THE ZENITH SECRET

His wife calls from the kitchen, "Hon, your coffee is ready." He reaches for the telephone next to the bed to call his staff partner.

Reuben Carbajal, in Phoenix, was Morales' lifelong friend. They were planning a business venture together when Morales died. Carbajal is devastated with grief. He would attend the funeral. As he prepares to depart and during the four hour drive to Wilcox, he remembers much of David's early history, growing up together and attending school in the tough Mexican barrio of South Phoenix during the late 1930s and early 1940s. Carbajal and another boyhood friend of Morales, Del Lewis, recall that David Morales had every reason to be an overachiever. He was the youngest of five children. His parents were dirt poor. The Carbajals practically raised him. And although he was a three-sport athlete in high school, the U.S. Army rejected him because of his enlarged heart when he tried to enlist in 1944. He had a penchant for a good fight, with a quick, violent temper. He feared no one as a youth. Morales enrolled in college, but a high school advisor wrote on Morales' transcript: "a natural leader with no great scholastic urge. Physical type."

The drive to work for his government remained paramount in Morales' mind. After drifting from one college to another, he found a way to satisfy it. If he couldn't work for his country overtly, he would do it covertly. The circumstances of Morales' recruitment by the agency remain unknown. He apparently was accepted into the U.S. Army for a brief period of time, served as an enlisted man in Germany returned to the U.S. for CIA paramilitary training, and then went back to Europe.

It's possible one of his first major covert assignments was a part of the CIA clandestine group that were involved in the Berlin tunnel operation in the early 1950s.[40]

Meanwhile in Wilcox, the undertaker, Carlstead, makes final preparations for the funeral. What began as a simple burial for a local resident, Morales, known as a former State Department official, has taken some strange twists. A government representative has appeared to coordinate the service; an unidentified official contingent would be arriving from Tucson. Morales would be buried with full military honors, a team of casket bearers, a bugler and an honor guard detachment would be sent up from nearby Fort Huachuca. There would be some government security men present at the church and graveside. It's apparent this would not be an ordinary Wilcox burial ceremony. Carlstead is puzzled but discreet.

Mrs. Morales and the children prepare to attend their father's funeral. There had been nothing approaching normality in her life with David. Morales' brothers, Raymond and Robert, are now en route by car to Wilcox for the funeral.

There are six cars in the CIA entourage on their way to the funeral. (The occupants in one or more cars are former CIA agents who have become publicly prominent for one reason or another—including Ted Shackley.)

Morales was one of the first six covert operatives of the Central Intelligence Agency. The agents running the covert operations section had virtual carte blanche. They could design their own manuals. They could pick their own tools and strategies. They could formulate their own list of do's and don'ts. They were creating a new branch of government to bridge the gap between war and diplomacy.

There was a lot of room to play in that gap. Could unfriendly governments be sabotaged from within, without having to send in the Marines? Could left-leaning despots be deposed by insurrections led by people in their own land?

BRADLEY E. AYERS

Could propaganda be used to turn a country's population against its government? Could it be used to prop up political parties to oppose the government?

For the CIA, the possibilities were virtually limitless. So, too, were the possibilities for its new covert action specialists. These were the good old days, when a dedicated, aggressive agent could write his own ticket.

At the same time, the Scottsdale attorney Bob Walton, is en route to Wilcox for the funeral. He and Morales had become friends, over a period of years, and Morales had shared some very sensitive information with Walton concerning some of his CIA activities, particularly his assassination assignments, his feelings about the Kennedy family and covert operations. When Morales retired, Walton handled business and real estate matters for both Morales and Carbajal. When Morales died, Joan Morales asked Walton to assist with the settlement of their affairs. She also discussed the call from Langley suggesting no autopsy be performed and giving assurance of lifelong financial security for herself and their children. Walton reflects on these matters as he makes the long drive to Wilcox.

Exhausted and still nursing my head wound, I returned to Minnesota and completed a detailed preliminary report of the Morales investigation and sent it to Dorff. He called me after receiving the package to say he'd send my information on to Dallas.

THE ZENITH SECRET

CHAPTER 27

Besides the basic biographical reconstruction of Morales' life, my report set forth critical data relating to El Indio's career with the CIA and presented a number of areas that would become important to me as the situation developed.

The hubris that came to dominate the CIA stemmed partly from its early successes, some of which seemed ridiculously easy. No campaign engendered more of that sentiment than the overthrow of the left-leaning government in Guatemala in 1954. That was also the campaign that first put Morales in the spotlight within the CIA.

The operation was a bluff. There was no popular revolt against president Jacobo Arbenz. He had been democratically elected. He had the support of the business community, the military and the moneyed elite. His only mistake was to turn to the Soviet Union for economic aid, a move that alarmed Washington.

Morales organized a small band of less than two dozen guerrillas. That was nowhere near the force required to defeat the Guatemalan army, so Morales staged a daring show of force. He and his warriors barged into a public building near the presidential palace and announced they had assumed control of the government. When air force fighters commandeered by other CIA agents flew over the palace just as Morales was making his bold claims, Arbenz panicked. He resigned, and Morales' men took control before Arbenz realized he'd been fooled. The cost of this coup to the U.S. government: very few dollars, and most important, no lives. Morales was one of the three agents to personally brief president Eisenhower on the operation.

Engineering the overthrow of Cuban president Fidel Castro was one of the dominant obsessions of U.S. foreign policy architects from the moment Castro took power in Cuba on the first day of 1959. It was an obsession for Morales, too.

The CIA operative was there from the start. He was working in the U.S. embassy in Havana when Castro launched his revolution. While most employees promptly returned to the U.S., Morales stayed behind, masterminding a series of small-scale operations that would form the basis of the U.S. anti-Castro campaign for the next several years. Among other things Morales planted radios with anti-Castro sympathizers, used later by U.S. commandoes infiltrating Cuba. Morales found ingenious ways of hiding the transmitters, placing many of them with nuns. When Castro shut down the U.S. embassy in the summer of 1959 and expelled all U.S. government personnel, Morales intensified his anti-Castro campaign from U.S. shores. In 1962, he was named chief of operations for JM/WAVE, the CIA's component of the anti-Castro campaign launched by President Kennedy in the wake of the ill-fated Bay of Pigs invasion. From that post, Morales reported directly to Ted Shackley, the ghost behind CIA covert operations who would rise to become the agency's associate deputy in 1976 under CIA Director George Bush.

Morales was at the center of the CIA-mob alliance. Before the Castro revolution, he met and befriended many of the mobsters running the casinos. Later while with JM/WAVE, Morales and Shackley assisted Rosselli in launching the Castro assassination attempts. The attempts failed, but Morales came out of the Cuban operation with new power and new alliances. From then on, he would be a close ally and associate of Shackley. And when deemed appropriate by his superiors, he would work closely with mobsters.

Morales' reputation as a master of covert operations was schizophrenic: government officials in capitals recognized him across Latin America, but he was unknown in the American public and most U.S. public policy makers. He was infamous elsewhere on the continent because by the late 1960s there were few South American countries in which he hadn't operated. Public records indicate that at various times during his career he was stationed in Guatemala, Havana, Lima, and Caracas. But these were his cover assignments. Like most CIA agents, Morales wasn't restricted to working in the country in which he was stationed. He roamed as needed. In 1964, he personally mowed down dozens of the Tupamaro guerrillas in Uruguay. While he was stationed in Lima in 1965 had helped pave the way for the invasion of the Dominican Republic by entering the country surreptitiously and knocking out a radio transmitter. The public record doesn't indicate any work in Bolivia, but in 1967 he helped engineer the capture of Cuban guerrilla Ernesto "Che" Guevara there.

Morales was chief of operations for the agency's mission in Laos in the mid-1960s, when the CIA mission was to enlist local tribal people in its effort to cut down on the movement of supplies by the Vietcong along the Ho Chi Minh trail into South Vietnam. The agency had to virtually create a political and military force from the ground up. The Meo tribes didn't seek out this role. It was thrust upon them. When some of their leaders said they could trade support for the U.S. campaign for help in getting their opium to foreign markets, the agency ended up giving aid and comfort to drug dealers. It was a bargain that would later haunt the U.S. in time; the war against communism in Southeast Asia was lost. And the battle to control the use of illegal drugs required opening a second, domestic front. That war, too, was a failure.

In Vietnam the CIA started the counter-insurgency Phoenix Program in 1967 with the mission of rooting out the Vietcong infrastructure. The man behind Phoenix, former CIA Director William Colby, told a congressional panel in the early 1970s that the program was a massive failure. Phoenix became a mass assassinations program in which tens of thousands of South Vietnamese were killed as suspected Viet Cong sympathizers. Public outrage undercut support for the South Vietnamese government. The head of the CIA's station in Na Trang from 1968 through 1969—when the Phoenix Program was at its peak— was David Morales.

Staff investigators of the House Select Committee on Assassination located the passages in my book *The War That Never Was,* concerning "Dave," the Big Indian, and his function as Chief of Operations under Ted Shackley at JM/WAVE, the agency's Miami station. They cross referenced other sources and tentatively identified Morales as having used the operational aliases of El Indio and Pancho in covert actions, including suspected assassination efforts.

Morales was the CIA "control" of reputed mobster John Rosselli while they worked on the CIA's anti-Castro JM/WAVE project during the early 1960s. They were buddies in every sense of the word. My own observations echoed in my mind. Rosselli was one of the few people who had direct access to Morales' office. Their relationship was based on camaraderie, mutual trust, respect, and frequent joviality. Rosselli was the only one who could make Morales laugh. Morales gave him the same authority and responsibility as CIA case officers.

Morales was trusted by leaders of both CIA and the mob because he was the CIA veteran with a background in assassination planning, and because he'd been in Cuba in the final weeks before Castro took over, when the mob was running the casinos in Havana. After the House Assassination Committee concluded its probe of the Kennedy killing, evidence surfaced implicating Rosselli in the assassination. A witness said she'd seen Rosselli meet with ex-FBI agent Guy Banister in New Orleans in the summer of 1963. Banister, a Bay of Pigs veteran, ran a private detective agency out of an office with an address used by Lee Harvey Oswald for his anti-Castro campaign literature that summer.

Assassination researchers such as "JFK" screenwriter Zachary Sklar suspects Banister was controlling Oswald on behalf of federal intelligence agency contacts.[41]

Other witnesses say Rosselli was present in Dealey Plaza in Dallas on the day Kennedy was killed. One says Rosselli had a rifle with him. Rosselli was never asked about any of this. He was killed before the House Select Committee was formed. What is known is that the FBI—which had been trailing Rosselli in 1963—lost track of him on November 19th. They didn't catch up with him until November 27th, five days after Kennedy was killed.

What's significant about the evidence tying Morales to Rosselli, and Rosselli to the assassination, is that this links the two main theories about the killing. What's more likely than that either the CIA or the mob did it, is that both powerful entities cooperated, just as they did in attempts to kill Castro.

If the cooperation extended to killing Kennedy, the two people in the best position to forge the link would have been Morales and Rosselli. Operations in which Morales may have been involved include the Letelier car bombing murder on Embassy Row in Washington, D.C. in 1976. This is a very painful matter.

For many former CIA agents, the line between government and private work is easily blurred. The skills they acquire on the public payroll are easily transferred. The loyalties and friendships they form with their fellow agents survive retirement. They can rely on their colleagues still with the agency for information and resources. What they do after retirement doesn't have the official sanction of the U.S. government, but frequently it has the government's fingerprints all over it.

Morales' name first came to the attention of the HSCA in the odd internal staff memo dealing with the Letelier assassination. This is the document alerting HSCA investigators to Morales' history as a career agency officer possibly involved in foreign and domestic assassination. Was Morales, if involved, a private agent or, if "retired," acting at the behest of his former government superiors? A public agent called back from retirement to handle one last tough assignment? Or an innocent bystander implicated only because he was in the wrong place at the wrong time, in the company of people with blood on their hands?

One of Morales' closest agency associates was arms dealer Edwin Wilson. Wilson was also implicated in the Letelier bombing. Although he was never charged in the case, prosecutors traced the explosive devices used in the bombing to him. In 2003 a federal judge in Texas threw out the 1983 conviction of Edwin P. Wilson, a former Central Intelligence Agency officer, for selling tons of explosives to Libya, ruling that prosecutors knowingly used false testimony to undermine his defense.

Morales and Wilson masterminded the bombing, according to the unidentified author of a memo obtained by House assassinations committee investigators in the late 1970s. Committee staffers didn't pursue the lead because the assassination wasn't what they were probing, but the memo's author had valid information and correctly asserted that Morales and Wilson were close associates, something not publicly known at the time.

Subsequent to the committee's work, other evidence emerged, implicating other CIA personnel in the killing. Michael Townley, the expatriate American eventually convicted of killing Letelier, was a former contract agent. His control was veteran CIA officer David Phillips, one of the stars, along with Morales, of the agency's operation to overthrow the Arbenz government in Guatemala in 1954.

If, in fact, Morales was interred in Sunset Cemetery outside of Wilcox, Arizona, in the Southwestern desert, he was next to unknown settlers, cowboys, miners and railroad pioneers—not military heroes—surrounded by yellowed prairie sod and scraggly sagebrush—not lush greenery and lavish mausoleums doubling as national monuments. There's a steel archway at the entrance. The boot hill section is dominated by multiple gravesites and family plots dating back to the 1880s when Europeans first populated the area. There are a few overturned vases and urns, some with withered dry flowers. But there aren't many footprints in the muddy topsoil.

Morales' gravesite and headstone are similar to those that surround his final resting place. You had to be at his burial to have even a hint of who he was or what he had done. And even then, you would have had to have inside knowledge to know that the men wearing dark suits and thin ties at the service were some of the highest ranking agents in the history of the CIA.

Obviously, agency officials were not about to let Morales' death expose his—and their—work. The CIA brass made sure it stayed that way. They lied to make sure the story of Morales' career as an assassin for America was buried with him. The headstone they laid him to rest under says he was a sergeant first class in the Army. Not really. That was his cover assignment. The headstone says he served in World War II and Korea. He hadn't. That was merely an extension of Morales' cover, a way for the CIA to maintain plausible deniability for his real work. Even dead, Morales threatened too many secrets.

The HSCA investigators never found Morales. It would have been a fruitless search under any circumstances because he was dead. The HSCA, riddled by controversy and lack of funds, was disbanded in 1979, before Fonzi and Lopez could track me down.

Officially unexplored is one of the most intriguing aspects of Morales' CIA career: the indication he played a role in the plot to kill John F. Kennedy. Morales claimed a hand in the killing. According to one Arizona friend, Morales never displayed a political bent, except when the subject of Kennedy came up.

"He lit up on that one," his lawyer Robert Walton once said to me. "That no good SOB," Morales had said angrily, blaming Kennedy for the indecision on whether to send in air support to back the CIA-trained Bay of Pigs invaders. But Morales' mood would lighten Walton said, as Morales would say, "We got that SOB." "He was describing the assassination as retribution for the Bay of Pigs decision," Walton said. "And he was taking credit for it."

With my head still throbbing, I returned to the sanctuary of my Minnesota townhouse to begin my preliminary report. I knew I'd just scratched the surface of what would probably be the most important investigation of my life. And I needed time and a safe haven to collect my thoughts.

The information gathered in Phoenix, the multiple interviews with Morales' intimates fleshed out and essentially confirmed, reinforced, and expanded upon my prior personal impressions, perceptions, observations, informal research, and document discovery to date. As a wrap-up to the factual portion of my report to Dorff, I included the testimony of Dale Carlstead, the Wilcox undertaker who had been involved in Morales' emergency medical evacuation to

Tucson and the funeral in Wilcox that followed. Despite the fact it had taken place some 12 years earlier, Carlstead said it was a funeral the town had not yet forgotten. I asked him why Morales' headstone, had apparently been neglected and, unlike all the others around it, was allowed to be soil-covered and overgrown. He said he didn't know, but hadn't seen any family members for years. I left Carlstead not really knowing if he knew who the man believed to be buried in Plot 89 really was.

From what had been learned of Morales from my own experience at JM/WAVE and the information gathered since from all sources, it was reasonable to suspect that Morales may have had a hand in one or more domestic assassinations. The best link to the murder of the president was Morales' known connection to mobster John Rosselli and a few other characters that had emerged over time as having something to do with a conspiracy to murder JFK.

As a wrap-up to my report to Dorff, I decided to focus on the Rosselli factor, acknowledging that some of what I set forth could not yet be corroborated. (This was spring 1990.) I could testify on the basis of my own observations and experience that Rosselli was at JM/WAVE in the summer of 1963 and that he and Morales had a close relationship.

Rosselli had given limited testimony relating to his involvement with the CIA, Castro assassination efforts and other covert agency operations in the secret anti-Castro war of the early 1960s. Rosselli had been killed before he could be more fully questioned about these activities. There is some evidence that as early as 1954, Rosselli was in Guatemala at the time Morales was there orchestrating the overthrow of the Arbnez government. New Orleans private detective Guy Banister's secretary, Delphine Roberts, advised author Tony Summers *(Conspiracy,* 1980) in 1978 as Summers was researching his book, that Rosselli and former FBI agent Robert Maheu had been present in Banister's office in mid-1963.

FBI surveillance records place Rosselli and Jack Ruby together in the summer of 1963. The FBI had been following the activities of Rosselli for some time, but had "lost" or ignored him during periods when he was probably cooperating with the CIA. His handler/case officer during this time frame would have likely been Morales, based on my observations at JM/WAVE. I was unaware as this report was written, of other sources that would assert that Rosselli was seen in Dealey Plaza assisting a sniper on the grassy knoll and that the FBI had lost track of him from November 19 through November 27, 1963. I did know of the Warren Commission and other reports of a Latin-Mexican appearing man in and about Dealey Plaza on the day of the assassination, one alleging he was seen driving a Nash Rambler to which an Oswald look-alike fled and was hurriedly driven away.

I spoke with Dorff by phone several times in the days that followed and we discussed a continuing investigation agenda. He advised me to keep complete records, that big "things" were about to happen at the JFK Center in Dallas. During a conversation on March 16, he read me an excerpt from a cover letter he'd written to accompany my preliminary report on Morales he was preparing to send to Dallas:

> "The intersection between the mob and the CIA is documented, and the two key people standing at that intersection at the time Kennedy was killed are Rosselli and Morales. If you're looking for people who connect the mob and the CIA at an operational level, and who could have been used in a plot against Kennedy, Morales, and Rosselli are the ones." He concluded that

because of Morales' background, position and contacts, "it's highly probable, that at the very least, he orchestrated or helped orchestrate it."

There was much more work to be done and fertile investigative ground yet
to be tilled. I encouraged Dorff to facilitate my return to the Morales inquiry as
soon as possible. My head was much better, and with the first phase of the investigation completed, I rested easily for a change.

CHAPTER 28

The phone was ringing as I returned to my Woodbury, Minnesota townhouse on March 17 after an early spring afternoon training run. Still panting from the workout, I picked up the phone to hear Bob Dorff's voice in LA. He sounded distressed as he explained the entire Morales investigation file had disappeared from his desk that morning. He'd turned the office upside-down. Nothing. It apparently had been stolen. He'd called the Beverly Hills police and made a full report, and two cops came by to take his statement. Dorff said he'd been preparing the file to send on to the JFK Center in Dallas. Now, he had nothing.

I knew Dorff had some kind of a security system in place at his office. What the hell? How could this happen? Who and why? Should I send him a duplicate of my file? Oddly, he said no; his file might yet turn up. Was Dorff leveling with me, or was this Hollywood dramatics, for whatever reason? I was troubled.

I spent more time with Bob Walton and we reviewed much of what Ruben had said. Walton confirmed it, elaborated a bit, and also verified Morales' relationship with a Jack Murphy, now supposedly retired and living in California. He also talked about two other individuals, allegedly close to Morales, a Dale Weigert and a Tom Forsyth, a man I remembered as a former CIA-JM/WAVE counterpart. Walton now dropped a big bomb. He told me he'd been investigated, as having represented and partnered with Morales in real estate and business ventures, by the Arizona Bar Association. He told me that to remain in practice, he was ordered to destroy a memorandum from his files evidencing a Goldwater-Mafia connection in Arizona and suggesting possible links to the assassination of the Kennedys. The memo alleged the involvement of Las Vegas mob figures, including Joe Bonnano, and others with whom Morales was associated while with CIA. Walton, obviously in failing health, said he'd destroyed the memo to save his livelihood as a lawyer. He spoke freely to me now, with Morales dead, because he was no longer obligated by attorney-client privilege and felt it morally right to give me the information.

I was more pointed in my questioning of both Carbajal and Walton about Morales' complicity in the Letelier car bombing and brought up the murder of Don Bolles, the Arizona Republic investigative reporter also killed by a car bombing in 1976. Walton expressed his personal view that Bolles was looking into matters involving the Goldwater-Mafia connection that went far beyond local politics.

John Markley came quite prepared for his meeting in Independence, California some days after my sessions with Carbajal and Walton. We shop-talked special ops military stuff for a bit, then cut to the issue at hand. This muscular, aging covert operator was cordial, but no-nonsense. He talked of his work in Vietnam and Laos and his acquaintanceship with the Big Indian. He'd even brought an 8x10 picture of Morales as a remembrance of their work together in the Phoenix Program and related operations with the CIA in the 1967-1969 time frame. He described the Big Indian in considerable detail, his work habits, his role and performance, on and off duty behavior, his drinking, womanizing, and absolute focus on the mission—and his ruthlessness when it came to doing what had to be done. It all fit. But, there was a problem: Markley told me Morales had made and given him a Native American belt buckle as a token of their friendship in Laos and Vietnam. I didn't let my reaction show. The David Morales I knew making handcrafted jewelry? I didn't think so. Then he showed me the photo. It was not a picture of the David Sanchez Morales I knew.

I said nothing to Markley of my suspicions that we were talking about two different individuals identified as CIA career officers, using the name of David Morales. But, this was quite extraordinary. Was there a David Morales, El Indio, Pancho stand-in? Other sources available to me up to that point tended to confirm Morales' assignment in Southeast Asia during the time frame Markley claimed he served with him.

Based on all I knew of Morales to that point, I had been germinating a "hunch." In my briefcase was an uncaptioned photo of David Morales, from a 1959 Havana newspaper, that I'd been asked to verify early on as the man sought by Bob Dorff and the JFK Center. The photo was almost exactly as I remembered Morales from the last time I'd seen him, in the 1960s. I'd been working on another case with David Rabern, a private investigator in Scottsdale, Arizona. We hit it off and he volunteered the information that he'd worked as a security officer in 1968 and had been at the Ambassador Hotel the night Bobby Kennedy was killed. On a whim, I pulled the photo out and laid it in front of him. "Have you ever seen this man before and if so, when and where?"

The hair stood up on the back of my neck and a chill coursed down my spine as David responded to my question. "Yes, this man was in the Ambassador Hotel ballroom the night RFK was killed." I'd not said a word to David Rabern about my interest in Morales prior to his ID of the photo. His identification of Morales was entirely voluntary, spontaneous, and without influence of any sort.

I didn't explain my full interest in Morales to Rabern beyond explaining I'd been hired as an Arizona P.I. to do a background investigation of the man, and consummate professional as he was, he didn't press me. However, he did ask that I not use his name in connection with the inquiry without his permission.

When I arrived at Dorff's on April 15 he expressed an interest in Carbajal's intimate knowledge of various import-export business activities in Mexico and his contacts there. Dorff explained that he'd like to expand his heavy industrial machinery trading enterprise south of the border.

By now, I'd accumulated enough highly interesting information on Morales to believe, if further developed, it might provide the basis for a nonfiction book. I suggested this to Dorff in the form of a written proposal, outlining a joint venture with him upon completion of my work for the JFK Center and payment of their obligation to me. A release of information agreement would have to be negotiated with the Center, of course, in exchange for sharing book income with the Center. Dorff, with his Hollywood connections, could even market the film rights to the book for additional revenue. Dorff rejected the proposal flat out. When I asked him about the missing Morales file—had it been found and did he want another copy of the preliminary report, he said no, as he was paranoid about another loss of the material. He advised me to hold on to the report for delivery to Dallas at some point in the future.

I had taken on several writing and consulting projects and was cooperating as a source with author David Corn on his book on Ted Shackley during the later part of April, in addition to working via David Rabern on the Minnesota fraud defendant search.

I contacted Carbajal and Walton by phone and elicited their agreement to meet with Dorff at a convenient time in Phoenix in May. Before I could reach Dorff with this news, he called me on April 30 asking if I could fly to Dallas on

May 4 to brief Bernard Fensterwald and Gary Shaw on my progress thus far on the Morales investigation. Following the Dallas briefing, I would fly to LA, meet Dorff and return with him to Phoenix for the introductions to Carbajal and Walton. It worked for me, but I was curious why Dorff would not want to be part of the Dallas briefing given the significance of what I had to deliver on Morales.

Late in the afternoon on May 5, I was told to come to the Kempinski Hotel to brief Fensterwald. The reception was not what I expected. Both Fensterwald and Shaw seemed detached, almost bored, by what I had to convey. As I observed their reaction to my months of fairly risky hard work, I made a snap decision to withhold the addendum to the report covering my latest interviews with Carbajal, Walton, Markley, and Rabern. As I concluded my remarks and tried to impress upon Fensterwald and Shaw the potential importance of Morales in unraveling a conspiracy involving the CIA to murder the president, Fensterwald commented, "Oh well, there were a lot of those old CIA spooks running around back then. Morales was probably just another one of them." I couldn't believe my ears.

When I finished my briefing, I asked Fensterwald to send the report to Washington office after I got back to Minnesota. He just blew me off. Had they seen the report and a fee-expense statement before? The briefcase lost in the burglary of my car months earlier in Phoenix contained only rough notes, nothing had been refined or formally transcribed, but the file that Dorff claimed had been stolen from his office was complete, typed, and carefully prepared. It contained all I'd developed up to mid-March. I called Dorff and told him the Dallas meeting was a total bust as far as I was concerned. Dorff seemed oddly unmoved. I was glad I'd withheld the addendum portion of my report during the briefing. The entire situation was beginning to smell very fishy.

I was sick at heart with what had taken place with Fensterwald, et al. I was proud of my work on the Morales inquiry and the reaction I got was a professional put-down. Nevertheless, I continued to hope for a positive outcome.

Dorff met my flight at LAX and we spent the balance of the day going over plans for the Phoenix meetings. I was surprised to see Dorff driving an expensive new car and that he had moved to a more spacious condominium in an upscale Beverly Hills neighborhood. We drove to Phoenix and stayed at an expensive hotel, The El Capitio. The next day, I introduced him to Carbajal and Walton. In his conversations with them, Dorff focused on his business interests and activities, only casually throwing in a question or comment about his interest in the assassinations, the CIA, and related matters. Dorff hit it off with Carbajal and they went to the local horseracing track in the afternoon.

Was Dorff's interest in establishing a dialogue with Carbajal and Walton truly one of developing business, or was I coerced into making the introductions for other reasons—a ploy so that he and the Center could exploit the sources on their own after I'd found them and established their value?

Returning to Minnesota in the early morning hours on a red-eye flight from the West Coast, I stopped at a red light before making a turn onto the freeway. After allowing several cars to clear, my Mazda was struck from behind by a full-size, fast-charging sedan and I was thrown between the seat and the door, my left shoulder twisted and my head snapped to the rear. The immediate pain in all regions was immense. I knew I was hurt, but I had no idea how badly.

I'd been injured numerous times before in my 50-plus years of a very active lifestyle, but I'd never really been put down. I continued my work, fulfilled my writing and investigative undertakings on the West Coast, and tried to maintain a "normal" routine. Despite my frequent out-of-town trips, I had a new girlfriend, once again about 20 years my junior, a runner, and I tried to stay with her. Perri had kids and was looking for the usual—stability and security. I wanted that too, but was incapable of bringing it about knowing what I had to do with my life. I fell hard for Perri and tried to please her. Deep inside, I knew she didn't understand where I was coming from. But she was a terrific-looking, inspiring, bright, charming, motivating lady.

The doctors classified my injuries as fully disabling, imposing substantial limitations on my capacity to continue investigative and security work in the field. What's more, I had to report my physical limitations to the FAA, which eventually led to the loss of my flying certification.

My last interviews with Carbajal, Walton, and Rabern had provided so many intriguing leads: the possible Goldwater-Mafia-Morales connection, the work and death of Don Bolles and what he was really on to, and Rabern's ID of Morales in the Ambassador Hotel when Bobby Kennedy was killed. This was all part of the withheld addendum to my preliminary report to the Center. I was now glad I hadn't delivered it to anyone. On the other hand, I didn't have the resources or, now, the physical capability to continue the investigation myself. I was somewhat relieved when I finally received the certification of my copyright for "The Search for El Indio."

Except for Perri's occasional company I was pretty much alone—never really lonely, but without someone to confide in or share my, albeit not-so routine, interests. I tried, but I just couldn't seem to reach my sons, now married, and consequently, was deprived of any relationship with my growing number of grandchildren. Suzie and my sons' insecure wives did not help matters.

I'd get calls from staffers working for Independent Counsel Walsh and the Kerry Committee seeking additional information in connection with the Reagan administration's Iran Contra scandal. FBI Special Agent Michael Foster from Walsh's office flew in from Washington and grilled me for nearly four hours on DEA, Customs, and South Florida Task Force related matters. George H.W. Bush was now the president, and I didn't know what to expect. I spent hours preparing myself for what, surprisingly, turned out to be a very congenial meeting. Later, I was subpoenaed and had to fly to Miami to give testimony in connection with ABC-TV's defense of their story (Miami affiliate WPLG-TV, now CNN reporter Susan Candiotti) of CIA proprietary Southern Air Transport's involvement in the guns-for-drugs trade during the Reagan administration's covert operations against Nicaragua in the early to mid-1980s. I had carefully documented my observations and experiences with the DEA during this period and was able to contribute to the federal court's favorable finding for ABC and the eventual demise of the agency's Southern Air Transport which I knew to be totally corrupted by illegal secret interest.

The languishing Morales investigation was never far from my mind, despite all the other goings-on in my life. I was stymied in how to proceed. My physical condition was not improving as the months went by and, in fact, I was becoming weaker and suffering from the lack of sleep due to the pain in my shoulders. Unable to pursue the Morales inquiry myself, I cooperated, as I felt comfortable, with a number of authors working on books related to the CIA and covert operations against Cuba.

I was extremely cautious about responding to anyone, and decided to discuss, if questioned about Morales only what had been published in *The War That Never Was* and not get into the investigation I'd done for the JFK Center. I helped Becker and Rappleye with their book on Rosselli, *All American Mafioso,* published in 1991; Tony Summers as he was doing research beyond his earlier book, *Conspiracy;* Hinckle and Turner with *Deadly Secrets* (their sequel to *The Fish Is Red),* published in 1992. I also flew to Colorado at the invitation of free-lance writer Bryan Abas, a.k.a. Ryan Ross. At the time, he wrote for *Westward,* a regional weekly newspaper.

Bryan was initially interested in me as a source for a story on America's controversial war on drugs, but he became intrigued with my investigative work on Morales. Over time, I developed a good deal of trust in him and his skill as a writer. He proposed we collaborate on a nonfiction book based on my copyrighted "Search for Indio," and I shared with him on an exclusive, confidential basis, much of what had been included in the preliminary report for the JFK Center. I also cooperated extensively with a Minneapolis-St. Paul non-profit truth seek-ing organization called Minnesota Ground Zero headed by Michael Andregg, a part-time instructor at St. Thomas College and a peace activist. I did several TV interviews for Michael on my CIA and DEA experiences.

Ever since the publication of *The War That Never Was,* I'd occasionally receive harassing and threatening phone calls. I kept my number unlisted and gave it out only when absolutely necessary or to people I trusted. But, somehow the number would be compromised, and it was easily available to agencies of government. Following work on the Morales case and as I continued to acquire notoriety in connection with my outspokenness on America's hypocritical and failing war on drugs under Reagan and Bush, the frequency of the intimidating and insulting messages increased. If I answered, I'd simply hang up, but some callers enjoyed leaving their sinister or goofy messages on my recorder. Some callers spoke broken English or Spanish. The most annoying were those that came in the middle of the night when I was desperately trying to get a few hours of rest at a time when I was coping with severe physical discomfort.

Distracting as they were, by the early 1990s I'd come to accept tax audits, phone harassment, and possible monitoring as an unavoidable consequence of revealing information that, for one reason or another, the government wanted to conceal from the American people, ignoring the public's right to the truth. Two incidents were more sinister and frightening.

I received my mail at a box at the nearby Woodbury, Minnesota post office. I did that because of my frequent travels and wish to avoid having mail sitting in an insecure home delivery box for extended periods. Nevertheless, I'd period-ically check the box by my driveway for neighborhood flyers, junk mail and the like. One afternoon, I returned home to find the metal door ajar. There, inside, were two dead canaries with their legs severed and a note reading:

GREETINGS FROM YOUR FLORIDA FRIENDS. YOU ARE ALREADY A DEAD MAN. THE ONLY QUESTION IS WHERE AND WHEN. TO CON-TINUE WILL GUARANTEE THAT SOMEONE YOUNG AND VERY DEAR TO YOU WILL END UP LIKE THIS TOO.

The note was, I took, an obvious reference to my speaking out (a canary being the old prison term for an informant), the severed legs maybe alluding to the condition of Rosselli's corpse, and a possible threat to harm my sons, grand-children, or Perri. I took the birds and the note to the local police. Knowing my background and profession, they seemed to attach little importance to the threat. Other than the incident being noted some months later in an interview I did for a Minneapolis alternative newspaper, fortunately nothing ever came of the matter. It may have been someone's joke, but it got my attention.

I was at my desk concentrating on a proposal for my book on the infamous

South Florida Task Force and the war on drugs at my Woodbury townhouse on a snowy day in mid-February, 1991. Living alone in a neighborhood of white-collar semi-professionals who typically left early and returned about supper time following their daily work routines, and not expecting any special deliveries or callers, I was somewhat startled by a ring of the doorbell followed by a hard knock on the door. Looking out of my office-bedroom window, I could see two hefty men in trench coats at the entranceway. I could tell a cop from a mile away and this was probably going to be bad news.

I had no choice but to go to the door. Opening it, a badge case with U.S. Secret Service credentials was thrust in my face. Agents Wahl and Berglund out of Washington had come to see me. Apparently, someone had reported me as a threat to President Bush and they wanted to talk. They were interested in my writings, especially a letter I had written to some associates critical of Bush's decision to initiate what became known as the Gulf War. They were also curious about my CIA and DEA background and what had either been, or might be, published about those experiences. They told me this as they accepted my invitation to come in, stomped the slush off their shoes, and removed their snow-covered coats. I could see they were armed, carrying shoulder holstered pistols under their suit coats.

These were older guys, about my age, polite, congenial, to the point. They wanted to know what weapons I owned and I told them. They wanted to talk about my work as an investigator and I told them what I'd been working on, including the Morales case. We talked over coffee. "Tell me what you want," I kept thinking. An hour passed as we sat chatting. What the hell were they there for? These guys were pretty big, physically, and I was fairly well whipped by my auto accident injuries. So I cooperated with them in a straightforward, direct but unflinching way. I could tell they already had anything I'd written that was out there in the public domain or might have been obtained surreptitiously— there was no need for document production at this point. There was no mention of a search warrant, but I suspected they might have one. I had nothing to hide and off-handedly invited them to search my home. They declined. It became pretty clear they were on a Washington-ordered fishing expedition. Apparently satisfied, they left as the afternoon snows continued, anxious to get their flight back to D.C..

I later learned that Berglund and Wahl were not Secret Service agents, but were listed as staffers on Bush's National Security Council, apparently using Secret Service cover. Their visit would come back to blight my life in a rather bizarre development more than a year later. (Recall how alleged Secret Service agents appeared in Dealey Plaza on November 22, 1963.)

BRADLEY E. AYERS

CHAPTER 29

The Morales inquiry had brought me nothing but grief. My financial ruin was impending. Nevertheless, I might have my day of equity and justice. The tantalizing leads I'd developed were still out there, holding promise of fulfilling my belief they'd eventually reveal what I'd begun to call the *Zenith Secret:* the direct link of the CIA, via JM/WAVE, to the assassinations of JFK, RFK, and possibly MLK. I took some comfort in knowing what I had to do, if humanly possible, given my circumstances.

As if to exacerbate my distress, I learned, somewhat with the help of Bryan Abas, that Oliver Stone's proposed screenplay for the JFK movie included a character, apparently based on Morales, intimately involved in the plot to kill the president. Morales, after November 22, 1963, is portrayed as killing potential witnesses and even appearing, because of his high-level CIA credentials, during the official reenactments of the events in Dealey Plaza. Upon learning of this, I wrote to Oliver Stone and Camelot Productions asserting my rights to the information upon which his movie script was based. My communication was ignored.

The character in Stone's original version of the script is identified as the "Indian," and supposedly resembles Morales as his photos and I described him. When I eventually viewed the JFK movie after its release, the "Indian" character's role had been diminished to an appearance among the political and intelligence, and military officials meeting in Washington to finalize the decision to execute JFK. Was he cut from a major role because of the threat of my lawsuit?

We'll never know.

There is evidence Stone, or his people, were in direct contact with Dorff in L.A., and were aware of the work I'd done on Morales, et al. They never saw fit to talk with me. He and his bloated collaborators including the screenwriter Zachary Sklar ripped me off. But, in steam rolling me, they cavalierly discounted and ignored one of the key aspects the assassination conspiracy—the role of El Indio and the Arizona connection.

I found the Stone film to be shallow, convoluted, and critically flawed. In my opinion, it failed to make a convincing case for a conspiracy in the murder of the president. It ignored the critical political dynamics and personalities of the early 1960s that I discovered leading to the assassination of JFK and others. Nevertheless, the movie had a positive effect in that it moved Congress to create the Assassination Records Review Board a few years later.

And, help was forthcoming. My sons were somewhat aware of my plight and, I believe, guardedly sympathetic—not with my professional preoccupations and whistle-blower/anti-establishment pursuits (the perception here remained, I'm sure, an unrewarded, futile Don Quixote), nor with my apparent inability to establish a conventional, stable "normal" personal, romantic lifestyle. Yet because they felt a sense of obligation to at least try to help the "old man," who was in dire straits for a variety of reasons. My Woodbury townhouse was at risk of foreclosure, and two of my boys stepped forward to loan me $5000 to keep the wolves from the door. There wasn't much voicing of blame, which they knew would be futile. The boys had the money, thanks to a good education and excellent professional careers. They just did it.

A few reasonably well-situated friends and acquaintances, most knowledgeable of my whistle-blowing, investigative interests, and publishing effort, helped me out financially as I struggled to stabilize my situation and get on my feet. Some strongly encouraged me to go on with the Morales inquiry, but were reluctant to sign on as clients for formal sponsorship. They knew this was sensitive stuff and were concerned about repercussions. They knew the problems I'd been dealing with. Under any circumstance, I accepted help from those I felt had the resources and would be understanding and patient while awaiting repayment. These folks believed in me and my purpose, and their help was a huge boost to my morale and a demonstration of trust and confidence. I prayed not to let them down.

I was just regaining my equilibrium when the dark forces struck again. On Saturday morning, April 3, 1993, I received in the mail an official U.S. government envelope with the return address for the Department of Justice, U.S. Marshals Service, Minneapolis office. What it contained caused me to run from the post office and vomit. There was a brief, innocuous note accompanying the Caution Notice, reading:

> It appears that someone has started a smear campaign against you.
> I would suggest that if you have a legitimate complaint against someone that you contact the Inspector General at
> 1-800-869-4499. I believe this is being covered up.

I was infuriated. Except for my virtual statistics and photo, all lifted from my Minnesota driver's license, the most damning contents of the Reason for Caution were absolutely false. It was true that as a licensed Minnesota private detective I was permitted to carry a concealed weapon. I'd carried a gun in an ankle holster on my left leg when on an assignment requiring a weapon. But, because of my disabling auto accident, I had no need for a gun and hadn't reapplied for a permit. I hadn't carried for many months, and that was a matter of public record.

The first two sentences of the Reason for Caution had absolutely no foundation. They were blatantly discrediting. There was no history to support these scurrilous allegations. The instructions portion of the Notice, while advising no immediate arrest was authorized based on information set forth. Law enforcement was advised to challenge me if I interfered with their performance of duty. The implications of this were chilling, as anyone wearing civilian clothing could claim to be a federal law enforcement officer, exercising whatever force and authority they deemed appropriate upon encountering me, under any circumstance, including the use of deadly force. It had to be assumed I was carrying a concealed weapon.

Perri was one of the few people who knew that I used to carry my .380-pistol in the ankle holster. She also knew of the so-called Secret Service visit and had been dating a U.S. Marshal after I became more reclusive. Her betrayal was now complete and potentially fatal. As word of the Caution Notice would spread, I might as well have been dead, as my character and reputation were assassinated.

I realized, unless I responded quickly I was not only out of business in every professional area of my life, but also fair game for any cop or law enforcement agent that might take aim at me. I immediately went home and called the

Department of Justice Inspector General in Washington, filed a phone complaint, and faxed a copy of the falsified Caution Notice to that office. Fighting anger and something like panic, I then got on the phone, ignoring the fact it was a weekend, and began calling attorneys for advice. All I got were recordings and answering services, but I kept trying to get through to someone. Universally, came the critical question. "If the CIA or some government agency considered you such a threat, why wouldn't they simply have you exterminated, one way or another?"

That was a damn good, legitimate question, but my answer necessitated the listener to make the great leap into a realm of understanding that defied conventional wisdom, especially that generally held by attorneys. I was challenged to explain the crazy logic of my behavior and, in doing so, described a guiding precept for covert operators.

I saw a bronze plaque on the wall during one of my visits at CIA headquarters that read something like this:

"One must be prepared to undertake actions that are perceived to be self destructive in order to achieve surprise and strategic advantage."

That idea remained with me through all my years of so-called clandestine activities. I don't think I ever abused the principle professionally, but I did apply it personally in order to survive in my struggle with the dark forces I was facing as I pursued my search for the truth. At first blush, it might seem to be potentially destructive strategy. Given the nature of who and what I confronted I knew I might only survive if I stood without reservation in public light.

Few attorneys I spoke with were willing or able to fathom the simple concept embodied in the words in the hall at Langley which I interpreted, for my circumstances, this way:

"Over the years, understanding the seemingly crazy logic of covert operations, I've created my own life insurance. I've been open and forthright with official investigators and the media. I've never tried to conceal my actions; I've been scrutinized from all angles at every stage since I was involved in government service. I'm a goddamn Boy Scout. There are numerous media accounts and, most recently, high profile, credible nonfiction books documenting my history and work. The one thing the dark forces fear most are unintended consequences. They will avoid creating a martyr. In fact, I trust they pray I don't have a suspicious accident. There's too much out there now in the media and public realm about my background work and crusades for the truth to overtly take me out. What they can do is try to discredit me, hope I'll embarrass myself or self-destruct in some way—cave in mentally or physically under the pressure. My notoriety is the very thing that keeps me alive, but I still have to deal with the set-ups and dirty tricks."

My pleas for help fell pretty much on deaf ears. At the very least, I'd need $5,000 up front to get someone to file suit in federal court on my behalf. Before that, I would have to pre-fill an administrative complaint and claim against the Justice Department that would have to be prepared, processed, and considered.

In the days and weeks following the issuance of the falsified Caution Notice, I scrambled everywhere for financial help, advice, and legal counsel to

THE ZENITH SECRET

take my case. Out of desperation, I turned to old, trusted, now well-situated, high school friends. One was a prominent Minneapolis attorney, and the other a successful building contractor in my home town. I came away empty. Everything else became secondary. Even though the issuance of the Caution Notice was not common public knowledge, the word spread quickly throughout the professional community that I depended upon for 90 percent of my work as a writer and investigator. The Marshals Service portrayed me as some sort of Oswald-like psycho. It was devastating.

After I got over the emotional aspects of this latest personal and professional put-down, it only reinforced my determination to go forward with what was now becoming a well-defined agenda. Regardless of the costs and any other consideration, I had to go forward with the Morales investigation and try to complete my book on the drug war. I was so embarrassed by the falsified Caution Notice as it circulated that, as I completed the writing and investigating contracts I had on hand, I stopped reaching out.

Michael Andregg, my standby supporter, finally put me in touch with an attorney who might take my case against the Justice Department over the Caution Notice. I'd been living with pronounced paranoia of what might happen unless I could somehow come up with a legal advocate to formalize my complaint. I'd had no response, pretty much as expected, from the Justice Department Inspector General. A personal letter to Attorney General Janet Reno got no response. I also brought my situation to the attention of the entire Minnesota Congressional Delegation. The response was tepid. I was like a criminal pleading wrongful accusation and judgement. They didn't get it—apparently they deferred to intimidation by the Washington bureaucracy. The senators did try to help me with my FOIA requests and for that, alone, I was grateful.

I had to spend a lot of time with the attorney, Frank Mabley, who was preparing my suit against the Justice Department. The law firm was well connected with Minnesota Congressman Bruce Vento, and I thought his office might become interested in my case. The basic challenge I had was to not only produce documents confirming my history, but also to educate the attorney about the insidious nature of those entities trying to silence and destroy me. There were times I felt I was talking to a tree, but I kept my cool.

CHAPTER 30

David Corn's biography of Ted Shackley appeared (1994, Simon and Schuster, *The Blond Ghost*) and, in light of my cooperation with the author, I was quite disappointed in the work. Corn's book was a whitewash of Ted's history as a covert operator, the man I knew at JM/WAVE, was aware of during Iran-Contra, and subsequently, as I was searching for El Indio. Corn's book left me feeling empty, offering only a ghostly representation of the flesh and blood, spooky entity I knew.

I was constantly reminded of Shackley's behind-the-scenes presence as I continued work on my Iran-Contra era war on drugs book through the frigid winter months, hunkered down in my townhouse, going forth only to do battle with the VA over my claims, get medical treatment or files papers in federal court. Whatever logical investigative work came my way, I jumped at if I felt physically able to get the job done. Eventually, I had to surrender my Minnesota private detective license because I could no longer afford to pay the required professional insurance premiums.

It was spring 1994 before I completed the necessary legal work for my federal suit, recovered enough physically and pulled together the money necessary for a trip to the coast and a meeting with Dorff and prospective writing client, Jock Jocoy, a California race horse veterinarian for the rich and famous who wanted me to ghost write his autobiography. I met Dorff in Riverside for lunch. We talked a bit about the latest developments in assassination research, particularly matters relating to David Morales. I expressed in the strongest terms possible the need for someone to pursue the investigation in Arizona.

I wanted to get away from Dorff as quickly as I could, and go to Jocoy to cut some kind of ghostwriting deal with him. One thing Dorff mentioned stuck in my craw. He said his friend, Tony Summers, had recently commented to him that "[Tony] was coming around to believe Oswald was a lone assassin." That was interesting because all my dialogue with Summers suggested something entirely different. My unease and mistrust of Dorff was reinforced every moment I spent with him.

I met with Jocoy in Del Mar and he showed me the supporting material for what would be an autobiographical book. What he brought forth had merit, I felt, with a lot of work. His expectations were to have a draft manuscript completed in approximately six months. I went to work on the project immediately. With copies of his materials in hand, I drove back to Las Vegas, put the car in storage, and flew back to Minnesota to get on with the Jocoy project. En route to Vegas, I stopped in Phoenix to reestablish contact with Walton, Carbajal, and Rabern's office. My sources were still intact and I was relieved given the passage of time since we'd last spoken.

The staffing of the newly authorized Assassination Records Review Board had been announced, and upon my return to Minnesota I made an appointment to meet with then Deputy State Attorney General, John R. Tunheim who had been designated as chairman. I had much to talk to him about, particularly CIA, JM/WAVE, Morales, and John Rosselli.

I called to make an appointment with John Tunheim. The meeting went extremely well. Tunheim listened carefully as I summarized my experience with JM/WAVE. My impressions, observations, and encounters with personalities of the period. I told him of my efforts to unravel David Morales. Then, I gave him my copies of *The War That Never Was, Deadly Secrets, Conspiracy, All American Mafioso,* and *The Last Investigation.* I gave him a list of the true names of key individuals involved in the CIA's covert anti-Castro effort. I also offered my cooperation with the board to help fulfill their congressionally ordered mandate—the pursuit and public release of any and all records relating to the murder of the president.

When I finally received a response to my Army and CIA FOIA Privacy Act request in January 1995, I immediately forwarded a copy to the ARRB, with particular reference to a 1976 internal CIA memo stating that five sealed envelopes associated with my work with the agency had been withheld from examination by the House Select Committee on Assassinations and returned to the files at Langley. I urged the board to seek the release of the envelope's contents. Following that, I maintained close contact with the ARRB. Chris Barger, a staff analyst, flew in from Washington to spend about half a day with me to discuss what input I might provide as the board proceeded with its work in May 1995.

I'd been encouraged by the interview with Tunheim and I gave Barger everything I had on JM/WAVE and the Arizona connection. I followed up the interview with copies of all the documents I'd collected that might assist the pursuit of JFK assassination related records. I received a warm letter of appreciation for my efforts.

As the years passed, I kept in close contact with the ARRB, hoping that something might turn up reinforcing the investigative work I'd done on Morales and promoting interest on someone's part to pursue the leads I'd developed. It didn't happen.

While awaiting the board's final report and the release of documents, my life continued to disintegrate. My home in Woodbury was broken into and files were taken—nothing else. Then, my 1994 Mazda Navajo SUV was impounded by the leasing company in a dispute over warranty repairs and payments. All of my investigative gear, gun, and camera disappeared without explanation and were never recovered. Despite the efforts of Senator Wellstone and others of the Minnesota Congressional delegation, the VA refused to acknowledge my service-related disability claims because of the absence of Army-CIA medical records. Eventually, I exhausted my resources for legal fees and had to carry the suit against the Marshal Service forward on my own. In 1995, it was heard in federal court in Minneapolis and dismissed with prejudice by Judge Rosenblum on grounds of national sovereignty. But the U.S. Marshals involved were supposedly reprimanded for violating policy. Nevertheless the damage was done.

In the summer of 1996, I sought the advice of an attorney who was well read into my history, lifestyle, and the torments resulting from my "whistleblowing"efforts. He told me to get out of town, permanently, and as quickly as possible. He'd done some investigating. "They"—and he wouldn't be specific but thought I should know—were out to destroy me. It wasn't as if I didn't already understand that, but hearing it from someone else I trusted made the threat all that much more real.

It was time to leave, no question about it. But I was broke, with no car and no specific destination in mind other than the state of Arizona. I had medical problems. My shoulders limited what I could do physically and my skin condition was periodically disabling when fissurings failed to heal and became infected. The VA had declared me fully and permanently disabled and awarded me an interim pension of $600 per month, pending the settlement of other service related claims. Bottomed out as I was, I felt damn lucky to get that, but the award precluded my acceptance of any other income without penalty. I was in a box. I would not have received the pension had it not been for Senator Paul Wellstone and the efforts of his staff on my behalf.

The CIA continued to hold my medical records and my Army file could not be found. As had been the case in so many critical situations in my life, when all seemed hopeless, someone or some event interceded at the last moment that allowed me to go on. Michael Andregg and others who believed in me as a man with a mission pitched in to help me financially.

Ron Williams, a member of Ground Zero Minnesota, Michael Andregg's peace activist group, had taken an interest in my investigation of Morales and my plight. I'd shared with him what I wanted to accomplish in the Southwest, extending my inquiry beyond what had already been done. Now, he came forth to help me. He loaned me the money to recover my impounded car and purchase replacement investigating equipment. He supplemented my VA pension. With his help, I would be able to travel and survive.

It was time to go. I surrendered my home to HUD, put my personal property into storage, sent a note of farewell to my sons, and headed west. Personal survival was priority number one. Second on the agenda was my pursuit of the Arizona connection.

CHAPTER 31

Homeless, with my personal and professional life in shambles, and under constant fear of more drastic threat and intimidation by the dark forces, I opted to try to begin a new life in Arizona. I was still licensed as a PI there, had good area knowledge, and, being unknown, might have some chance of reestablishing myself professionally if I kept a low profile. I'd previously reconnoitered the area around Flagstaff and Sedona, and felt comfortable in the mountainous area of northern Arizona, where seasonal changes were comparable to the upper Midwest. With the financial and moral support of Ron Williams and a few other friends who understood and believed in me, I set off with my dogs and cats in a U-Haul truck with the basic necessities for reestablishing a home.

My plan, on arrival in Arizona, was to press for the release of my medical records from Special Warfare, CIA, and Army intelligence, to get my private detective business up and operating, and to work on a book about my DEA experience and America's failed war on drugs. I hoped I could do this in relatively obscure fashion, so I settled in a small cabin on a slope of the White Mountains in the tiny community of Pine-Strawberry, a few miles north of Payson. Phoenix and the VA hospital were about an hour and a half southwest, as was the VA Regional Office where I would press my service-related disability claims.

Just down my priority list was the hope I might pursue the Arizona connection to the assassination of President Kennedy. Despite all the grief associated with the investigation of Morales, and even though I didn't have an investigative client as required by my PI licensing in Arizona, I hoped to develop leads that connected Morales and his CIA and Mafia associates to the death of the president. My prior work had developed some tantalizing possibilities, but I knew I'd have to go about any fieldwork very discreetly. If I came up with enough, possibly I could find a sponsor to fund a more substantial inquiry.

I was physically and emotionally drained when I arrived in Pine-Strawberry in the fall of 1996. Almost robot-like, I unloaded the U-Haul, got my pets comfortably sheltered. I set up for the winter in the 500 square foot cabin perched on the hillside among towering Ponderosa pines. With my animals for companionship, I went to work on the war on drugs book and tried to establish some semblance of normality in my life. I planned to keep a very low profile in the small community. If anyone asked, I'd say I was a writer seeking privacy and solitude while finishing a book. Living pretty much as a typical disabled veteran recluse, I had to make do on my pension. Fortunately, my earlier benefactors who believed strongly in my purpose, continued to supplement my finances. I reluctantly accepted whatever help might be available, knowing I had to survive to find the truth.

After the gravely intimidating battering I'd experienced in Minnesota over the past three years, I was wary of doing anything that might draw attention to myself. However, it was impossible to remain completely hidden because of professional and personal contacts that were essential to the continuation of my book research and investigation. Charlie Winton, a book distributor in San Francisco, was working on the placement with a publisher of my uncensored rewrite of *The War That Never Was.* Jim DiEugenio and Lisa Pease published articles in *Probe Magazine* mentioning my name and CIA connection relating to President Kennedy's murder with my authorization. However, my location in the mountains was kept secret. Several months after my arrival in Arizona, I was contacted by an independent TV documentary producer working on a series on the assassinations, their researchers encouraged me to cooperate with Howard Moytle, and just before Christmas, he and a film crew flew in from Chicago and taped a four hour interview with me in the Pine cabin. I allowed this to go forward with the assurance the documentary would not be aired for many months, and I felt by that time my books would be in the hands of a publisher and my "message" delivered. The dark forces could take all the shots at me they wanted after that.

The stresses of the past two years had aggravated some of my physical problems and I had to establish a connection with the VA hospital in Phoenix for regular care. During my excursions to the valley for medical treatment, I reestablished contact with Morales' attorney Bob Walton and El Indio's lifelong friend, Reuben Carbajal. I kept the dialogue with them low key. (I learned that Noel Twyman had followed in Fonzi's steps in quizzing them about Morales, but had made no mention of this or all that had transpired relative to the Morales story since I'd last spoken with them.) I hoped, in so doing, that something spontaneous might surface if I played it cool—I was convinced they both had information that had yet to be disclosed to anyone. All the while, I kept confidential contact with Judge Tunheim, and AARB staffers Jeremy Gunn and Chris Bargar. Privately, I remained curious about Goldwater's possible connection to the murder of Don Bolles, an *Arizona Republic* investigative reporter, who died in a 1976 car bombing. Bolles' murder took place around the same time as the Washington, D.C. Letelier car bombing assassination to which Morales was suspected of having links by HSCA investigators.

Ron Williams had given me the contact information for several potential sources in Phoenix, who were knowledgeable of the Arizona political scene of the preceding 30 years or more. They proved to be valuable as I went about my Goldwater background research. I picked up a copy of Lake Headley's 1990 book, *Loud and Clear,* on the Bolles murder and absorbed its thesis. Shoumatoff's *Legends of the American Desert* was also very helpful in background research. My trips to the valley were brief but fruitful, and the isolation and solitude of the mountain cabin provided an ideal setting in which to ponder the information I was accumulating.

I learned the Goldwaters had led a very active, socially and culturally engaged political life in Arizona for more than half a century. They mingled with the elite of the Phoenix-Scottsdale community as well as the working class, Mexican Americans, Indians, poor farmers, and ranchers. I already had testimony that the senator and his family members were patrons of Carbajal's El Molino Restaurant and knew the Morales family as early as the 1950s. From my new Phoenix sources and the Headley book, I learned that Senator Goldwater and his neo-conservative clan were deeply involved in all kinds of political manipulations in Arizona, virtually controlling the electoral process in the state as well as water and mining resources. It was a commonly held belief that Senator Goldwater had close ties to gambling interests and organized crime despite his upright public image and iconic, militant, right-wing, national stature.

After several months of this low-key research, I had exhausted my available sources. Senator Goldwater's health was failing, but the family remained socially active and prominent in the Scottsdale area. I wanted to get some flavor for the upper crust, the rich, powerful, the exclusive of Phoenix, with whom the Goldwaters associated. I began attending the plentiful cultural and social-political events in the valley, introducing myself as a writer doing research on a biography of the senator. I gave no hint of my interest in assassinations or anything related. I was amazed how easy it was under this cover to insinuate myself into Scottsdale's active upscale set. It was a great indulgence for me to emerge every month or so from my cabin, showered and looking sharp, to travel to the valley to crash a cocktail party, listen to live classical music, attend an art show, a reading, or a lecture. Unfortunately, I didn't have much luck probing the dark side of Arizona politics and uncovering the Goldwaters' unpublished history, despite long conversations with people who knew the family well.

As with so many other extraordinary developments in my investigation of Morales and related matters, there came a big break. During the course of attending cultural lectures or "salons" as the Phoenix intelligentsia called them, I was introduced to a couple who had organized some of the events. They had heard of my writing and my CIA-special operations background. They asked if I might like to make a presentation at a spring event for the "Spirit of the Senses" salon. Despite wanting to maintain a low profile, I saw the invitation as a way of further ingratiating myself with the elite inner sanctum who might know where all kinds of skeletons are buried. I suggested to the sponsors that I do a reading from the book I was writing about the war on drugs and they approved.

I made my presentation in mid-May, in a darkened theater with a single overhead spotlight over the podium. Unable to see the audience because of the lighting arrangement, I had no idea of the attendance, nor could I establish eye contact. I was introduced by Wyatt Earp, the grandson of the famous cowboy, who elaborated on my bio. I read a gentle, sentimental story I'd written about the loss of one of my dogs that contrasted what would follow. Then I read a chapter from my unpublished book on the war on drugs, about a major drug smuggling operation I had worked on while serving with the DEA. I read it to the surprising approval of the social elite, even with all the street talk, violence, and obscenities common to the drug subculture.

Following the reading, I was approached by a petite, well-dressed Hispanic woman who had graying black hair. Refined, matronly, and attractive, she introduced herself and complimented me on my reading. Her name was Pearl and she'd read Fonzi's book and knew of my investigations of Morales. It caught me completely off guard. She wanted to talk to me in private sometime.

I had plans to meet with Wyatt Earp, Brian Quig and his sidekick, and two of my Phoenix sources after the reading. Pearl gave me a number to call where I could leave a message the next time I came down to the valley. Had I known at that moment how significant meeting Pearl was, I would have cancelled any other plans for that night.

I called the number Pearl gave me and left a message telling her when I'd be at the VA hospital. I could meet her in the lobby there after my appointments. I received no confirming call back and began to have doubts that I'd see her again.

Near the end of May, I returned to the VA hospital in Phoenix as scheduled, and after my appointment, loitered in the reception area for 45 minutes. Pearl was nowhere to be seen. When I finally went to my car, I found a note under the windshield wiper. Pearl said she would meet me at the pavilion in the old Indian School area just west of the hospital complex. How she knew my car from all the hundreds parked there I'll never know. The wide expanse of park-like open

THE ZENITH SECRET

space where the historical Indian School had stood was deserted. Pearl was sitting alone at a picnic table in the roofed pavilion when in the warm spring afternoon I approached her.

She was dressed smartly, and a white medical smock lay on the bench beside her. Well-groomed, with sparkling brown eyes, she greeted me and we shook hands. She wore no rings. We made small talk at first. She seemed to know a great deal about me, and apparently had access to my files at the VA hospital since she knew my appointment history. She declined to give me anything more than her first name and asked that I promise not to divulge any identification without her approval. She described herself as a medical consultant. She said she was in her mid-40s and had children. I asked her about her heritage and she explained that her father was Mexican and Native American. Her mother was Caucasian. Her manner was poised and she spoke with just a hint of an accent. She was quite articulate and became more relaxed as we chatted about our personal backgrounds. Early on in the conversation she asked me for my solemn word that I be absolutely discreet about our meeting and future conversations. I was not to follow her or tape record anything she said. This highly piqued my interest.

Then Pearl was silent for several minutes. Gazing at her hands clasped in her lap, I saw tears welling in her eyes. I said nothing, waiting. She said she was thinking of her father and what he told her before he died in 1991 at the age of 65. He had lived for some days after a heart attack before succumbing to pneumonia. Pearl's mother had already passed on. Pearl had spent the last days with her father while he was still in intensive care. She carried the burden of his deathbed confidences with considerable guilt and moral conflict. But, with the recent revelations about Morales and all that it might imply, she felt obliged as an American to speak to someone about what he had divulged. Without sounding patronizing, and in a very dispassionate way, she said she felt I was someone who had the courage and integrity to pursue the information she had to offer while protecting her interests and privacy. Was this for real, or was I being conned? This was a dilemma given what I had already experienced in the toxic atmosphere surrounding the Morales story and the JFK assassination research. I would take this one slow and easy.

I learned early on, as an apprentice newspaper reporter, that when encountering a source such as Pearl, an interviewer is most successful when simply allowing the subject to talk, and by sharing a little of oneself. After about an hour of such an exchange, we had established a pleasant comfort level.

She had grown up in Tempe, a suburb of Phoenix. She married a man she met an college, but divorced after four years. She had never traveled on her own outside the Southwest on except occasional visits to D.C. to see her father who worked on the staff of Senator Barry Goldwater. Pearl volunteered for the Peace Corps and spent three years as an animal health specialist in Central and South America. When her service ended, Pearl returned to Phoenix, and was accepted to medical school. She met and married a widower. He died two years later in a plane crash. She continued to raise his children until they went off on their own. She said she no longer dated and was devoted to her work as a specialist. Church, salons, and cultural events, were really her only social indulgences.

I was impressed by Pearl in a number of ways. This was a woman who did not seem to function on whim or impulse.

Although I'd not broached the subject, and before I asked Pearl to tell me about her father, with her eyes cast to the sky, she said she remembered vividly the day when President Kennedy was killed. She was 13, in school that day, and the nuns at her Catholic school took all the students to church to pray. That night, her father called from Washington or somewhere and said he wouldn't be home on his usual schedule (alternating two weeks in D.C., with two weeks at the senator's office in Phoenix). When her father finally returned a week or so later, she saw he'd begun drinking heavily. She was in high school when Robert Kennedy and Martin Luther King, Jr. were murdered in 1968. Her father, who had moderated his drinking, spent more and more time at the office in Phoenix or traveling, returned to heavy drinking and would often take long walks in the desert by himself. No one in the family seemed to be able to comfort him, and he would not talk about his work or what was bothering him.

Who was Pearl's father? Over the next nine months, meeting sometimes for a few minutes or up to an hour, I met with Pearl in a variety of out of the way sites in and about the Phoenix area, usually after my appointments or emergency care at private or VA facilities in the valley. The rapport was comfortable, even friendly, never approaching a romantic nature. She did not want to meet in any publicly active environment. The procedure was always the same. I would call ahead to the VA to confirm a previously scheduled appointment or make one if I needed out patient care. I had no way of contacting Pearl directly and respected her wish to meet with me at her discretion. I would then find a note on my car in the VA hospital parking lot advising me when and where we should meet. It was sometimes the old Indian School pavilion by the hospital, but other times we'd meet at the fountain in Fountain City and or at the Superstition Mountain trailhead. Not once did I see her park or emerge from a vehicle which could be traced by license plate. She came on foot and left on foot, and although I instinctively wanted to, I did not follow her out of consideration for her requests. I didn't want to jeopardize my access to her as a source.

Pearl's father, Pepe, or Papa, as she referred to him, was born an illegitimate child of American Indian-Mexican parentage in Gallup, New Mexico in 1926 and was put up for adoption. The procedures for dealing with such situations were (by today's standards) quite primitive. He was a sickly child and was taken to a Catholic-funded hospital in Phoenix. He matured in an orphanage and in foster homes. Regarding his genetics and ancestry, Pearl injects that Papa asserted he was of Zuni origin on his mother's side and not Navajo or Apache. His father's true ancestry is unknown except for what Pearl found in tracing the birth record which had him as "Indian-Mexican."

During the 1920s and 1930s, in the relatively unsettled American Southwest, the care of children given up at birth, especially minorities, typically fell to a church or missionary organization on the Indian reservations and surrounding communities. The Catholic church was most instrumental in the process, but record keeping was haphazard at best. Pearl said she knew little of the early years of her father's life, except that he remained sickly until he was five or six. Papa was a small, skinny boy with poor eyesight. She assumed he was somewhat introverted, unable to contend with the bullying kids in the rough neighborhood. But he was a good student and a hard worker. The Catholic families that fostered him were hardscrabble, laboring, and strictly disciplined. Pearl's father had chores to do every day after school, and by the time he was 12, it was expected he find full time summer work. His first real job, she'd explained, was working in the horse barns and fields on property owned by the Goldwater family. It was to be a connection that would affect his entire life.

The smart, wiry, hardworking youngster caught the eye of the ranch supervisors, and by the time "Papa" entered high school, he had a regular job with the Goldwaters. He'd overcome his childhood illnesses, but remained slight, bespectacled, dark-haired, and sinewy, with delicate features. I take this image from Pearl's descriptions and from his high school yearbook photo she showed me. Papa was strong, but too small to engage in high school contact sports, so he became a distance runner. She believed he first came in contact with David Sanchez Morales, then a student at Phoenix Union High School, at track meets in 1942 and 1943. Papa said Morales stood out as a big, powerful competitor in a number of events.

Bookish, intent, unlike so many other kids from the poor settlements around Phoenix, Papa earned favor with the Goldwaters, and when he graduated from high school in 1943, the Goldwater family arranged for a four year scholarship to Arizona State University.

From 1944 to 1948, Pearl's father majored in geology and hydrology with a minor in political science. There, in 1944 and 1945, he became friendly with Morales despite their contrasting qualities. Morales, who was more interested in girls and extracurricular activities, was not a good student, and her father helped him with his studies. Morales shared with him that he too was being helped through school by the Goldwaters. (It seems, as observed by Pearl, the Goldwaters selectively provided financial help to a number of minority youth in the 1940s and 1950s.) Morales did not return to ASU the following fall. Papa graduated in 1948 with a bachelor of science degree.

He did some graduate work at Northern Arizona University in Flagstaff studying mining and earth sciences, but left school without an advanced degree to go to work for Barry Goldwater's staff as a paid intern. Papa's primary duty was as a liaison between the senator and Arizona Native American tribes in matters concerning water and mining rights. There was also a strong political component with these interests as he went about his duties. Pearl said her father met and married her mother soon after going to work for Senator Goldwater.

Papa worked on the Goldwater staff both in Washington and Arizona. He had direct, personal, almost daily contact with the senator and various political figures. Papa became the key go-between for the senator in his financial and political dealings with the Indian tribes, the Bureau of Indian Affairs, ranching and water rights in Arizona and throughout the Southwest, especially in Nevada, from the early 1950s to 1974. As a senatorial staff member, he prepared papers and appeared with the senator at many congressional hearings.

The last word Papa had heard about Morales when he didn't show up at ASU, was that he'd gone to California and later joined the Army. (This coincided with what I'd learned in my background investigation of Morales. It also increased my suspicion that the Goldwaters subsidized Morales funding for attendance at USC between 1946 and 1948.) Her father said he was surprised in 1961, right after the Bay of Pigs fiasco, when Morales walked into Senator Goldwater's office in civilian clothes and gave him a big bear hug. Papa was stunned. By this time, there was word in Washington's most information-privileged circles that President Eisenhower was awarding certain successful CIA covert operators, including Morales. The big man of earlier, humbler days in Phoenix was boldly asserting his presence in the elite office of a U.S. senator. Pearl's father was quite taken aback, especially when he saw Morales walk into the senator's office without any preliminaries.

During one of my meetings with Pearl in late summer, I asked her why she was telling me all this; what did she expect to gain from our conversations? (The possibility lingered that I was being led down some primrose path.) Her reply was simple: "I just want to tell you where I think you should look." I had already concluded that Pearl was involved in some kind of medical consulting at the VA hospital in Phoenix, but on one stifling hot afternoon, when we met by the fountain pond in Fountain City, she put her partially open hand bag on the bench beside her and a plastic security admittance badge on a nylon cord slipped out. It was from the Mayo Clinic in north Scottsdale. The media was reporting that the ailing Senator Goldwater was under treatment there at the time.

What is set forth here is the correlation of information provided by Pearl during my series of discussions with her and includes my interpretation of what she had conveyed in a chronological framework.

Pearl told me her father became aware of a plot to neutralize or eliminate President Kennedy's presidency. He believed it began in earnest shortly after the 1962 Cuban missile crisis. The plot coincided with Senator Goldwater's expressed intent to run for the presidency against Kennedy in 1964. Pearl's father was not a party to the plot, but because of his intimate access to Goldwater's office, which included overheard communications and observance of various persons and goings-on as the political campaign developed, his awareness of a sinister, diabolical conspiracy increased. At first, it seemed like politics as usual, although he knew from experience, Goldwater was a no-holds barred, well-established, well-funded, and ruthless campaigner.

Senator Goldwater was the principle political figurehead for the most radical, right-wing elements of the Republican Party at the time. His philosophy of using whatever force necessary to defeat the "communist menace" in the world garnered him many supporters, including those in the military, the FBI, the CIA, Secret Service, and other top level agencies. The campaign strategy, following the Bay of Pigs disaster, the 1962 missile crisis, and the agreement with Khrushchev, was to paint the president and the Democrats as appeasers of the international Soviet-China threat. For the militant idealogues in the Goldwater camp, Kennedy's continued presence in the White House represented a potentially lethal threat to America. Kennedy had to be removed or defeated, one way or another.

Pearl's father, on the sidelines and dutifully doing his job for the senator on a variety of domestic issues, watched in silence as Goldwater's powerful inner sanctum asserted itself. Papa said the thought of assassination never entered his mind. He knew the senator to be a tough, hard-nosed politician with many rather unsavory connections. Yet, he also seemed as a generous and compassionate man, who tempered his will and ambitions. Pearl said he'd been very kind to her father and had helped financially to put her through college. That's why Papa had kept his silence about what was called the Gila Project among the select few in the Goldwater inner circle. (This was a cryptic, symbolic title for aggressive political action. It was chosen because of the lethal capability of the Southwest's Gila monster. It also had a cover in communications by a project on the Gila River in Arizona, in which the senator would logically have an interest.)

My conversations with Pearl led me to believe that Senator Barry Goldwater was at the heart of a conspiracy to eliminate what was considered by the highest conservative echelons, the scourge of JFK's presidency. This effort intensified, dramatically, as did Goldwater's outspoken Cold War rhetoric after the 1962 missile crisis and Kennedy's deal with Khrushchev. Morales and high-level people from the CIA and the Pentagon became frequent visitors to Goldwater's Washington office and always met with the senator behind closed doors. During one of Pearl's brief and infrequent trips to Washington to stay with her papa, Pearl recalled meeting General Curtis LeMay and FBI Chief J. Edgar Hoover.

As an experienced interviewer, I observed Pearl closely as we spoke during these meetings. I threw her curves, tried to casually distract her, used some tricks of interrogation. She had no problem in maintaining eye contact and I saw none of the typical body and facial signs of deception. Again, I came away feeling there was something going on with this woman, but skeptical and cynical as I innately was, I would be damned if I could put my finger on it. She never asked for money or favors.

Despite all of my efforts to stay inconspicuous in Pine, on the evening of August 1, 1997, someone took shots at me with a high-powered rifle as I was crossing a firebreak with my dogs in the wooded area south of my cabin. I walked my three adopted Weimaraner dogs about the same time each evening among the Ponderosa pines, pretty much along the same trail, before feeding them as a matter of routine. That night, the dogs may have saved my hide as they lunged for a rabbit just as we were about to cross the firebreak. I had them leashed to a waistbelt harness, but they took off in unison with such force that I was pulled into a stooped, half-falling position, stumbling forward in somewhat of a running crouch, as I was literally pulled across the five yard open lane of the break.

I heard the shot whistle just over my head and caught a fleeting glimpse of a rifleman braced on the hood of a vehicle in the ravine about 100 yards to my left and below me. As I fell to the other side of the firebreak, another shot rang out and as I lay there, I heard the vehicle speed off.

I hightailed it back to the cabin and barricaded myself there for the next three days. The shooting was not accidental. The area where I walked the dogs was off-limits to hunting. It was too close to the village of Pine and a main highway. I could think of no motive for the incident other than to interdict my investigation in Phoenix. I waited for the next shoe to drop—a home invasion or fire bombing—and I pondered whether to report the incident to law enforcement. To do so would quite flagrantly reveal my presence in Pine and might lead to all kinds of questioning by police that might expose the details of my pursuit of the Arizona connection. I was alone and defenseless in the little cabin in an out-of-the-way location on the side of the mountain, and, obviously, I'd have to emerge from the house to sustain myself and my animals. I decided, eventually, to report the incident to the Gila County Sheriff, the law enforcement agency that had jurisdiction in the rural wilderness area, as discreetly as possible and hope for the best. What bothered me most was the fact the brief glimpse I had of the shooter and vehicle somewhat resembled the color and type commonly used by the local sheriff.

On August 4, I drove to Payson and met with a sheriff's deputy. I described the incident and provided him a sketch of the area where the shooting had occurred. The deputy took the report in a matter-of-fact manner and said only it would be placed in the file. He asked me no questions after I identified myself and I volunteered nothing about my investigative work.

The shooting was a major distraction to my ongoing dialogue with Pearl, and I decided to let things cool for a few weeks before returning to Phoenix. I adjusted the scheduling of my next appointment at the VA accordingly, with the expectation Pearl would, as in the past, access the change. I had become so intrigued by what Pearl was telling me, I found the need to lay low very frustrating.

Things were unusually quiet for a while. I resumed walking my dogs each morning and evening, ever vigilant now of anything suspicious. I hoped the shooting incident would just blow over. But, that was not to be.

BRADLEY E. AYERS

I'd been in Pine for 10 months, living as unobtrusively as possible while carrying out my agenda of working on my war on drugs book and venturing into the valley to carry on my pursuit of the Arizona connection to the Kennedy assassination. I'd spoken to no one about my ongoing dialogue with Pearl. My first thoughts after the shooting incident postulated my contact with her had been compromised, and someone or some larger entity was motivated to lethally shut me down. There was another possibility. The somewhat remote, backwoods northeast area of Arizona referred to by the natives as the "rim" because of its mountainous, plateau elevation above the south central desert valley had become a haven for a diverse mix of people. Retirees seeking the solitude and relatively inexpensive cost of living in small, out-of-the-way communities, well fixed professionals from Phoenix building expensive rustic get-away homes to escape the stultifying summer heat in the valley, and eclectic mix of low income locals with family ties and jobs in the area: semi-poverty level artists, writers, and craftsman (I include myself in this category) and a whole variety of social drop outs, misfits, and people hiding from their spouses, the courts, or the law. It was truly an interesting place to live. I even became friends with a Hollywood screenwriter who would flee to the rim whenever the L.A. scene got too much for him.

Among the foregoing, there was a sinister element. The remoteness of the area, the rugged terrain, limited road access, absence of regular law enforcement patrols and the general Old West cultural atmosphere of people keeping to themselves made the rim an ideal haven for drug traffickers. The proximity of urban Phoenix, high living Sedona, college campuses Tempe and Flagstaff presented readily accessible markets for illegal narcotics. Nearly everyone living on the rim and near Highway 87 was aware of the area's thriving dope industry. Marijuana, crack cocaine, and speed were the staples, but meth was growing in demand.

I had little personal interaction with the citizens of Pine-Strawberry—a stop at the convenience store for gas and a few groceries, a local bar for happy hour, the post office and print shop, etc. However, I quickly picked up on the demographics and cultural atmosphere of the community. Now, pondering a possible motive for the shooting incident, I had to consider that someone, mistaking me for someone involved in the drug trade, motivated by vengeance or business encroachment, fired the shots. Maybe the shooting was totally unrelated to what I was doing covertly in the valley.

About a week or so after the incident, when Beth Counseller, a reporter for the *Payson Roundup*—the major newspaper in the region—asked to interview me. I found that she's learned that I was writing several books (I'd told the sheriff deputy this, but not the specifics, when I made the shooting incident report), but Beth seemed to have more information from other sources. I decided, in view of my concerns, that I was being identified as a drug dealer because of my cloistered lifestyle. I again relied on my pragmatic view that being out front with the media was a form of life insurance. It had kept me intact this far. I prevailed upon Beth, in return for a no-holds-barred interview, that she not mention the shooting incident. I was concerned about being publicly portrayed as some sort of paranoid nutcase.

The interview was published in late August and I agonized over what effect it might have on Pearl if she had access to the paper. But, that wasn't my only distraction. I had been badgering my so-called literary agent in San Francisco to get something done on the placement of an expanded version of *The War That Never Was* with a publisher. While sweating out the shooting incident and the

THE ZENITH SECRET

fallout of the *Payson Roundup* article, I got a call from Charlie Winton and in his laid back manner, advised me he had someone who wanted to publish my books. He said that a Henno Lohmeyer of United Publishing Group in Norwalk, CT would be in touch with me with a proposition. I was delighted.

The manuscript, absent until the current Arizona connection research was completed, could be delivered in a matter of months, and I really needed the money. For months I'd been struggling to get a publisher, not only working with Charlie Winton and the *Probe* editors on the West Coast, but other writers who had published in the CIA/conspiracy theory/whistle-blower/ non-fiction genre. Doug Valentine and Frank Camper had both tried to help me find publishers. Doug, Tony Summers, and even Gaeton Fonzi went so far as to try to put me in contact with Tom Clines for an interview on Morales, et al. None of this produced fruit, and now suddenly here was Lohmeyer.

Lohmeyer offered me an advance of $7,500 on *The Zenith Secret*. But, before any contract could be finalized, I'd have to fly to Connecticut and meet him in person. Difficult as it was to put him off, I told him I needed to look at my schedule. After the shooting incident and the article in the newspaper, I was uneasy. There was something about Lohmeyer's tone and his interest in getting me away from my mountain "sanctuary"—without even seeing my full manuscript—that made me uncomfortable.

Despite my pent up frustration over getting *The Zenith Secret* published, there was something far more important going on. The promise of more revelations by Pearl, if that dialogue could continue despite the recent distractions, at least temporarily outweighed anything else. If what Pearl was telling me could be supported, I was on the track of possibly exposing the conspiracy that resulted in the death of President Kennedy. I rescheduled my appointments at the VA in Phoenix for October. I called Lohmeyer to smoke him out a bit further—I told him I would fly out immediately, unannounced, or I'd have to wait until after my next round of treatment at the VA in Phoenix for October. Lohmeyer wouldn't buy it. He wanted me in Norwalk on his terms and schedule. My instincts kicked in. I sensed a set up. That ended any possible deal with United Publishing Group. Lohmeyer never called me back and Winton in San Francisco began to distance himself from me.

I thought to hell with them. I had something going with Pearl in the valley that transcended anything else. No matter how desperate and frustrated I was. I was not to be disappointed.

The note on the car was there at the VA. We met late on an October afternoon at the Superstition Mountain Trailhead. She walked up to me out of a shallow dry wash almost hidden by underbrush. She was in hiking clothes and carrying a feathered carcass. We exchanged pleasantries, but before I could explain my reasons to for changing my VA schedule, she reached into her vest and pulled out a copy of the August 27 article in the *Payson Roundup,* the page with Beth Counseller's interview article. "Why did you do this?" she asked, her eyes flashing. What could I say? I then had to explain, the shooting incident, my rationale for the interview, assuring her there'd been absolutely no compromise of my contact with her.

Then she did something quite surprising to me. She pulled out a cigarette out of a pack in her breast pocket, lit it, and inhaled deeply. She was silent. I thought, oh shit, I've blown it. I'd watched sources before and this was not a reassuring act. Before she could speak, I asked her what was with the huge owl that was laying on the gravel. She took another draw on the cigarette. "Some ignorant SOB killed it, used a gun by what I see. Look at it's head. The stupid bastards executed it because they saw it as a threat." It was the first time I'd heard this refined woman use profanity.

This was strange. She talked on in a kind of rambling way about life and death. I endeavored, when I thought it appropriate in the conversation, to explain my views on the life experience. She did not place any great significance on what had happened to me on August 1 in Pine and said she already knew everything about me appearing in the *Payson Roundup* piece by Beth Counseller. I was extremely relieved, feeling we'd breached a possibly major obstacle to continuing our conversation. Nevertheless, my guts told me there was something else going on now in our dynamic.

I knew I had to press on very carefully.

It was almost dark when Pearl said she had to leave. The trailhead parking area was deserted when I'd arrived and no other cars entered the gravel plot while Pearl and I were there. Now, at dusk, a cold wind was blowing up the narrow ravine, swirling dust around us. The sky was leaden, the sheer rock cliffs menacing, the scene surreal, hostile. I asked Pearl if I could give her a lift somewhere, but she declined. Before leaving, she nonchalantly told me she might not be able to meet me again soon because she was going into the hospital for some tests. Then, she walked off into the shadows, down the same gully from which she'd emerged, carrying the dead owl. I knew there were no inhabitants or vehicle access roads for miles around. The Superstition Mountains were a rugged, desolate, wilderness protectorate famous for hidden treasure mysteries and Old West legends. I was concerned for her, but could do nothing more under the circumstances but to drive back to Highway 87 and return to Pine.

Pearl had given me much to think about. The conversation that day was one of the most provocative we'd had up to then. When I was finally able to steer our discussion back to Pearl's father and his relationship with Senator Goldwater, Pearl elaborated on that crucial period of 1962-1964 when he worked out of the senator's offices in Washington, D.C. and Phoenix. Papa had been hired by Goldwater primarily to advise on earth sciences and environmental matters of political interest. The political machinations, active campaigning, and manipulations were a very secondary concern to her father, although he loyally supported the senator's plans. Over the preceding decade, Papa had acted in behalf of Goldwater in numerous negotiations, lobbying, and deal making. He performed liaisons with a wide variety of powerful special interest constituencies—land management, ranchers, water rights people, mining companies, the Indian tribes, and the Bureau of Indian Affairs. While remaining a low key figure on the senator's staff, he apparently became one of Goldwater's most trusted employees. Pearl said her papa never turned down an assignment from the senator.

Her father told her that the early summer of 1963, the presidential aspirations of the senator were formalized and the organization of the campaign dominated the activities of the staff in Washington and Phoenix. High ranking, influential figures in the Republican Party, including the senior Bushes, Richard Nixon, and senators and congressmen from Southwestern states were frequent visitors to the senator's offices. The senator had meetings with members of the JCS and individuals her father knew were from the CIA and FBI. Her papa was often present at his desk when the visitors arrived, but never a party to the closed door meetings that followed. Occasionally, he would overhear senior staffers make reference to the Gila Project which he understood to be the code name for a covert program to discredit President Kennedy and his administration before the 1964 election. A fairly frequent visitor to the senator's office during this time was David Morales, accompanied by Richard Helms, who Pearl's father knew to be a CIA type. Morales always greeted her father cordially and introduced him, usually by first name only, to whomever accompanied him. By October 1963, the political comings and goings reached a fever pitch, overshadowing most all other activities in the Goldwater camp. Papa told Pearl he just tried to stay out of the way, true to his retiring, unobtrusive manner.

By this time in our discussions, I had a pretty good idea of the man Pearl called Papa. She continued to want to talk about him, obviously in love and admiration for what he represented in her life. Often, I had to bite my tongue out of deference to her.

That afternoon, she had dropped a bombshell on me. Senator Goldwater called Papa into his office in mid-November 1963. Papa knew he was stoking his bid for the Republican presidential nomination, but he wasn't part of the burgeoning campaign. So when the senator called him into his office to ask him to carry out a political task, Papa was quite surprised. Goldwater asked Papa to drive to Nevada to pick up a campaign donation and bring it to Phoenix. Goldwater said the people that were making the contribution were folks that Pearl's father had met and would recognize, and they knew him. Two days later, Papa drove to Las Vegas, made a call to a number Goldwater had given him, and was directed to an office in a building on the Las Vegas strip. There he met Robert Maheu and Joe Bonnano, who had both visited Goldwater's offices in D.C. and Phoenix on several occasions over the years. It was rumored that Bonnano was some sort of Las Vegas entrepreneur with possible underworld connections, but it was accepted by Goldwater's staff, as was the ethical political standards of the period, that to succeed as an elected official, one had to deal with a wide constituency, even some unsavory types.

Winning an election in America in the 1960s was a knock down, drag out game. There were other reputed mobsters that had come through the doors of Goldwater's office. Papa said Maheu handed him two large suitcases, probably weighing 40 pounds each, and hustled him off to Phoenix. As instructed, he delivered the suitcases to the Goldwater compound in Scottsdale in the early morning hours of the following day, no questions asked.

A day or so later, Papa said he received a call from the senator asking him to deliver the campaign donation to some people working for him in New Orleans and Dallas. Her father picked up the suitcases at the Goldwater ranch and drove to Dallas. Again, he called a phone number the senator had given him and was directed to a motel near the Dallas airport. At the desk, he called the room of a Mr. Gordon. Gordon turned out to be a CIA man that had accompanied Morales on visits to the senator's D.C. office in preceding months. Recognizing Mr. Gordon and a man named Tony, to whom he was introduced, Papa gave Mr. Gordon one of the suitcases and continued on to New Orleans. I wondered if this Tony might be Tony Sforza.

Pearl's papa said he drove all night, napping in his car, and arrived in New Orleans around mid-morning. Again he called a number that had been given him. He was told to come to a motel near the New Orleans airport and call at the desk for Mr. Sanchez. He did as instructed. Mr. Sanchez, much to Papa's surprise, turned out to be David Morales. They went to his room where Morales introduced him to another man by first name only—Johnny. Papa delivered the suitcase and the three went to breakfast at a nearby restaurant. Johnny, introduced as a, presumably Republican, political consultant, was from Chicago. There was little talk about anything other than Morales' recollections of the old days in Phoenix, his days at ASU with Papa, and how he was looking forward to leaving government service. Johnny, said little. (Papa later recognized him from pictures in the media in the mid-1970s as the mobster Johnny Rosselli.)

I had done my best to maintain my composure as Pearl told me about what, apparently, was the covert transfer of cash at Senator Goldwater's bidding to individuals already suspected of having some role in the assassination of the president. This was extraordinary. And, the Goldwater-Bonnano-Maheu connection reinforced what Morales' attorney Bob Walton had shared with me in the course of several interviews.[42]

The question was, what the hell do I do with this? My personal living situation in Pine was at best, uneasy, and the matter of future meetings with Pearl was unclear. I began to feel overwhelmed by the situation. I needed space and time to work things out. I wrestled with the obvious journalistic and investigative question: who else might possibly know of what Pearl had been telling me? I also had some pressing personal issues that had to be resolved.

The wheels were coming off my living arrangement in Pine. I'd flown back to Minnesota for a few days in late July to settle the strong arm, false arrest personal injury suit against Rainbow-Fleming Floods. With the help of my legal counsel, Joe Hoffman of Minneapolis, we settled for nearly $10,000. By the time I paid Joe his contingency fee and made payment against my debt to my benefactor, Williams, reclaimed a car I had in storage, and paid a few other bills remaining when I departed Woodbury the previous fall, I had about $1,000 in my pocket. I drove back to Arizona and detoured to Lone Pine, California to make my annual trek up Mt. Whitney. Pumped up with wrapping things up in Minnesota and with what I had going with Pearl as a promising source in Phoenix, I literally raced up and down the mountain setting a new record for uninterrupted ascent and descent for a person over 60 years of age. (My hometown newspaper in Minnesota, the *Stillwater Gazette,* got hold of the story and did a congratulatory article several weeks later.) I finally got back to Pine and used my last $500 to pay the overdue rent on my cabin.

Then, I had car problems, and there went my August and September VA pension checks. Now, in October, after paying another month's rent, I was broke. What was worse Williams announced he had run out of money and was no longer able to help me with the $400 to $500 he'd been sending so I might pursue my investigative effort in the valley. Ron Williams had been my friend, confidante, and supporter for more than a year and was extraordinarily well-read on assassination lore and related subjects. He was the first and only person to whom I first alluded to the development of a source pointing to a Goldwater connection to the Kennedy assassination and he had dismissed it. And he could not understand why I'd not accepted the publishing deal proposed by Henno Lohmeyer.

I struggled with my thoughts that night as I drove the dark, winding mountain grade of Highway 87 from the valley, back up to the rim. I had made a $500 security deposit on the cabin when I moved in a year earlier, so I probably could get by without paying more rent until the lease expired December 1. Something would have to break between now and then if I were to remain there. If only the VA would honor my disability claims or Winton would come through with a believable book deal. If not, I'd truly be homeless, with winter coming on and with three dogs, two cats and nowhere to go—and with someone possibly gunning for me.

Back in August on my way to Pine from Mount Whitney, I'd stopped for a drink at a popular tavern in Strawberry, just up the road from Pine and my cabin. Still feeling good about my ascent and descent record, I was sitting quietly at the end of the bar when I was approached by a young woman appearing to be in her mid-30s. I looked like some sort of scruffy mountain man with long hair, an earring left over from my drug undercover days, a hat pulled low, and I was unshaven—I could dress this way commonly, blending in seamlessly with the locals as long as I kept my mouth shut. We struck up conversation and Nancy told me she had just arrived in the area from the valley and was looking to buy a home in surroundings that would be suitable for a writer looking for peace and solitude while completing a book. We chatted a couple hours, interrupted by the loud country music on the jukebox. We hit it off nicely. I'd been without female companionship for more than a year, and she was quite charming, smooth, articulate, aware, and male ego-enhancing at half my advanced age. I was a foolish old man who should have known better.

I told her I might be moving from my cabin in a few weeks and, as a rental, she might want to look at it. We agreed she would call me in a few days. It probably was inevitable that we'd end up in bed together and she came to stay with me off and on over a period of weeks in the fall of 1997. She had no idea of what I was all about other than I was a writer doing a book.

Nancy was a very gifted, good looking young woman with great potential, but as our relationship developed, I learned she had a drug problem and was trying to escape a domestically violent and poisonous relationship. As the compulsive rescuer of so many human shipwrecks, I tried to help her recover her car, find a decent place to live and get her life on track. She would stay at my cabin and look after things when I went to the valley. But there were times I'd return to find indications she'd been stashing dope at the cabin which caused me great concern. Was I being set up for discreditation again? The last thing in the world I needed was a trumped up drug charge. I was beginning to have strong feelings for Nancy, and on my way back from the valley one night after meeting Pearl, I knew the days ahead would be tough ones. I had to make crucial survival decisions.

At the end of November, with a couple hundred dollars cash to my name, and with my animals in a trailer I'd built in the weeks before, I said goodbye to Nancy, put my few personal belongings in storage, and left Pine. I had no specific plan as I headed west, only that I had to figure out how to continue my dialogue with Pearl. I would live from my car as long as I could, with my animals as companions. In reality, I was just another stressed out, aging, disabled veteran hanging on the fringe of American society. The words "homeless derelict" echoed in the once-proud Army officer's mind. As I drove down the gravel road from the cabin, I felt like I was descending into a large black abyss. I broke down and cried like a baby.

I was not naïve about the socio-economic marginalized environment I was entering. I made certain rules for myself—keep myself presentable daily, no matter how difficult, shave, wear decent clothes, clean the car, keep the animals totally under control and well cared for, stay clear-eyed and absent of obvious anger or discontent, and always with ID and other documentation to present to law enforcement if requested. My story would be that I was ex-military, partially disabled, semi-retired, researching a book and casually looking for a home in the Southwest. If pressed, I always had my P.I. credentials for verification of identity. Even in 1997-1998, prior to 9/11, being adrift anywhere along the southwestern U.S./Mexican border was a potentially risky situation in which to find oneself.

To maintain a relatively innocuous presence, I could not remain in any one area very long; and not for more than a day or two, especially with the animals that had to be aired and exercised regularly. So, I moved about cautiously and discreetly almost every day. I would let the dogs out of the trailer at rest stops and picnic areas and set up my typewriter on a picnic table or on the back of the car. I continued to write daily, summing up notes made after my conversations with Pearl and further developing my war on drugs book. Some months earlier, my friend Mike Andregg had invited me to be a panel member at a public affairs conference in Minnesota scheduled for the spring, and I worked on my presentation assuming I'd be able to somehow travel back to the Midwest to make an appearance. As I prepared the presentation, I was unaware the invitation to this event would have profound ramifications.

For the next six months I traveled around the Southwest, living from my car. I felt I was on to something with Pearl and wanted somehow to keep that dialogue going. My eldest son and his family lived in Southern California, and reluctant as I was to involve them in my "stuff," I spent Christmas with them and went back many times to grab a few days of sanctuary, decent sleep, do laundry, clean myself up, regain some sense of civility, and to free the animals from the trailer for a time. When travelling about, I seriously tried to find some place where I could reestablish a home, but I had no money and, with the VA continuing to stall my service-related disability claims, I had no leverage with which to maneuver my way into a home or even rent one. It was scary as hell, and I wasn't getting any younger.

I went back to Phoenix several times, met with Bob Walton again and went over his recollections of the Goldwater-Mafia connection. I said nothing to him about my contact with Pearl. It was not until January of 1998 when I had to return for treatment at the Phoenix VA hospital that I met again with Pearl.

CHAPTER 32

I returned to Phoenix for an appointment at the VA hospital just before Christmas. The stress of living in my car, had aggravated my chronic skin condition and I was on the verge of a serious infection. I was pleased to find a note from Pearl on my car and we met in the deserted pavilion on the Old Indian School grounds near the hospital on a brilliant Arizona winter afternoon with gentle breezes, warm sun, temperatures in the 70s, and not a cloud in the sky.

Despite the gorgeous weather, Pearl seemed depressed, but I didn't pry. I told her I had left Pine and was searching for a new home. She suggested I look around Tucson where she'd gone to college. Pearl seemed unusually nervous. She was in a hurry, so I directed the conversation back to the revelations of our last meeting. By this time, I'd done a lot of reading on Goldwater's alleged connections to organized crime in Arizona and the Southwest. I was amazed at the documented scope of the senator's apparent involvement with the underworld and a whole range of shady characters.

She said Papa himself, would never knowingly have become involved in any illegal activities. The senator knew that. But, there were others on his staff that did the dirty work. She basically confirmed what was well documented in the books by Lake Headley and Alex Shoumatoff.

I asked how many people close to Goldwater might have had knowledge of the movement of cash in the weeks before the assassination of the president. She thought it would have been very few. Papa had been sworn to secrecy and had scrupulously maintained his silence until his final days. She already told me Papa was a devout Catholic. I asked her how he reconciled his suspicions about the senator's involvement in the Kennedy assassination with his conscience. She didn't know, but, that question got us started talking about religion. Pearl brought up the fact that while Barry Goldwater was Jewish, he was very close to the Mormon church. Some even suggested he practiced the faith. Something clicked.

Years earlier, while in contact with columnist Jack Anderson, I had the growing feeling that Anderson knew of, or discovered, the conspiracy that resulted in Kennedy's death. Anderson was a devout Mormon. In passing, during one of our earlier conversations, Pearl told me Papa mentioned that Goldwater had a cordial, ongoing dialogue with a lot of journalists in Washington. Was Anderson one of them? Did she know? Yes, in fact, Papa said the friendships between Goldwater and Pearson, and later with Anderson, made him uneasy because he was always concerned about the muckrakers doing a column on one of the "deals." Papa was involved with public relations and knew that public disclosure would jeopardize the outcome. Anderson never did, apparently, maybe out of deference to the friendship he shared with Goldwater. The Mormon tie can be very tight.

This line of discussion led me to ask if Papa mentioned any other media person that might have had some inkling of the covert money transfer and the Gila Project? Her answer blew me away.

Shortly before the post-Watergate hearings began—about the time the

Church Committee convened—Papa was effectively retired from the Goldwater staff.

Papa had been with the senator for nearly 25 years. From that point forward, Pearl said her father, and she, never had serious financial concerns. She said Papa went to work for a Brazilian land investment and development company, married, and bought a substantial home in Brasilia and traveled to the States infrequently. Pearl said she was upset with her father during this time because his company was tearing up the Amazon rainforest. Her tuition at Arizona University was never a problem, but she didn't take advantage of her father's apparent wealth. Papa only came back to Phoenix to live with Pearl until two years before his death. She didn't know what happened to his second wife, only that she occupied the home in Brasilia for a while and then it was sold. During all of this period, Pearl said she was fully engaged with her own life.

It was obvious Pearl was anxious to leave, but I had to go back to a thought that kept running through my mind.

"Was your father in Phoenix in 1976, possibly spring or summer?"

"I don't think so, why do you ask?"

"It was that spring that *Arizona Republic* reporter, Don Bolles, was car bombed. As you know, there's always been many questions surrounding the motive for his murder, despite the convictions and all. Is it possible that Bolles was on to something more in his investigation of Goldwater? Did Papa ever say anything to you about that?"

"Papa told me once that in late 1975, a reporter from the Phoenix paper was calling him at home and work in Brasilia about a story he was doing on Arizona politics. He knew Papa had served on Goldwater's staff. The man apparently called several times, but Papa did not return the calls."

Only after Bolles death did Papa tell Pearl this. The man who called was Bolles.

"Pearl, do you think Bolles had gotten wind of the Gila Project?"

She replied, "I don't know, of course, but I think so. It's common knowledge there was much more at stake in that investigation than rotten Arizona politics."

I flashed back to a meeting I'd had with *Minneapolis Star Tribune* chief investigation reporter John Ullman in 1985. He was interested in my observations as a DEA operative in the so-called war on drugs and the then developing scandalous Iran/Contra and Reagan/Bush revelations. Apparently establishing his credentials with me, we talked about the investigation of government cover-ups. Ullman said he'd experienced a "doozy." John had played a lead role in the rally and subsequent outside investigation by the Investigative Reporters and Editors, Inc. that descended on Phoenix in the wake of fellow member Don Bolles murder. Ullman said they encountered stonewalling from every entity that might have provided assistance in the investigation, from Bolles' employer, the *Arizona Republic*, to all law enforcement agencies, local and federal. In the end, the intrepid journalists spent their time drinking, eating, and lying by the pool. The investigation went nowhere. [43]

As I had observed earlier, Pearl seemed jumpy during our meeting. She frequently looked around. I saw no one. I had to remain focused. It was my practice to go somewhere and write down everything we'd discussed when our meetings concluded.

Rather abruptly one day, Pearl said she had an appointment, and wished me Merry Christmas and good luck in my hunt for a new home. She walked off toward the hospital. She appeared to be limping slightly, and did not look particularly well.

Pearl's remarks about Bolles were exceedingly provocative in light of everything else I knew or suspected about his murder. His dying words, "It was the Mafia," seemed unusual at the time, but fits well with the scenario of developments that preceded his demise. Would Morales and his CIA and underworld cohorts have been in Phoenix in June 1976? Was Bolles murdered because he was on to Goldwater's 1963 Gila Project and the covert transfer of cash just before JFK's assassination?

That night, I stayed over in Phoenix, sleeping in the car at the Squaw Peak trailhead at the north end of Central Avenue. Early the next morning, I went to headquarters of the *Arizona Republic* newspaper to see what I could find out on my own about the Bolles case. The editorial department abruptly turned me away, referring me to the newspaper library morgue; the only information the paper would release was what had been printed in the days and weeks after the murder and several follow-up articles and columns. Headley had all of this and more in his case. I'd been to the paper before in my search for anything on Morales, and other than a photo and clip dating to 1973, there was nothing. I then called Reuben Carbajal.

"Was Didi [Morales] in the area in the spring of '76?"

Reuben said, "Sure. He was supposedly retired, but that's the time they were building the home in Wilcox. David was back and forth to Washington and we were putting some deals together."

I didn't tell Reuben why I was curious or even mention the Bolles murder. At least, now, I had Morales in the area of the crime. I then went to the Phoenix Police Department and the local ATF and FBI offices on the outside chance I might be able to gain access to some public files relating to the Bolles murder. I had to show my ID, of course, and explain my purpose for the request. I was not surprised when I was turned away and advised the official records were sealed.

I tried to reach Delbert Lewis, the manager of the local ABC-TV affiliate who I'd spoken with back in 1990. The reader will recall he was a friend of Morales in the early days. Now, I wanted to find out what behind the scenes stuff he might know about the Bolles murder. Mr. Lewis wasn't available.

I was out of money, barely enough gas to get back to California and spend Christmas with my son and his family in San Clemente. Earlier in the month, I'd stumbled on a possible home on Big Bear Mountain, north of Riverside. I was desperate to at least have the hope of settling in somewhere and getting myself and my animals off the road. On the way back to San Clemente, I went back to Big Bear, made an offer on the home on the outskirts of the quaint high elevation town. Big Bear in December was frigid and snow covered, just like home, and I felt in tune with the surroundings. I went to my son's home for the holidays.

I was still at my son's home, post-Christmas, when a UPS package for me was delivered to the door, It was Noel Twyman's *Bloody Treason*. Lisa Pease and Jim DiEugenio of *Probe* magazine had sent it to me. The book was extremely well-done, professional non-fiction. Twyman had used my book, *The War That Never Was*, extensively as a source and reference. What troubled me, however, was his liberal use of the information I'd developed on Morales in the early 1990s without accreditation. Now we had Fonzi, Oliver Stone, Bryan Abas, and Lord knows how many others using the report I'd delivered to Fensterwald, Dorff, et al., in 1990 as if it were their independent work.

I called to thank Lisa and Jim for the book. We talked in very general terms about my continuing investigative work in Arizona, but I made no mention of Pearl. I still wasn't sure in my mind where all of that was going. Then I contacted Noel Twyman who resided, conveniently for me, in an upscale community just north of San Diego. He agreed to meet with me.

I met with Noel at a restaurant in Del Mar on New Year's Eve. I was impressed and somewhat disarmed by this congenial, refined, articulate older gentleman. I complimented him on *Bloody Treason,* putting aside for the time my feelings of frustration and resentment.

Noel explained that his primary source for information about me came from *The War That Never Was* and his friend, Bob Dorff, who put him on to my report on the 1989-1990 investigation of Morales. Dorff allegedly claimed the report was his property, although I'd been retained by the JFK Center and I'd delivered the report in person to Bernard Fensterwald, et al. in Dallas in the spring of 1990. Dorff allegedly told Twyman he paid me in full for the investigation. I asked Noel how much. He said Dorff claimed he paid me $5,000. I found out Twyman also was an acquaintance of the veterinarian, Jock Jocoy, who, more recently, ripped me off for some work I did for him.

"Noel, these two men are liars. The JFK Assassination Center has never paid me for the work I did for them, and Dorff only paid me $1,000 and covered expenses when I was in L.A. The center owes me in excess of $20,000 and I've never been paid in full for my Morales investigative work. Further, I copyrighted my work under the title *The Search for El Indio* in 1991, and you, Fonzi, Oliver Stone's Camelot Productions, and there may be others, who have simply ignored my copyright, and I've had no money to contest it. Noel, while I am in huge admiration of your work, you should have talked to me while you were putting the book together. There's a hell of a lot more to he Morales/Arizona thing than is out there! I might have shared it with you because I don't have a publisher of my own."

We talked some in general terms about the book and some of his sources which I told him were bogus and diminished the credibility in his work. I then explained I was trying to hang on in the Southwest in the hope of pursuing leads that had grown out of my earlier investigation of Morales. For the first time, with someone other than Ron Williams, I used the term, "the Arizona Connection," but I said nothing about Pearl and what I'd learned from her. I told him, as a professional, experienced investigator, I felt strongly about what I could do with a base of operations, a client, and some resources.

Twyman pulled out his check book. "Brad, this is not payment for violating your copyrights—I don't think I did—or to keep you from suing me, but I want to make things right with you. I'll give you $1,000 to help with your situation. I hope you'll keep in touch with me." I promised I would.

I drove back to San Clemente with renewed hope in my heart. At least I had something to run on for a while, maybe a deal on a home for myself and my animals. Maybe 1998 would be the year things would begin to come together. My son and his spouse had no comprehension of the reasons for the smile on my face as we opened a bottle of bubbly that evening.

I made the mistake of sharing Twyman's book with my son and his wife. She was in the advanced stages of pregnancy with what was already acknowledged as a boy, my first male grandchild. They of course knew of my "spook" background. My son, the eldest, was eight years old when I was with the CIA in Miami, and the trauma and turmoil of that time was vivid in his mind. They couldn't understand why I would be coming forth with revelations that could possibly put my family at risk, that had proven so disruptive and damaging to me personally, in virtually every aspect of my life. They could not understand why I couldn't settle into some kind of normalcy, find a niche somewhere and be content.

Putting aside my intense interest in pursuing the Arizona connection, I went back to Big Bear. The more I thought about it, the house deal there seemed too good to be true, so I took $500 of the money Twyman had given me and ordered an independent appraisal. The house rested on unstable, earthquake prone terrain. I had no choice but to move my stuff into a storage unit and go back to living out of my car. I was really upset with myself. My animals, good naturedly accepted the continued ride in the trailer. They looked at me with eyes that said I'd been a fool.

If things had been desperate before, my predicament was now in reinforcement mode. I decided to travel south and east, the Tucson area and maybe another visit to Wilcox to see if anything changed there. I kept thinking about the Morales gravesite. So many years had passed since the alleged interment of the casket in 1978 and when I finally uncovered the headstone in the spring of 1990. Other graves reflecting the burials of the late 1970s appeared to have a normal, regrown prairie sod covering. But it struck me that the Morales plot, #89, suggested some fairly recent upheaval of the soil, despite that the headstone itself was buried. I hoped to go back to Wilcox and reexamine the site. Few people were aware of my search for El Indio which began in 1989. But, among those few was Ted Shackley. In fact, he'd put me on to Morales' death in Arizona. With all the compromises that occurred along the way, is it possible the body was removed from the grave? Why? Would it be to conceal an independent examination of the body which might show some sinister cause if death? Or did the casket really contain the body of the Big Indian or somebody else, or was it empty? Maybe Morales was living the good life in some South American country, chuckling over the whole charade. I visualized the old gang, all those supposedly deceased—Pancho, Rip, Sforza, Artime—sitting under a thatched roof in the tropics sipping pina coladas and talking about the old days.

I spent several days looking around the Tucson and Green Valley area for a home. The realtor, Lee Simmons, was helpful, but it was discouraging. I drove over to Wilcox. The Morales plot now looked like the others in the cemetery. Since I'd been there eight years earlier, the grave had been landscaped and sodded. I tried to find the mortician, Carlstead, to see if there was anything more I could learn from him, but he was away on business.

Back to living from my car, the predictable aggravation of my skin condition occurred. I needed medical treatment. I was using almost a half box of bandages a day to cover the spontaneous fissures on my hands and feet. An infection was virtually inevitable without more antibiotics and wound protection. So, I called ahead and made an appointment at VAMC in Phoenix where my records were located. I hoped to meet with Pearl once again. I had some specific ideas in mind if she'd be willing to help me.

There was no note on my car when I finished my visit to the dermatologist and picked up my prescription. All kinds of things could have happened that would result in a misconnection with Pearl. I thought it wise to hang out for a while and walked across the street to the deli to get a cup of coffee. A few minutes later, as I sat reading the paper, I saw Pearl at the window. She motioned to me and I joined her as she walked away.

She was limping, pronouncedly, and the skin on her face appeared tightly drawn. She looked almost emaciated. As we walked together around the park-like Old Indian School acreage next to the VA hospital, she chain-smoked as we talked. About her limp she said she'd had a small accident, but her expression suggested something more. I didn't pry.

After an exchange of small talk, I asked, "Pearl, did your father tell you anything about what went on in the senator's office after JFK was killed?"

"I remember Papa came home for a while. He was very distraught as we all were, even I as a little girl. Papa started drinking heavily, something I never saw him do before; and he was very depressed. But, after Christmas, 1963, he went back to Washington. He said Goldwater's office was a madhouse of political activity right through November, 1964 and the election. Papa was with the senator when he was nominated as the Republican candidate at the convention on the summer of 1964. After Kennedy was killed, he said he never heard another word of the Gila Project."

"Was there ever any mention of your father's relationship with Lyndon Johnson either before or after the assassination?" I asked.

Her reply suggested that Goldwater and Johnson, despite their political affiliations, were quite close. They served in the senate together for many years, were on a first name basis, and spoke frequently with each other. Papa said some of the studies and research he did on southwestern U.S. land use matters were shared with the Johnson people. Both Johnson and Goldwater had close ties to the labor movement and unions all over the country, and they worked together on many of these issues. Of course, after Kennedy was killed, Goldwater and President Johnson were of one mind on Vietnam. The Castro problem never came up much in the Goldwater camp, as far as Papa knew. Then she added, "But keep in mind that my father was not involved in foreign policy or strictly political matters in Goldwater's office. He was really a scientific specialist and sometimes, a sort of confidante-errand boy, but he wasn't party to grand strategy."

We headed back toward the hospital. It was then, after a good deal of consideration, that I asked Pearl to go the extra mile. "I haven't had any success in securing any of the medical evidence, coroner's reports, death certificates, or even the official investigative reports on either Morales or Don Bolles. Do you think, with your medical community connections, you might be able to help me? One of the things that would be most helpful is anything that indicates an exhumation of Morales' body in the early 1990s." And I added, "Can you bring some documentation of your father's association with the senator?"

Pearl said, "I'll try," and then walked away toward the emergency room entrance.

The situation for me, both personally and professionally, was developing in a way I could never have anticipated. I needed to establish some direction and stability so I could move on, for better or for worse. I decided to travel north and continue looking for a possible landing site along the way, but eventually ended up in San Francisco and forced a face to face meeting with Charlie Winton, a book distributer. I'd hoped that the publication of Twyman's book might generate some publisher enthusiasm for my proposed uncensored, expanded version of *The War That Never Was*. Lisa and Jim at *Probe* magazine had published some provocative stuff. I still hadn't shared any of my investigation of Morales post 1990 or the Arizona connection, and I was conflicted about the wisdom of doing so. I thought maybe I should with Winton.

Returning to Southern California in late February, my next move was to arrange another meeting with Noel Twyman. I'd been sending him letters and faxes apprising him of my continuing investigation of the Arizona connection without divulging my dialogue with Pearl, but suggesting I was on to something significant. We met at a Denny's restaurant in Del Mar on February 20. I explained I was in poor shape, but felt I was on the track of a JFK assassination conspiracy connection to Senator Barry Goldwater.

With that, the old man's face blanched, and he replied, "I've made my contribution to assassination research at considerable expense with *Bloody Treason*. I'm not about to do anything more. A revised version of the book may be coming out, but I don't want to be involved beyond that." That, essentially, was the end of the conversation. He wished me well and left. I sat there, numb to all that was going on around me as the restaurant began to fill.

The doors were closing around me. That night, after the meetings with Twyman, I did as I did so many other nights—went back to my car, looked after the animals, crawled into my sleeping bag, and with my rosary in place, I beseeched the Great Spirit for patience, courage, and guidance.

From the time I departed Minnesota in the fall of 1996, I had kept in contact with a number of people I knew to be aware of my Morales and assassination conspiracy investigation, my financial plight, and personal travails. These confidantes were a reassuring connection, in the absence of any friends in the Southwest, and I tried to keep them informed of where I was and what I was up to. I had a telephone when I lived at the cabin in Pine, but now had no phone readily available. I wrote many letters, or sent faxes whenever I could.

While I mentioned in these communications that I had developed some new sources in Arizona, I said nothing of my conversations with Pearl. But, I encouraged them to read Headley's and Shoumatoff's books, and the recently released, *Bloody Treason,* for background and to provide some inkling of the direction of my field work. From time to time, they'd respond to my sometimes depressing communiqués with money, $100 or so, and their help was gratefully received. [44]

More than a year earlier, I'd promised Mike Andregg I'd participate in a symposium on international affairs at St. Thomas College in St. Paul where Mike and his spouse were instructors. The conference was scheduled for March 18. Months ago, I'd prepared an abstract. Now, with the conference looming, I began to seriously prepare my talk which would focus on JM/WAVE and the CIA's secret war against Cuba.

Financially stressed as I was, John Woods in Colorado and Mike Andregg sent me enough money for a red-eye flight back to Minnesota to make my appearance at the conference. I knew I'd have to beg money for a return ticket, but I'd cross that bridge when I came to it as I'd done in so many situations in recent years. While I looked forward to participating in the International Studies Association symposium, I had mixed feelings about returning to Minnesota under circumstances of high visibility. The anguish of my last years there was an open wound. But, I'd promised Mike I'd go, and I began planning to exploit what I'd recently developed in pursuit of the Arizona connection.

Following the disappointing meeting with Twyman, I headed back to Arizona to clear a few things from a storage unit I still had there, recover my notes stashed from earlier meetings with Pearl and other sources, and, hopefully, meet with Pearl again before finalizing plans for the return to Minnesota. I made an appointment for a dermatological check up at the VAMC in Phoenix.

We met at a park in Fountain City. The day was unusually cool, with a leaden sky and light rain. She arrived bundled up in an Indian shawl, walking with a cane, and looking a dozen years older than when I'd last seen her a few weeks ago. I was shocked at her appearance. She carried a large, brown envelope.

We sat opposite one another at the picnic table. The fountain had been turned off. What I could see of her face and skin looked almost mummified. I looked like hell, myself. I had gone days without cleaning up or shaving. My eyes were red and ringed darkly due to lack of decent rest. My wrinkled, soiled clothing smelled of sweat and animals. I apologized for my appearance as she lit a cigarette.

"I brought this for you; I hope it's going to be helpful." She handed me the envelope. Opening it, I found an 8x10 black and white photo of Senator Goldwater, a small Native American man who fit the description of Pearl's father, and David Sanchez Morales, exactly as I remembered him from JM/WAVE. The three smiling men were posed shoulder to shoulder in what appeared to be an official office with plaques the U.S. and Arizona state flags on either side. What appeared to be Goldwater's signature and a notation that read, "Good luck, David and Pepe," and the date January 12, 1963 inscribed below. I was flabbergasted. Here was the senator, Morales, and Pearl's father almost arm-in-arm. But the photo wasn't the only thing in the envelope. There was a rubber band bound stack of greeting cards. Pearl explained there were some 20 Christmas cards that Senator Goldwater had sent to Papa over the course of his employment as a staffer. Pearl said I could take the photo and have it duplicated, but the cards were part of her keepsake chest in memory of her father. I promised to return the photo once I was able to get a good duplicate made if that was alright with her.

"You must promise not to tell anyone where you got the photo until…." She didn't continue and I didn't ask her to finish the sentence. In hindsight, I wish I had.

After thanking her for the contents of the envelope, I asked her if she'd had any luck in getting the official medical reports or grave exhumation information I'd asked for at our last meeting. She said she was trying to figure out a way of requesting the documents, if any existed, without being personally identified with the request. She'd continue to try, but it wasn't going to be easy or happen quickly.

She lit another cigarette and said she had to go. "Do you have any idea of what the situation was like in the Goldwater office later, after the 1964 election and Johnson's victory?" I asked. Pearl said she had the impression things returned to normal, but Goldwater came away with a lot of Washington clout. "Papa said he came out of the election with more power than he'd had before. He was so well connected in Washington and at the Pentagon he could influence just about anything."

I wondered, of course, if that meant the Warren Commission proceedings and subsequent Congressional hearings into the late 1970s. I didn't press the issue. What about immediately before and following the assassination of Martin Luther King and Bobby Kennedy? Pearl said she didn't know, Papa never really talked much about that period. "I know he did run into Morales at Washington National Airport and the Phoenix terminal around that time as Papa was doing a lot of back and forth travel in connection with his work for the senator. I know that for a fact because Papa came home drunk several times and said he'd run into Morales and some of his CIA buddies and they had a few drinks before and during their flight." She added for the umpteenth time that it was so out of character for her father.

As Pearl rose to leave, she reached under her shawl and brought forth a very small box. "I promised to show you this when we first began to talk." She opened the box and displayed a huge oyster pearl, almost half an inch in diameter. "I want you to have this. I know you're having a very difficult time and you've got a lot of work to do and maybe a very tough road ahead. You can sell it or pawn it and it'll get you by for a time, maybe until you can make something of what I've shared with you."

I choked, overwhelmed with her gesture. "Pearl, I'm deeply grateful, but I can't take anything like that from you. You've already given me more than I can deal with in ways that are not material. And, if I were to accept anything with immediate monetary value from you, it would tarnish the integrity of our relationship. You must understand that if it was ever revealed that I'd accepted something of material value from you, it could be construed that you paid me to accept your account of your father's life experience. I'm deeply honored by your wish to help me beyond what you've already given, that is, your trust in me. Hold on to the pearl, dear lady, for what it represents in your life and now between us. God bless you."

She understood. She had tears in her eyes as we wordlessly shook hands and then hugged. She turned and walked like an old woman up the path and out of the park. The fountain pond was still, silent. I sat there, overcome with emotion. The heart-wrenching situation came crashing down on me. With tears welling and my heart in my throat I put my head on the table, sobbing. I sensed I might never see Pearl again. I had many more questions for her and there wasn't a damn thing I could do.

I drove back to California depressed and emotionally conflicted. Where should I go from here?

I arrived back in San Clemente for a final brief stay with my son to see my new grandson again and prepare for my trip to Minnesota. I had to have several days off the road to prepare myself, pack, and review what I intended to present at the conference. My investigative efforts in Arizona of the preceding 18 months had opened up a whole new vista, but I wasn't sure how to handle what I'd developed, especially the information that came from my meetings with Pearl. I knew that former Minnesota Republican Senator Dave Durenburger was going to make a presentation at the ISA symposium. Mike Andregg had introduced me to the senator some years earlier. He was a moderate Republican, was familiar with my background, and tried to help me recover my medical records from the CIA. Since that earlier contact, Durenburger had been smeared by scandal that many said was politically engineered by conservative Republicans with the help of the Justice Department and intelligence agencies. I had been thinking about sharing the Arizona connection revelations with someone who might give some guidance about delivering what I'd learned to the proper authorities. Durenburger and I were slated to speak on the same day of the conference, around the same time. I decided to synopsize my recent Arizona connection discoveries and try to corner Durenburger long enough to discuss them and seek his advice. I said nothing about this idea to anyone as I pushed myself to make preparations to return to what had once been my home area and now seemed quite threatening and hostile.

I tried to keep to myself and remain as unobtrusive as possible, but the tension in my son's home, because of my earlier presence, increased. I decided to leave a few days earlier than planned. I'd made reservations to board my animals near my storage unit in Lake Elsinore. The lady that ran the facility volunteered, for a price, to drive me to the Los Angeles Airport for my flight on March 16. By this time, in my search for a home, I'd been in contact with realtors all over rural Southern California. I received a call on March 12 from a broker in Pine Valley, a quaint little community off Interstate 8 east of San Diego,

THE ZENITH SECRET

who said he had a home he thought I'd be interested in. So, the following day, I said farewell to the household and headed in the direction of Pine Valley. My plan was to be back at Lake Elsinore on the morning of the 16th, and later that day fly back to Minnesota for the conference.

By now, I typically drove with an eye on the rearview mirror. Several times, since my last meeting with Pearl, I had the feeling I was being followed. I would usually pull off the road or alter my route abruptly to shake off any possible tail. I didn't notice anything particularly unusual as I made my way southeast, stopping randomly along the way to look at other areas where I might find a home. Late in the day, I met the realtor and viewed the home. I wasn't impressed. Since I had a couple of days at my disposal and was all set for the trip to Minnesota, I decided to drive further east on Interstate 8 and get some feel for the Imperial Valley community of El Centro.

Having received my March VA pension check a week or so earlier, I had enough cash to rent a cheap motel room. I was still trying to get myself mentally and physically squared away for the challenges that lay before me in Minnesota. With a night of decent rest and a good shower, I'd be as ready as possible for the drive to Lake Elsinore and my flight later that day. As I drifted off to sleep in the smelly, little room that night, I had no notion that in a few hours I would experience another of life's convulsions. The events of the following 48 hours are described in minute detail in the statement I provided the U.S. Customs and the Border Patrol in connection with case number 98-025402-B. The following is an excerpt of the official statement:

> This written statement is made voluntarily by the undersigned as a follow-up to verbal statements made by telephone to the U.S. Border Patrol Station in Campo, CA and subsequently in person to the U.S. Border Patrol Captain Delaney at the Buckman Springs checkpoint, and to San Diego County Deputy Sheriff David Wilson at the Sheriff's substation located off I-8 near the Boulevard/Campo exit at approximately 0715.

> For the past weeks I have been traveling about southern Arizona and California, reconnoitering the area for possible relocation of my residence from north central Arizona (the town of Pine). I have been traveling in a tan 1994 Mazda Navajo SUV, towing a tan 1989 Aros two-wheel trailer on which is mounted a homemade plywood kennel containing my three Weimaraner dogs and two cats.

> During the course of my travels over the past weeks, (I have reason to believe), I've been periodically followed by various unidentified cars, trucks, and four-wheel vehicles, including some marked with standard U.S. Border Patrol insignia.

> Bearing upon this statement is the fact that I was scheduled to present a research paper at a conference of the International Studies Association in Minneapolis, MN on the morning of March 19, 1998.

> I was prepared to make certain revelations that may have significant historical import on the murder of President Kennedy in 1963. These revelations are based upon my investigation and research in Arizona, Nevada, and Florida since 1989.

> With the foregoing as the setting, I departed El Centro at 0400 on Monday, March 16 after gassing my vehicle and clearing my motel room.

> During the drive from El Centro I observed considerable U.S. Border Patrol vehicular activity on the Interstate exits/on-ramps, frontage and service roads, often searching the roadsides with spotlights.

BRADLEY E. AYERS

After five or 10 minutes of driving, a vehicle with bright headlights pulled up to the rear of my kennel trailer. The bright light in my rearview mirrors was blinding. Almost immediately thereafter, a figure came around my vehicle and stood shining a very bright flashlight through my closed driver's side window, directly into my eyes. As I cleared my head and became alert, he moved slightly to the front of my car and stepped back. The light he held now shown through the windshield as well as the side window. I could make out that the figure was apparently male, large, 6' and 1/2" tall, 180-200 lbs., wearing military-style camouflage fatigues, a dark ski mask pulled over his head, gloves on his hands, and, with the hand not holding the flashlight, pointing a carbine-type (Mini 14?) automatic weapon at me.

He then said in a stern, clipped, fairly moderate tone, "U.S. Border Patrol: Get out of the car, move to the right side of the vehicle, and spread eagle yourself on the ground, head to the front, east, face to the ground." His voice had a distinct "military" quality conveying that he meant business. I did as he ordered and he kept the flashlight and weapon trained on me from about six feet away as I lay down. My dogs continued to bark and scratch the sides and doors of the plywood kennel. Then, another male voice, much in the same manner and tone of speech as the man holding the gun over me, said, "Quiet those fucking dogs or I blow them away." This was the first indication that there was a second man. The voice came from near the driver's side of my vehicle.

As the dogs settled down, the second man began to search my vehicle, driver's side first, then the rear and the passenger side. I could hear things being moved about in the car, but when I tried to turn my head to see, the man with the gun and flashlight trained on me said, "I told you to keep your head and eyes to the front." I followed his instructions.

At first I thought the unfolding event was some kind of hoax; however, within minutes I became convinced that the situation was dead serious. This realization hit as I lay helpless on the ground and the thought that the man holding the gun on me might fire at any moment caused me to break out in a cold sweat. I tried to control my breathing and be calm, but I could not hold my (coffee-filled) bladder and began to wet my pants. I remained motionless, fully expecting that I might die at any moment. It seemed as though I lay there for 15 or 20 minutes, but, realistically, it was probably no more than 10 minutes.

Finally, the man with the gun on me said, "Stay right where you are." Then he moved quickly, apparently toward his vehicle. At the same time I heard car doors closing, but I could not tell if they were the doors of my car or the vehicle to the rear of the mobile kennel trailer. The second man came to where I was lying on the ground and dropped a small object right in front of me, saying, "Here's a fortune cookie from your old Miami friends, asshole."

Moments later, I heard the vehicle behind the trailer rev its engine and as I turned around to look, the vehicle made a 180° turn and sped off in the direction (west) of Jacumba.

I got a flashlight out of the rear of my vehicle and went over to the object that had been dropped in front of me. It was a semi-clear plastic bag containing the dismembered/mutilated remains of a rodent-like animal (probably a squirrel). Upon examining and probing the bloody contents of the bag, it was apparent that the animal's legs had been cut off, its throat slit, and its tail removed. The eyes appeared to have been gouged out. Inside the bag was a message on 8 1/2" x 11" white paper.

THE ZENITH SECRET

The only interpretation I can attach to the message is one of threat and intimidation.

After reviewing the message, I rewrapped it in the plastic bag with the animal remains, just as I found it, and placed it in a compartment in my trailer for whatever law-enforcement agency would investigate the incident.

As the sky became light, a dense fog began to settle over the mountainous Jacumba area. I drove directly to the convenience store I had stopped at earlier near the I-8 Jacumba exit and asked the attendant for directions to the U.S. Border Patrol Station and he told me to go west on I-8.

On arrival at the checkpoint, I gave Captain Delaney a brief verbal account of what had happened. He stated that he knew of no Border Patrol personnel or operations/activities of the nature I described. He took notes, made several phone calls (one or more to his supervisor, I believe) to determine what agency would have jurisdiction in any investigation of the incident. After checking my documentation, ID, etc., he sent me back to the east on the Interstate, to the San Diego County Sheriff's substation at the I-8 Boulevard exit where I met Deputy Sheriff Dave Wilson.

Upon meeting Deputy Sheriff Wilson, I gave him a fairly detailed verbal statement/account of what had happened that morning at the Jacumba airport entrance.

Wilson advised me that he would investigate the "event," which he referred to as the oddest or strangest he had ever encountered in his 26 years of police work. I departed Campo/Boulevard and drove west to Pine Valley to collect my thoughts, plan a course of action, and eat breakfast.

With respect to the "strangeness" factor as Deputy Wilson had commented, I add the following observations and comments for the record:

I believe that the tone and content of the message, the manner in which it was produced and delivered, are very specifically intended to dissuade me from my investigative and writing work (as previously described herein) and, specifically, to discourage me from making the presentation at the forthcoming ISA conference in Minneapolis. The bizarre nature of the entire incident smacks of the modus operandi of certain federal intelligence and law enforcement entities who must use covert means to quiet critics, whistleblowers, and others who seek to expose wrongdoing and corruption, and who cannot be attacked and/or discredited by any other means.

Bradley E. Ayers
March 16, 1998

CHAPTER 33

Mike Andregg was not pleased when I contacted him shortly after the incident at Jacumba and reported what had happened. Everything for my ISA presentation, including the money for the trip to Minnesota was gone. The most critical items were the notes of my conversations with Pearl and the photo she'd given me. I could not present myself for the ISA conference on March 19. Andregg was not ameliorated as I tried to give him some of the details.

I was struggling with an avalanche of emotions. I was confounded by what had taken place on the morning of the 16th. It was truly surreal. How could a shakedown like this take place on U.S. soil? But, then, look at the past. Who was responsible? What kind of threat did I represent that justified this sort of covert operation? The paramilitary thugs that cornered me apparently knew exactly what they were looking for. This suggested fairly extensive prior surveillance. Was Pearl involved; had my meetings with her been observed? And, why didn't they just kill me instead of delivering a very strange, intimidating message?[45] To compound the mystery was the cavalier response of the law enforcement officials, both San Diego County and federal. Were they aware of the operation, and did they whitewash it? The only answer I could come up with suggested my investigation of the Arizona connection had provoked a very deliberate response from what I could only refer to as the "dark forces." It seemed that whomever was responsible for ordering and conducting the operation was intent on obtaining the contents of my briefcase and interdicting my trip to Minnesota where I would have presented my findings.

While all of these questions were tumbling about in my mind, I had to consider my immediate circumstances. Now that someone had the essentials of my investigative file, what would be the next step? I had no death wish; I'd survived to this point for a reason. With what I learned from Pearl I had even greater purpose. Yet, I was cowed; I could only imagine what I was up against if, I was onto something that might unravel the most controversial and historically telling events of our day. And, what were the implications for Pearl? I was responsible for protecting my source. This was a terrible situation. Anxiety, fear, and confusion gave way mostly to anger and determination. No matter what their motivation, I would not let those bastards put me down. That was to some extent sheer bravado, but it got me through trying to reconcile what had happened.

I decided to go to the High Sierra to lay low and get my thoughts in order. I had a few possessions at my son's house in San Clemente, and on my way north I stopped to pick them up. I told him of the Jacumba incident, and to accept any calls and or notes from the authorities to whom I'd made my reports. As it turned out, there were none, or at least I never found out about them. Apparently, there was to be no official follow-up to the events of the 16th. My son's displeasure with my presence at his home was almost palpable. I was now compromised, badly damaged property, and a potential liability for anyone who might have sympathy for my predicament.

I was well aware of that as I tried to formulate a plan. As I moved about in the more sparsely populated areas of California, never remaining in one place for more than a day and night, and always vigilant for anything unusual, I kept

THE ZENITH SECRET

pondering the shakedown at Jacumba. What motivated those responsible, assuming they had governmental approval or sanction, to resort to covert means to find out what I had? If I were some kind of threat to national security, an enemy of the state, or on a personal level, a danger to some government official, why not a court-approved search warrant or a contrived arrest? While I tried to maintain a low profile as I went about my investigation, I certainly wasn't out of sight of those entities that might have an interest in my work. The predawn paramilitary approach seemed almost ludicrous. But, it sure as hell sent a message and, to some extent, put a freeze at least temporarily, on my pursuit of the Arizona connection. I wondered constantly about Pearl's situation, if she'd been rolled up too, or possibly had known of the Jacumba encounter and the loss of so much sensitive information she'd provided. Part of me wanted to head immediately to Phoenix to try to connect with her, but I was too shaken to attempt another meeting so soon. Plus, I was broke. April 1 and my next VA pension check were many days away. What little cash I always concealed in a waterproof nylon pouch in the windshield-washer reservoir in the car was for gas and food for my animals.

I did a damage assessment. Among the items taken at Jacumba were my handwritten notes of my meetings with Pearl. These and the photograph Pearl had given me were the most sensitive and revealing materials. I had carried them with me as I hoped to use them in my planned discussion with Senator Durenburger. Now, I kicked myself for not getting the photo of Goldwater, Papa, and Morales duplicated. I'd been too preoccupied with preparing to return to Minnesota for the ISA conference.

One positive was that my post-meeting notes were handwritten, and it would be a major challenge, even for CIA or FBI codebreakers, to decipher my hieroglyphics. The typed abstracts,[46] along with a ton of my work on the Arizona connection, were stashed in the storage unit in Lake Elsinore. I had cached them in a place where I felt no one could find them without tearing down the concrete and steel building.

The other positive was that over the past 18 months, I'd diligently kept in contact with people who were aware of my background, investigative history, and work on the Arizona connection. I reached out to them and let them know my predicament. I continued to feel that the more others knew of my efforts, the less likely it would be that I'd be completely taken down. Ron Williams, Mike Andregg, Arnie Hymanson, Jim DiEugenio, Lisa Pease, John Woods, J.R. Freeman, all received and accepted my communications, some responding with a few bucks of funding or words of support that helped me survive and stay on the run. I thought about the gem that Pearl had offered and how its value would have been so helpful, but not for a moment did I regret my decision to refuse it. She was never far from my thoughts.

I began to plan a return to Arizona as soon as possible after April 1. I would receive my VA pension check and try to reconnect with Pearl. I was angry and now more anxious than ever to go after the Goldwater leads.

I did not anticipate the limbo I found myself in following the events at Jacumba. As I bounced around rather confusedly from one location to another in the outreaches of Southern California high desert to the mountains, I knew where I could hang out without attracting much attention, and I had a lot of think-time on my hands. Living in your car with only animals as true company has its pluses and minuses. Long trail runs and walks in the woods gentle one's soul.

Introspection, which I have engaged in starting at a young age, (my father

BRADLEY E. AYERS

referred to it as "listening to the little man upstairs") clearly reflected that I did not do well in situations in which I could not beneficially influence or control the outcome, at least in part. I pondered the significance in my behavior over time. Was this characteristic the manifestation of narcissism, selfishness, deep-seated insecurity, or absence of self-identity? And what was the social-behavioral manifestation of this need to control? I examined my purpose: were my actions honorable, moral, and, in my heart, in the best interest of all involved, despite the immediate pain and discomfort of anyone concerned, including myself? I prayed that to be true.

Self-pity was not on my agenda. My existentialist realization said that it doesn't matter how you feel in the grand scheme of things. Nevertheless, I was in one of the worst possible circumstances, psychologically and physically helpless and vulnerable. I'd violated no law, yet I was like a criminal on the run. Worse, I didn't know who was after me. I contemplated what I would do if I were cornered and had the opportunity to fight back.

Fatalist that I was, I also had to think about how I might react if faced with another situation like that at Jacumba. I'd long ago rejected violence as a means of resolving matters. Nevertheless, a realist at heart, with a healthy lust for life, I carried a 12-gauge shotgun and my trusted .380 caliber Sidekick pistol in the car. These were my ultimate fallback in self-defense. While I'd kept myself in good shape, both of my shoulders were weakened by fully torn, irreparable rotator cuff injuries. I was 63-years-old and knew I could not sustain myself for long with a younger adversary. The presentation of a weapon, even in self-defense, would be provocation, especially for law enforcement or someone posing as such, to take me down lethally. In addition, I recoiled at the thought of someone harming my animals. Could I ever again use a gun to harm anyone or any living thing? Any decent rest after the Jacumba incident was virtually impossible. I was on high alert, the adrenal level super high. Sound, healthy rest had been a problem for years because of shoulder pain and what I considered a mild case of post-traumatic stress syndrome. The recent shakedown amplified the problem a hundredfold. The old nightmares became quite frequent. As with so many veterans, it didn't take much to bring it all back. The perceived moment of extinction at Jacumba with a gun at my head, resurrected the scent of oleander, fresh human blood, the penetrating chemical odor of black, neoprene rubber body bags, embalming fluid, and funeral flowers, the heavy small of cordite, explosives, and gunpowder. It took hours in the middle of the night, lying there in my sleeping bag in the back of the Navajo, to regain a grip on things and plan for the dawn that would come blessfully soon.

I had my rear end hung out a mile and no real plan to cover it. I needed to act. So, it was with great reluctance and vigilance that I prepared to down from the mountain and emerge from the high desert to pick up my mail and receive my April 1 VA pension check in San Clemente. Things had gotten so bad that for the last few days in March, I'd resorted to sharing my animal's canned food and drinking from mountain streams. I was living anyone's worst fears—sixty-plus years old, homeless, in poor health, broke, and living in a car. I was now a member of America's underclass, just another displaced veteran. And I had another problem. During the regular trips to the VA hospital in Phoenix over the preceding year, I'd gone again and again to the VA regional headquarters to see if there had been any progress on my expanded disability claims. The answer was always, "No. Your active duty service medical records (including your file from the CIA) are incomplete and your claim remains in appeal."

I longed to talk with someone who might understand my predicament and

THE ZENITH SECRET

maybe offer some advice. I'd grown to trust Jim DiEugenio and Lisa Pease, and since I'd be traveling via the outskirts of LA, I called and asked to meet with them. I was a visual mess when we met at a restaurant in the suburbs amid a Sunday morning breakfast crowd on March 29. Knowing about the Jacumba incident, Jim and Lisa quickly picked up on my situation, and we discussed options for my survival. They bought breakfast and gave me $200 in cash. Their help was a financial backstop if there was some sort of interference with my VA check.

The old adage, "If you think things can't get any worse, just wait," was about to be borne out as I drove up to the strip mall in San Clemente where I received correspondence, faxes, and calls. Constantly on edge, I parked my car and animal trailer in front of the Post Stop. When I came out moments later, the driver's side door of my vehicle was unlocked and my Arizona private detective badge case, with all my personal identification was gone. It was one of the few really significant items that hadn't been taken at Jacumba. Now, all of my personal credentials, my PI licensing certificate, my driver's license, my VA medical care card, were gone. I was devastated, and immediately called the Orange County Sheriff, knowing that I'd have to fully expose myself in the course of making a theft report.[47]

My VA disability check came through and I hung around San Clemente for a day or so, searching the strip mall area for any trace of my credentials. Fortunately, I'd taken my address book into the Post Stop when the badge case disappeared, so I had that to work from. I talked to the sheriff several times, but there was no sign of the badge case. I searched every dumpster and garbage can in a two-block area around the Post Stop, but didn't find it. A typical thief would likely look for money, take it, and discard any identifying information. Nothing, not a trace. And how did anyone get such quick entry into my locked vehicle? I could only think of the Jacumba dark forces taking what they overlooked on March 16. They must have found the extra key to my car I'd stashed behind the ashtray. I looked. It was gone.

Obviously, given my delicate circumstances, I couldn't be driving around the Southwest without a driver's license and personal identification. I'd now have to go back to Arizona, for better or worse, to reconstitute my credentials.

En route to Phoenix, I went by my storage unit in Lake Elsinore. Everything seemed intact. I'd spun my own code on the combination lock and sealed it with clear fingernail polish, an old trick in the security business. There was no sign of tampering. After going over my accumulated investigative files, I set out for Arizona to try to put my identity back together. As I drove across the desolate, rugged terrain east of the California coastal hills, what grated on my psyche more than anything else was that I'd been totally distracted from pursuing Goldwater-Morales related investigative leads or even being able to concentrate on the war on drugs writing project. I had been forced into a wheel-spinning" mode, and it made me angry.

The need to return to Arizona was most disconcerting, but a practical necessity. I left California on the back roads out of Lake Elsinore, traveling across the interior, descending to the desert, skirting the Salton Sea and El Centro, and south to Interstate 8 near Yuma. I picked up a tail as soon as I crossed the Colorado River on the outskirts of Yuma; two men, in an unmarked mid-size sedan, with civilian plates as far as I could determine and definitely not Arizona tags.

I had no choice but to continue on to Phoenix and spend the next several days applying for a duplicate driver's license and private detective certification.

BRADLEY E. AYERS

Everywhere I went around the city, there was the same or a similar vehicle behind me. Whoever it was, they made no effort to camouflage the surveillance as if they wanted me to know I was being watched. It was disturbing and I thought several times of simply stopping and confronting them, But, I was still spooked by the Jacumba Airport shakedown, and felt a confrontation might just give the people in the car an excuse to further interdict my freedom. Under the circumstances, I delayed going to the VA hospital to get my medical care authorization recertified. I remained extremely anxious to try to connect with Pearl, but a visit to the hospital might compromise my contact with her if it were not already known. I spent two sleepless nights in the cargo delivery parking lot at Phoenix International Airport in the glare of overhead lights that flooded the area. It was virtually impossible for anyone to approach my vehicle or the animal trailer without my being aware of it. I was sure I was watched, but no one bothered me. This was an extremely tense situation. I felt I'd be stopped at any moment for some trumped up violation and I was quite helpless to do anything about it.

I wanted to get out of Phoenix as quickly as I could, and with the business I had to take care of there completed insofar as possible, I decided to drive to the Tucson area for another meeting with Lee Simmons, the realtor in Sonoita, AZ that I met with several times before in my search for a home. I hoped by some slim chance I'd yet be able to find a place to live for my animals and me in Arizona where I could get back to work on my drug book and try to reconnect with Pearl. My tail disappeared about 20 miles south of Phoenix.

Even though I expressed the urgent need for Simmons to find something for me, he wasn't able to help. I spent the next several weeks living in the car while looking around the area from Green Valley to Sierra Vista. Even if I'd had a small bankroll and a modicum of income, there was nothing I could afford. Unable to return to Phoenix for any reason because of the surveillance there, I dejectedly drove back to California to await my May 1 pension check and plan the next move. I holed up in Lake Elsinore at my storage unit hoping to discover some direction. I spent a lot of time praying and distance running, hoping for some kind of good news or inspiration.

I learned that author Gus Russo was trying to reach me as I went about my business in San Clemente and San Juan Capistrano. I wasn't familiar with the man who apparently was writing a book about the Kennedy assassination. I got in touch with Jim DiEugenio before calling him. Jim advised that Russo was pursuing the theory that Fidel Castro was directly responsible for the death of the president. This thesis smacked of the old CIA line. Who was Russo working for? I decided not to establish a dialogue with him, suspicious he was on some sort of fishing expedition, and I already had a full agenda of my own. I spent the next two weeks just wandering about Southern California, totally at loose ends. I was going nowhere and running out of money. Something had to give.

On Sunday, May 10, I awakened in the parking lot of the Catholic church in San Juan Capistrano with the intention of attending Mass later in the morning. I was only able to move my left leg with great difficulty. My left foot was swollen and very painful to the touch, and a thin red line led from my toes halfway to the knee. The weeks of living in my car, showering at YMCA's, trailer parks, marinas, and other semi-public facilities with questionable sanitation had taken its toll.

I'd suffered with chronic fissuring of the skin since 1953 when I'd experienced frostbite at Ft. Riley. It has been aggravated by mild radiation and mustard gas exposure at Fort McClellan in 1955, and further skin damage from soakings with a defoliant agent in 1963 while with the CIA. I'd pretty well managed to avoid a major infection with the self-treatment and the medications provided in recent years by the VA, but this one had gotten out of hand, and I knew the symptoms of blood poisoning when I saw them. I was in potentially serious trouble. Like it or not, I was going to have to return to Phoenix for treatment at the VA hospital where all my records were located. Within minutes after Mass ended, I was on the highway eastbound, regardless of the consequences.

By Sunday afternoon my leg was aching and throbbing so badly I could barely continue driving. I arrived in Phoenix in the wee hours, oblivious to anyone who might have followed me. I went immediately to the Urgent Care Emergency entrance, but had to wait until the Outpatient Clinic opened in the morning. I had no appointment of course, so I had to wait to be seen after the inpatients had been cared for. It was about noon before VA physician Dr. Hawkins performed surgery on my foot and prescribed heavy-duty antibiotics. Although continued IV treatment was in order, the doctor deferred to my request to release me from the hospital so I could tend to my animals in the trailer in the parking lot. At risk of permanent damage to my foot, I went away with a ton of pills and orders to check back in daily.

I looked for a note on my car from Pearl when I got back to it that evening, but there was nothing. By that time the pain killers had kicked in, and after tending to my animals, I crawled into my sleeping bag in the back of the car, lost to the world.

I had to spend the week in the Phoenix area for outpatient treatment at the hospital, returning periodically for an intravenous infusion of antibiotics. I felt lousy, hobbling around with crutches, my leg in pain and my system disrupted by a variety of medications. There was no indication I was under surveillance as I had been during my last visit to the city. There was also no sign of Pearl. Finding no notes on my car, I donned a hospital gown and wheelchaired myself through the maze of hospital hallways in the chance I might spot her in one of the offices or wards. No Pearl. When not required to be at the outpatient clinics for treatment, and very much in a nostalgic frame of mind, I drove up to park in Fountain City and the trail head in the Superstition Mountains and sat there for an hour or two on the chance she might show up. I even went to Mayo Clinic near Scottsdale where I thought she might be working. I shuffled my way through the corridors, but I did not see Pearl. Back at the VA hospital, waiting for treatment, I sat reading for hours in the pavilion on the Old Indian School grounds. Not a soul approached me. I worried that something had happened to her. And, other than actively searching for her and disregarding her security, there was nothing I could do. The stress of physical pain, lack of sleep, and dwindling funds began to overwhelm me. I had to act as soon as my treatment was completed. But, where to go remained an underlying question.

I realized, under the circumstances, I had to put aside my writings and investigation, at least for now, and concentrate on personal survival. I visited the VA Regional Office in Phoenix to see if any progress had been made in processing my appeal for service-related disability claims. The case remained in limbo absent the Army's and CIA's cooperation in the release of certain of my active duty records. On crutches, I went to the local office of the Disabled American Veterans, my appeal advocate, and pleaded my situation. The response was less than encouraging. There was nothing more the DAV could do as long as my records were being withheld by officialdom. I then went to the Social Services offices at the VA hospital to meet with a counselor and hopefully get some assistance as a homeless veteran. He gave me several vouchers so I might stay in a nearby motel until my treatment was completed. Staffer Ron Bowen then gave me his evaluation of the situation. "Mr. Ayers, you're approaching mid-60s, your disability appeal is in limbo and may never be adjudicated, you've got some serious health issues and may never be able to work again. My advice to you is to go somewhere, maybe back to Minnesota where you'll be near your friends or family that can help you. I just don't see anything else in the immediate to get your situation stabilized. If you continue as you are, your health is going to continue to deteriorate and you're going to lose whatever you have left."

His words hit me like a punch to the gut. It wasn't that I was unaware of my predicament, but to hear someone else say it was brutal.

I told Bowen I'd consider his advice and make a decision in the next day or so. That night, lying in the downtown Day's Inn, feeling almost human after cleaning up and eating a decent meal, I did a lot of soul searching. Bowen's perception of my situation was quite right. The next morning, I went back to see him. First, I authorized him to contact the one family member in Minnesota who might have some appreciation for my predicament and could begin to try to find a place for me there. I also explained to Bowen, having just paid the rent on my storage unit in California, I had no money to travel back to the Midwest. Bowen referred me to the Salvation Army and a Catholic charity in Phoenix for a gas fill and a supply of canned food for the road. I didn't mention to Bowen that, before leaving Minnesota, I wanted to drive back to Lake Elsinore and remove some items from storage. The main thing I wanted was my investigative files. I could live without the rest of the stuff until I got situated somewhere, if that ever happened.

Knowing I'd be short of the funds needed to complete the trip west and then northwest, I contacted Wyatt Earp who agreed to loan me $300. I was to meet him in Prescott where he was doing a show at the famous Palace Bar mimicking his great-grandfather. With that loan, I knew I could make it as far as the Twin Cites assuming I had no breakdowns en route. Before leaving Phoenix, not ready to fully abandon my inquiry in to the Goldwater-Morales connection, I made a farewell call to Bob Walton. We met at a Chinese restaurant in Paradise Valley. Bob was not in the best of health and was living with his daughter. We spent about an hour together, rehashing much of what we'd talked about in earlier meetings.

I explained I was having some physical problems—I had just gotten my last treatment at the VA hospital earlier in the day—and was going back to the Midwest to recuperate. He bought lunch and slipped me $20 for gas. While I did not mention my encounter with Pearl, I told Bob I'd developed a source that elaborated considerably on what he'd told me about Senator Goldwater and the senator's link to organized crime, militant right wing activists, Morales and various CIA people. Bob reiterated that he'd nearly lost his license to practice when he at first refused to destroy certain papers that had tied these entities together. I asked him if he'd heard of the Gila Project and his face flushed. He was silent for several moments, eyes downcast. "Yes," he said. "I was familiar with that. You're on the right track." When I asked him to go on, he declined, pleading concern for his own safety and that of his family, and I wasn't comfortable pressing him further. Bob and I parted with a handshake, an embrace, and his wish of good luck. Bob was a true patriot. He looked ill and I wondered if I'd ever see him again. I then headed to California to pick up my files and other critical personal items.

THE ZENITH SECRET

On May 18, I returned to Phoenix, picked up some prescriptions and my medical files at the VA hospital, received the gas vouchers and food from the Salvation Army and St. Vincent DePaul charity, and drove to Prescott to meet Wyatt. I watched his show that evening and met him later. He was only able to advance me $150. This was going to make the trip to Minnesota a real challenge financially. My foot was bothering me. That night, as I drove north to Flagstaff and the Interstate, I knew it was going to be an ordeal. I continued to be absolutely amazed at how well my animals were handling the situation. They seemed quite content in the small cubicles in the trailer and with the regular stops along the way for airing, exercise, and elimination. They remained my sole companionship and major comfort in an otherwise depressing, tension-filled existence. While I was traveling, just as I'd done over the preceding weeks while moving about in Arizona or stuck in Phoenix at the VA hospital, I kept in touch with my most trusted associates, Ron Williams, Doug Valentine, John Woods, Jim and Lisa from *Probe* magazine, and my middle son who was monitoring my travel. I was somewhat embarrassed to have to tell my investigative contacts it was necessary for me to turn away from my quest in the Southwest. After selling or trading anything marketable en route, I arrived in Minnesota on May 28 with the flare up of the foot infection and what would later be diagnosed as walking pneumonia. With mixed emotions, I heard the news that Senator Barry Goldwater had died as I drove across the state line.

I didn't realize how stretched I was, physically and intellectually, by the circumstances and events I'd experienced in the Southwest in the preceding two years. And, I didn't find much immediate comfort with the VA Regional Office and DAV in connection with my disability claims appeal. Meanwhile, I continued to live primarily in my car, animals in the trailer and all. My son tried to help me find a home and Ron Williams loaned me money to have my personal property shipped back from the West Coast. It was several months before I started to feel healthy again and resumed a regular routine of running and working out.

The Minneapolis-St. Paul area held only bad memories for me. I was haunted by the gut wrenching experiences with the authorities during my last years in Woodbury. I shunned the metropolitan area as a possible place to find a home—the cities were way beyond my financial means. So, I concentrated my search along the rural St. Croix River near the area where I'd grown up, searching for a small hideaway where I could resume my writing with some sense of security and look after my animals without interference. The estrangement from my family continued, except for infrequent contact with my middle son who was somewhat sympathetic to my situation. But, save for Ron Williams, no one really was conscious of the dynamics that had brought me to where I was. After a series of false starts, I was finally able to lease for the winter an aging little farmhouse in northwestern Wisconsin, about 75 miles from the Minneapolis-St. Paul metro area. I was still unpacking as the snow began to fall, It wasn't much, but at least I wouldn't have to spend another night in my car or cause my beloved animals to spend anymore time in their cramped trailer quarters.

I couldn't (or wouldn't) easily put thoughts of Arizona and Pearl out of my mind. The whole episode spooked me more and more as time passed. I spoke in general terms about it to Ron Williams; and I made a point to keep in contact with my old assassination research associates. I struggled with the idea of revealing my conversations with Pearl. If I did I would violate my commitment to her and possibly jeopardize reestablishing contact with her and going back to the Southwest to continue my work on the Goldwater assassination link.

BRADLEY E. AYERS

Not long after my return, I got a letter from Doug Valentine that puzzled me. He expressed his sympathy for my continuing travails and apologized for his failure to convince Tom Clines to talk with me. He said Clines still referred to me as "the swamp man." Then Doug asked, "I was wondering if you would tell me which private investigator David Morales put out of business?" My thoughts flashed immediately; Doug must have gotten this from Clines. He had good dialogue with him. But "private investigator," no. Investigative reporter, yes. Don Bolles most probably; this undoubtedly revealed to Clines by Morales in one of their drinking sessions before the Big Indian died. Clines just didn't have his description of the victim correct. My reply to Doug was not revealing. I hadn't really the opportunity to dig into the Bolles car bombing before I had to leave Arizona and I wasn't sure of my ground.

Then, there was the letter from Brian Quig[49] one of my sources on Arizona politics. This was high energy stuff in light of what I'd learned from Pearl and had been working on in Arizona.

Stuck away in my tiny sanctuary in the North Woods, these communications were agonizingly provocative. But, I had no way of following up on them with barely enough resources to sustain myself.

Confronted with the task of trying to stabilize my situation and survive on less than $1,000 per month was an all-consuming undertaking (it should be kept in mind that the interim VA disability pension I accepted in 1996 precluded the acceptance of any other income without the penalty of having whatever I earned deducted from the monthy government allotment). With physical disabilities that prevented me from even part-time work to generate income that might supercede the amount received from the VA, I was really in a box until my service-related injury claims were adjudicated under appeal.

Soon after arriving in northern Wisconsin, I appealed to the office of Senator Russ Feingold to become involved in my effort to free up the withheld service records from the Army and the CIA. Staffer Matt Nikolay went to work on my case almost immediately after I had a personal meeting with the senator. Concurrently with that effort, Washburn and Polk County veteran service officers Carl Krantz and Rick Gates became involved in my case with the VA. They reviewed my background, my unique military, CIA, and DEA service and began assisting me with administrative actions that reinforced my original claims and the urgency for some resolution. Dr. Favour at the VA hospital in Minneapolis took an interest in my physical problems and established a protocol for tests and treatment that further confirmed the medical diagnostic basis for my disability claims. Bringing all this together was time-consuming and nearly became a full time effort, but at least I now had some expert help in seeking the benefits to which I had rights as an honorably discharged veteran. Nevertheless, my case remained confounded, primarily by the agency's continued refusal to release my operational and medical records of the 1963-1964 period. At the urging of Senator Feingold's office, I submitted a second request for my files under the Freedom of Information-Data Privacy Act.

My primary hope remained to establish some degree of financial security and a permanent home, so I could resume my investigative work and renew my pursuit of the Arizona connection if even from a distance. My old friend Ron Williams came to my aid and helped me arrange for the recovery of my stored household goods in Minneapolis. Gradually, I realized my decision to return to my home area was the right one. Even so, my thoughts were never very far from the tantalizing prospects posed by the investigative leads I'd developed in the Southwest. As time permitted, I returned to work on my book writing projects and began to refine the notes and interview abstracts. The more I got into these, and as my health improved, the more anxious I became to exploit what I now felt was information that could lead to unraveling the plots that led to the death of JFK and possibly Bobby Kennedy. Over the winter months, I shared some of my thoughts and findings with Ron Williams and, guardedly, with other assassination researchers I trusted. I did not go into detail about my conversations with Pearl, still holding out hope that somehow that dialogue might be renewed if she again emerged.

Ron Williams was heavily into assassination lore, had an extensive library and was well resourced via the Internet and other researchers of all stripes. He was aware of my interest in going after the Goldwater-Morales-Mafia links, and in a general way, my wish to renew the Arizona connection inquiry. He had become aware of a private research group called JFK Lancer Productions and Publications located in the Southwest. The group was apparently funded and headed by Deb Conway, with the sponsorship of her wealthy husband. Ron suggested Conway might be interested in hiring me as a private investigator and funding the continuation of my work in Arizona. I thought about it, and finally in the spring of 1999, called her. The introductory conversation went quite well and I was excited by the prospect of eventually getting back in the field even though I had huge reservations about trying to work in Arizona again. Obviously, I could not talk in detail about my Goldwater-Morales-Mafia findings and other relevant aspects of leads I'd developed in our initial conversation, so I prepared an express mail packet of general information for Conway to review, an overview of my work, and a brief agenda for continuing inquiry.

I spoke with Conway again after she'd received and reviewed the brief and background information I'd sent. She seemed sincerely enthusiastic about working out some arrangement for me to go work for her group. I explained to her I couldn't accept income because of my interim VA pension arrangement, but could receive advances and reimbursement for expenses. She talked about me flying out to meet her to discuss a working relationship. We'd talk again in a few days.

I was really enthused. I pretty much had recovered my health, my VA situation was solidly in process, the lease on my farmhouse where I spent the winter had expired and I was living in a dilapidated, filthy old house trailer while again looking for a new home. I'd found a good boarding kennel for my animals and was ready, willing, and able to undertake a new adventure. I began to feel like a viable, professional once again after so many months of being out of action. I craved to get back into the thick of things, and I had some new ideas about unraveling the Arizona connection. Anxious to continue the exchange with Conway, on June 9 I prepared yet another packet of information for her and sent it off by priority mail. The following day she called me and tersely informed me there would be no working arrangement. Her husband had reviewed the matter and vetoed the deal. JFK Lancer couldn't afford it.[50]

I was stunned, my hopes dashed. When I hung up the phone, I looked around. There was a crumbling old house trailer, with a toilet that backed up and a rotting floor, stinking so bad even my animals preferred being outdoors. Trying to hang on to some grand idea that I might be able to find out who killed my president had turned all our lives upside down. It was ridiculous. I was beating my head against the wall. My sons, who viewed me as a Don Quixote, were right. Nobody got it. I'd had enough.

It took me the better part of another month of relentless searching along back roads and trails of the North Woods to finally find the place I trust will be my refuge and sanctuary for the balance of my life. I'd prayed for guidance and direction as I drove about, looking for something I could afford and was available for immediate occupancy. Suddenly, it was there; a 500 square foot log cabin with stove and refrigerator on a dead end road overlooking a small wilderness lake. It had never been occupied, and when I drove down the overgrown driveway to the house, I knew immediately that's where my animals and I belonged. It'd need lots of work and improvements, but to the exclusion of nearly everything else in my life, I knew I could do it. I immediately got in touch with a kindly old gentleman for whom I'd done investigative work in the '70s and '80s. John Timmerman, a truly extraordinary human being, had come to my aid several times over the years, and he knew my background and character. He advanced me the money for the down payment and assumed the mortgage on the property. I, together with my beloved animals that shared so much of my tumultuous existence over the years, have been here on Somers Lake since the summer of 1999. The years following the unsettling events of the 1990s have been relatively tranquil and time has passed more quickly than I would like. My days, typically 12 to 15 hours of concentrated activity, have been filled with projects, tasks, and interests: looking after my pets, working on improving my home, making Indian walking sticks, running, snowshoeing, kayaking, and walking in the woods with my dogs, and reading all variety of non-fiction books. I live alone, the sole year-round resident on a small lake surrounded by forest. I neither hunt nor fish, preferring to leave nature unviolated. My lifestyle is sparse, and might be considered bleak and austere by the standards of others, but it is socially unfettered, rigorous, healthy, and blessed with the beauty and inspiration of precious north country surroundings and the inspiration of the Great Spirit.

Despite that I've not been able to continue my field investigation of assassination plotting, my interest in the Goldwater-Morales-Mafia connection has not dimmed. It's a pity I've not had the resources to pursue the inquiry. But, I've maintained informal contact with those involved in private assassination research, and I continue work almost daily on an account of my experience over the years as it may contribute to understanding the dynamics of the time and identifying those I believe may be responsible for death of President Kennedy, his brother, and Martin Luther King, Jr. What is printed on these pages is the end product of that effort.

The years have been kind to me since the trauma of the 1990s. Except for some so far treatable skin cancer, my health has stabilized and I'm able to lead a very active life, both physically and intellectually. Despite the CIA's continued refusal to release my records, some of my disability claims have been favorably adjudicated, thanks to VA Regional Advocate Charlie Wolden and VSO Rick Gates. I'm treated exceedingly well at VA facilities. I still compete regularly in my age group in distance running and snowshoe race events. I'm a community-environmental activist and write regularly for some of the regional papers. I've acquired a growing collection of mounted native wildlife to the extent that I'm running out of living space in my cabin. And, I continue to adopt and take care of abused and orphaned dogs and cats. While I recognize I'm still vulnerable to the dark forces for my actions and what I represent, they know where I am. There are some negatives, the estrangement from family being the major one. I've never been able to reconcile my values and purpose with those of my sons and their spouses. Thus, I am denied any access to my grandchildren. I have come to accept this as the price to be paid for my chosen lifestyle and the quest for adventure and enlightenment that has more or less influenced my life. I've had to reconcile the fact that in contemporary American society there are few

THE ZENITH SECRET

who would understand my purpose, philosophy, and definition of patriotic citizenship.

And that is why I'm flying solo. I compare my life to a distance run, where there is no place for self-pity and the truly important thing is to show up at the starting line every day and finish feeling you've done the best you can. It is too much to expect anyone else to accept and live with my acknowledged intensity and single-minded existentialist drive. It is too much to expect anyone else to comprehend the odyssey that has been my life. I wouldn't expect anyone else to run in my moccasins.

If I could musically theme my life, it would be a progressive symphony of Gregorian chants, Bobby Vinton, Dave Brubeck, Sousa marches, Beethoven, Janis Joplin, Crosby, Stills, Nash, and Young, Bob Marley, Santana, Mozart, Pink Floyd, Brad Mehldau, and Native American drum songs—an eclectic composition that reflects the moods, social backdrops, and dynamics of my years. "Freedom is nothing more/than nothing left to lose," from Joplin's "Bobby McGee," has stuck with me from the day I first heard it. How right the lady was!

While I remain frustrated I've not been able to fulfill many aspects of what I have defined as my mission, I have found contentment in having made, and continuing to make, the effort. I pray that this journey will not have been in vain and that I will have served a useful purpose in my troubled time on Mother Earth.

EPILOGUE

As the years passed following my return from Arizona in 1999, I began to accept the fact that my efforts to reveal the Arizona connection might never be acknowledged in a manner that could inspire further inquiry. Preoccupied with health considerations and the effort to stabilize my living situation, I did not aggressively pursue the publication of the evolving book manuscript I titled *The Zenith Secret*. From time to time I'd become aware of a publisher with an interest in whistle-blowing CIA/government conspiracy-assassination subjects and would send my detailed proposal off for consideration. Invariably, there would be either outright rejections or demands that I submit the full manuscript for review. The rejections were boilerplate and laughable for the most part, and I accepted them in stride as any published writer must do. Those editors demanding the full manuscript without a contract offer were talking to the wrong guy. I wasn't about to expose what I had, gratis, in view of all the misery that had gone before. So, while I continued to refine my manuscript, I kept my focus on the immediate—getting my life back together after the turmoil of the 1990s.

"Dormancy" aptly describes my interest and personal involvement in assassination research for nearly five years. Other than periodically sending off my book proposal under the title of *The Zenith Secret* and continuing to refine the manuscript when I felt moved to do so, I was disengaged.

From time to time, there would be inquiries from other writers asking for my cooperation, and I complied with their requests insofar as I felt comfortable. There were also invitations to do media interviews, appear on panels, or speak on possible CIA connections to domestic assassinations. I turned them down because I had intellectually distanced myself from a public discussion of matters that I'd not yet worked out privately. I had fixed in my mind that if and when the right opportunity came along, I would reveal what I knew in the form of a non-fiction trade book that would be a credible, permanent, reasonably scholarly contribution to recent history, and not just self-promoting, attention-motivated white noise. If I couldn't do it that way, such was fate.

I lulled myself into this view, and in so doing was able to get on with creating a new life for myself. I was not completely without frustration though as I watched so many of the key players in what I had reason to believe was a pervasive conspiracy leave the human scene, and they took their secrets with them to the grave. Icons Barry Goldwater and my original confessor, Jack Anderson, are gone. Shackley, the major CIA figure I personally knew, has passed: there were others who I believe had inside knowledge, but they are now suffering from dementia or in such poor health that they are no longer viable sources of information. Save for myself, to the best of my awareness, only Tom Clines, Edwin Wilson, and Carl Jenkins are still potentially viable ex-CIA-Mongoose-JMWAVE sources. CIA Director Porter Goss would not talk under any circumstance. There may be others out there, some referred to by other writers as sources, but it might be difficult to get them to free their tongues despite the fact that we're all not far away from meeting our Maker. A sense of personal conscience is not a virtue essential or desired in covert operatives, especially ideologues or those dependent on CIA pensions.

My sense of detachment neutralized the frustration I'd lived with for so long because of my inability to pursue the Arizona connection. I thought a good deal of Pearl and wondered where she might be, if still living. Gradually, I came to accept the reality that I would probably never be able to speak with her again, and it would be up to me to decide how to handle what she divulged. For that reason, I would be very cautious and selective about the how and when I revealed her as a source and make her full role in my investigative work known to others.

Dale Gustafson, with my friend Ron Williams, visited me from time to time at Somers Lake, and we'd chat about assassination subjects and related matters. The name of University of Minnesota tenured professor Dr. James Fetzer came up several times. Fetzer had long been active as a JFK assassination writer and lecturer, and had edited the book *Assassination Science,* published in 1998. The seventh printing for the highly regarded book was due out in 2003. Fetzer was said to have several other assassination-related books in the works. Since I was within reasonable driving distance of the Duluth, Minnesota campus where Dr. Fetzer taught, Gustafson suggested that it might be useful if the professor and I met to share information. I agreed, and Gustafson facilitated the contact. A lunch rendezvous was arranged.

Our first meeting began what has developed into a very stimulating and cordial friendship. Our relationship eventually contributed to the placement of this book with a publisher. The professor, in his mid-60s, was a former Marine officer who had seen service during the Vietnam War. With somewhat common military backgrounds, Fetzer and I hit it off well. He had read my 1976 book, *The War That Never Was,* and was generally familiar with my background. I agreed to share some of my assassination-related investigative files with him. Specifically, he was interested in a character that claimed to have been a marginal figure in the plot to kill JFK, a man by the name of Tosh Plumlee, whom I'd met and discounted after investigation years earlier. The Plumlee field inquiry had been funded by Peter Lemkin, a private assassination researcher, with money provided by a foreign benefactor. I was unable to verify any of Plumlee's claims in the course of a weeklong, harrowing return to Miami in 1992, where I apparently was recognized as a former CIA-DEA operative.

My conversations with Dr. Fetzer were far-ranging, and because of my extensive background in aviation and as a former commercial pilot, the subject of Senator Paul Wellstone's death in a Minnesota plane crash in October 2002 inevitably came up. There were many questions surrounding the tragedy, and there was a good deal of talk in the media and on the Internet about the senator's death being a result of a political conspiracy. Fetzer surprised me when he said that he and another professor-writer, Dr. Don Jacobs, aka Four Arrows, of Arizona, had investigated the alleged weather-pilot error related accident and were writing a book exposing the crash as a Bush administration-orchestrated political assassination. Given that I'd flown into the Eveleth, Minnesota airport many times as a charter pilot, under a variety of flight-conditions and had known and respected the senator (whose office had been instrumental in the mid-90s in the VA's award of my interim disability pension), Dr. Fetzer invited me to review the book on release for the publisher, Vox Pop, of Brooklyn, NY. I agreed, honored to be asked and happy to have the opportunity because I, quite independently, felt the official explanation for the Wellstone crash was seriously questionable.

When the book, *American Assassination: The Strange Death of Senator Wellstone,* was distributed in 2004, I wrote a lengthy review that was widely published, generally supporting the thesis of the book and the quality of the investigation work done by Fetzer and Jacobs. The book went into several printings and did fairly well in the marketplace. My friendship with Dr. Fetzer has positively evolved and flourished over time, and I consider him one of my closest confidants and allies. Yet, we freely agree and disagree on a variety of issues. He has given me enormous support as I've gone forth with my own publishing efforts as represented by this book and another on my war on drugs experience that will follow. The contact with Dr. Fetzer and the completely unanticipated literary developments that ensued are quite indicative of the serendipitous occurrences that I've come to accept in the course of my life, particularly in matters relating to my interest in the assassinations.

The year 2004 held yet another "out of nowhere," important, and unexpectedly productive development. (In retrospect, I wonder if it didn't have something to do with the fact that I'd begun replaying some of my old Pink Floyd albums.)

Gary King, editor of the *Leader*, the major regional paper in northwestern Wisconsin, called me in mid-August 2004, asking if he could give my phone number to a British TV documentary producer who was working on a project associated with U.S. domestic assassination. I'd kept my telephone number unlisted for the sake of personal privacy, but had given it to Gary in connection with various published articles and my submissions dealing with local issues. Gary said that the caller had been directed to the *Leader* by Noel Twyman, who was aware that I wrote for the paper from time to time. Gary advised the UK caller seemed to be sincere and well-grounded, from what he could tell on the phone. As had always been my practice, when I felt that the inquiry came from an established professional researcher, I responded favorably. Jason subsequently contacted me. Although I expressed my concerns about security of anything to be discussed in view of the fact that we had to communicate internationally, a dialogue by phone, fax, and mail, with some help from Gary King and his Internet capability, was initiated. Jason introduced himself as a well-resourced and industry-connected freelance producer doing research for a television documentary on the murder of Robert Kennedy for worldwide distribution. He'd already done extensive study of the June 1968 assassination, absorbed all the available literature, accessed the AARB and other archives, and had spoken with a number of sources who were contributing to his development of information. While Jason claimed to have approached his research without bias, the more he studied RFK's death, the more he became convinced that it was the result of a conspiracy.

The producer advised that his review of all that he'd accumulated thus far suggested the possible conspiratorial involvement of the CIA. With that in mind, he'd begun to focus on known CIA operatives at JM/WAVE. This, of course, led him to my book, *The War That Never Was,* and subsequently published information on Morales that resulted from my investigations of El Indio in the early 1990s. Jason was not aware of the additional information I'd developed since then, which constitutes the later portion of this book. He was extremely well read on Morales and some of his associates, and I was quite impressed with the young producer. I agreed to assist him in any way I could.

It was clearly understood that there would be no monetary compensation for my cooperation, and that we'd ascribe to strict journalistic standards in all aspects of our work together. I advised Jason in the early stages of our association that I'd really never focused on Bobby Kennedy's murder in my investigative work, but shared his suspicion that Sirhan Bishara was, like Oswald and James Earl Ray, a patsy. I told the producer, however, that it was the death of

THE ZENITH SECRET

Robert Kennedy that moved me to go public about my experience at JM/WAVE and write *The War That Never Was*. Our initial conversations were general in nature, as I needed to trust him, and become thoroughly confident in his motives and his adherence to the cardinal rules of investigative journalism. The more I communicated with Jason, the more comfortable I became, and because our association continues as he goes on with his work, we have an exceedingly harmonious, mutually complementing relationship.

This is what I personally knew about Bobby Kennedy and his murder, and, in the course of our dialogue to date, have related verbally, in writing and on camera:

1. I was an eyewitness to RFK's presence with CIA career and contract operatives at JM/WAVE in 1963. (These meetings are described in earlier chapters in this book.)

2. Well-credentialed, highly respected private investigator David Rabern spontaneously identified David Sanchez Morales' photo in 1990 as a man he recognized being present in the Ambassador Hotel ballroom the night RFK was murdered.

3. The Vietnam photo alleged to be Morales, shown to me by source John Markley, was not the David Sanchez Morales I knew, which suggested that there may have been a stand-in that would have permitted Morales to be elsewhere during the critical spring 1968 period when both RFK and MLK were killed.

4. Testimony from both Robert Walton and Reuben Carbajal, supplemented by information provided by Pearl based on her father's remarks, indicate that Morales was present in the U.S. in the spring of 1968.

5. I had received information from a variety of secondary sources, but had been unable to confirm solidly and independently, that Robert Kennedy had embarked on his own investigation of his brother's death, and was involved in that inquiry in California, in addition to pursuing his political agenda in June 1968.

6. Columnist Jack Anderson questioned me about RFK's presence at JM/WAVE when he and Les Whitten interviewed me in 1971. Articles published by Anderson and others during the period following the assassination of JFK suggested that RFK suffered serious remorse after the death of the president and the fact that as head of the Special Group he had been personally involved in sanctioning the CIA plots to kill Castro. There is also extensive evidence to suggest that RFK was in serious conflict up to his death with Lyndon Johnson, the FBI, right-wing zealots, and certain heads of the U.S. military over Vietnam and related issues, as well as those in Congress and government opposing the evolving Civil Rights movement.

7. From my experience at JM/WAVE, I believed it possible that Robert Kennedy became aware, as I did, that the CIA in 1963 was deliberately providing misleading, or withholding from the Special Group, intelligence indicating that the covert war was not succeeding and there was little or no chance for an internal uprising in Cuba that might overthrow Fidel. By reporting this to his brother, RFK would have alienated the agency militant Cold Warriors and the Mongoose-JM/WAVE cabal.

Jason already had a fairly good understanding of the foreign policy and domestic political atmosphere that existed at the time Bobby Kennedy was killed and had done extraordinary research on RFK's personal and public life. The producer also had an excellent grasp of the history of the 1960s in America

BRADLEY E. AYERS

and had great insight into the machinations of political figures and the ideological dynamic that prevailed at the time. It was a pleasure to work with him because, as I had to do so many times in the past with other young media types, it wasn't necessary to educate him on historical background and setting to understand the socio-cultural environment in which the assassination(s) took place.

But, what I could deliver to Jason would be my human sources as well as my own testimony and observations. The producer revealed to me in October, 2004, that he had videotape footage of the Ambassador Hotel ballroom on the night Bobby was killed. I was not aware that anything of that sort existed. Jason asked me to look at several of the stills that he'd been able to lift, with the technology at his disposal and his expertise, from the video footage. I agreed to look at what he had, and he sent them along, first by fax in very poor quality, but then via the *Leader* website. I was bowled over when I got them. There was Morales, or an incredible likeness, but even more importantly for me, because of my close personal experience with the man and all I'd learned since, was the likeness of Gordon Campbell in another photo from the ballroom. My God, could they really have been there? If these photos are legitimate, Morales was there just as David Rabern said, and of huge significance was the man I knew as Gordon Campbell. A Mr. Gordon had been mentioned by Pearl as one of those receiving the Bonnano money just before JFK was killed.

Jason called me after he'd confirmed that I 'd received the photos. I told him, expressing some reservations because of the electronically transmitted quality of the photos, that I would be willing to identify one of the figures in the photos to a 90 percent degree of assurance, as the Morales I knew at JM/WAVE. Then, surprising him, I told him that I thought a figure in other photos of the ballroom was Gordon Campbell.

I then reiterated what I knew about Campbell and reviewed my association with him while I was with the CIA. I was at least 80 percent sure of my identification of Campbell in the photos. I then suggested that Jason go to the photo section of Fonzi's book, *The Last Investigation,* and look at the artist's sketch of the man described by Antonio Veciana as his CIA case officer, "Mr. Bishop," who Fonzi theorizes was David Atlee Phillips. The reader will recall Veciana alleges he saw Bishop with Lee Harvey Oswald. I remind the reader that Campbell controlled Karl, the operative I've described as a dead ringer for Oswald and who met his end in the "fall" from the chopper at Eglin in my presence in 1964. I'd long contended, with anyone who inquired, that Phillips was not the man in the Veciana sketch. I had seen both Phillips and Campbell at JM/WAVE, and the Veciana sketch resembled Campbell almost to a hair. No wonder Veciana could not ID his old case officer at the infamous 1976 luncheon encounter arranged by Fonzi: They're different people. I told Jason that I'd reserve final judgment until I actually saw the videotape footage he had of the Ambassador Hotel ballroom. Nevertheless, this development was hair-raisingly extraordinary because we were possibly moving toward a completely spontaneous, independent reinforcement of my long-held suspicions and the general corroborative testimony of many of my sources. To establish this by true journalistic criteria, we needed unallied confirmation.

My best potential source for identification of the Morales figure in the photos was David Rabern, the Arizona private detective I'd not spoken with since 1990. I'd promised David that I'd not mention his ID of Morales without his OK. I was a licensed Arizona private detective, and I knew Rabern's business in Scottsdale had grown exponentially over the years. He had an excellent, high-profile reputation among professionals in the valley. I decided that it was time to call him to confirm our 1990s discussion and his ID of the El Indio photo. I hadn't spoken to Rabern in nearly 14 years. I picked up the phone, adrenaline surging. I got David directly, introduced myself, and we chatted briefly about various professional matters. Then I explained to David the purpose of my call. Would he talk with Jason? Rabern, being a stand-up guy and a person of integrity, recalled our meeting, the Morales photo, and agreed to speak with the producer, despite any risk of public embarrassment or damage to his business image.

The rather grainy, blurred contrast photos off the Internet, or even duplicates by mail, were of insufficient quality on which anyone could be expected to pass reasonably confident judgment, especially given the significance of the issue at hand. Jason arranged to fly to the States in January 2005 and bring with him the actual videotape of the ballroom scene. He had lined up a number of witnesses on the West Coast on his own, and, at my advice, he would see and interview Bob Walton, Reuben Carbajal, possibly Robert Morales, and David Rabern in Phoenix. I would meet with him to be interviewed and view the ballroom footage as he traveled across the country to the East Coast for further research.

Jason called me on his arrival in L.A., and I anxiously awaited word on the outcome of his contacts and interviews. Would anyone back me up on my identification of the Internet-transmitted photos from the producer? And, if in fact my opinion was supported, what were the implications? Certainly, there would be a strong circumstantial basis for possible CIA involvement in RFK's murder. Why else would two known agency people, suspected of having links to other assassinations, be in the ballroom that night? What was their business?

How would I respond to my viewing of the actual tape? My tentative identification of Morales had more or less set the stateside inquiry in motion, but I was relieved to know that Jason would talk with others and show them the video footage before my viewing. Thus, there'd be independent verification or contradiction, exactly what's useful in empirical research.

Jason kept in touch with me as he traveled eastward from the coast. After on-camera interviews there, he went to Phoenix. He interviewed Reuben and Bob Walton. Reuben, quite expectedly, denied his old friend Didi would have been involved in the assassination of RFK. Bob Walton's health had dramatically deteriorated over the years. But both men confirmed their extended discussions with me and all that I'd documented and reported about Morales. Of course, I had no idea of Pearl's whereabouts and no way of locating her. Even if I did, I'd not been relieved of my commitment to protect her identity.

The prize development for Jason, and a great boost for my early identification of the figures of the photos, was David Rabern. He confirmed the likeness to Morales to about the same degree as I had. But of equal and possibly greater significance, he confirmed the likeness of Gordon Campbell to a man with whom he had semiofficial contact while with various security and law enforcement entities in LA in the 1966-68 timeframe. Rabern said it was known that the man was CIA-connected and was involved in covert intelligence activities. Jason has established a continuing dialogue with Rabern, who has provided a considerable amount of information about the events and circumstances surrounding the RFK murder. These conversations are ongoing and will become part of the documentary the young producer is putting together. When Jason reached Minnesota, I spent half a day in an on-camera interview with him. I finally had the chance for multiple viewings of the Ambassador Hotel ballroom videotapes, and my initial identifications of Morales and Campbell were confirmed for the record. Since the interviews in January 2005, I've continued my dialogue with Jason, and even as this book is being written, continue to provide him the names of sources, offer covert operations and tradecraft tips, paramilitary tactical advice, suggest other leads, and exchange information with him. I fully anticipate his forthcoming documentary will thoroughly shake those who believe that Sirhan alone was responsible for the death of Robert Kennedy and provide a credible argument for CIA involvement in the murders that dramatically altered the course of our history.

Coming so late in the game, Jason's independent corroboration of many of my suspicions and findings has been quite gratifying. Further, while I've certainly been very troubled by the assassination of the president and focused on his murder over the years, I've been bothered even more deeply by the untimely death of Bobby Kennedy. He was our last hope for freeing America from the Zenith Secret influence that took control of our country by political assassinations in the 1960s.

END NOTES

1. My classmate in one of the advanced courses was then West Point Captain Norman Schwartzkopf, later to become four star general and the commander of U.S. Central Command and a national hero as he led the allied coalition against the Iraqi army that had invaded Kuwait in early August 1990, known as the Gulf War. While at Fort Benning, Schwartzkopf, a.k.a. "Stormin' Norman" during the Gulf War) and I enjoyed a respectful friendship and reviewed each other's articles for the *Infantry Journal*.

2. Years later, long after my CIA assignment, I learned that William Roth Bond, a 52-year-old full colonel in 1963, had risen to the rank of brigadier general and in 1970 was the commander of an infantry brigade in Vietnam. He was killed as he stepped from a helicopter, the only star-ranked officer to die in Vietnam. See epilogue for further commentary on Bond and his demise.

3. I was eventually given three separate cover identities, each for use under different, special circumstances. One was the Army civilian employee ID/ cover under my true name. The second was to be used in any internal CIA communications, reports, memos, accounting records, etc.—anything that would go into the agency files. I was to identify myself and sign-off as Anthony P. Darguzis, supposedly a fictitious name. Later, I learned the CIA used the London telephone directory to come up with this and other pseudonyms for in-house purposes. At JM/WAVE, I was given another operational cover identity, to be used in external activities while working with the Cuban exiles, in any capacity. This was Daniel B.Williams who would be listed as a legitimate employee of a variety of corporations set up to cover covert operations against Cuba. A plausible personal history was fabricated and memorized for use with both the Army cover and the covert operational cover. Cover documents, IDs, drivers licenses, etc. were produced by the agency cover branch and appeared to be absolutely legitimate.

4. I got early impressions that the agency recruited, besides Cubans, other non-U.S. operatives in the secret war against Cuba. This was later confirmed when I encountered contract agents from a variety of countries: Germany, France, Italy, Belgium, and even Eastern Europe, Czechs, Lithuanians, etc.

5. Outside agents were American or Cuban CIA employees who were not cleared for entry into the undercover headquarters. These employees were either too "hot" because of exposure to exiles or did not have proper security clearance. Contact with these persons was always made clandestinely on the outside, using individually assigned operational cover; in my case, the Paragon Air Service cover.

6. The Rex and the Leda were converted WWII Naval vessels configured and maintained by the JM/WAVE Maritime branch for use in the station's covert paramilitary operations against Cuba. Each vessel had an American case officer that managed the crew, coordinated missions, arranged dockage in the U.S. and elsewhere undercover, and dealt with all the financial details associated with

the operations of the ships. The Operations and Maritime Branches were closely intertwined but often at odds.

7. Sometime later I learned the Plantation Key complex had, in fact, been a base for paramilitary operations prior to my occupancy, apparently by commando groups directly under Morales' control. The site had a good, small seaside basin for securing V-20s. It had been vacated because neighbors had become suspicious.

8. During the summer of 1963, following the incident with the U.S. Fish and Wildlife officer, as I supervised the maritime and survival small unit tactics training programs, my assistants and I were "asked" on three occasions to transport unmarked five gallon cans of liquid to a larger craft positioned off Dynamite Pier under the cover of darkness—despite my objections. I did not know the contents of the cans, but they were often leaking, particularly in the rough seas, and the odor of the liquid was the same as that I had experienced with the wildlife officer. It was impossible for me and the Cubans to avoid direct contact with the chemical in the cans. Many of us experienced skin rashes, fissuring, and dermatological outbreaks following contact with the chemical and had to seek medical treatment.

9. I observed Rosselli frequently when I had occasion to visit the operations or intelligence branches. I observed him in and emerging from the offices occupied by Dave Morales and Bob Wall, and in the plans room with Roderick during the summer of 1963. I also saw him with Roderick, Morales, and a case officer by the name of Tom Clines lunching or having cocktails at the State Bar, (a favorite JM/WAVE staff watering hole) on U.S. 1 not far from the station, and at the Perrine New England Oyster House. I got the distinct impression Rosselli and Morales were quite close and Roderick confirmed this in conversations I had with him. By the middle of summer 1963, it was commonly known that Rosselli was a mobster hitman type hired by the agency to conduct covert operations designed to kill Castro. There was virtually no secret about this at JM/WAVE. Following my introduction to Rosselli in Wall's office, my contact with him was brief, casual, and cordial and did not involve operational matters.

10. Billionaire Howard Hughes had long been linked to organize crime principals. Those associated with his private and business activities would later emerge as figures possibly associated with foreign and domestic assassinations. This was unknown to me in 1963 and I assumed the convenience of the Cay Sal refuge was solely a patriotic, altruistic gesture on the part of Hughes.

11. There were a few environmentally protected areas, either land or sea in and about the Keys in the early 1960s and there were no restrictions on spearfishing. Our training area encompassed what later became the Pennekamp State Park and Marine Sanctuary off Key Largo. Today, that entire area is protected and human encroachment is rigidly controlled.

12. Karl was not Cuban. By speech and appearance he was European, possibly Belgium or French, but he spoke excellent English with an accent. He appeared in his mid-20s, with slightly balding dark hair, and a trim, muscular build at about 6' tall. I never learned his last name and I suspect Karl was an alias.

BRADLEY E. AYERS

13. During my visits to the intelligence branch, I was able to read the daily summaries of information relating to the covert war against Cuba and some raw intelligence coming from paramilitary infiltration teams that had successfully integrated themselves into Cuban society, or were living black and reporting, via radios that were operated from clandestine sites. I also saw reports from other sources, diplomatic, foreign visitors/tourists, commercial visitors from a variety of countries and view U-2 photographs. I continued to read reports of the destruction of Cuban cane fields, tobacco crops, and other agricultural resources by fire and toxic chemical dissemination. However, the most disconcerting information suggested there was little foundation for the CIA opinion that the covert operations were succeeding, and that internal unrest, disillusionment with Castro's leadership, and economic and political turmoil would soon cause the Cuban people to assert themselves, overthrow Castro, and drive the Russians off the island. There were also reports from sources in Cuba indicating Russian nuclear tipped missiles were still present on the island.

14. There was a small, private refreshment room a few doors down the hall from Shackley's office. From time to time, after delivering my Pentagon-bound activity report to Maggy for Ted's approval, and obviously ignoring or tolerating my unkempt appearance and noxious smell, she would invite me to have coffee. We would retire to the coffee room and spend a few minutes making small talk. She was well aware of my conflict with Morales, and, when I inquired, she would casually mention that the Big Indian was away, usually in Mexico or Las Vegas. When visiting downstairs with Bob Wall, his comments to me suggested that, with Morales conspicuously absent, he was running the operations branch. The tone of Wall's remarks suggested he was not particularly happy with the workload on top of running his own agents. Roderick confirmed this in our conversations. During one of these visits with Rod I asked about his buddy, Rosselli. Ed told me Rosselli had been given another assignment and was no longer at the station as far as he knew. The time period of my visits to the station was September through early November 1963.

15. I later met Porter on one of my visits to the station while training the commandos on Elliott Key. Porter was in his mid-20s, I estimated, and by build, manner, appearance, and facial features, he might have been a youthful clone of Gordon Campbell. I believe this man was Porter Goss, President George W. Bush's appointee to head the CIA in 2005.

16. Gordon Campbell gave me several Miami-Homestead area phone contact numbers to use for secure communications with him or Karl. One number I tried was answered by a woman with the greeting, "Mr. Bishop's office." I concluded I'd either dialed incorrectly or Campbell had given me the number by mistake, or I may have erred in recording it when he gave it to me. However, several times when talking casually with Maggy, she dropped the name Bishop when referring to Campbell. I didn't know what to make of it, but I ceased using that number for the contact with Mr. Campbell.

17. When the Dallas Police brought Lee Harvey Oswald forth for transfer to another holding facility, Suzie and I were watching the unfolding events on TV. It was the first time I had seen Oswald close-up. When I saw him, my breath caught in my throat and a chill ran up my spine. Oswald was a "dead ringer" for Karl, Campbell's right-hand man who had been assisting me with the Elliott

Key operation. The resemblance was quite incredible and I thought it very strange.

18. Cal was truly a kind, compassionate, sensitive man. He was aware Suzie and I were having problems. My mother and father, concerned about the stability of our marriage and the long-term welfare of our sons, decided to fly from Minnesota to Miami to spend a few weeks with us. Sensing what the parental visit was really all about, Cal, with Rudy, bent all kinds of rules, and allowed me to take my father fishing several times in JM/WAVE boats. Rudy even accompanied us on one trip to the Flamingo area. Although not formally briefed, my parents came away from that vacation with a much better understanding of my assignment at JM/WAVE and appreciation for the circumstances under which Suzie, the boys, and I were living.

19. Barry Goldwater, the Republican candidate, with his honesty, strategic logic, and political realism, was in tune with the times, but he was overwhelmed at the polls by Johnsonian doubletalk and Democratic promises of a "Great Society." Goldwater, although defeated, enjoyed strong support from the military, the intelligence committee, big business, and the militant right in America. Many years later, because of what I learned about the assassination of President Kennedy, I began to re-evaluate the political dynamics of the 1963-64 period and the forces and personalities which may have had an interest in the elimination of the sitting president.

20. I found Miami rife with rumors about the Kennedy assassination, but preoccupied with the turmoil of my life at the time, I did not pay particular attention to what I heard. The militant Cuban exile community in and about Little Havana seemed convinced that Castro had killed the president, preempting Kennedy's plan to eliminate him. That had been the CIA line at JM/WAVE during the post assassination period when I was the station. Less often heard, sometimes even uneasily whispered, was a connection of the CIA with organized crime, Cuban exile and foreign agents had exacted revenge against the president for the Bay of Pigs failure and anticipated withdrawal, of U.S. and Kennedy administration support for the overthrow of Castro. At the time, whatever might be the case, I considered all the talk to be irrelevant to my actions. Only years later did I begin to consider seriously what I believed in 1965 was just street talk.

21. In the early 1970s, when I returned to north Key Largo to document all that had gone on there during the CIA's secret war against Cuba and the Castro assassination plots, I went back to Pirates' Lair and the old Point Mary safehouses. Quite by accident, I found evidence of the cache in the form of weathered, tattered $20 bills within several hundred feet of where the "legend" suggested it might be. There is more about this later in the book.

22. Had I sought psychological treatment at the time, by contemporary clinical criteria, I would probably have been diagnosed as suffering from post traumatic stress disorder. There was no recognition of this condition by the psychiatric community in the 1960s and 1970s. Soldiers returning from war were usually considered to be suffering from "battle fatigue" in that era.

23. Besides transporting human passengers, including skydivers, and a wide

variety of scientific and commercial clients, I adapted my aircraft to carry live animals, porpoises, even a lion; frequent cargo included caskets/human remains, auto and plumbing supplies (to the Bahamas), dynamite, furniture (for British royalty), wild game harvested by hunters and fishermen, baby chicks and turkeys, fresh seafood, fresh flowers and the latest fashions out of New York and Paris that. Nearly every flight was a new and challenging experience. Tropical storms and North Country icing and winter flying added to the excitement.

As more and more U.S. servicemen were killed in Vietnam, I was frequently chartered to fly remains from major airports to smaller communities not served by the airlines. These flights were always exceedingly painful for me as a former professional soldier.

24. Lee told me she had worked in television in Southern Louisiana in the past. She seemed quite knowledgeable of the inner workings of the politics of the area, how the system worked and was controlled, and the various power brokers in and about New Orleans in the 1960s. Implicit in her remarks was personal access to parties close to Garrison. I had no knowledge of anything of Louisiana politics and my only connection with that area was flying charters for oil interests out of Lafayette.

When talking about culture and people of the bayou country, Lee, in good humor, referred to them as "coon asses" (despite her class and refinement, she proudly referred to herself as a "coon ass," someone who had grown up on the bayous). The natives of the Florida panhandle were referred to as "fish heads."

25. A time-honored, entrenched Bahamian socio-cultural tradition required that one must be laid to rest on the island of one's birth. Accidents among itinerant workers were frequent—long hours at labor, drunkenness, careless driving, and too much "ganja" took its toll. Body bags or caskets, I always found it rather laughable when the mortician would demand a twin engine airplane for transport of the remains from one island to another. Before embarking with a body (and upon landing) a death certificate would have to be presented to Customs. Never did any Customs inspector open the casket or body bag to verify if, in fact, it contained human remains. Neither did I. But, given the ongoing political unrest and narcotics trade in the Caribbean at the time, the caskets and bags may well have contained guns, explosives, or dope. I was often tempted to sneak a peek, but with a death certificate in hand and payment guaranteed it was none of my damned business.

26. I once accepted a charter assignment to redeem a bad check that a member of British royalty had issued in payment for a lion cub sold to him by an animal importer in Miami. The check was for $2500 and, if redeemed, I'd get half plus expenses, the air charter fee, etc. I went to the Barclay Bank in Nassau where the check had been drawn, and was referred to the maker. I tracked the Duke down and confronted him at his mansion on the sea. We had tea and drinks, but he said he was broke. Finally, I told him I'd have to take the lion. He led me to the cage. The cub was now nearly full grown, but gentle as a baby. The old Duke was shedding tears as I led the lion away, put him in the front seat of my rented car and drove off. The lion "cub" snoozed soundly in the back seat of my plane all the way back to Miami where he was delivered to my client. I got a $500 bonus for the trip. This is an example of some of the bizarre assignments I got.

THE ZENITH SECRET

27. Lee and I married in 1967 by a Justice of the Peace in South Dakota, but the marriage was never properly recorded and legalized due to an apparent noncomformance with waiting periods, etc.

28. The terminology, "black bag job," is the slang description for an officially unauthorized surreptitious search and removal of suspicious materials or alleged evidence sought by law enforcement or other governmental agencies. These operations are sanctioned verbally when there are insufficient grounds for a court ordered search warrant, and they typically are carried out when the subject of surveillance or investigation is absent from the place to be searched.

29. Carlos Santana's music was quite popular during this period, especially a newly released album titled, "Abraxas." The music seemed to fit our setting and lifestyle in Florida at the time; and the idea that our newly acquired boat would be a vessel of good fortune for us made the Greek term, with its definition, appropriate as a name for the boat.

30. Many years later, in the course of my work with John Kelly, a stateside producer for the BBC working out of Washington. I learned that my name had appeared on a top secret special White House Plumber's whistle-blower hit list, thus confirming my suspicion that the entire false rape incident was a botched attempt to neutralize me as a source of information following the publication of the Jack Anderson column series.

31. In 1991, John Kelly shared with me that he had been friends with a member of the Gervasi family. Apparently, Tom Gervasi, on his deathbed in the late 1980s, confided that as an editor, he had been on the CIA payroll as a counterintelligence specialist. Under James Angleton, he intercepted and sanitized publications that might embarrass or damage agency interests, mine being one of them.

As *The Zenith Secret* was in production, the CIA, in a rare letter of denial, responded to an inquiry from a regional newspaper in northern Wisconsin. The agency representative refuted that my original manuscript had been censored. (Please see a copy of the letter in the inside cover of this book.)

32. The assignment to FEMA seemed somewhat routine at the time. However, in September 1981 I was selected to participate in a brainstorming study, with other officer and civilian experts, exploring how terrorists might exploit vulnerabilities in attacking homeland America. One area we discussed in detail was the scenario that unfolded in New York and Washington, D.C. on September 11, 2001.

33. I refer the reader again to my forthcoming non-fiction book, *Out of Pocket: Rotten Deals* for the full story of my war on drugs "adventure."

34. WPLG-TV (Channel 10) in Miami reported that Southern Air Transport (SAT), a known CIA proprietary airline operating out of Miami International Airport at that time, was intimately involved in the re-supply of the Contra army during the mid-80s, and particularly was involved in smuggling narcotics from Barranquilia, Colombia. WPLG-TV based its reports on testimony of a cartel wife turned informant, Wanda Palacio, and the findings of DEA agent Bradley Ayers and Customs Inspector Joe Price. The airline denied the allega-

tions, and sued WPLG for libel and defamation. WPLG won the lawsuit.
http://ciadrugs.homestead.com/files/bradleyayers.html

35. Allen Dulles, *Craft of Intelligence* (New York, NY: Harper & Row, 1963)

36. Oliver Stone and Zachary Sklar, *JFK: The Book of the Film* (New York: Applause, 1992)

37. Livingstone, Harrison Edward. *Killing the Truth* (New York:Carrol & Graf, 1993) pp.259-260

38. Allen Dulles, *Craft of Intelligence* (New York, NY: Harper & Row, 1963)

39. The principle sources for the Guatemala operation are the books, *Bitter Fruit: The Untold Story of the American Coup in Guatemala*, by Schlesinger and Kinzer, (Doubleday, 1982) and *Night Watch* by David Phillips, (Atheneum, 1977). Phillips confirms Morales' involvement in the operation. Both books are important in that they establish the early relationship between Morales and other key agency and covert paramilitary specialists, and describe situations in which their activities were directly controlled by the highest levels of CIA management, circumventing normal command and control channels within the agency. David Phillips, in his book, makes reference to a Morales counterpart who was involved in the Guatemalan operation, a man named Hector. New Orleans District Attorney Garrison's office received an anonymous letter during its investigation advising that a certain Hector Aguero was a key figure in the assassination of JFK. The name Hector came up several times in my various activities at JM/WAVE and with Orlando Bosch, but I could never put the name together with a face or other identification. Tony Sforza, like Morales, looked Hispanic and spoke fluent Spanish and he would be a likely suspect as the Hector figure.

40. One of my bosses at JM/WAVE was career agency employee, Ernie Sparks. Sparks supervised the on-sight field training of Cuban exiles in Guatemala in preparation for the Bay of Pigs invasion. Sparks is identified as "Sitting Bull" in Haynes Johnson's book, *The Bay of Pigs*, (Norton, 1964). Sparks spoke to me in some detail of Morales' activities in preparation for and during the Bay of Pigs invasion. There were varying accounts of El Indio's being in an observation plane over the invasion beach or on a nearby ship as the operation unfolded.

41. While I'd not spoken to Dorff or anyone else about it, with the suspicion of a Morales-Sforza connection to the Letelier car bombing raised by HSCA investigators, I was aware of the media outrage over the 1976 car bombing in Phoenix that claimed the life of investigative reporter Don Bolles of the *Arizona Republic*. Bolles, purportedly, had been looking into politically and financially sensitive matters involving the Goldwater family, connections to organized crime, and related issues. I made a mental note to explore this incident further if I had the opportunity.

42. My gathered impression of East Coast-based Bonnano was that he was not a major figure in Mafia hierarchy, but would have been a key intermediary for the top echelon of the period—Marcello in New Orleans, Trafficante in Tampa, and Giancana in Chicago—as well as a relatively low profile cut out for the more

visible, notorious kingpins. See Rappley's book reference on Bonnano, Goldwater, et al.

43. Killing someone covertly, that is, somewhere outside the realm of declared combat, is an extremely complex undertaking fraught with all sorts of unintended consequences. A rigged suicide or contrived "accident" is the preferred method by those involved in black operations around the world, including the CIA.

The alternative is a public execution, such as in the murders of President Kennedy, Martin Luther King, and Bobby Kennedy. This approach to assassination is designed to send a message, but it's also risky in terms of attribution. With possibly hundreds looking on and capable of giving testimony, a successful public assassination depends on the predictable confusion and panic at the scene. The planting of obfuscating and contradicting charades adds to the conflicting reports and testimony surrounding the event. And, there is generally the need for a plausible explanation for murder patsy with an alleged motive, a throw-down weapon, muddled forensics, and a cover-up that sticks to camouflage attribution. All of this requires a great deal of planning and preparation and ultimately involves a number of people, thus secrecy becomes a major problem both before and after the event.

Arson typically leaves a huge evidentiary footprint, plus, if murder is involved, the victim has to be immobilized or disabled so as to be confined to the site of the fire.

A car bomb, on the other hand, is relatively innocuous. Most of the incriminating evidence is destroyed in the blast, especially if the bomb can be rigged to ignite the vehicle's fuel tank concurrently with the explosion designed to kill the target.

A bomb wired to the car's ignition is indiscriminate. Once set, whomever gets into the car and turns on the ignition is going to be blown up. Even a timer-activated bomb, once placed, detonates regardless of who's in the car.

The preferred technique for car bombing is one that employs a remotely controlled ignition device. The necessary components for rigging such a mechanism are quite generic. The perpetrators conduct prior surveillance of the target, study patterns of behavior, select a detonation site where collateral damage will be minimal, and find a position from which they can observe the target entering the vehicle, thus assuring positive identification and also providing the option to delay activation if the circumstances are not ideal.

Pro and anti-Castro Cuban exiles had been car bombing one another for years in Miami. Usually, the victims were leaders of political factions or journalists. The mechanics for executing such an act requires only crystal set electronic skills. I went back to my reading of the CIA tradecraft manual, recalling the appropriate chapters of the 1960's era. The paramount consideration in any assassination was the positive identification and isolation of the target who either voluntarily or by artifice moves into the killing zone. The exquisite simplicity of sliding a quarter pound of explosives (then C-3) under the driver's seat if the target's car was self-evident. Access to most any car was not a problem. The explosive package, if wired to the car's ignition required only a blasting cap or primer cord, but could easily be spotted by a paranoid targeted individual.

The preferred technique was remote triggering, a remotely controlled ignition when one was positive the target was positioned behind the wheel or, at least, a passenger in the vehicle. A controlled detonation reduced the risks involved, always a major consideration in covert operations.

Remote ignition devices in the 1960-1970 era were becoming commercially available, in the form of radio-controlled model aircraft, garage door openers, phone message retrievers, dictaphone activators, etc. With the remote signal mechanism attached to small batteries, the bomb was no larger than a kid's lunch box. It did not require rocket science to blow someone up, mortally shred the target's lower torso, and possibly set the car on fire, which would further destroy any evidence. Car bombing was and is a gruesome form of execution, but typically it leaves little evidence that might lead to perpetrators.

I've tried diligently over the years to gain access to the actual investigative and forensic reports on both the Don Bolles murder and that of Chilean Ambassador Letelier, but have not been successful. I wanted to analyze and compare the two. In the absence of official documents, I've read all the literature available to me about both assassinations. Based on this research, I'm reasonably convinced the bombings were carried out by the same parties, one occurring in June, 1976 and the other in September, 1976.

44. I will be eternally grateful for the moral and financial support given me during this extremely difficult period by some of the people listed in the acknowledgements, especially Ron Williams and John Timmerman. Without their good words, encouragement and support, large and small, I'm not sure I would have been able to continue my quest, much less keep body and soul together. Ron Williams, my closest friend, was the single person to whom I'd hinted I'd found a source offering extraordinary information on a Morales-Goldwater connection.

45. That is a logical and legitimate question. I was then, and remain so today, of the belief there are three essential reasons for my longevity to this point.

When I went public about my experience and observations while at JM/WAVE in 1963-64, there was considerable suspicion the CIA's secret war against Cuba and the plots to assassinate Fidel Castro were internally spawned and conducted independent of sanction by President Kennedy and his advisors—in the descriptive terminology of the day, a rogue operations by ideologues and disenchanted agency paramilitary cowboys following the disaster at the Bay of Pigs. I was one , if not the only, acknowledged agency operative who offered first person testimony to the fact that Attorney General Robert Kennedy was on the site in south Florida monitoring everything that was taking place. I became useful to the CIA as a source, albeit embarrassing because I could also testify to the presence of Mafia operative John Rosselli on the scene, really deflect the "rogue elephant out of control" charges brought against the agency in the 1970s.

From the moment I decided to go public, I made a deliberate effort to cooperate with the media and achieve a degree of high public profile. As my account was substantiated by the press and numerous other respected authors, literally hundreds if not thousands became aware of my testimony and I became widely recognized in those media and literary circles focusing on 1960s CIA covert operations and domestic assassinations. I've never sought celebrity , nor have I tried to financially exploit my decision to go public. I think I've remained a relatively low-key witness to some of the most history altering events of our time. I've also been universally recognized for my credibility in an environment that is toxic with charlatans, attention seekers, and pretenders. My death, no matter how that might come about, would in the eyes of the dark forces, focus even more attention on my revelations and investigative work. Thus, personal harassment, sinister efforts to discredit, threaten, and intimidate me have become the methods of choice by those who hope to dishonor and discredit me.

THE ZENITH SECRET

There is a terminology in the intelligence business known as "limited hangout." This describes the deliberate release of sensitive information to deflect attention from that which is even more secret, embarrassing or compromising. I can't say for sure if I've been used in this way by the dark forces, but it's a possibility . We'll see what the fallout from this book will be and how uncomfortable those holding the family jewels become with this account. Another utilization of a designated limited hangout is that he/she may be tracked to find out to what extent other than unreleased, protected information might be at risk of compromise. This is classic CIA counter intelligence modus operandi perfect by the likes of James Angleton and David Phillips. Time will tell whether I've overstepped the invisible boundary and gotten too close to the fire as a limited hangout out of control.

46. Long ago, based my experience in government service with CIA and DEA, I made it a personal rule not to utilize electronic means of recording and storing sensitive information. Thus, I avoided the use of word processors and computers in so far as possible in my investigative work. I'd seen how virtually any electronically filed data could be surreptitiously extracted by the authorities from anyone's data base. I also saw how a database or computer hard drive or software could be covertly subverted and contaminated without ever gaining physical access to the equipment , with false and illegal downloading, contrived email and chatroom use to substantiate the search and seizure of a person's materials. Thus, everything I wrote was done the old fashioned way, with a typewriter. Access to electronic communications is a common practice by the authorities. I've followed my fundamental rule, much to the grief of my publishers. I'm the brunt of all kinds of ridicule by my peers, but I never have an excuse for not writing. I'm not subject to power outages, computer failure, or unanticipated , uncontrolled loss of data (except in the case of black bag jobs and shakedowns such as what happened at Jacumba).

47. Case number 98/15425, dated 4/01/98 from the Orange County Sheriff.

SELECTED REFERENCES

1. Publications referring specifically to the author's background and work:

Corn, David. *Blond Ghost: the Shackley Biography*. New York: Simon & Schuster, 1994.

Fonzi, Gaeton. *The Last Investigation*. New York: Thunder's Mouth Press, 1993.

Hinckle, Warren and William W. Turner. *The Fish Is Red: The Story of the Secret War against Castro*. New York: Harper & Row, 1981.

Leamer, Laurence. *The Kennedy Men*. New York: William Morrow and Sons, 2001.

Rappleye, Charles. *All-American Mafioso: the Johnny Rosselli Story*. New York: Doubleday, 1991.

Russo, Gus. *Live by the Sword*. Baltimore: Bancroft Press, 1998.

Shackley Theodore. *The Third Option*. New York: McGraw Hill, 1981. (Mr. Shackley was my CIA station chief at JM/WAVE.)

Summers, Anthony. *Conspiracy*. New York: McGraw Hill, 1981. (Expanded version published in 1989 by Paragon House.)

Turner, William. *Rearview Mirror*. Roseville, CA: Penmarin Books, 2001.

Twyman, Noel. *Bloody Treason*. Rancho Santa Fe, CA: Laurel Publishing, 1997.

2. Publications relating to the general subject matter of this book:

Aucoin, James L. *The Evolution of American Investigative Journalism*. Columbia, MO: University of Missouri Press, 2005.

Bluhm, Raymond K. *U.S. Army: A Complete History*. Army Historical Foundation. Westport, CT: Hugh Lauter Leven Associates, 2005.

Boorstein, Edward. *Allende's Chile: An Inside View*. New York: International Publishers, 1977.

Branch, Taylor and Eugene M. Propper. *Labyrinth: How a Stubborn Prosecutor Penetrated a Shadowland of Covert Operations on Three Continents to Find the Assassins of Orlando Letelier*. New York: Viking Adult, 1982.

Califano, Joseph Jr. *Inside*. New York: Public Affairs, 2004.

Camper, Frank. *The Mk/Ultra Secret*. Savannah, GA: Christopher Scott Publishing.

Conason, Joe. *Big Lies*. New York: St. Martin's, 2003.

DiEugenio, James and Lisa Pease, eds. *The Assassinations*. Los Angeles: Feral House, 2003.

Dinges, John. *Assassination on Embassy Row*. New York: McGraw-Hill, 1981.

Dowbenko, Uri. *Bushwhacked*. Pray, MT: Conspiracy Digest, 2002.

Edwards, Lee. *Goldwater: The Man Who Made a Revolution*. Washington, D.C.: Regnery Press, 1995.

Fetzer, James H., ed. *Assassination Science*. Chicago: Catfeet Press, 1998.

___, ed. *Murder in Dealey Plaza*. Chicago: Catfeet Press, 2000.

___ ed. *The Great Zapruder Film Hoax*. Chicago: Catfeet Press, 2003.

Freed, Donald. *Death in Washington: The Murder of Orlando Letelier*. Chicago: Lawrence Hill, 1980.

Galanor, Stewart. *Cover-Up*. New York: Kestrel Books, 1998.

Goldberg, Robert Alan. *Barry Goldwater*. New Haven, CT: Yale University Press, 1997.

Hancock, Larry. *Someone Would Have Talked*. Southlake, TX: JFK Lancer Publications, 2003.

Haslam, Jonathan. *The Nixon Administration and the Death of Allende's Chile: A Case of Assisted Suicide*. New York: Verso Books, 2005.

Headley, Lake and William Hoffman. *Loud and Clear*. New York: Henry Holt, 1990.

Iverson, Peter. *Barry Goldwater: Native Arizonan*. Norman, OK: University of Oklahoma Press, 1998.

Klaber, William and Philip Melanson. *Shadow Play*. New York: St. Martin's, 2003.

Lane, Mark and Dick Gregory. *Murder in Memphis*. New York: Thunder's Mouth Press, 1993.

Macnitt, Ben. *Murder of Don Bolles*. New York: Ballantine Books, Date Unknown.

Newman, John M. *JFK and Vietnam*. New York: Warner Books, 1992.

___. *Oswald and the CIA*. Berkeley, CA: Carroll and Graff.

Pepper, William F. *Orders to Kill*. Berkeley, CA: Carroll and Graff, 1995.

Perlstein, Rick. *Before the Storm: Barry Goldwater and the Unmasking of the American Consensus.* New York: Hill and Wang, 2002.

Rentschler, William H. Goldwater: *A Tribute to a 20th Century Political Icon.* New York: McGraw-Hill, 2000.

Schotz, E. Martin. *History Will Not Absolve Us.* Brookline, MA: Ulmer and DeLucia, 1996.

Shackley, Ted and Richard Finney. *Spymaster.* Dulles, VA: Potomac Books, 2005.

Shoumatoff, Alex. *Legends of the American Desert.* New York: Alfred Knopf, 1997.

Trento, Joseph J. *Prelude to Terror.* Berkeley, CA: Carroll and Graff.

U.S. Department of the Interior. National Park Service. *Cold War in South Florida,* 2004.

Weisberg, Harold. *Martin Luther King: the Assassination.* Berkeley, CA: Carroll and Graff, 1971.

THE ZENITH SECRET

INDEX

A

ABC, trial of, 206
Ambassador Hotel, and Robert Kennedy assassination, IV, 155, 204, 206
Anderson, Jack (columnist), 162-173, 176, 233
Andregg, Michael, 207, 212, 215, 231, 239, 241, 245, 246
Arizona connection. 209, 214, 215, 217, 224-226, 237-239, 241, 245, 246
ARRB, *see Assassination Records Review Board*
Artime, Manuel, 41, 115, 116, 122, 124, 138, 145, 163, 188, 237
assassination, of JFK, 102-104, 142, 144-146, 155, 201, 213 *See also Kennedy, John F.;*
    and the CIA's secret war, XII, 104, 157, 163, 180, 209
    and Dave Morales, 181, 185, 198, 201, 209, 220
    and Fidel Castro, 104, 139, 249
    and the JFK Assassination Information Center, 181, 185, 198, 201, 209, 220
    and the JM/WAVE operation, V, XI, XII, 142, 155, 158, 177, 181, 209
    and Johnny Rosselli, 155, 158, 176, 198, 199, 201
    as retribution for Bay of Pigs, 200
assassination investigation, of Dave Morales, 179-202
Assassination Records Review Board (ARRB), 209, 213, 214
Avilas, Eleana (cook at Elliott Key), 89-93, 96, 97, 101-103, 107-109, 112, 114, 137
Avilas, Mr. and Mrs. (cooks at Pirates' Lair), 89
Ayers, Bradley Earl, 21p, 136p. See also *The War That Never Was*
    and assassination investigation of Dave Morales, 179-202
    cover of *See Williams, Daniel B. (fictitious identity of author)*
    JM/WAVE recruitment of, 1-15
    resignation of, 1, 2, 121, 122, 124, 127, 133-135
    as suspect of crime in Minnesota, 171-173
    and suspension of flying license, 151,152
    war on drugs book project, 181. 206, 207, 213, 217, 219, 223, 231, 234, 248
Ayers, Suzie, 5, 12, 39, 40, 45, 48, 52, 53, 58-60, 76, 77, 81, 83, 85
    kicking out of Ayers, 89
    and move to Minnesota, 106
    and President Kennedy's assassination, 103
    press for Vietnam, 106, 122, 123

B

Bahamas, Ayers in, 149, 151
    and Freeport Flight Service, 149-152
    and suspension of flying license, 151, 152
Barger, Chris, 214
Bay of Pigs, X, XII, 11, 28, 41
    and assassination of JFK, 157, 187, 197

and rescue-extraction mission, 118, 119, 121, 122, 124
surf-landing program, 127
UDT program, 59, 77-79
V-20/fishing trawler mission to Puerta Sagua de Grande, 61-75
V-20 training, at Pirates' Lair, 83, 84, 100
visit from Ted Shackley, 58
withdraw of support for, 109, 111, 112

F

FBI, (Federal Bureau of Investigation) 103
    and surveillance of Johnny Rosselli, 199-201
    and withdraw of support for exile operations, 126
FEMA, (Federal Emergency Management Agency) evacuation planning at, 178
Fensterwald, Bernard, 181-183, 205, 236
Fernandez, Julio, 63-67, 69, 118, 119
Ferrie, David, 155, 157, 170, 174
    disguise of, 157
Fitzgerald, Des, 13, 41, 56
Flesh, Henry, 160, 162, 163
Florida. *See Coconut Grove safehouse; Coral Gables safehouse; Dynamite Pier
    training site; Elliott Key safehouse; JM/WAVE operation; money cache,
    finding of, at Point Mary; Pirates' Lair safehouse; Plantation Key safe-
    house*
Fonzi, Gaeton, 177, 179, 181, 193, 226
Franklin, Dick, 159
Freeport Flight Service (Bahamas), 149-152

G

Garret, Lieutenant Colonel Frank, 7, 9, 11, 41
Garrison, Jim, 142, 150.
Garrison Investigation, 154, 155, 170
    omissions of JM/WAVE activity, 157, 158
Gervasi, Tom, IV, 175, 177
Giancana, Sam, 176
Gila Project, 223, 228, 233-235, 238, 251
    and Bob Walton's knowledge of, 251
Goldwater, Barry, 221, 222, 227
    death of, 252
    and Gila Project, 223
    and Lyndon Johnson, 238
    Mafia connection of, 203, 206, 209, 212. 218, 233, 251
    and presidential campaign, 223
    and transfer of money, 228, 229
Goss, Porter, 266
Guatemala, overthrow of government, and the CIA, 186, 197, 198, 201

H

Harvey, William, IV, 13, 41, 56, 80, 167, 186

THE ZENITH SECRET

Helm, Richard (Head of CIA Covert Operations), 41, 228
Higginbotham, Ted, 160
Homestead safehouse, 121, 125, 129, 133
HSCA (House Select Committee on Assassination), V, 177, 179, 181, 185, 189
    and Dave Morales, 199, 200, 218
Hughes, Howard, 64
Hunt, E. Howard, 41, 173

I

The Invisible Government (Wise and Ross), 104
Iran Contra scandal, 179, 206

J

Jacumba incident, 245-249
    official statement about, 242, 243
Jerry (CIA case officer), 46
JFK Assassination Information Center, 181, 182, 201, 203-207, 236
    surveillance of, 184, 185
"JFK" (movie), and Dave Morales, 209
JM/WAVE operation, IV-VI, XI, XII, 14,43, 50, 53, 57, 74, 75, 116, 119, 125, 130,
    133, 137, 145, 146, 150, 151, 155, 157, 162, 163, 166, 167, 170, 175-181,
    184-186. 197, 198, 201, 203, 209, 213, 214, 239, 240, 264, 265, 267, 270, 272
    See also Campbell, Gordon; CIA; Coconut Grove safehouse; Coral
    Gables safehouse; Dynamite Pier training site; Elliott Key safehouse;
    exile training program; Morales, Dave; Pirates' Lair safehouse;
    Plantation Key safehouse; Shackley, Ted; Zenith Secret; Zenith
    Technical Corporation
    and accusation of conspiracy to kill JFK, 104
    anti-Kennedy talk at, 142, 158
    Karl's familiarity with staff of, 92, 130
Jocoy, Jock (writing client), 213
Johnson, Lyndon (U.S. president), 104
    Cuban policy of, 112, 115, 124
    phasing out of paramilitary operations under, 109
    and Barry Goldwater, 238

K

Karl (JM/WAVE officer), 88, 92, 98, 104
    death of, 127-134, 146, 175
    familiarity with staff of JM/WAVE, 92, 130
    resemblance to Lee Harvey Oswald, 142, 157, 170
Kennedy, John F. (U.S. president), *See also assassination of JFK,*
    Orange Bowl Address, X, XI
Kennedy, Robert,
    assassination of, IV, V, 155, 157, 221
    assassination of, and Dave Morales, 181, 204
    assassination of, and the Zenith Secret, 209
    meeting at Waloos Glades Hunting camp, 86

pleasure craft, disguise of, 21, 74p, 80,
Psychological Operations Battalion, at Ft. Snelling, 178

R

S

THE ZENITH SECRET